MISCELLANEA
NEOTESTAMENTICA

VOLUMEN PRIMUM

SUPPLEMENTS TO
NOVUM TESTAMENTUM

VOLUME XLVII

LEIDEN
E. J. BRILL
1978

MISCELLANEA
NEOTESTAMENTICA

STUDIA
AD NOVUM TESTAMENTUM PRAESERTIM PERTINENTIA
A SOCIIS SODALICII BATAVI
C. N.
STUDIOSORUM NOVI TESTAMENTI CONVENTUS
ANNO MCMLXXVI
QUINTUM LUSTRUM FELICITER COMPLENTIS
SUSCEPTA

EDENDA·CURAVERUNT

T. BAARDA • A. F. J. KLIJN • W. C. VAN UNNIK

VOLUMEN PRIMUM

LEIDEN
E. J. BRILL
1978

ISBN 90 04 05685 8

CONTENTS

LIST OF ABBREVIATIONS

ACR	*Australian Catholic Record*
AIHI	Archives internationales d'histoire des idées
Akten IKBS	*Akten des ... Internationalen Byzantinisten-Kongresses*
AnBib	*Analecta Biblica*
ANTT	Arbeiten zur neutestamentlichen Textforschung
AThANT	Abhandlungen zur Theologie des Alten und Neuen Testaments
BBB	Bonner biblische Beiträge
BEThL	Bibliotheca ephemeridum theologicarum Lovaniensium
Bib	*Biblica*
BIH	Bibliographisches Institut Hochschultaschenbücher
BJRL	*Bulletin of the John Rylands Library*
BNTC	Black's New Testament Commentaries
BSt(F)	Biblische Studien (Freiburg)
Bijdr	*Bijdragen, Tijdschrift voor Philosophie en Theologie*
BZ	*Biblische Zeitschrift*
CBG	*Collationes Brugenses et Gandavenses*
CB.NT	*Coniectanea biblica, New Testament Series*
CBQ	*Catholic Biblical Quarterly*
CChr	Corpus Christianorum
CChr.SL	Corpus Christianorum. Series Latina
CHaer	Corpus Haereseologicum
CNT(K)	Commentaar op het Nieuwe Testament (Kampen)
Conc	*Concilium*
COT	Commentaar op het Oude Testament
CSCO	Corpus Scriptorum Christianorum Orientalium
CSEL	Corpus Scriptorum Ecclesiasticorum Latinorum
CSHB	Corpus Scriptorum Historiae Byzantinae
CUFr	Collection des Universités de France
EHPhR	*Études d'histoire et de philosophie religieuses*
Eranos	*Eranos, Acta Philologicae Suecana*
ET	*Expository Times*
ÉtB	Études bibliques
EThL	*Ephemerides theologicae Lovanienses*
EvTh	*Evangelische Theologie*
Exp	*The Expositor*
FGNK	Forschungen zur Geschichte des neutestamentlichen Kanons
FThSt	Freiburger Theologische Studien
FTS	Frankfurter Theologische Studien
GNT	The Greek New Testament
GThT	*Gereformeerd Theologisch Tijdschrift*
HNT	Handbuch zum Neuen Testament
HTC	Herder's Theologischer Kommentar zum Neuen Testament
ICC	The International Critical Commentary

IDB	Interpreter's Dictionary of the Bible
JA	*Journal Asiatique*
JBL	*Journal of Biblical Literature*
JBW	*Jahrbücher der biblischen Wissenschaft*
JJS	*Journal of Jewish Studies*
JMUEOS	*Journal of the Manchester University Egyptian and Oriental Society*
JRAS	*Journal of the Royal Asiatic Society of Great Britain and Ireland*
JThS	*Journal of Theological Studies*
Kairos	*Kairos. Zeitschrift für Religionswissenschaft und Theologie*
KatBl	*Katechetische Blätter*
KBANT	Kommentare und Beiträge zum Alten und Neuen Testament
KEK	Kritisch-exegetischer Kommentar über das Neue Testament
KeTh	*Kerk en Theologie*
KNT	Kommentar zum Neuen Testament
LeDiv	*Lectio Divina*
LV(B)	*Lumière et Vie (Brugge)*
MBPF	Münchener Beiträge zur Papyrusforschung und antiken Rechtsgeschichte
MGWJ	*Monatsschrift für Geschichte und Wissenschaft des Judentums*
MSSNTS	Monograph Series. Society for New Testament Studies
Muséon	*Le Muséon*
NBG	Nederlandsch Bijbelgenootschap
NedThT	*Nederlands(ch) Theologisch Tijdschrift*
NGWG.PH	Nachrichten von der Gesellschaft der Wissenschaften zu Göttingen, Philologisch-Historische Klasse
NHS	Nag Hammadi Studies
NJKA	*Neue Jahrbücher für das klassische Altertum (etc.)*
NLC	New London Commentary on the New Testament
NT	*Novum Testamentum*
NTA	Neutestamentliche Abhandlungen
NTS	*New Testament Studies*
NT.S	Supplements to Novum Testamentum
OrChr	*Oriens Christianus*
OrChrA	Orientalia christiana analecta
ParPass	*La Parola del Passato*
PBA	Proceedings of the British Academy
PCB	Peake's Commentary on the Bible
PG	Patrologia Graeca
Pharus	*Pharus, katholische Monatsschrift für Orientierung in die gesammten Pädagogik*
PL	Patrologia Latina
PLB	Papyrologica Lugduno-Batava
PO	Patrologia Orientalis
PUD	Publications de l'Université de Dyon
RAC	Reallexikon für Antike und Christentum
RB	*Revue Biblique*
RE	Realencyklopädie für protestantische Theologie und Kirche
RevSR	*Revue des sciences religieuses*

RSR	*Recherches de science religieuse*
RThPh	*Revue de théologie et de philosophie*
SC	Sources chrétiennes
SCP	Scriptores Christiani Primaevi
Scrip	*Scripture, Quarterly of the Catholic Biblical Association*
SGKA	Studien zur Geschichte und Kultur des Altertums
SPAW.PH	Sitzungsberichte der Preussischen Akademie der Wissenschaften Berlin, Philosophisch-historische Klasse
StANT	Studien zum Alten und Neuen Testament
StC	*Studia Catholica*
StT	Studi e Testi
StUNT	Studien zur Umwelt des Neuen Testaments
ThLBl	*Theologisches Literaturblatt*
ThLZ	*Theologische Literaturzeitung*
ThQ	*Theologische Quartalschrift*
ThR	*Theologische Rundschau*
ThStKr	*Theologische Studien und Kritiken*
ThWNT	*Theologisches Wörterbuch zum Neuen Testament*
ThZ	*Theologische Zeitschrift (Basel)*
TTh	*Tijdschrift voor Theologie*
TU	Texte und Untersuchungen zur Geschichte der altchristlichen Literatur
UMS.HS	University of Michigan Studies, Humanistic Series
UnSa	*Unam Sanctam*
VAKMF	Veröffentlichungen der Alexander Kohut Memorial Foundation
VD	*Verbum Domini*
VigChr	*Vigiliae Christianae*
VoxTh	*Vox Theologica*
VT	*Vetus Testamentum*
WI	*Welt des Islams*
WThJ	*Westminster Theological Journal*
ZÄS	*Zeitschrift für ägyptische Sprache und Altertumskunde*
ZNW	*Zeitschrift für die neutestamentliche Wissenschaft (und die Kunde der älteren Kirche)*
ZPE	*Zeitschrift für Papyrologie und Epigraphik*
ZThK	*Zeitschrift für Theologie und Kirche*

THE STUDY OF THE NEW TESTAMENT
IN THE NETHERLANDS, 1951-1976

W. C. VAN UNNIK

This collection of essays in the field of the New Testament studies is published in order to celebrate the 25th anniversary of the "Conventus Novi Testamenti Studiosorum".

The "founding-fathers" of the Conventus were two veteran scholars F. W. GROSHEIDE, since 1912 Professor at the Free University of Amsterdam, and J. DE ZWAAN, who worked first in Groningen (1914-1929) and then in Leyden (since 1929). For many years they worked together as members of the committee, preparing a new translation of the N.T. which appeared in 1939. Both had reached the retiring-age, which is 70 years of age in the Netherlands, and a new generation of their pupils was going to take over the work. Since we are dealing here with the period since 1950, it falls beyond the scope of this essay to sketch the work of these two men, whose activities fell in the pre-war period. But this much should be said, that they have held an important place, each in his own way, in the religious life and in the field of theological scholarship in the Netherlands. In calling together the SNTC, they passed on, as it were, their heritage to a younger generation. We cannot but start by remembering these predecessors with deep gratitude for their fine scholarship and friendship.

There were two reasons which gave an impetus to this new society:

a) the foundation of the "mother-society", the S.N.T.S. which also owed its origin to the initiative of DE ZWAAN. Since not all people interested in the Netherlands could become members of the S.N.T.S. because of its rules of admittance, it was thought worthwhile to make a local group to foster that interest by bringing them together in regular meetings in the frame-work of a national society.

b) students of other theological disciplines like Old Testament, Church History and Comparative Religion in the Low Countries had already started such groups and proved the effect of such an enterprise. It would be missing a chance, if their example would not be followed by their colleagues in the N.T. field.

It is not my task to relate the history of the SNTC. But the completion of a period of 25 years offered a good opportunity for a short historical survey of N.T. studies in Holland during that span of time. It will be incomplete, but may give some impression of the way in which Dutch N.T. scholarship has developed.

In the course of the past decades since World War II, great changes have taken place on the Dutch scene which also affected the study of the New Testament.

What did not change, however, is the geographical scene, which was and is still of importance for a good evaluation of the present position. From the very beginning of their national existence, the Netherlands have had strong connections in trade and culture with the three surrounding countries France, Germany and England. Its vernacular spoken by a small population was a barrier to mutual exchange, but forced upon the Dutch the necessity of learning foreign languages if they wanted to do business with their neighbours. They have greatly profited from this one-way-traffic, because they could "prendre leur bien où ils le trouvent".

As far as religion is concerned, the country was up till the 1960's clearly divided between a Roman Catholic and a Protestant part. The former was very faithful to Rome and culturally influenced by French Catholicism. The training of the clergy took place along strict, traditional lines. Protestantism stood predominantly in the Reformed stream and had little contact with the churches outside the country, because they belonged to different confessional families. The ministry was trained at the universities; knowledge of the classical languages and Hebrew was and still is required. During the last century, Dutch theology was deeply influenced by the writings of German-speaking theologians without loosing its own character and following all the meanders of German theology; this difference is largely due to the variety in ecclesiastical background. Contacts with theology in the English-speaking world were slight, though N.T. scholarship formed to some extent an exception (KIRSOP LAKE was professor in Leyden between 1905-1913; DE ZWAAN studied in England and both he and D. PLOOY had strong links with England, particularly with J. RENDEL HARRIS).

One more factor in the theological picture of Holland must be considered. In the 1880's a split took place in the Dutch Reformed Church. One of the main issues was the doctrine of biblical inspiration or the attitude towards higher criticism. In the Dutch Reformed

Church a variety of opinions was held, going from fundamentalism to the position of the so-called Dutch Radicals, whereas in the separated Churches a very strict doctrine of biblical inspiration was upheld. Many of the sharp edges that existed up till World War II have disappeared, but the break itself is not healed yet. The theological faculties of the Free University and the Theological School in Kampen belonged to these "Re-reformed Churches", whereas the ministers of the Dutch Reformed Church were and are trained at the faculties of the three State universities (Leyden, Groningen, Utrecht) and the Municipal University of Amsterdam. In each of these schools there was one chair for N.T. studies. Finally, it may be added that the Roman Catholic Church has had a university at Nijmegen since 1923. Its theological faculty was very small, because it had graduate studies only and many of the Dutch clergy who continued their studies after seminary were sent by their bishop abroad.

This was the situation when SNTC made its start in 1951. Members were the professors and those of their pupils who had taken their doctor's degree in the N.T. field or were preparing a thesis, while ministering to parishes, sometimes in big cities. Here, as in other branches of theological learning, the relation between university and churches has been rather strong, even though there was not a direct connection. It should be remembered that in the churches of the Reformed family biblical exposition was an important element in the sermons which formed the central part of the church-services.

What were the changes that came about since 1951 with regard to N.T. studies? Six points to illustrate this may be singled out.

1) The greatest differences in organisation are seen on the Roman Catholic scene. They are connected with the alterations that took place in this Dutch province of the R.C.C. and which cannot be discussed here. They were partly stimulated by the 2nd Vatican Council, but had also internal causes. One of the consequences was the closing-down of a multitude of seminaries and the concentration in new faculties in Amsterdam (professors for N.T.: P. L. AHSMANN and B. HEMELSOET); Utrecht (TH. C. DE KRUYF), Tilburg (G. BOUWMAN), Heerlen (J. J. A. KAHMANN). The faculty of Nijmegen was also opened for undergraduate studies (professor W. K. GROSSOUW and B. M. F. VAN IERSEL). In this period, the fruits of the famous Encyclical Letter "Divino Afflante Spiritu" of 1943 were showing itself in the stronger emphasis on biblical studies among the Catholics as compared with past centuries. In the last decade the attention of many students

moved away from this biblical renewal in the direction of political and social *engagement*.

2) On the Protestant side, there was not such a change in the field of organization. The number of faculties remained the same and their status has not altered. But there were of course changes in the personal sphere.

In *Leyden* J. DE ZWAAN retired in 1953 and was succeeded by G. SEVENSTER, formerly professor on behalf of the Dutch Reformed Church in the same university; when the latter reached the retiring age he was replaced by M. DE JONGE (1971), who had been reader for Intertestamental Studies in Groningen. At *Amsterdam* the younger brother of the Leyden professor, J. N. SEVENSTER, occupied his chair in the Municipal University till his retirement in 1975; his place was taken over by J. SMIT SIBINGA, who had previously held a post in Leyden. Biblical Theology is taught in Amsterdam by the professor of the Lutheran Seminary C. H. LINDIJER. In the *Free University* (V.U.) R. SCHIPPERS has been the successor of F. W. GROSHEIDE since 1951. As to *Groningen* J. TH. UBBINK retired in 1955; in his place came P. A. VAN STEMPVOORT, who for reasons of health was forced to retire in 1967; A. F. J. KLIJN transferred from Utrecht, where he had been reader for N.T. studies, to Groningen. The Reformed Theological School in *Kampen* has been served in this field by H. N. RIDDERBOS who laid down his office last year, but has not found a successor yet. During the last 25 years there was no change in Utrecht. Finally two more schools may be mentioned here, because their professors of N.T. have become members of our Conventus, viz. a second seminary in Kampen of the reformed churches that were seperated from the main-stream in 1944; the incumbent since 1967 is J. VAN BRUGGEN; and the seminary of the Christian Reformed Churches in Apeldoorn where the N.T. has been taught by J. P. VERSTEEG since 1971.

3) A remarkable change took place in another direction too. After World War II the Dutch universities have been steadily growing as elsewhere in the world; this fact resulted in an expansion of the teaching staff. The theological faculties also benefitted from this development on a modest scale. New posts for readers, instructors and assistents have been created. We cannot mention here all names of the junior staff-members. But a few may be selected. At the Free University two new chairs were provided for Tj. BAARDA and H. MULDER, the latter having also a part-time job at the Protestant Theological Faculty of Brussels; they came to share the responsabilities

of R. SCHIPPERS. In Utrecht a new lecturership for N.T. studies was first held by A. F. J. KLIJN and after his departure for Groningen by J. REILING, who is at the same time professor at the Baptist Seminary. In Leyden the teaching-load of the professor was relieved by the help of J. SMIT SIBINGA, K. BERGER and B. DE HANDSCHUTTER respectively, whereas H. J. DE JONGE functions in the same capacity in Amsterdam. Research-posts for the "Corpus Hellenisticum" are held in Utrecht (see below, p. 12) by G. MUSSIES and P. W. VAN DER HORST. At Nijmegen, S. VAN TILBORG and A. P. VAN SCHAICK work as instructors. This extension of Staff at the universities took place gradually, mainly in the sixties. It opened the possibility for more research.

4) In connection with this expansion a special development may be noted which is closely related to N.T. studies (taken in a narrow sense). Keeping pace with the new and growing interest in so-called Intertestamental Studies, it was possible to establish a chair for that subject in 1962 at Utrecht (J. W. DOEVE), a lectureship at Groningen since 1965 (M. DE JONGE; H. E. GAYLORD). In Leyden J. C. H. LEBRAM is working in this field. It may be remarked in this connection that the greater part of Qumran-Studies is done in our country by Old Testament scholars, of whom J. P. M. VAN DER PLOEG (Nijmegen) and A. S. VAN DER WOUDE (Groningen with a Qumran-institute) are the leading men. Special emphasis on later Judaism (rabbinics) is found in Amsterdam, where M. BOERTIEN holds a chair in the Faculty of Arts and at the Catholic Schools of Amsterdam and Utrecht under the guidance of rabbi J. ASKENASY.

5) A special feature of this period has also been a closer contact with colleagues in Belgium, in particular with its leading centre at Louvain. This new development is a symptom of tendencies which make themselves felt in much wider areas. We did speak already of the considerable change in Roman Catholic Theology that had its impact also in the relation with the Protestants which became much more open. At the same time in the field of politics and culture the two countries Belgium and Holland came to a much better understanding and mutual relation. So the border-line was more or less effaced and this became also true in this particular case. It will be remembered that L. CERFAUX and J. COPPENS, professors for New and Old Testament at Louvain, started in 1950 the "Journées Bibliques". At first these conferences, held at the end of August each year, were meant to make seminary-teachers and interested members of the clergy of Belgium acquainted with progress in biblical studies. But, without

losing this goal, they have gradually moved more in the direction of conferences for scholars, both of Old and New Testament. The themes of these meetings are taken from both parts of the Bible, though in the last decade for some reason or another the N.T. had the greater emphasis. The papers and communications presented to these conferences are published in French, German or English (the latest volumes have been devoted to the study of respectively Luke, Matthew, Mark and John, the editors being F. NEIRYNCK, M. DIDIER, M. SABBE and M. DE JONGE). The Dutch have participated in these conferences in growing numbers, attracted by the hospitality of their southern neighbours. On the other hand, Flemish students of the N.T. have joined the S.N.T.C. and we hope that this fruitful collaboration and exchange will continue and be intensified. I know that this hope is shared by the present professor for the N.T. at Louvain F. NEIRYNCK and his colleagues.

6) Since roughly speaking 1968, the Dutch universities also shared in the universal unrest prevailing in academic circles and created a climate that was not very favourable for research in the fields of the Humanities and Theology. On the one hand we see — confining ourselves to the study of the N.T. — an ongoing specialization, an ever widening and deepening of the scientific apparatus required for a proper understanding of the N.T., and on the other hand we hear the question, even the cry: what has this work in textual criticism, philology, introduction etc. to do with the great challenges Christianity has to face? Should we not come to a thorough contextualisation in the present critical times? Even while admitting that a serious problem is laid at our door, I am convinced that we cannot betray our heritage but for the sake of a better understanding of the N.T. itself, which by its very existence requires such an approach. We do not do it as a pass-time, but as an essential contribution European, also Dutch, scholarship can make, has to make to the understanding and effectiveness of the N.T. in the world of our times.

Almost a century ago in 1886 the Leyden-professor Willem Christiaan VAN MANEN gave a survey of the contributions Dutch scholars had made in the field of the N.T. studies in the 25 years since 1859. That starting-point was not so arbitrarily chosen as might seem at first sight, for it was the year in which a previous historian had finished his account. VAN MANEN published his survey first in German in the "Jahrbücher für protestantische Theologie" (1883-1885) and then in Dutch in a separate volume of 268 pages: "Het Nieuwe Testament sedert 1859" (Groningen 1886). It gives summaries of all books and articles, ordered by the main topics of the N.T. Introduction and following the order of the canonical books.

In planning this introduction for this jubilee-volume I asked myself whether I should follow this example in looking back over the past 25 years. Or had the material to be ordered after a different principle, e.g. according to author's name? With a very few exceptions all members of our society have kindly put their bibliographies at my disposal by which my own notes could be checked.

On due consideration it appeared that both ways were impracticable, were it alone for reasons of space. After all I had not been invited to write a catalogue, but an introduction to this volume. Moreover, the excellent bibliographies of "Biblica" and "New Testament Abstracts" offer sufficient information, also concerning the work of Dutch scholars; so there is no need to waste paper by duplication. Hence it was thought much more appropriate to combine restrospective observations with an indication of the direction in which the main streams of interest in the N.T.-field flow for Dutch students. However it seemed useful to give a list of doctoral dissertations in this area defended at the Dutch universities by way of appendix.

Dutch theology in general has always been and still is in direct relation to the life of the concrete churches. The character of that relation varies. So there is no official link between the state-universities and the Dutch Reformed Church whereas the ties between the Roman Catholic hierarchy and the theological schools, between the so-called Re-reformed Churches and the Free University and the theological school at Kampen are rather close.

This general rule does also hold good, if we look in the direction of N.T. studies. A most conspicious case in this connection is H. N. RIDDERBOS who has been greatly involved in the life of his denomination, influenced that work by many articles on actual issues and has almost the status of a "church-father". A book of TJ. BAARDA on the "synoptic question", "De betrouwbaarheid der Evangeliën" (1967), caused unrest in his communion. Much work by members of our society, many of whom are parish-ministers, is done to serve the churches and their members, and not for purely scientific reasons. This point may be illustrated not so much by a list of specific books and articles in churchpapers as by two general facts.

In the first place, I should like to draw attention to the activities of some of our members on behalf of the Bible Societies. — As a consequence of the renewed interest in the Bible among the Roman Catholics the "Willibrord Vereniging" published a new translation of the N.T. (1961) into which W. K. GROSSOUW has invested much of his work during many years. On the Protestant side there was work on the revision of the translation of 1939 (G. and J. N. SEVENSTER, R. SCHIPPERS, P. A. VAN STEMPVOORT, W. C. VAN UNNIK); a new translation of the Old Testament Apocrypha was prepared by the same group together with J. W. DOEVE and the O.T. professor M. A. BEEK, which after many vicissitudes appeared in 1975. — A. F. J. KLIJN helped in the revision of the Dutch N.T. and prepared annotations for fascicules with notes. M. DE JONGE was active in preparing a version of the N.T. in present-day Dutch. He and J. REILING wrote together with the linguist Dr. J. L. SWELLENGREBEL two volumes for the series "Translator's Handbook" of the United Bible Societies (The Johannine Epistles and Luke: Gospel respectively). R. SCHIPPERS served for many years as chairman of the Committee on Translations whereas the present writer is General President of the Dutch Bible Society since 1967. — A plan to make an "Oecumenical Translation" together with the brethern in Flanders has been abortive; its realisation shall have to wait till a new generation will take over the task.

In the second place, we may mention the fact that there are already three series of commentaries in Dutch which are not written for scholars only, but also to serve the needs of the parish ministers. But that does not mean that they belong to that category which is called "practical" or "layman's". All three of them discuss points of Greek grammar and lexicography. They vary in character, method and size. Each of them has a different ecclesiastical background. Two of them continue series that started before World War II, but publish now completely new volumes. The oldest and most voluminous is the "Commentaar op het Nieuwe Testament", written by scholars of the Calvinistic school ("Re-reformed Churches") and stands in that solid tradition. The second series is called "De Prediking van het Nieuwe Testament"; it started in the thirties when the call for a "theological" interpretation of the Bible was voiced, to a great extent inspired by Barthian theology; hence not only N.T. scholars have contributed to this series, but also systematic theologians (background, Dutch Reformed). Since 1965 the Roman Catholics started a series under the name "Het Nieuwe Testament vertaald en toegelicht" under redaction of W. K. GROSSOUW, B. M. F. VAN IERSEL and F. NEIRYNCK, which reflect the collaboration of Flamish and Dutch scholars.

All this work, serving the home-church, can only be done on a solid scientific base. The N.T. books came into existence in and for the church, delivering the message and "for the equipment of the saints" (Eph. 4:12); hence a direct contact with the church of our time is a duty for N.T. scholarship. This interaction between study and church is not one-way-traffic, but a form of exchange that is fruitful in both directions. There are dangers lurking along that way, but they are seen by an open eye and overcome with a critical mind that knows of the Spirit that "will guide into all the truth" (John xvi 13).

This part of N.T. Scholarship we have dealt with so far may be styled "applied science". It is now time to turn to those areas where "pure scientific research" takes place, where Dutch scholars try to break new ground and to discover what new material can be found to understand the N.T. in the world and in its uniqueness. For reasons of space only those areas will be mentioned where certain clusters are found, while specific problems had to be left out. In identifying a certain number of them I hope not to have made too arbitrary a choice.

1) In the sphere of *Intertestamental Studies* M. DE JONGE is preparing an edition of the "Testamenta XII Patriarcharum" for the Berlin corpus of the "Griechisch christlichen Schriftsteller". His thesis on that book of 1953 reopened the discussion about the origin of that important Pseudepigraphon. He published a small edition of that book according to one manuscript (1964) and together with his collaborators a volume of Studies (1975). These books form part of the series "Pseudepigrapha Veteris Testamenti Graece", resp. "Studia in Veteris Testamenti Pseudepigrapha" of which he is the redactor together with A. M. DENIS. For that project J. SMIT SIBINGA is preparing a new edition of the Testament of Abraham. Others are to follow. This new enterprise is a great stimulus for future research in an area that was known and yet neglected, and not thoroughly investigated. — J. W. DOEVE studied the hermeneutical principles of the rabbis, as compared with the N.T. (1953); in later years he turned his attention to the historical problems connected with the 2nd century B.C. and the dating of Qumran texts. In passing we may mention here the publication of the Job Targum by J. P. M. VAN DER PLOEG en A. S. VAN DER WOUDE.

2) It need hardly be said that the good offices of G. QUISPEL

(professor for the History of the Early Church at Utrecht) made it possible for Dutch Scholars to participate, right from the beginning, in the work on the Nag Hammadi codices and the rethinking of the problems, connected with that large umbrella "Gnosis". QUISPEL not only published very important texts such as those contained in the Jung-Codex and the "Gospel of Thomas", but also wrote scores of articles, now collected in the two volumes of his "Gnostic Studies" (1975-1976). He stimulated work in this particular field and in some others to which we shall turn presently. And though not all his theses met with general approval, he deserves the honour for having opened new perspectives. The present writer made a number of contributions in this field, starting with a paper on the relation of the Gospel of Truth and the N.T. (1954). We cannot discuss the whole problem of Gnosticism here, but it is quite certain that it is extremely important for N.T. studies to have clarification here, because of the role attributed to this religious phenomenon by R. BULTMANN and his followers. In the light of this Library of Nag Hammadi and new research on Mandaeism and Manichaeism, the whole problem of origin, history, spread etc. of Gnosticism, also in its relation to Greek philosophy and oriental religions must be completely revised and statements based on the insufficient material available before 1950 are unfounded. Much work of interpretation and historical evolution still lies ahead of us. Great caution in these matters will be wise, but hypotheses take on a life of their own and can be hard to eradicate. It will not be out of place here to mention the fact that not only N.T. scholars work in this field: the Egyptologist J. ZANDEE had his share in previous publications and is now preparing an edition of "the Teachings of Silvanus". H. J. W. DRIJVERS, professor in Semitic Languages at Groningen, who wrote his dissertation on "Bardesanes" (1966) is studying the problems involved with regard to syncretism in Mesopotania. So there is a lively interest in the enigma, called Gnosticism, in the Netherlands, and it can be said for certain that it will continue.

3) One of the other branches of N.T. studies that was effected by the discovery of Nag Hammadi, more particularly by the publication of the "Gospel of Thomas", was *Textual Criticism*. QUISPEL in various articles drew attention to the fact that this gospel in sayings parallel to synoptic material reveals readings which deviate from the Egyptian or Byzantine texts, but have affinities with the so-called Western text and with various branches of the descendants of Tatian's Gospel

Harmony. Tj. BAARDA, then assistant to R. SCHIPPERS, took up the gauntlet and contributed a chapter to SCHIPPERS' book "Het Evangelie van Thomas" (1960) on: Thomas and Tatian. Since then he has written several articles on textual problems connected with the mysterious Tatian, crowned so far by his dissertation on the variants of the Fourth Gospel, found in Aphrahat (1975).

In the meantime A. F. J. KLIJN continued his studies in the Western text and gave a second survey of the researches in the 20 years since 1949 (1969). G. QUISPEL in his "Het Evangelie van Thomas en de Nederlanden" (1971) argued that traces of Tatian's work can still be found in mediaeval "Lives of Jesus" in western Europe, and also in the German poem the "Heliand". He continued with much more material a line that D. PLOOY, professor at Amsterdam/Utrecht, had drawn in the 1920s. His thesis, however, is not accepted by the Leyden professor of Mediaeval Church History C. C. DE BRUIN, who has devoted the greater part of his scholarly life to the history of Bible-translation in the Middle Ages (editor of the "Corpus Sacrae Scripturae neerlandicae medii aevi" in many volumes). — Quite recently J. VAN BRUGGEN did question the criteria on which the modern text of the N.T. since Westcott-Hort is based and pleads for the value of the Textus Receptus ("De Tekst van het Nieuwe Testament", 1976).

4) In yet another direction the influence of the "Gospel of Thomas" was felt, viz. in that of new research in the *history of Jewish Christianity*. It was again G. QUISPEL who pointed out the similarity between variants in this gospel and in Jewish Christian sources. That led him into the investigation of the origins of Christianity in Edessa, where this Gospel with all likelihood was at home, and in Syria in general. In his view that country received its Christian faith directly from Jesus of Palestine, in a stream of tradition different and independent from that which we all know, the development in a western direction which is reflected in the N.T. and the early Fathers. The best presentation of his position may be found in an article of 1968: "The discussion of Judaic Christianity" (now in: *Gnostic Studies* II p. 146ff.). Though these theses are not generally accepted either and form part of the discussion in the scholarly world at large, they bring that enigmatic world of Jewish Christianity in a new perspective. A. F. J. KLIJN and G. J. REININK did therefore a very great service to scholars in bringing together all the "Patristic evidence for Jewish-Christian sects" (1973). Much is here still in debate, but whilst it is a very difficult subject, it is important to see here new possibilities.

5) The research in the *Synoptic Question* is done both in Nijmegen and Louvain. In the former university a group round B. M. F. VAN IERSEL studies the characteristics of language in the gospels with emphasis on syntactical structures, the differences in tenses, the use of the participle etc. The results will be published in four volumes, the first of which will be ready by the end of this year. A somewhat different line is followed by F. NEIRYNCK who collected the first-fruits of his labours in his book "Duality in Mark, contributions to the study of the Markan redaction" (1972). As may be seen from the subtitle of this book the phenomenon of pleonasm, repetition etc. that has often attracted the attention of students is not used here as a criterion for source-criticism, but to describe part of redaction-history.

6) The centre of research in Utrecht is found in the "*Corpus Hellenisticum Novi Testamenti*" where the present writer works together with J. REILING, G. MUSSIES and P. W. VAN DER HORST, each of whom had their training in classics before reading theology. In my address as rector of the university, I have given an exposition of the long history and aims of this project (an English translation is found in *Journal of Biblical Literature* 83 (1964), 17ff.). As will be known the Judaic-hellenistic side is provided for in Halle under the leadership of G. DELLING; a group of American scholars under H. D. BETZ (Claremont) is taking part in the work by working on the writings of Plutarch. Three volumes of "Subsidia" have appeared so far, one of which is that of G. MUSSIES on "Dio Chrystom and the N.T." (1972). The same author treated the language of the Johannine Apocalypse in his doctoral dissertation "the Morphology of Koine Greek" (1971); at the moment he is engaged among other things in a study of the traditions about Diogenes as compared with those about Jesus. J. REILING is studying prophecy in the early Church and published the first results in his thesis "Hermas and Prophecy" (1973). VAN DER HORST is preparing a dissertation on the collection of ethical precepts under the name of Phocylides: and gave already some articles in *Novum Testamentum*, e.g. on "Musonius Rufus and the N.T." (1974, 306ff.). My own contributions are of a more thematic nature, the elucidation of certain verses or conceptions of the N.T.; out of numerous articles I mention here only the last: "Het Godspredikaat 'Het Begin en het Einde' bij Flavius Josephus en in de Openbaring van Johannes" (1976). This work has greater implications than giving a simple illustration of a certain text, as may be seen from my

"Tarsus or Jerusalem, the city of Paul's youth" (1962) and "Oog en Oor, criteria voor de eerste samenstelling van het Nieuwe Testament" (1973). It is much more than collecting "parallels"; it requires careful evaluation of these parallels which helps us as to realize how the words were understood by the contemporaries of the N.T. and brings to light certain contexts that for them were real while for us, living in another world, they are hidden under the surface. It may be said with great confidence that much work is still lying ahead of us, not only because of the vastness of the classical literature to be studied, but also through the on-going extension of our knowledge of the Hellenistic-Roman world. Apart from this Corpus, but also dealing with the study of the N.T. in relation with the "Umwelt" are three books of J. N. SEVENSTER: "Paul and Seneca" (1961); "Do you know Greek? How much Greek could the first Jewish Christians have known?" (1968), which has a direct bearing on many problems connected with the character of traditions embodied in the Gospels; "The roots of pagan anti-semitism in the ancient world" (1975), the importance of which leaps to the eye in thinking of the christian mission in the first century.

7) Finally a new field is opened in exploring the often neglected *history of N.T. exegesis*. Since the days of Erasmus there has been a strong exegetical tradition in the Netherlands. The most famous names in this connection are Hugo GROTIUS and J. J. WETTSTEIN, who being exiled from his hometown found a new fatherland in Holland. For the monumental new scientific edition of Erasmus' Opera, that is on its way, sponsored by the Royal Dutch Academy, H. J. DE JONGE is preparing the volume of the "Annotationes", whereas the famous 1516-text of the N.T. will be reprinted thanks to the good offices of Bruce M. METZGER (Princeton). In 1971 DE JONGE presented to participants of the S.N.T.S. meeting in Holland an interesting booklet on: "Daniel Heinsius and the Textus Receptus of the New Testament"; to the volume, celebrating the 4th centenary of Leyden University (1975), he contributed a learned study on Scaliger. Within the framework of the "Corpus Hellenisticum" some predecessors of Wettstein are studied, because these gentlemen who had such an amazing, intimate knowledge of the classics have many valuable insights that have been lost in later generations, which was a loss indeed.

These are the main areas in which Dutch N.T. scholars are engaged in their research. Is it working in the margin of the N.T. itself?

The answer is: No! It is carried by the conviction that the N.T., being a collection of occasional writings, made for certain people in specific circumstances, in a sphere of religious and cultural life that is not ours, demands an intimate knowledge of the world in which it came into existence, which is there without being made explicit. New material has become available and must be explored for its bearing on N.T. problems. In the material that is known for several centuries much is still unexploited. The N.T. cannot be read in isolation: it must be studied in relation to what has gone before in the Jewish and pagan world, to its contemporary setting and also to what followed (it cannot be separated from patristic study; this wholesome insight that was self-evident for the generation of the end of the last and the beginning of this century has too often been forgotten in the last decades). The advance in N.T. scholarship cannot be achieved by great slogans, a ping-pong game of hypotheses, but only by careful minute analysis and assessment of factual data. It need not to be stressed that such a study of details is only fruitful when done with the greater totality in mind.

It goes without saying that the work in more familiar fields is also continuing apart from commentaries (see p. 8f.). In this respect we may point to the voluminous study of H. van der Loos on "the Miracles of Jesus" (1965) and the full-size discussion of Pauline theology in H. N. Ridderbos' "Paulus" (1966, also translated in English and German) with the subtitle "a sketch of his theology" which is rather an understatement for a book of 650 pages. The work on the Synoptic Gospels by groups in Nijmegen and Louvain has been mentioned before. The studies of M. de Jonge concentrate on Johannine problems, the work for the "Corpus Hellenisticum" leads the present writer to pay special attention to Luke-Acts, Paul and the Apocalypse. Questions of chronology are taken up again by J. van Bruggen.

It is somewhat striking that the interest in the great issues that were raised by R. Bultmann and his school (Quest of the historical Jesus, Hermeneutics) during this period, were not themselves reflected in the publications of Dutch scholars. This "defect" — if it may called by that name — can be explained in this way that in Holland grave question-marks are put at the foundations on which Bultmanns structure has been built. J. N. Sevenster investigated in his collected essays "Bultmanniana" (1969) the criteria applied by Bultmann and his followers to the synoptic tradition and Paul's indebtness to

Hellenistic communities, and found them not valid. Bultmann's conception of Johannine eschatology was tested and rejected in the dissertation of L. van Hartingsveld (1962). The work on the Gnosis, referred to before (p. 10) makes by implication the influence of that current of thought on Paul and John as held by the Bultmann school rather questionable. And when the foundations are so shaken a discussion is not very promising. As to Hermeneutics it may be said that in the Dutch theological context largely dominated by Barthian theology the problem had a different aspect. And finally: *non possumus omnia omnes*.

Let me conclude with expressing my hope that this short survey of Dutch N.T. scholarship with all its shortcomings may give our colleagues abroad a good impression of what is going on in this field on the borders of the North Sea and serve as a helpful framework for the contributions that follow in this volume. My heartfelt wish applies to the S.N.T.C. at this jubilee: may it fulfil its function of meeting place and stimulus also in the years ahead: *vivat, floreat, crescat Conventus noster!*

APPENDIX

Theses in the field of the New Testament, defended at Dutch Universities 1951-1975*

1951

Utrecht:

Kwa Joe Liang, *Het begrip deemoed in I Clemens, bijdrage tot de geschiedenis van de oud-christelijke ethiek*, Utrecht 1951, 144 pp.

Amsterdam, VU:

Dondorp, Arie, *De verzoekingen van Jezus Christus in de woestijn*, Kampen 1951, 186 pp.

1952

Amsterdam, SU:

Lindijer, Cord Hendrik, *Het begrip sarx bij Paulus*, Assen 1952, 239 pp.

Nijmegen, RKU:

Linssen, Gerardus, *Het apostolaat volgens St. Paulus. Een bijbelstheologische studie van I Kor. ix*, Nijmegen 1952, 171 pp.

1953

Leiden:

Doeve, Jan Willem, *Jewish Hermeneutics in the synoptic Gospels and Acts*, Assen 1953, IX, 232 pp.

---

* These dissertations, when written in Dutch, have a summary in English, French or German.

Leiden:

Flesseman - van Leer, Ellen, *Tradition and Scripture in the early Church*, Assen 1953, 210 pp.

Jonge, Marinus de, *The Testaments of the twelve Patriarchs. A Study of their Text, Composition and Origin*, Assen 1953, 184 pp.

Royen, Paul David van, *Jezus en Johannes de Doper. Een historisch onderzoek op grond van de synoptische evangeliën naar hun onderlinge verhouding sedert de arrestatie van de laatste*, Leiden 1953, 118 pp.

Groningen:

Plenter, Jan Derk, *De blijdschap in Paulus' brieven. Een studie met diens brieven aan de Filipenzen als uitgangspunt*, Assen 1953. 219 pp.

Utrecht:

Schoonheim, Pieter Leendert, *Een semasiologisch onderzoek van Parousia met betrekking tot het gebruik in Mattheus 24*, Aalten 1953, 316 pp.

Amsterdam, SU:

Elderenbosch, Pieter Adriaan, *De oplegging der handen*, den Haag 1953, 156 pp.

1955

Utrecht:

Andel, Curt Pieter van, *De structuur van de Henoch-traditie en het Nieuwe Testament*, Utrecht 1955, 131 pp.

Amsterdam, VU:

Swigchem, Douwe van, *Het missionair karakter van de Christelijke gemeente volgens de brieven van Paulus en Petrus*, Kampen 1955, 276 pp.

1956

Amsterdam, VU:

Wind, Anne, *Leven en dood in het Evangelie van Johannes en in de Serat Dewarutji. Met een elenctische confrontatie*, Franeker 1956, 334 pp.

1957

Groningen:

Woude, Adam Simon van der, *Die messianischen Vorstellungen der Gemeinde von Qumran*, Assen 1957, 274 pp.

1958

Utrecht:

Vliet, Hendrik van, *No single Testimony, a Study on the Adoption of the Law of Deut. 19:15 par. into the New Testament*, Utrecht 1958, 162 pp.

1959

Leiden:

Kosmala, Hans, *Essenismus und Christentum*, Leiden 1959, 85 pp.

Amsterdam, SU:

Leeuwen, Gerrit van, *Christologie en anthropologie. Studie over de christologische fundering van de theologische anthropologie*, den Haag 1959, 332 pp.

Amsterdam, VU:

Holwerda, David Earl, *The Holy Spirit and Eschatology in the Gospel of John. A Critique of Rudolf Bultmann's present Eschatology*, Kampen 1959, 141 pp.

Kampen:

Du Plessis, Paul Johannes, ΤΕΛΕΙΟΣ, *the Idea of Perfection in the New Testament*, Kampen 1959, 255 pp.

1960

Utrecht:

Verweys, Pieter Godfried, *Evangelium und neues Gesetz in der ältesten Christenheit bis auf Marcion*, Utrecht 1960, 382 pp.

Amsterdam, SU:

Kossen, Hendrik Bernardus, *Op zoek naar de historische Jezus, Een studie over Albert Schweitzers visie op Jezus' leven*, Assen 1960, 300 pp.

Amsterdam, VU:

Young, James Calvin de, *Jerusalem in the New Testament. The Significance of the City in the History of Redemption and in Eschatology*, Kampen 1960, 168 pp.

1961

Leiden:

Cramer, Albert Willem, *Stoicheia tou kosmou. Interpretatie van een nieuwtestamentische term*, den Haag 1961, 179 pp.

Amsterdam, SU:

Meuzelaar, Jacobus Johannes, *Der Leib des Messias. Eine exegetische Studie über den Gedanken vom Leib Christi in den Paulusbriefen*, Assen 1961, 188 pp.

Amsterdam, VU:

Cruvelier, Jean Marc Étienne, *L'exégèse de Romains 7 et le mouvement de Keswick*, 's-Gravenhage 1961, 215 pp.

Kistemaker, Simon, *The Psalm Citations in the Epistle to the Hebrews*, Amsterdam 1961, 167 pp.

Nijmegen:

Iersel, Bastiaan Martinus Franciscus van, *"Der Sohn" in den synoptischen Jesusworten, Christusbezeichnung der Gemeinde oder Selbstzeichnung Jesu?*, Leiden 1961, 194 pp.

1962

Utrecht:

Hartingsveld, Lodewijk van, *Die Eschatologie des Johannesevangeliums, eine Auseinandersetzung mit R. Bultmann*, Assen 1962, 271 pp.

Dreyer, Andries Johannes Gerardus, *An Examination of the possible Relation between Luke's Infancy Narratives and the Qumran Hodayot*, Amsterdam 1962, 135 pp.

Amsterdam, VU:

Boer, Willis Peter de, *The Imitation of Paul, An exegetical Study*, Kampen 1962, 235 pp.

Roels, Edwin D., *God's mission. The Epistle to the Ephesians in Mission Perspective*, Franeker 1962, 303 pp.

Smith, William Sheppard, *Musical Aspects of the New Testament*, Amsterdam 1962, 187 pp.

Kampen:

Walt, Tjaard van der, *Die Koninkrijk van God-Nabij! Exegetiese verkenning van die toekomstperspectief van Jesus Christus volgens die getuigenis van die synoptiese evangelies*, Kampen 1962, 332 pp.

Du Plessis, Isak Johannes, *Christus as Hoof van Kerk en Kosmos. 'n exegeties-theologiese studie van Christus se hoofskap, veral in Ephesiërs en Kolossense*, Groningen 1962, 148 pp.

1963

Leiden:

Smit Sibinga, Joost, *The Old Testament text of Justin Martyr I, The Pentateuch*, Leiden 1963, 162 pp.

Kampen:

Roberts, John Henry, *Die opbou van die Kerk volgens die Ephesebrief*, Groningen 1963, 200 pp.

1964

Leiden:

Ru, Gerrit de, *De kinderdoop en het Nieuwe Testament*, Wageningen 1964, 295 pp.

Amsterdam, SU:

Meerburg, Philippus Pieter, *De structuur van het koptische Evangelie naar Thomas*, Maastricht 1964, 190 pp.

Amsterdam, VU:

Bandstra, Andrew John, *The Law and the Elements of the World. An exegetical Study in Aspects of Paul's Teaching*, Kampen 1964, 209 pp.

Nijmegen, RKU:

Ruys, Rembertus C.M., *De struktuur van de Brief aan de Romeinen, Een stilistische, vormhistorische en thematische analyse van Rom. 1:16-3:23*, Utrecht 1964, 297 pp.

1965

Leiden:

Waard, Jan de, *A comparative Study of the Old Testament Text in the Dead Sea Scrolls and in the New Testament*, Leiden 1965, 101 pp.

Groningen:

Smid, Harm Reinder, *Protevangelium Jacobi, A Commentary*, Assen 1965, 200 pp.

Buitkamp, Jan, *Die Auferstehungsvorstellungen in den Qumrantexten und ihr alttestamentlicher, apokryphischer, pseudepigraphischer und rabbinischer Hintergund* (proefschrift fac. der Letteren, 1964), Groningen [1965], 158 pp.

Amsterdam, VU:

Vos, Louis Arthur, *The synoptic Traditions in the Apocalypse*, Kampen 1965, 245 pp.

Nijmegen, RKU:

Willemse, Johannes Joseph Cornelis, *Het vierde evangelie, Een onderzoek naar zijn structuur*, Hilversum 1965, 344 pp.

Reijnders, Gerardus Quirinius, *The Terminology of the Holy Cross in early Christian literature as based upon Old Testament Typology*, Nijmegen 1965, 230 pp.

1966

Leiden:

Watteville, Jean de, *Le sacrifice dans les textes eucharistiques des premiers siècles*, Neuchatel 1966, 234 pp.

Amsterdam, GU:

Hanhart, Karel, *The intermediate State in the New Testament*, Groningen 1966, 248 pp.

1967

Leiden:

Grünberg, Madeleine, *The West-Saxon Gospels. A Study of the Gospel of St. Matthew, with Text of the four Gospels*, Amsterdam 1967, 414 pp. (proefschrift fac. der Letteren).

Amsterdam, VU:

Oostendorp, Derk William, *Another Jesus. A Gospel of Jewish Christian Superiority in II Corinthians*, Kampen 1967, 103 pp.

Nijmegen, RKU:

O'Malley, T.P., *Tertullian and the Bible, Language, Imagery, Exegesis*, Nijmegen 1967, 186 pp. (proefschrift fac. der Letteren)

Kampen:

Lategan, Bernard Christiaan, *Die aardse Jezus in die prediking van Paulus volgens sy briewe*, Rotterdam 1967, 280 pp.

1968

Amsterdam, VU:

Combrink, Hans Jacob Bernardus, *Die diens van Jesus, 'n Eksegetiese beskouing oor Markus 10:45*, Groningen 1968, 201 pp.

Knight III, George William, *The faithful Sayings in the Pastoral Letters*, Kampen 1968, 162 pp.

Groningen:

Nielsen, Jan Tjeerd, *Adam and Christ in the Theology of Irenaeus of Lyons, An examination of the Function of the Adam-Christ Typology in the Adversus Haereses of Irenaeus, against the Background of the Gnosticism of his time*, Assen 1968, 109 pp.

1969

Leiden:

Kwaak, Hans van der, *Het proces van Jezus. Een vergelijkend onderzoek van de beschrijvingen der evangelisten*, Assen 1969, 300 pp.

Roon, Aart van, *Een onderzoek naar de authenticiteit van de brief aan de Epheziërs*, Assen 1969, 366 pp.

1970

Amsterdam, VU:

Timmer, John, *Julius Wellhausen and the Synoptic Gospels, A Study in Tradition Growth*, Rotterdam 1970, 127 pp.

Nijmegen, RKU:

Orban, Arpad Peter, *Les denominations du monde chez les premiers auteurs chrétiens*, Nijmegen 1970, 247 pp. (Proefschrift fac. der Letteren).

1971

Amsterdam, VU:

Budiman, Rudy, *De realisering der verzoening in het menselijk bestaan, Een onderzoek naar Paulus' opvattingen van de gemeenschap aan Christus' lijden als een integrerend deel der verzoening*, Delft 1971, 235 pp.

Ridder, Richard Ralph de, *The Dispersion of the People of God, The Convenant Basis of Matthew 28:18-20 against the Background of Jewish, pre-Christian Proselyting and Diaspora, and the Apostleship of Jesus Christ*, Kampen 1971, 239 pp.

Versteeg, Johannes Pieter, *Christus en de Geest, Een exegetisch onderzoek naar de verhouding van de opgestane Christus en de Geest van God volgens de brieven van Paulus*, Kampen 1971, 449 pp.

1972

Leiden:

Middendorp, Theophil, *Die Stellung Jesu Ben Siras zwischen Judentum und Hellenismus*, Leiden 1972, 186 pp.

Kampen:

Nicol, Willem, *The Sēmeia in the Fourth Gospel, Tradition and Redaction*, Leiden 1972, 155 pp.

1973

Utrecht:

Bruggen, Jakob van, *"Na veertien jaren", de datering van het in Galaten 2 genoemde overleg in Jeruzalem*, Kampen 1973, 263 pp.

Verheule, Anthonie Frans, *Wilhelm Bousset, Leben und Werk*, Amsterdam 1973, 435 pp.

Vos, Johannes Sijko, *Traditionsgeschichtliche Untersuchungen zur paulinischen Pneumatologie*, Assen 1973, 152 pp.

Reiling, Jannes, *Hermas and Christian Prophecy, a Study of the Eleventh Mandate*, Leiden 1973, 197 pp.

Amsterdam, VU:

Cruz, Virgil Ambrose, *The Mark of the Beast. A study of XAPAΓMA in the Apocalypse*, Amsterdam 1973, 150 pp.

Nijmegen, RKU:

Mc. Dermott, Brian Owen, *The personal Unity of Jesus and God, according to Wolfhart Pannenberg*, St. Ottilien 1973, 504 pp.

1975

Amsterdam, VU:

Baarda, Tjitze, *The Gospel Quotations of Aphrahat, the Persian sage, Aphrahat's text of the Fourth Gospel*, Amsterdam 1975, 520 pp.

A FRAGMENT OF PAUL AT AMSTERDAM (0270)

J. SMIT SIBINGA

Among the treasures of the University Libraries in the Netherlands there are a few — not many — manuscripts of the Greek New Testament. Two of these are written in uncials: the Codex Boreelianus, dating from the 9th or 10th century (F, 09) in Utrecht, and a quite different book, Joseph Scaliger's Greek-Arabic lectionary, dated 1265, (*l* 6) in Leiden.[1]

To these well-known manuscripts a third, and again rather different, uncial witness has been added: the fragment 0270, a leaf from a small vellum codex, written in a handsome 'biblical majuscule', to be dated to the early 5th or late 4th century, and containing parts of Paul's First Letter to the Corinthians, ch. XV. It was recently acquired by the library of the University of Amsterdam; about its provenance and past no information is available.[2]

In publishing and discussing this fragment we first of all print, side by side, a diplomatic transcript and a reconstruction such as a modern reader would require, spacing words, proposing restorations, etc. After this we intend to give a description of the fragment, also paying attention to such aspects as its paleography and date. Next, particular points in the transcript and reconstruction are set forth, and finally the text of the fragment is studied.

---

[1] See: Henk Jan DE JONGE, Joseph Scaliger's Greek-Arabic lectionary ..., *Quaerendo* 5 (1975), 143-172.

[2] The shelf mark is GX 200. I am indebted to Dr. P. J. SIJPESTEIJN, who very kindly brought the fragment to my attention and gave every help that was needed; to Dr. K. A. WORP, also of the Department of Papyrology of the University of Amsterdam, and to the staff of the Library for their advice and cooperation at every stage, and to professor dr. S. VAN DER WOUDE, chief librarian, for his permission to publish the fragment. The help of Dr. K. JUNACK and professor Dr. K. ALAND of the *Institut für neutestamentliche Textforschung* at Münster/Westf. is also gratefully acknowledged. Dr. S. P. BROCK, Oxford, kindly corrected the English.

A

```
]ΝΕΚΟΠΙΑΣΆΟΥΚΕ̣ΓΩ[
    Ἡ̄Θ̄Ῡ
]Α̣ΡΙΣΣΥ̣ΝΕΜΟΪΕΙΤΕ[
]ΤΕΕΚΕΙΝΟΙ̣ΟΥΤΩ[
]Μ̣ΕΝΚΑΙΟΥΤΩΣΕΠ[
    ]ΕΙΔΕΧΣ̄Κ̣Η̣ΡΥΣΣΕΤ[              5
        ]Ο̣ΤΙΕΓ̣ΗΓΕΡΤΑΙΠ Ω[
        ]ΝΫ̈ΜΙΝΤΙΝΕΣΟΤ̣Ι̣
    ]ΝΕΚ̣[   ]Ω̣ΝΟΥΚΕΣΤΙΝ˙
    ]Α̣Σ̣[   ]ΝΕΚΡ̣ΩΝΟΥΚ̣
    ]ΧΣ̣[   ]Γ̣ΗΓΕΡΤΑΙ:ΕΙΔ Ε        10
]Γ̣ΗΓΕΡΤΑΙ.ΚΕΝΟΝΑΡΑ
]Ρ̣ΥΓΜΑΗΜΩΝΚ̣Ε̣ΝΗ
                 Υ
Κ̣Α̣Ι̣ΗΠΙΣ[   ]ΙΣ̣ΗΜΩΝΕΥΡΙ..Ο̣Μ Ε
ΘΑ̣ΔΕΚΑΙΨΕΥΔΟΜΑΡΤΥΡΕ̣ΣΤΟΥ
Θ̄Ῡ.ΟΤΙΕΜ̣Α̣Ρ̣Τ̣Υ̣ΡΗ[       ]Κ̣Α̣Τ̣Α     15
Τ̣ΟΥΘ̄ῩΟΤΙ[
    ]Κ̣Η̣Γ̣ΕΙ̣[
    ]Υ̣ΚΕΓ̣[
```

A

1 Cor xv	*number of letters*		*line*
10 πάντω]ν ἐκοπίασα οὐκ ἐγὼ [δὲ	22	15+7	
ἡ θ(εο)ῦ			
11 ἀλλὰ ἡ χ]άρις σὺν ἐμοί εἴτε	21	15+6	
οὖν ἐγὼ εἴ]τε ἐκεῖνοι οὕτω[ς	22	14+8	
κηρύσσο]μεν καὶ οὕτως ἐπ[ι-	21	13+8	
12 στεύσατε] εἰ δὲ χ(ριστὸ)ς κηρύσσετ[αι	24	14+10	5
ἐκ νεκρῶν] ὅτι ἐγήγερται πῶ[ς	23	14+9	
λέγουσιν ἐ]ν ὑμῖν τινες ὅτι	22	13+9	
ἀνάστασις] νεκ[ρ]ῶν οὐκ ἔστιν	23	13+10	
13 εἰ δὲ ἀνάστ]ασ[ις] νεκρῶν οὐκ	22	11+11	
14 ἔστιν οὐδὲ] χ(ριστὸ)ς [ἐ]γήγερται. εἰ δὲ	24	14+10	10
χ(ριστὸ)ς οὐκ ἐ]γήγερται κενὸν ἄρα	22	16+6	
καὶ τὸ κή]ρυγμα ἡμῶν κενὴ	20	13+7	
ὐ			
15 καὶ ἡ πίσ[τ]ις ἡμῶν εὑρι[σκ]όμε-	23	20+3	
θα δὲ καὶ ψευδομάρτυρες τοῦ	23	23+0	
θ(εο)ῦ ὅτι ἐμαρτυρή[σαμεν] κατὰ	22	17+5	15
τοῦ θ(εο)ῦ ὅτι [ἤγειρεν τὸν χ(ριστὸ)ν ὃν	22	8+14	
οὐ]κ ἤγει[ρεν εἴπερ ἄρα νεκροὶ	24	5+19	
ο]ὐκ ἐγ[είρονται	—	4	

B

]N̲Θ̲

]ΩΝΑΝΘΡΩΠΩΝΕΣΜ[

]ΝΙΔΕΧ̅Σ̅ΕΓΗΓΕΡΤΑΙ[

]Α̣ΠΑΡΧ̣ΗΤΩΝΚΕΚΟ̣[

]ΕΠΕΙΔΗΓΑΡΔΙΑΝΘΡΩ̣[

]Τ̣ΟΣΚΑΙΔΙ.Ν̣ΘΡΩΠΟ̣[5

ΝΕΚΡ̣Ω̣Ν̇ Ω̣ΣΠΕΡ[   ]Α̣[

ΠΑ̣ΝΤΕΣΑΠΟ̣[   ]Ν̣Η̣[

Τ̣ΩΣΚΑΙΕΝΤΩΧ̅Ω̅[

ΟΠΟΙΗΘ.ΣΟΝ[   ]ΑΙΕ[

ΕΝΤΩΙΔ̣ΙΩΤ[   ].   .[10

Χ̅Σ̅ΕΠΕΙΤΑΟΙΤΟΥΧ̅Υ̅[

ΡΟΥΣΙΑΑΥΤΟΥΕΙΤΑ..[

ΤΑΝΠΑΡΑΔ̣ΙΔ̣ΩΤ.Ν...[   ]ΕΙ[

Τ̣Ω̅Θ̅Ω̅ΚΑΙΠ̣Α̣ΤΡΙ[   ]..ΝΚΑΤΑΡ

ΓΗ̣[   ]ΚΑΙΠΑΣΑΝ   15

                 ]Μ̣Ι̣Ν̇ΔΕΙΓΑΡ[

                 ]ΧΡ[   ]Ο̣Υ[

                    ]Ϋ̈Π̣Ο̣[

B

1 Cor xv		*number of letters*	*line*

]ΝΘ

19, 20	τ]ων ἀνθρώπων ἐσμ[έν νυ-	18	13+5	
	]νὶ δὲ χ(ριστὸ)ς ἐγήγερται [ἐκ νεκρῶν	23	15+8	
	]ἀπαρχὴ τῶν κεκο[ιμημένων	21	13+8	
21	]ἐπειδὴ γὰρ δι' ἀνθρώ[που θάνα-	23	16+7	
	]τος καὶ δι' [ἀ]νθρώπο[υ ἀνάστασις	25	14+11	5
22	νεκρῶν ὥσπερ [γ]ἀ[ρ ἐν τῷ ἀδὰμ	22	12+10	
	πάντες ἀπο[θ]νή[σκουσιν οὕ-	21	11+10	
	τως καὶ ἐν τῷ χ(ριστ)ῷ [πάντες ζω-	20	12+8	
23	οποιηθ[ή]σον[τ]αι ἕ[καστος δὲ	22	12+10	
	ἐν τῷ ἰδίῳ τ[άγματι ἀπαρχὴ	21	9+12	10
	χ(ριστὸ)ς ἔπειτα οἱ τοῦ χ(ριστο)ῦ [ἐν τῇ πα-	21	15+6	
24	ρουσίᾳ αὐτοῦ εἶτ[α τὸ τέλος ὅ-	23	14+9	
	ταν παραδιδῷ τ[ὴ]ν [βασιλ]εί[αν	23	15+8	
	τῷ θ(ε)ῷ καὶ πατρὶ [ὅτα]ν καταρ-	21	18+3	
	γή[σῃ πᾶσαν ἀρχὴν] καὶ πᾶσαν	22	10+12	15
25	[ἐξουσίαν καὶ δύνα]μιν δεῖ γὰρ[	24	9+15	
	[αὐτὸν βασιλεύειν ἄ]χρ[ι] οὗ [θῇ	23	4+19	
	[πάντας τοὺς ἐχθροὺς] ὑπὸ [τοὺς	24	3+21	

* * *

0270 consists of two adjoining fragments of one leaf. The larger piece contains parts of 15 lines (ll. 1-15) and measures 9.2 × 8.8 cm. The small fragment, measuring 2.8 × 3.9 cm, supplies some extra portions of ll. 13-15 as well as the remains of three more lines, ll. 16-18.

The vellum, thin and of fine quality, is now darkened in some places and bleached in others, suffering, amongst others things, from humidity. The surface is much more uneven than would appear from a photograph.

From the way in which the fragments fit together, some inferences may be drawn as to what happened to the leaf. At the lower right corner of the *verso*, as shown in the photograph, there seems to be a gap between the large piece to the left and the small fragment to the right. In fact there is, at this point, no vellum missing. A small part of it, measuring no more than a few square millimetres and belonging to the larger fragment, is folded over. Apparently, the two fragments were only separated in the process of unfolding, long after the folio had dried out and lost its flexibility. Earlier, the leaf must have been folded together in such a way that the *verso* of the small fragment covered, and so protected, the lower lines, i.e. ll. 10-14, of the *verso* of the larger piece. This would explain the specific form of the fissure near the fold and the shape of the discoloured but still legible patch from B 10[3] ..ΩΙΔΙ.. downwards. These letters, belonging to the words τῷ ἰδίῳ (1 Cor xv 23), were covered by the far end of the small fragment, at the end of l. 15, which at that time already had its present shape. The outline of the missing part at the end of l. 14 fits the stain which made the Ω of ἰδίῳ disappear. If, as we are inclined to suppose, the fragments were only separated in recent times, this would account for the fact that the two pieces have reached us together. In its undivided but folded state the leaf clearly was already separated from its companion, that is, from the other half of the double folio. Also, it was already much reduced in size. During the period of its worst exposure, the *recto*, including the small part which was folded over, suffered less than the *verso*, which is the flesh side. Simply because writing on the hair side is more durable — or because of some material protection, such as part of another leaf from the same codex?

---

[3] I refer to the *recto* as A and to the *verso* as B. B 10 means: *verso*, line 10.

In the left margin of the *verso* and the right margin of the *recto* the photographs exhibit seven dots of the smallest size in one vertical row: for the purpose of ruling the leaf, the vellum was perforated with a sharp tool. The imprint of the ruling is occasionally visible. It was made on the *verso*. The writing of both sides stands exactly on the lines for which the pricks were made, one for each line of the page.[4] The distance between the lines is 0.45 cm, taken up by approximately 2 mm of writing and 2.5 mm of free space. The length of the line is c. 6.5 cm. There is one column to the page, of which, as the transcript shows, 18 lines are preserved in part or in full.

With the exception of B 1, the length of the line is between 20 and 24 letters. There is a high degree of regularity. Of 34 lines, 10 contain 22 letters each, 9 have 23 letters. If on the *verso*, which is the flesh-side, the lines tend to be slightly shorter than on the *recto*, this is perhaps natural for the leaf of a small codex. On a left-hand page, the scribe may have felt somewhat less free near the end of a line than near the right-hand margin of a *recto* page.[5]

Because the number of letters to a line varies so little, the number of lines missing from page A can be calculated without much difficulty, if we can, for 1 Cor xv 16-19, suppose the text to be as close to Nestle as elsewhere in 0270.[6] After l. 18, eight more lines with an average of 22 to 23 letters would fill the lacuna, and bring the number of lines to the page up to 26.[7]

---

[4] That is, two for each *folium*, to be ruled before folding. The prickings for the lines 8 and 10-15 are preserved. Cf. H. J. MILNE, T. C. SKEAT, *Scribes and Correctors of the Codex Sinaiticus*, London 1938, 73-78. More recently, the subject was investigated by L. W. JONES in several papers, listed in "Ancient Prickings in eighth-century Manuscripts", *Scriptorium* 15 (1961), 14-15 and in B. M. METZGER, *The Text of the New Testament*, Oxford ²1968, 8. At first, prickings were made inside the text, later in the outer margins of a "bifolium". The change took place gradually about 450-500 A.D. In JONES' opinion the "outer-marginal" system, of which 0270 is an example, indicates a date later than 450 A.D. See, e.g., *Miscellanea Giovanni Mercati* 6 (St T 126), 1946, 80f. As far as early New Testament manuscripts are concerned, the subject is open for further investigation.

[5] Cf. H. A. SANDERS, *A Third-century Papyrus Codex of the Epistles of Paul* (UMS.HS 38), Ann Arbor 1935, 6. For a different point of view, see S. Y. RUDBERG, 'Eine Eigentümlichkeit der Schrift griechischer Pergament-Kodizes', Akten IKBS XI München 1958, München 1960, 528-530: the flesh side, with its smoother surface, always has more letters to a line than the hair side. See also A. DAIN, *Les manuscrits*, Paris 1964, 26.

[6] It is impossible to say whether 0270 contained the disputed reading ἐστιν in v. 17. Cf. G. ZUNTZ, *The Text of the Epistles*, London 1953, 187.

[7] O. STEGMÜLLER, *Berliner Septuagintafragmente*, Gräfenhainichen 1939, 21, mentions 22-24 as a normal number of lines for parchment codices of the bible.

The height of the column of writing must have been approximately 11.5 cm, the width some 7 cm. For the page one may assume a size of about 15×11 cm $(6 \times 4^{1}/_{4}$ inches).

The *verso* has preserved traces of its page-number, but this is sadly mutilated and very uncertain. It may or may not have been made by the original scribe. The first letter that we can discern is possibly the right half of a N. To the left, where there may have been a letter for the hundreds, the vellum is gone.[8] The last letter seems to be Θ, or perhaps E. In any case we have an odd figure, ending in -5 or -9, and so p. 1 was a left hand page also, while the first page of the first leaf of the codex was left unnumbered, and possibly without text.

Two pages of 0270 contain as much text as one page in Nestle's edition of the Greek New Testament. So, in the codex to which 0270 once belonged, any part of the New Testament must have covered roughly twice its number of pages in Nestle-Aland. That is to say, 1-2 Cor. must have required about 100 pages; the Pauline corpus would fill some 360 pages or 180 folios. In the Chester Beatty-Michigan papyrus of the Pauline epistles, about 100 folios probably held the corpus paulinum *minus* the pastoral epistles.[9] The same amount of text would take up some 160 folios of the size of 0270. So in all probability the codex to which our leaf belonged was a fat little book.

The size, though smaller than most biblical manuscripts, is by no means exceptional. Among the more recent uncials of the Greek New Testament,[10] V (031, four gospels, 9th century), measuring 15.7×11.5 cm,[11] Π (041, four gospels, 9th century), measuring 14.5×10.5 cm,[12] and some fragments of other codices are comparable.[13]

---

[8] As the position of the two remaining letters is a little beyond half way the line I should think this was a three letter figure.

[9] See F. G. KENYON, *The Chester Beatty Biblical Papyri ...*, fasciculus iii, supplement, *Pauline Epistles, Text*, London 1936, viii-xi.

[10] For most of the following data we depend on K. ALAND, *Kurzgefasste Liste der Griechischen Handschriften des Neuen Testaments*, I. Gesamtübersicht (ANTT 1), Berlin 1963, supplemented in K. ALAND (ed.), *Materialien zur neutestamentlichen Hand-schriftenkunde*, I (ANTT 3), Berlin 1969, 7-37, and *Bericht der Stiftung zur Förderung der neutestamentlichen Textforschung für die Jahre 1972 bis 1974*, Münster/Westfalen 1974, 11-13.

[11] See W. H. P. HATCH, *The Principal Uncial Manuscripts of the New Testament*, Chicago, Ill. (1939), plate xlv.

[12] See HATCH, *o.c.*, plate lii.

[13] 0135 (Gospels, 9th century, c. 14.3×12.5 cm); 0140 (Acts, 9th/10th century,

I. Amsterdam University Library, MS. GX 200, *recto.*

II. Amsterdam University Library, MS. GX 200, *verso*.

Among the remains of older manuscripts of the same type one could mention 0220 (fragment of Romans, 3rd century, c. 15 × 13 cm, c. 24 lines to the page) as the earliest example, and a good number of other examples from the same period as 0270, that is, from the 4th or 5th century:

0231 (Matthew, 2 columns, number of lines: 15) of c. 15 × 11 cm.
059-0215 (Mark, number of lines: 18)[14] of c. 15 × 11 cm.
0171 (Luke, two columns, number of lines: 24) of about 15 × 11 cm.
0206 (1 Peter, 8 lines) of 13.5 × 10.1 cm.
0228 (Hebrews, c. 23 lines to the page) of c. 15 × 12 cm.

These fragments are all dated to the 4th/5th (so 059-0215) or to the 4th century. From the 6th century 060 (John) and 0222 (1 Cor.) can be added. Among early Coptic manuscripts this comparatively small size seems to be no exception. For example, the three Chester Beatty manuscripts described by Sir Herbert THOMPSON in 1932 measure (A) 15.2 × 13 cm, (B) 12.0 × 10.2 cm and (C) 10.5 × 8.5 cm.[15] In the period and area in which these books and the books to which these fragments once belonged were made, there must have been a specific demand for codices of this size.[16] It seems likely that they

---

c. 14.5 × 9.2 cm, see H. HAHN in K. ALAND, *Materialien*, I (see note 10), 186), and 0255 (Matthew, 9th century, c. 15.5 × 10 cm, see K. JUNACK, *ibidem*, 213).

[14] Not "c. 19" as stated in ALAND, *Liste*, 42 and 54.

[15] See H. THOMPSON, *The Coptic Version of the Acts of the Apostles*, Cambridge 1932, x-xv. The Scheide Library, Princeton, N.J., recently acquired a 4th or 5th century codex of Matthew, measuring c. 12.5 × 10.5 cm; see B. M. METZGER, "An Early Coptic Manuscript of the Gospel according to Matthew", in J. K. ELLIOTT (ed.), *Studies in New Testament Language and Text*, Essays in Honour of George D. Kilpatrick (NT.S 44), Leiden 1976, 301.

[16] I am not sure the term "miniature size" ("Miniaturformat", JUNACK, *a.c.* (see n. 13) 213 and others) should be applied to these books, obviously intended for some normal use. For 0169 (9.5 × 7.8 cm) the editor, A. S. HUNT, spoke of "miniature proportions" (*The Oxyrhynchus Papyri*, 8, London 1911, 15), Metzger of "truly a pocket edition" (B. M. METZGER, *The Text of the New Testament*, Oxford ²1968, 67). Perhaps "miniature size" could be reserved for the very smallest type of codex, such as P[78], of which each leaf is 5.3 cm wide by 2.9 cm high (i.e. the whole double leaf is 10.6 cm wide by 2.9 cm high). Thus Mr. P. J. PARSONS in a private letter, dated Oxford 20 July 1976. Small manuscripts were listed and discussed by W. H. WORRELL, *The Coptic Manuscripts in the Freer Collection* (UMS.HS 10), New York 1923, xi-xiii; L. AMUNDSEN, Christian Papyri from the Oslo Collection *SO* 24 (1945), 126-129, in the *editio princeps* of P[62]; William H. WILLIS, An unrecognized Fragment of *First Peter* in Coptic, in: Ch. HENDERSON, Jr., (ed.), *Classical, Mediaeval and Renaissance Studies in honor of Berthold Louis Ullman*, Roma 1964, I, 270; A. HENRICHS, L. KOENEN, Ein griechischer Mani-Codex (P. Colon. inv. nr. 4780 ...), *ZPE* 5 (1970), 100-103. See also E. G. TURNER, Some Questions about the Typology

were intended for private rather than for liturgical use. However, this particular format, which is by no means rare among minuscule manuscripts,[17] is found in lectionaries as well.[18] So it is perhaps wise, at least for a later period, to reckon with a variety of uses.

In 0270, the number of lines to the page is 26. Among the other examples, mentioned above, only V has more: 28. Among the rest, we have 0171 with 24 and 0222 with 20 lines to an equally small page. So, among manuscripts of its own period and size, 0270 has an unusually full page. Yet — as far as we can judge from one mutilated leaf — it seems the scribe has succeeded in making the elegance and beauty of his handwriting prevail, without any suggestion of a crowded mass of text — which testifies to his skill and good taste.

The ink is of a dark brownish colour, for which the word sepia seems appropriate.

The writing is a small-sized "Biblical Majuscule", written in a firm and careful hand, showing a marked difference between thin horizontals and heavy verticals and, partly, obliques. It keeps strictly within two imaginary horizontal lines, but *rho* and, somewhat less, *upsilon* reach below the line, *psi* above and below. The fragment has no example of *phi*.[19] In some letters breadth exceeds height: *mu*, *omega*, but also *eta*, *kappa*, *nu*, *pi* and *tau*. The circle of *omikron* and *theta* is somewhat flattened, *epsilon* and *sigma* conforming. Letters are always strictly separated and on the whole evenly spaced. At the end of the line there is, as far as one can tell, no crowding of letters, and no stroke above a vowel indicating final *nu* (see A 8 ἐστιν). The last letter of A 10 and 13, however, is a miniature *epsilon* in high position,[20] and the last letter of A 6, Ω, is written in the same way. In terms of the number of letters, A 12 is the shortest line of its page,

---

of the Codex, Akten des XIII. Internationalen Papyrologenkongresses (*MBPF* Heft 66), München 1974, 427-438. — I owe the last three references to the kindness of Mr. Parsons.

[17] See, for the New Testament, e.g., 2ᵃᵖ, 4ᵃᵖ, *6*, *49*, *199*, *530*, *2224*, *2599*; for the Septuagint, Rahlfs n. *277*, *1912*.

[18] See, e.g., *l* 56, *l* 348, *l* 472b, *l* 478, *l* 1213, *l* 1325, *l* 2117.

[19] *Beta*, *zeta*, *lambda* and *xi* are also missing.

[20] Compare, e.g., the Codex Sinaiticus in Matth xxviii 6:

...ΚΑΘΩ͛Σ
ΕΙΠΕΝΔΕΥΤΕΕΙΔᴱ
ΤΕΤΟΝΤΟΠΟΝΟΠΟΥ

and 0189 (4th century) in Acts v 15:   ...ΤΟΥΣΑΣΘᴱ
ΝΕΙΣ..

(see *ZNW* 26 (1927), 113).

with only 20 letters. Here ἡμῶν is written over such a wide space, that the end of the line projects into the margin. This could have been easily avoided; so one is tempted to guess a particular reason. Still the whole impression is one of regularity, precision and elegance, achieved without much effort.

Terminal dots, when present at the extremities of thin horizontals, are mostly slight. For *gamma*, see A 6, 11 γη-, 17, B 2 (but none in A 10 and 11 -γερται, 12 κήρυγμα, B 4 γάρ). In *epsilon*, the top end as a rule has a small knob, the cross-bar sometimes, the bottom end never. *Tau* shows a finial at its left end only, *kappa* as a rule at the ascending oblique. In this letter, the two obliques usually meet at some distance from the vertical. In some cases, the meeting-point is not joined to the vertical (see A 3 ἐκεῖνοι, 9 νεκρῶν). In *upsilon* there is a well-marked terminal dot at the end of the oblique ascending from left to right, and a different and smaller ornament at the other side. At its base, the middle stroke ends chisel shape, sometimes with a tiny leftward curl. In one case, the vertical of the *rho* slightly bends to the left at its lower end (A 10). In the *mu*, the slanting stroke going up from left to right is often very thin; the same is occasionally true for the oblique of the *nu*. The middle angle of *mu* always touches the bottom line and is slightly rounded off at this point in a characteristic way, while still maintaining its V shape. In *pi* the two verticals rise just above the thin cross-bar, which does not project beyond them. At the right corner, it seems, the pen was not lifted from the writing surface. *Alpha* and *delta*[21] are not entirely symmetrical, but lean over to the left, the right oblique being longer and in a more sloping position than the left one. The obliques tend to meet a little below the top.

All this goes to say that we have, in 0270, an example of the biblical majuscule very near the period of its full perfection, as described by CAVALLO.[22] It was written by a fully trained professional scribe, whose work must have been considered as first rate. Though probably a good representative of its style, the hand is quite distinct from others we have seen so far.[23]

---

[21] As stated, there is no example of *lambda*.

[22] G. CAVALLO, *Ricerche sulla maiuscola biblica*, Firenze, 1967.

[23] Dr. K. JUNACK writes (letter of 12 April, 1976): "Trotz intensiven Suchens ist es mir bisher nicht gelingen, unter den schon bekannten Unzialfragmenten eine Handschrift zu finden, mit der Ihr neues Fragment in Verbindung zu bringen ist".

A date not too far from the year 400 seems likely. Assigning
a date to a formal bookhand, however, is nearly always very uncertain.
So we at least would like to keep our margin of doubt fairly large,
suggesting the end of the 4th and the beginning of the 5th century.[24]
About the place of origin nothing can be said, though Egypt would
seem a fair guess.

For the *nomina sacra* θεός and χριστός contractions are found.[25]
Ἄνθρωπος and πατήρ are written in full. There is nothing unusual
about this.[26]

The punctuation appears to be original in one case: at the end of
1 Cor xv 13 the pause after ἐγήγερται is marked by a colon in a small
extra space before *v.* 14 εἰ δέ. One of the points of the colon seems
to be by the first scribe. The other one was meant as a correction
rather than an addition — if our suspicion is correct that a colon is
difficult to account for at this point in the text. Another, certainly
later hand has supplied a variety of punctuation marks at a number
of places. As normal, the strongest division is marked by the high point:

A	1	ΕΚΟΠΙΑΣΑ˙	(1 Cor xv 10)
	2	ΕΜΟΙ˙	(*v.* 10, end)
	8	ΕΣΤΙΝ˙	(*v.* 12)[27]
B	6	ΝΕΚΡΩΝ˙	(*v.* 21)
	16	ΔΥΝΑΜΙΝ˙	(*v.* 24)

The low point is inserted where modern editions use the comma:

A	3	ΕΚΕΙΝΟΙ.	(*v.* 11)
	6	ΕΓΗΓΕΡΤΑΙ.	(*v.* 12)
	11	Ε]ΓΗΓΕΡΤΑΙ.	(*v.* 14)
	15	Θ(ΕΟ)Υ.	(*v.* 15)
B	5	ΘΑΝΑΤΟΣ.	(*v.* 21)

---

[24] Dr. JUNACK writes (letter of 12 April 1976): "Ich stimme mit Ihnen überein,
dass die Schrift recht alt sein muss und bestimmt auf das 4.-5. Jh. zu datieren ist.
Man könnte evtl. ihrer sauberen schmucklosen Form wegen vielleicht noch einige
Jahrzehnte zurückgehen. Hier möchte ich mich aber nicht festlegen ...".

[25] In B 14 the stroke above ΘΩ is doubtful, but I cannot see a reason why it should
have been omitted. 1 Cor xv 10-25 has no example of κύριος.

[26] Cf. A. H. R. E. PAAP, *Nomina sacra in the Greek Papyri of the first five Centuries A.D.* (PLB 8), Leiden 1959, 119f.

[27] Strictly, this high point may have been made by the first scribe; after all,
it seems unlikely.

The middle point is employed once:

B 11   Χ(ΡΙΣΤΟ)Σ ·   (v. 23: ἀπαρχὴ χριστός),

where modern editions also have a comma.

The difference between high and low point is, on the whole, clear. The end of v. 13 would, in accordance with the use elsewhere in this fragment, ask for a high point. So it seems likely that the reader who, studying the text, put in the extra punctuation, found a low point and added the high one.

Apart from the beginning of v. 14 and, probably, v. 20,[28] which are marked off by extra space, there is no separation between words.

The two cases of initial upsilon are marked by the diaeresis in the form of two dots: A 7 ῠ̈ΜΙΝ (1 Cor xv 12) and B 18 ῠ̈ΠΟ (v. 25). The only case of initial iota is not marked,[29] nor is the upsilon in the correction or alternative reading ὑμῶν in A 13.

There are no breathings in the text as written by the original scribe. However, in the variant ἡ σὺν ἐμοί instead of σὺν ἐμοί (1 Cor xv 10) in A 2, the article ἡ has the rough breathing. This does not necessarily mean that this correction in A 2 is by a much later hand. But both from the breathing and from the shape of the eta it is evident that it was not made by the first hand. At this point, the text seems to have been subject to two corrections, of which this was the second.

The problem is: how does one account for the word θ(εο)ῦ, added between the lines A 1 and 2, above the Σ and Υ of σὺν ἐμοί and very much faded? A reading ἡ χάρις ἡ θεοῦ σὺν ἐμοί[30] is not recorded in the manuscript tradition and does not really make sense; so it is not likely to have been intended by a corrector. We are led to assume that a first corrector, on finding the (exceptional) text ἡ χάρις σὺν ἐμοί, added ΤΟΥ Θ(ΕΟ)Υ, in order to arrive at the reading ἡ χάρις τοῦ θεοῦ σὺν ἐμοί. The proper place for the two words τοῦ θεοῦ was above -ις and συ- in χάρις σὺν ἐμοί, or perhaps above the two sigmas and the upsilon. After this, a second correction seemed necessary. Someone wanted the text to read ἡ χάρις ἡ σὺν ἐμοί — also an exceptional reading, but, from a certain point of view, preferable to the reading of the *prima manus*. So this second corrector cleaned the vellum thoroughly at the place he needed for

---

[28] See below, p. 38, on νυνί in B 1-2 or 2.

[29] B 10 ΙΔΙΩ (1 Cor xv 23).

[30] See below, p. 38-42, for a discussion of the variants in 1 Cor xv 10.

the extra article ἡ, which he was going to put in, i.e. at the place of the first corrector's TOY. Θ(ΕΟ)Υ was effaced only partly and superficially: it is still there. But its position, to the right of the place between χάρις and σύν shows that it was not all, but only part of the first correction.

In contrast with the corrections in A 2, the alternative reading ὑμῶν instead of ἡμῶν in 1 Cor xv 14, indicated by an Υ above the H of ἡμῶν in A 13, seems to be part of the original text and may derive from the exemplar.

The orthography is faultless throughout.

* * *

In the diplomatic transcript and in the reconstruction of the text of 0270 there are several points that call for some comment.

In a few cases, an alternative restoration of the text is proposed. Generally, however, the reconstructed text is fairly certain. The transcript shows the punctuation of both the first and the later hand (or hands), and also the corrections that were made in A 2 and 13. The reconstruction also presents these corrections, unmistakable as such by their position between the lines, but it omits the additional punctuation. The transcript uses square brackets] [ ] [where the vellum is gone, and dots on the line, ..., where a number of letters is obliterated. In the reconstructed text round brackets ( ) serve for the expansion of the *nomina sacra*, and square brackets enclose letters lost in the original and restored by the editor. Dots below the line as a rule mark those letters which are damaged but not seriously doubtful. As for the number of letters to a line, 15 + 7 means: 15 letters visible or partly visible in the original, 7 letters restored by the editor.

For the *recto* side it can be noted that the beginning of line A 15 is undamaged. It follows that we also have the first letters of A 13, 14 and 16. As for the right hand margin, the lines A 7-14, and by inference also A 2, are well preserved at the end. This provides the basis for a reconstruction of the missing parts of the text. And it seems that the regularity of the writing and the quality and character of the surviving text are such as to make it possible to arrive at a reasonably certain reconstruction of the two pages of 0270.

A 1-2   Alternative :

πάντω]ν ἐκοπίασα οὐκ ἐγὼ   20   15 + 5
δὲ ἀλλ'ἡ χ]άρις σὺν ἐμοὶ εἴτε   22   15 + 7

2   About the corrections *τοῦ θεοῦ and ἡ, added by two different hands, see above, p. 35-36.

4-5   For the division ἐπι/στεύσατε, see, e.g., P⁴⁶ in 1 Cor iv 2 πι/στος; xiv 22 απι/στοις (twice); xv 11, 14 πι/στις.

4-7   Compare P⁴⁶, fol. 57ᵛ, l. 15-18 :[31]

ουτως κηρυσσομεν και ουτως επι
στευσατε' ει δε χρς κηρυσσεται
εκ νεκρων οτι εγηγερται πως
λεγουσιν εν υμειν τινες αναστα

6, 12   The readings ἐκ νεκρῶν ὅτι (v. 12) and καὶ τὸ κήρυγμα (v. 14), though not actually found in the surviving parts of 0270, are required by the available space, and virtually certain.

13   Y above the H of ἡμῶν: an alternative reading by the original scribe. The H in HMΩN A 13 is the only one in 0270 in which the cross-bar ascends, however slightly, from left to right. In writing this eta the scribe had the small supralinear Y in mind.

Of σ and κ in the word εὑρισκόμεθα no trace is left.

15   Some letters of the words ἐμαρτυρήσαμεν and κατά are, partly, visible from the verso side, as the edge of the vellum is folded over. Notably -τυ-, but also small parts of -ρη- and -ατα are clearly discernible.

17   Alternative :   οὐ]κ ἤγει[ρεν εἰ γὰρ νεκροὶ   21   5 + 16
                  ο]ὐκ ἐγ[είρονται

with D syᵖ etc. This reading cannot be excluded. However, with two occurrences of iota, several of rho and no broad letters such as mu, sigma and upsilon, the number of letters in line 17 is more likely to be 24 than 21.

Of the verso a few lines, notably B 8, 9 and 10 have suffered badly. Of many letters only bare traces are left, and so a dot below a letter sometimes involves serious doubt, as inspection of plate II will make clear.

---

[31] See F. G. KENYON, The Chester Beatty Biblical Papyri ..., fasciculus iii, Supplement, Pauline Epistles, Text, London 1936, 87.

B 1-2   In P⁴⁶, *v.* 20 νυνί is not marked off in a special way. In 0270
it must have been. An open space of at least a few letters is as good
as certain, but it is impossible to specify. NY- reaching into the
margin at the beginning of l. 2 is also possible.

3, 5   To the right of the vertical of the *tau* in τῶν, one vertical
of the *nu* in ἐκεῖνοι, A 3, shows from the *recto*. Similarly, in B 5
δι'ἀνθρώπου the line crossing the *delta* belongs to the *rho* in κηρύσσεται, A 5.

14   The ink of the letters -ν κα- has completely disappeared. It is
not faded, but rubbed off or eaten away, in any case gone. However,
their outline and position is, in a somewhat lighter colour, perfectly
clear on the surface of the vellum.

* * *

As far as the character of its text is concerned, 0270 is on the whole
obviously close to ℵ and B. The text of 0270 was probably, in several
respects, a very good old Egyptian text.

We select for discussion the five readings in which 0270 differs
from Nestle-Aland. This is, of course, a completely one-sided
approach and as such unsatisfactory. But it may, for the time being,
reveal some interesting features, notably in the variants of 1 Cor xv 10.

1.   *1 Cor xv 10*

As to the last words of 1 Cor xv 10, the manuscript tradition varies
a good deal. There are at least[32] six variants, attesting either one
or two adjuncts after the noun χάρις, and either using or omitting
a second article before the prepositional phrase σὺν ἐμοί or the like.
At most stages influence from two expressions in the immediate
context, *v.* 10a χάριτι .. θεοῦ and ἡ χάρις αὐτοῦ ἡ εἰς ἐμέ[33] is evident.

1.1.1   ἡ χάρις τοῦ θεοῦ ἡ εἰς ἐμέ   P⁴⁶
1.1.2   ἡ χάρις τοῦ θεοῦ ἡ σὺν ἐμοί   ℵᶜADᵇKP...[34]
1.1.3   ἡ χάρις αὐτοῦ ἡ σὺν ἐμοί   255 1738 2143[35]

---

[32] We neglect the variant .. ἡ ἐν ἐμοί, found in patristic quotations, see
C. Tischendorf, *Novum Testamentum Graece*, editio octava, Lipsiae (1872), *ad loc.*
[33] Om. ἡ² D*FG 1245.
[34] See K. Aland, M. Black et alii (ed.), *The Greek New Testament*, 1966, *ad loc.*
[35] See H. von Soden, *Die Schriften des Neuen Testaments* II, Text, Göttingen 1913,
ad loc.: Jᵃ² 184 ³ 164 174.

1.2   ἡ χάρις τοῦ θεοῦ σὺν ἐμοί   ℵ*BD*G 0243 (0270ᶜ¹?) 1739...³⁶
2.1   ἡ χάρις ἡ σὺν ἐμοί   0270ᶜ² 1611³⁷
2.2   ἡ χάρις σὺν ἐμοί   0270

In the variants 1.1.3, .. αὐτοῦ .., and 1.1.1, ..(ἡ) εἰς ἐμέ, the text is assimilated to *v.* 10a. In repeating the article ἡ, the readings 1.1.1, 1.1.2, 1.1.3 and 2.1 likewise agree with the context. The words ..ἡ εἰς ἐμέ (1.1.1) in P⁴⁶ show that this assimilation was at work before the earliest of our witnesses was copied. Even at this early stage it was carried further than in the *textus receptus* (1.1.2). Variant 2.1 is now known to be ancient: it is attested in 0270 to antedate minuscule 1611, from the 12th century, which until recently was its only witness, by many centuries. In principle, any reading may antedate its witnesses by an unknown number of years. Therefore it seems best to discuss the variants without undue respect to the date of the manuscripts or their number.

The variants 1.1.1, 1.1.2, 1.1.3 and 2.1 all read a second article before the prepositional phrase; only 1.2 and 2.2 do without. Grammarians are not in full agreement as to the necessity of the article in a case like this, where a prepositional phrase follows an articular noun as its only (2.1 and 2.2) or as a second adjunct (the other variants), instead of being inserted between article and noun — which would be, in this case, ἡ (τοῦ θεοῦ) σὺν ἐμοὶ χάρις.³⁸

It seems undeniable that emphasis, contrast and clarity are served by the use of a second article, appearing before the prepositional expression.³⁹

---

³⁶ See *The Greek New Testament, ad loc.*

³⁷ Von Soden: *Iᶜ¹* ²⁰⁸. On the affinities of its text, see VON SODEN, *o.c.* I iii, 1932.

³⁸ See: R. KÜHNER, B. GERTH, *Ausführliche Grammatik der griechischen Sprache, Satzlehre*, I, 4. Auflage [reprint], Hannover 1955, 615-616; E. SCHWYZER, A. DEBRUNNER, *Griechische Grammatik* II, München 1950, 26; F. BLASS, A. DEBRUNNER, *Grammatik des neutestamentlichen Griechisch*, Göttingen ⁹1954, § 269. For a characteristic difference in emphasis and starting-point, compare N. TURNER, *Syntax* (J. H. MOULTON, *A Grammar of New Testament Greek* III), Edinburgh 1963, 221: "... the repetition of the article is necessary for the sake of clarity" and BLASS-DEBRUNNER-FUNK: "The repetition of the article .. is not generally required ... but only in those cases ..." (*A Greek Grammar of the New Testament*, Cambridge-Chicago 1961, 140; cf. F. BLASS-H. St. J. THACKERAY, *Grammar of New Testament Greek*, London ²1911, 160).

³⁹ E.g.: L. RADERMACHER, *Neutestamentliche Grammatik*, Tübingen ²1925, 117: "Auch ein präpositionales Attribut sollte der Deutlichkeit halber stets durch den Artikel an das zugehörige Wort gebunden werden .."; BLASS-DEBRUNNER, *o.c.*, § 272 "... der Deutlichkeit wegen besonders nötig ..".

However, there are many instances to show that, if the first of two adjuncts is a genitive without repeated article — (ἡ χάρις) τοῦ θεοῦ, not (ἡ χάρις) ἡ τοῦ θεοῦ — the second attributive may also do without an extra article.[40] This is the case of variant 1.2.

Also, there are early instances in which a prepositional phrase as the only adjunct after the noun lacks the article.[41] This usage, which is well attested in the papyri,[42] is occasionally found in the LXX[43] and also in related literature.

Gen. iii 6	τῷ ἀνδρὶ αὐτῆς μετ᾽ αὐτῆς] ... τῷ μετ᾽ αὐτῆς
Epiph I 28	
ix 9	τῷ σπέρματι ὑμῶν μεθ᾽ ὑμᾶς[44]
Lev. iii 5	ἐπὶ τὰ ὁλοκαυτώματα ἐπὶ τὰ ξύλα τὰ ἐπὶ τοῦ πυρὸς τοῦ θυσιαστηρίου[45]
xx 17	ὃς ἐὰν λάβῃ τὴν ἀδελφὴν αὐτοῦ ἐκ πατρὸς αὐτοῦ
Josh. xiii 12	πᾶσαν τὴν βασιλείαν Ωγ ἐν τῇ Βασανίτιδι
xx 7	τὴν Καδης ἐν τῇ Γαλιλαίᾳ ἐν τῷ ὄρει τῷ Νεφθαλι
Wisdom ii 2	καπνὸς ἡ πνοὴ ἐν ῥισὶν ἡμῶν
Henoch xiii 6	τὰς δεήσεις περὶ τῶν πνευμάτων αὐτῶν
xviii 6	τὰ ἑπτὰ ὄρη ἀπὸ λίθων πολυτελῶν
Joseph and	
Aseneth iv 13	ὁ υἱὸς τοῦ ποιμένος ἐκ γῆς Χανααν[46]

[40] Thucydides 2.65 ἡ πρόνοια αὐτοῦ ἐς τὸν πόλεμον (KÜHNER-GERTH, o.c. I, 616). For the New Testament, see BLASS-DEBRUNNER, o.c., § 269:2. E.g.: Acts xxvi 4 (+ v.l.); Rom iii 26; iv 1; ix 3; 1 Cor ix 18; Eph i 19; ii 7; iii 4; Phil i 5; iv 19; Col i 4; 2 Thess iii 14.

[41] Herodotus 5.108 ἡ ἀγγελίη .. περὶ τῶν Σαρδίων; Thuc. 2.52.1 ἡ ξυμκομιδὴ ἐκ τῶν ἀγρῶν ἐς τὸ ἄστυ; 3.37 διὰ .. τὸ καθ᾽ ἡμέραν ἀδεὲς καὶ ἀνεπιβούλευτον πρὸς ἀλλήλους; more examples in G. B. WINER, G. LÜNEMANN, Grammatik des neutestamentlichen Sprachidioms, Leipzig [7]1867, 129. The statement in BLASS-DEBRUNNER, o.c., § 272 ".. und so ist das Fehlen des Artikels aus Klassikern keineswegs genügend zu belegen" seems to be pointless; cf. A. T. ROBERTSON, A Grammar of the Greek New Testament ..., London, s.a., 783.

[42] See, for the Ptolemaic period, E. MAYSER, Grammatik der griechischen Papyri aus der Ptolemäerzeit II/2, Satzlehre, Berlin-Leipzig 1934, 161, table, "Typ IV", 166-7 sub d).

[43] As noted by M. JOHANNESSOHN, Der Gebrauch der Präpositionen in der Septuaginta (NGWG.PH 1925, Beiheft), Berlin 1925, 365 for Gen, Ex and 1 Macc. For other books, see E. PERCY, Die Probleme der Kolosser- und Epheserbriefe, Lund 1946, 60.

[44] For similar formulae, see, e.g., Gen xvii 7, 9, 10; xviii 19; xlviii 4; Ex xxix 29; Num xxv 13; Test. Levi vii 1; Luke i 55.

[45] With variants; cf. K. HUBER, Untersuchungen über den Sprachcharakter des griechischen Leviticus, Halle a.d. S. 1916, 46.

[46] Also vi 5; xiii 10; cf. xviii 7.

Test. Levi iii 2 τὰ πνεύματα τῶν ἐπαγωγῶν εἰς ἐκδίκησιν τῶν ἀνόμων.

In the New Testament,[47] most examples are from Paul.[48] In fact, the frequency of this idiom in Paul is exceptionally high[49] — as readers, scribes and correctors in antiquity must have noticed. Verbal force of the noun and a predicative function[50] of the adjunct help to understand the omission of the article. There is no need to go into the details. The main point is that the need of another article was evidently not felt so much[51] — at least not by Paul.

Variants, in which the article is added, appear in, e.g.,

Rom x 1 ἡ δέησις πρὸς τὸν θεόν] ἡ δέησις ἡ πρὸς τὸν θεόν
KL al pler[52]
1 Cor xi 24 τὸ σῶμα ὑπὲρ ὑμῶν P⁴⁶] .. τὸ ὑπὲρ ὑμῶν ceteri[53]
2 Cor vii 14 ἡ καύχησις ἡμῶν ἐπὶ Τίτου] .. ἡ ἐπὶ Τίτου P⁴⁶ Cℵ..
Gal iv 14 τὸν πειρασμὸν ὑμῶν ἐν τῇ σαρκί μου] .. τὸν ἐν τῇ σαρκί μου
Col i 4 τὴν πίστιν ὑμῶν ἐν Χριστῷ Ἰησοῦ] .. τὴν ἐν Χ' Ι'
1 Thess iv 10 πάντας τοὺς ἀδελφοὺς ἐν ὅλῃ τῇ Μακεδονίᾳ ℵ*A D*G latt] ... τοὺς ἐν ὅλῃ τῇ Μακεδονίᾳ Bℵpl.

As the presence of the article assimilates the style to normal Greek usage, these variants should, as a rule, be interpreted as stylistic corrections.

In 1 Cor xv 10 a change from ἡ χάρις σὺν ἐμοί (2.2) into ἡ χάρις ἡ σὺν ἐμοί (2.1) as well as a change from ἡ χάρις τοῦ θεοῦ σὺν

---

[47] Cf. J. F. FISCHER, *Prolusiones de vitiis lexicorum Novi Testamenti*, Lipsiae 1791, 326 (Prolusio xiii, n. 21): at this point the N.T. writers followed Hebrew idiom. As far as I see, Bp MIDDLETON did not discuss the subject. When reading his discussions of, e.g., Gal iii 11; 2 Thess iii 14; 2 Tim i 8, one wonders whether he was aware of it. See Th. F. MIDDLETON, *The Doctrine of the Greek Article*, ed. H. J. ROSE, London 1833, 348, 383, 391 and cf. 302 on Paul's anarthrous style.

[48] See N. TURNER, *Syntax*, 221f.

[49] E. PERCY, *Die Probleme*, 54: "...in einem Umfang..., der ohne Gegenstück in der sonstigen griechischen Literatur zu sein scheint".

[50] 1 Cor xv 10 seems to be inspired of Wisdom ix 10, where it is said in a prayer: ἐξαπόστειλον αὐτὴν (i.e. τὴν σοφίαν) ... ἵνα συμπαροῦσά μοι κοπιάσῃ. Cf. PERCY's interpretation: "In [1 Cor] 15, 10 ... dürfte ,.. σὺν ἐμοί Prädikativ sein mit zu ergänzendem οὖσα". (*Die Probleme*, 55, n. 58).

[51] A. T. ROBERTSON, *A Grammar*, 783.

[52] Cf. Hen xiii 6 τὰς δεήσεις περὶ τῶν πνευμάτων αὐτῶν.

[53] Many witnesses add a verb after ὑμῶν and so change the grammatical function of ὑπὲρ ὑμῶν. Cf. B. M. METZGER, *A Textual Commentary on the Greek New Testament*, London-New York (1971), 562, who fails to bring out this aspect.

ἐμοί (1.2) into ἡ χάρις τοῦ θεοῦ ἡ σὺν ἐμοί (1.1.2) is explicable along these lines. That is to say, either 1.2 or 2.2 is original; the other variants are secondary.

So it is quite likely that the (second) correction in 0270, the addition of ἡ between χάρις and σὺν ἐμοί, was intended to improve upon grammar and style in a way which fitted the immediate context in v. 10a.

Comparison of the variants 2.2 and 1.2 suggests that such an improvement could also be achieved by the addition of τοῦ θεοῦ. In other words, the purpose of the earlier correction in 0270 may have been similar to that of the one which replaced it, although they of course came from different sources, unknown to us. Because the adjunct τοῦ θεοῦ does not ask for an extra article to be added after the noun, the absence of the article before the second adjunct is no longer objectionable.[54] This is of some importance when we have to decide between the variants 1.2 and 2.2.

By itself, the variation between ἡ χάρις (2.2) and ἡ χάρις τοῦ θεοῦ (1.2) is fully understandable, and each of these variants is acceptable within the terms of Paul's diction; there is no difference in meaning. There are firm examples of the full expression[55] and of the short one.[56] This variety in Paul's diction caused a certain amount of textual variation in several passages.[57] Especially when ἡ χάρις is repeated a number of times,[58] no difference in meaning or emphasis is discernible. So it is difficult to decide whether the words τοῦ θεοῦ after χάρις were perhaps added from the context or from a similar passage in order to give the sentence some extra weight and fullness, or were dropped as superfluous and repetitious. As far as the variation in 1 Cor xv 10 is concerned one could argue both ways. Both the long and the short expression provide good sense and fall within the possibilities of Paul's diction as far as we know it. The difference is simply that the short expression has fewer words than the long one.

---

[54] See BLASS-DEBRUNNER, o.c., §269:2, and compare the examples in KÜHNER-GERTH, o.c., I, 615: most of them have such a genitive.

[55] See Rom v 15; 2 Cor vi 1; viii 1; ix 14; Gal ii 21; Col i 6; 2 Thess i 12; Tit ii 11, etc.

[56] See, e.g., Rom v 17, 20; Eph iv 7. Compare the use of ἡ χάρις in the final greetings of Eph, Col, 1 and 2 Tim, Tit with the longer formulae elsewhere.

[57] See 1 Cor i 4; iii 10; Eph iii 2, 7; Rom xii 3, 6; Gal ii 9; Eph iii 8. VON SODEN in his apparatus criticus rightly refers to related passages, see, e.g., Rom xii 3.

[58] So in Rom v 15-21; xii 3, 6; 1 Cor xv 10; Eph iii 2-8.

2. 1 Cor xv 12

As witnesses to the readings discussed so far, 0270 and 0270ᶜ² stand quite alone (2.2) and almost alone (2.1). In the next variant P⁴⁶, 0270 and Origen have strong Western affiliation.

1 κηρύσσεται ἐκ νεκρῶν ὅτι ἐγήγερται P⁴⁶ D* et ᶜ EFG 0270 ... Origen
2 κηρύσσεται ὅτι ἐκ νεκρῶν ἐγήγερται *ceteri*
3 κηρύσσεται ὅτι ἐγήγερται ἐκ νεκρῶν *sine teste*? Tischendorf 8ᵃ ⁵⁹

In both variants (1) and (2) there is *hiatus* after κηρύσσεται and both variants have a second *hiatus* after ὅτι. Word order in (1) is perhaps more impressive and elegant because of the ὑπερβατόν.⁶⁰ It makes ὅτι ἐγήγερται sound as an echo of the formula in *v.* 4, and at the same time makes it clear that ἐκ νεκρῶν was no part of that formula. TISCHENDORF commented on the quality of this reading⁶¹ but did not adopt it into the text of his *editio octava*. So far, no other case of ὑπερβατόν with ὅτι in Paul has come to my attention.⁶²

3. 1 Cor xv 14a

1 κενὸν ἄρα τὸ κήρυγμα ἡμῶν   P⁴⁶ᵛⁱᵈ BL pm lat sy Ir
2 κενὸν ἄρα καὶ τὸ κήρυγμα ἡμῶν   ℵ*ADGK 0270 pm Or

The distribution of witnesses is such as to make editors since LACHMANN hesitate.⁶³ It does not seem that 0270 changes the situation. Context (*v.* 14b .. καὶ ἡ πίστις, *v.* 15 .. δὲ καὶ ψευδομάρτυρες .., *v.* 18 ἄρα καὶ ..) and perhaps assonance (κενὸν .. (καὶ) τὸ κήρυγμα .. κενὴ καὶ ..) would rather induce addition of καί than omission. So internal criteria seem to be slightly in favour of the short reading (1).⁶⁴

---

⁵⁹ Also in Tischendorf's *editio critica minor*, Lipsiae 1877, and rather puzzling. We omit this reading from our discussion. It was corrected by VON GEBHARDT.

⁶⁰ See E. VON DOBSCHÜTZ, Zum Wortschatz und Stil des Römerbriefs, *ZNW* 33 (1934), 51-66, 59: "Die bei den Griechen so beliebten verschränkten Wortstellungen sind bei Paulus äusserst selten ...", and cf. BLASS-DEBRUNNER-FUNK, *o.c.*, §477:1.

⁶¹ C. TISCHENDORF, *Novum Testamentum Graece*, editio octava critica maior, Lipsiae (1872), II, 551: "(: : quae lectio non nemini praeferenda videbitur)".

⁶² Rom x 5 is perhaps of some interest.

⁶³ LACHMANN, VON SODEN, *The Greek New Testament*, and perhaps others, use square brackets; WESTCOTT and HORT give καὶ as an alternative reading in the margin. See VON SODEN, *Die Schriften des Neuen Testaments*, I/iii, 1911, 1929: "Schwieriger ist es, wo sich die *H*-Zeugen in die *I*- und die *K*-Lesart teilen".

⁶⁴ VON SODEN's comment is well worth reading, *ibidem*, 1930.

4.　1 Cor xv 14b

1　ἡ πίστις ὑμῶν　ℵADᵇᶜGKP 0270ᵇ...
2　ἡ πίστις ἡμῶν　BD* 0243 0270ᵃ ...[65]

When preparing his eighth edition, TISCHENDORF was made to change his mind over this variant. HORT pondered over it, witness his marginal reading. The variant was discussed by VON SODEN[66] and by METZGER,[67] who both — and probably rightly — decided in favour of ὑμῶν. Of the ancient codices, B is now joined by 0270ᵃ and ℵ by 0270ᵇ, and the uncertainty seems to go back to its *exemplar*.[68] However, it must have existed only for the reader and student of this passage, not for anyone who listened to it.

5.　1 Cor xv 24

1　παραδιδοῖ　BFG
2　παραδιδῷ　P⁴⁶ℵADEP 0270 ...
3　παραδῷ　KL al pler Or

The old witnesses agree against the *textus receptus* and Origen (παραδῷ) in reading a subjunctive of the present tense. The form παραδιδω (παραδιδῷ) is more commonly attested than παραδιδοι, 'an obviously vernacular form' (of the subjunctive), which HORT in 1 Cor xv 24 treated as 'Western only' and rejected.[69] This last form occurs in B, followed by TISCHENDORF and B. WEISS, and so it appears in NESTLE-ALAND.[70] In reading παραδιδω 0270 joins a majority among the older witnesses. Similar variants occur elsewhere.[71] They are a matter of orthography.

---

[65] See K. ALAND, M. BLACK e.a. (ed.), *The Greek New Testament, ad loc.*

[66] See VON SODEN, *ibidem*, 1974.

[67] B. M. METZGER, *A Textual Commentary*, 567f.

[68] See *above*, p. 36 and 37.

[69] B. F. WESTCOTT, F. J. A. HORT, *The New Testament in the Original Greek* II, Introduction, Appendix, London 1907, Appendix, 175.

[70] Kuenen and Cobet already drew attention to the confusion between ΟΙ and Ω (pro φ) in B. See A. KUENEN, C. G. COBET, Η ΚΑΙΝΗ ΔΙΑΘΗΚΗ, *Novum Testamentum ad fidem codicis vaticani*, Lugduni-Batavorum 1860, LX-LXI.

[71] See, e.g., Eph iv 29; 1 Thess v 15. Cf. BLASS-DEBRUNNER, *o.c.*, § 95:2; J. H. MOULTON, W. F. HOWARD, *A Grammar of New Testament Greek* II, Edinburgh 1929, 210f.

LC. XXIV 12
LES TÉMOINS DU TEXTE OCCIDENTAL*

F. NEIRYNCK

Depuis WESTCOTT-HORT, l'examen de l'authenticité de Lc. xxiv 12 se fait normalement dans le cadre d'une discussion des *Western non-interpolations*.[1] C'est le cas pour J. JEREMIAS qui, à partir de 1949, défend l'authenticité du verset dans les différentes éditions de son ouvrage sur *Die Abendmahlsworte Jesu*,[2] mais également pour les études nouvelles qui ont suivi la publication de P[75] et dont celle de K. ALAND est sans doute la plus importante.[3] Depuis lors, le nombre de ceux qui préfèrent parler simplement de *Western omission* a considérablement augmenté.[4] Il est d'autant plus frappant que les

---

* Article rédigé en vue d'une conférence à la réunion annuelle du *Studiorum Novi Testamenti Conventus*, qui s'est tenue à Ede, le 26 mai 1975.

[1] Cf. B. F. WESTCOTT, J. A. HORT, *The New Testament in the Original Greek II: Introduction, Appendix*, London 1881, 175-177 (§ 240-244) et 294-295 (§ 383). Sur Lc. xxiv 12 voir *Appendix, I. Notes on Variant Readings*, 71. — Déjà avant WESTCOTT-HORT, Lc. xxiv 12 avait été relégué dans l'apparat critique par TISCHENDORF ([5]1849-[8]1869). GRIESBACH lui avait donné la note de *lectio forsitan delenda* ("omissio minus probabilis") (1774; [2]1796); "adstipulante Schulzio", D. SCHULZ qui dans la troisième édition (1827) ajouta une réflexion de critique interne: "Cf. Io. xx, 6,7. Absentem hunc totum vs. haud facile desideres. Παρακύπτειν, ὀθόνια, ἀπῆλθε πρὸς ἑαυτόν, (cf. Io. xx, 10) ut a Lc. sint aliena, ita undique produnt Ioannem".

[2] J. JEREMIAS, *Die Abendmahlsworte Jesu*, Göttingen [2]1949, 70-75; [3]1960 = [4]1967, 138-145, spéc. 143-144. Traduit en anglais (Oxford 1955; London 1966) et en français (Paris, 1972).

[3] K. ALAND, Neue neutestamentliche Papyri II, *NTS* 12 (1965-66), 193-210, spéc. 205-206; repris, légèrement retravaillé, dans *Studien zur Überlieferung des Neuen Testamentes und seines Textes* (ANTT 2), Berlin 1967, 155-172: *Die Bedeutung des P[75] für den Text des Neuen Testaments. Ein Beitrag zur Frage der "Western non-interpolations"*, spéc. 168. Voir E. HAENCHEN, *Die Apostelgeschichte* (KEK 3), Göttingen [4]1961, 667-670; [5]1965, 666-669, spéc. 668; B. M. METZGER, *A Textual Commentary on the Greek New Testament*, London-New York 1971, 191-193: "Note on Western Non-Interpolations"; K. SNODGRASS, Western Non-Interpolations, *JBL* 91 (1972), 369-379, spéc. 373 et 379.

[4] Cf. B. M. METZGER, *A Textual Commentary*, xix: "since the acquisition of the Bodmer Papyri many scholars today are inclined to regard them as aberrant readings". — Pour une réaction contre ce mouvement, en ce qui concerne Lc. xxiv 12, voir K. P. G. CURTIS, Luke xxiv, 12 and John xx, 3-10, *JTS* 22 (1971), 512-515; suivi par J. K. ELLIOTT, The United Bible Societies' Textual Commentary Evaluated, *NT* 17 (1975), 130-150, 145. L'article de CURTIS ne mentionne même pas P[75]. Il est critiqué par J. MUDDIMAN, A Note on Reading Luke xxiv, 12, *EThL* 48 (1972), 542-548;

témoins de cette omission ne sont guère discutés. L'apparat critique de *Greek New Testament* en donne l'énumération : "D it[a,b,d,e,l,r1] syr [pal mss] Marcion Diatessaron Eusebius [1/2]".[5] Il m'est apparu que la valeur de ces témoins mérite un nouvel examen.

La variante du codex Bezae est signalée déjà dans la Polyglotte de B. WALTON (1657)[6] et puis dans l'édition du Nouveau Testament de J. MILL (1707).[7] En 1751 J. J. WETTSTEIN y ajoute le témoignage de manuscrits latins : "D Codices *Latini*"[8] et, sur ce point, une information plus précise est fournie dans l'édition de J. BIANCHINI (1749) : en plus du codex *Cantabrigiensis* (*d*), le *Vercellensis* (*a*) et le *Veronensis* (*b*) n'ont pas le verset.[9] Ce sont encore les témoins qui en 1774 sont connus par J. J. GRIESBACH : "D Veron. verc. cant.".[10] Le *Rehdigeranus* (*Rd* = *l*) y sera associé par D. SCHULZ en 1827,[11]

F. NEIRYNCK, The Uncorrected Historic Present in Lk. xxiv. 12, *ib.*, 548-553. Sur les rapports entre Lc. xxiv 12 et Jn. xx 3-10 voir F. NEIRYNCK, John and the Synoptics, dans M. DE JONGE (éd.), *L'Évangile de Jean. Sources, rédaction, théologie* (BETL, 43), Gembloux-Louvain 1976, 73-106, spéc. 98-104; ΠΑΡΑΚΥΨΑΣ ΒΛΕΠΕΙ. Lc 24,12 et Jn 20,5, dans *ETL* 53 (1977), 113-152.

[5] K. ALAND, M. BLACK, B. M. METZGER, A. WIKGREN, The Greek New Testament, Stuttgart 1966; = [2]1968 (+ C. M. MARTINI). Pour la troisième édition, aucun changement n'est signalé par B. M. METZGER, *A Textual Commentary*, 184. — Seul le Diatessaron n'est pas repris dans la liste des témoins donnée par K. ALAND (cf. *supra*, n. 3 : dans *NTS* 12, 196; = *Studien*, 157). L'auteur signale que son apparat est celui de *GNT* (dans *NTS* 12, 197 : "in Anlehnung an...") dont la première édition n'avait pas encore paru à ce moment (1966), mais il ne s'explique pas sur l'absence du Diatessaron (omis également pour Lc. xxiv 6.36.51; xii 39; xxii 43-44; Jn. iv 9; cf. 196-199). De même, K. SNODGRASS (cf. n. 2) qui reprend les données de ALAND. — Note ajoutée après la parution de la troisième édition de *Greek New Testament* (1975) : *GNT*[3] ne signale plus "Eusebius[1/2]" comme témoin de l'omission. C'est d'ailleurs, avec *Eusebius* (sans 1/2) parmi les témoins du texte, le seul changement dans l'apparat de Lc. xxiv 12.

[6] La collation de Ussher dans B. WALTON, *Biblia sacra polyglotta VI. Appendix*, London 1657, n° XVI, 17 : "Hic versus deest in *Cant.*".

[7] J. MILL, *Novum Testamentum Graece cum lectionibus variantibus*, ed. L. KUSTERUS, Rotterdam 1710, 194 : "Deest versus iste in *Cant.*".

[8] J. J. WETTSTEIN, Η ΚΑΙΝΗ ΔΙΑΘΗΚΗ. *Novum Testamentum Graecum*, Amsterdam 1751, 823.

[9] J. BLANCHINUS, *Evangeliarum quadruplex Latinae versionis antique seu veteris Italicae*, Roma 1749, t. II, CCXCVIII-CCXCIX. Le texte y est donné d'après le *Corbeiensis* (*ff*[2]; seulement la fin du verset : "Et abiit...") et le *Brixianus* (*f*). — P. SABATIER imprime le texte du *Colbertinus* (*c*) et donne aussi la version du *Corbeiensis* (le verset entier), mais il ne signale pas d'autre omission que celle du *Cantabrigiensis*; cf. *Bibliorum sacrorum Latinae versiones antiquae seu Vetus Italica*, Reims, t. III, 1749.

[10] Dans sa première édition du Nouveau Testament grec (Halle 1774).

[11] Dans une troisième édition du Nouveau Testament de GRIESBACH (t. I, Berlin 1827); il avait étudié le manuscrit déjà en 1814.

le *Palatinus* (*e*) par F. C. Tischendorf en 1849,[12] et vers la fin du 19ᵉ siècle s'ajoutera encore le *Usserianus I* (*r*¹).[13] Le témoignage du Codex Bezae, seul parmi les manuscrits grecs, trouve donc une confirmation dans les vieilles latines. Notons toutefois que leur témoignage est divisé et que le verset est bien attesté par le *Colbertinus* (*c*), le *Brixianus* (*f*), le *Corbeiensis II* (*ff*²) et le *Aureus* (*aur*).[14] Nous y reviendrons. Voyons d'abord les autres témoins de l'omission.

1. *Les canons d'Eusèbe*

Il semble bien que c'est Tischendorf qui a introduit les canons d'Eusèbe dans l'apparat critique de Lc. xxiv 12. D'abord, en ⁵1849, il donne la simple mention: *Eus canon*; il la complète en ⁷1859: "nec magis Ammonius legisse videtur", et puis, en ⁸1869, il s'explique clairement: "cum enim verba v. 10 ησαν δε η μαγδ. μαρ. usque v. 35 εν τη κλασει του αρτου unum caput 339 efficiant comprehensa canone decimo, qui singulis propria continet, quae vero v. 12 narrantur debuerint cum Ioh 20,5 sq coniuncta canone nono poni, eis destinato quae Lucas et Iohannes communia habent, Eusebius versum 12 qui dicitur apud Ammonium nec invenisse nec supplesse censendus est. Quocum cohaeret quod Ioh 20,5 sq eodem canone decimo posita sunt, adnumerata quippe eis quae Ioh propria habet". D'autre part, il signale que le verset est attesté par Eusèbe dans *Quaestiones ad Marinum*, *Supplementa* 287 et 293 (avec citation).[15] Les canons d'Eusèbe con-

---

[12] Dans sa cinquième édition du N.T. (la 2ᵉ édition de Leipzig). Il est également l'éditeur du codex (Leipzig 1847).

[13] Édité par Abbott en 1884, on le trouve dans l'apparat de Wordsworth-White (1889-1898), Merk, Bover, Kilpatrick.

[14] Pour *c*, *f* et *ff*² voir déjà les éditions du 18ᵉ siècle (cf. n. 9), et l'apparat de Tischendorf (*octava*) et von Soden; Hort ne signale que *c* et *ff*². Pour *aur* (éd. Belsheim, 1878) voir l'apparat de Wordsworth-White. — Cf. A. Jülicher, W. Matzkow, K. Aland, *Itala. Das Neue Testament in altlateinischer Überlieferung*, t. 3: *Lukasevangelium*, Berlin ²1976 (*ad loc.*). — On comprend qu'une *editio minor* se contente d'une indication sommaire: *D it*, cf. Nestle-Aland (47: "omnes vel plerique codices..."; voir aussi J. Jeremias, *o.c.*, 143, comp. 138, n. 2), et les synopses de Huck-Lietzmann et Aland; ou *D VetLat*, cf. Vogels et la synopse de Benoit-Boismard. Mais le danger est réel de négliger les témoins qui attestent le verset, surtout lorsqu'il ne s'agit plus d'une abréviation; cf. M.-E. Boismard, *Commentaire* (*Synopse*, t. 2), Paris 1972, 445: "ce verset est omis par D et la *Vetus Latina*". Même chez un auteur qui est parfaitement au courant du problème, on peut lire: "Den Vers Lk 24, 12 ( ) lässt unter den Griechen allein D aus, wieder mit der gesamten Vetus Latina..."; cf. H. J. Vogels, *Handbuch der Textkritik des Neuen Testaments*, Bonn ²1955, 45. La phrase est reprise par H. Zimmermann, *Neutestamentliche Methodenlehre*, Stuttgart ³1970, 67.

[15] C. Tischendorf, *Novum Testamentum Graece* (editio octava), Leipzig ⁸1869, 723-724. — Cf. *PG* 22, col. 1000 (*Quaestio IX*): καὶ κατὰ τὸν Λουκᾶν... Πέτρος δὲ σπεύσας ἐπὶ τὸ μνῆμα ἀπαντᾷ, καὶ τὰ ὀθόνια θεωρεῖ.

stituent le seul témoin, à côté de D *a b e rhe*, qui a été retenu dans les *Notes on Select Readings* de Westcott-Hort (1881); on y trouve également la référence à "Eus. *Mar* (distinctly)". Comme désignation de ces données, l'édition de A. Souter emploie la formule "Eusebius $^1/_2$", qui est adoptée maintenant par *GNT*.[16]

La plupart des éditions et commentaires passent sous silence le témoignage des canons d'Eusèbe. Mais F. Blass et A. Harnack s'y réfèrent[17] et, plus proche de nous, K. Aland semble encore reprendre le point de vue de Tischendorf.[18] Et pourtant l'argument de Tischendorf est bien fallacieux : il est basé sur la supposition que, selon Eusèbe, la visite au tombeau de Lc. xxiv 12 est identique à celle de Jn. xx 3-10. Mais on ne peut exclure la possibilité qu'Eusèbe y voit deux visites, d'abord celle de Pierre en compagnie de l'autre disciple (Jn.), et puis la démarche de Pierre seul (Lc.). Dans ce cas, il est normal que Jn. xx 2-10 est considéré comme un texte propre à Jean (n° 210, canon 10) et que Lc. xxiv 12, étant propre à Luc, fait partie de la section du *Sondergut* lucanien de Lc. xxiv 10 à 35 (n° 339, canon 10). Il ne s'agit pas d'une possibilité purement théorique. C'est précisément une des questions posées dans les *Quaestiones ad Marinum* : Comment Luc peut-il dire qu'un seul disciple est allé au tombeau tandis que selon Jean ils étaient deux ? Eusèbe répond clairement que Luc nous rapporte une seconde visite de Pierre : παλινδρομαῖος ἐπὶ τὸ μνημεῖον μόνος παραγίνεται· καὶ αὖθις παρακύψας βλέπει τὰ ὀθόνια μόνα ὡς καὶ τὸ πρότερον· εἶτα ἀπῄει, πρὸς ἑαυτὸν θαυμάζων τὸ γεγονός· καὶ νῦν μὲν ἀπῄει θαυμάζων τὸ γεγονός,....[19]

Il semble donc que, dans l'apparat critique de *GNT*, on peut rayer le nom d'Eusèbe dans la liste des témoins de l'omission.[20] On gardera

---

[16] A. Souter, *Novum Testamentum Graece*, Oxford 1910; = ²1947. Cf. J. M. Creed (*Luke*, London 1930). — Le commentaire de P. Schanz donne le nom d'Eusèbe uniquement parmi les témoins de l'omission, et sans préciser (Tübingen 1883); de même, K. Snodgrass *a.c.* (cf. *supra*, n. 3), 373.

[17] F. Blass, *Evangelium secundum Lucam*, Leipzig 1897, 110; *Philology of the Gospels*, London 1898, 188 (with reference to Tischendorf); A. Harnack, *Marcion: Das Evangelium vom fremden Gott* (TU, 45), Leipzig ²1924, 247*.

[18] *Loc. cit.* (cf. *supra*, n. 3), 206 (= 168): "Eusebius scheint beide Textformen zu kennen".

[19] PG 22, col. 990 (*Supplementa Quaestionum ad Marinum*, IV).

[20] Voir déjà la remarque de Scrivener qui disait simplement : "surely not (omitted) by Eusebius' canon, for he knew the verse well"; cf. F. H. A. Scrivener, *A Plain Introduction to the Criticism of the New Testament*, Cambridge ³1883 (¹1861), 555, n. 2.

"Eusebius" parmi les témoins qui attestent le verset, mais sans l'addition de "$^1/_2$" qui n'a aucune justification. C'est encore en dépendance de Tischendorf que Cyrille d'Alexandrie y est cité comme seul Père de l'Église à côté d'Eusèbe.[21] On est en droit de se demander pourquoi l'apparat ne fait pas mention ici des Pères "occidentaux", Ambroise[22] et Augustin![23]

2. Le Diatessaron

Dans l'apparat critique de Lc. xxiv 12, le *Codex Fuldensis* apparaît pour la première fois avec l'*editio octava* de Tischendorf (1869).[24] La référence est reprise par Westcott-Hort, avec ce bref commentaire: "omitted ( ) in the harmonistic narrative of *fu*; but probably ( ) by accident".[25] L'indication de Wordsworth-White est plus précise: "F *Iohannem* (xx. 6-8) *sequitur*".[26] La première référence au Diatessaron arabe vient de F. C. Burkitt dans les *Supplementary Notes* de la séconde édition de Westcott-Hort (1896): "The passage is not in *Diat*. arab, the account in Jn. xx 3-8 being preferred".[27] H. J. Vogels[28]

---

[21] PG 72, col. 944 (*Comment. in Lucam*): καὶ τὴν τοῦ Πέτρου μαρτυρίαν τὰ ὀθόνια μόνον ἐπὶ τοῦ μνήματος ἑωρακότος... Le passage est cité dans l'*editio octava* de Tischendorf.

[22] *Expositio Evangelii secundum Lucam* X, 174: "(Petrus ergo vidit solus dominum; devotio enim parata semper et promta credebat et ideo studebat frequentiora fidei signa colligere). Alibi cum Iohanne, alibi solus, ubique tamen inpiger currit, ubique aut solus aut primus, non contentus vidisse quae viderat repetit intuenda..." (CChr 14, 396; SC 52, 214). Comparer le texte d'Eusèbe sur les deux visites au tombeau.

[23] *De consensu Evangelistarum, liber III*, c. xxv, 70: "Et ipse quidam Lucas Petrum tantum dicit cucurrisse ad monumentum, et procumbentem vidisse linteamina sola posita, et abiisse secum mirantem quod factum fuerat" (PL 34, col. 1204). Augustin ne distingue pas les deux visites et essaie de les harmoniser: "Sed intelligitur hoc Lucas recapitulando posuisse de Petro" (col. 1204); "Ita et Petrus intelligendus est primo procumbens vidisse, quod Lucas commemorat, Joannes tacet; post autem ingressus, sed ingressus tamen antequam Joannes intraret, ut omnes verum dixisse sine ulla repugnantia reperiantur" (col. 1205). — À noter que le témoignage d'Augustin est signalé par T. Zahn, *Das Evangelium des Lukas*, Leipzig-Erlangen ³⁻⁴1920, 714, n. 46; cf. H. J. Vogels, *Beiträge zur Geschichte des Diatessaron im Abendland* (NTA 8/1), Münster 1919, 83, n. 1.

[24] L'édition date de 1868; cf. E. Ranke, *Codex Fuldensis. Novum Testamentum Latine interprete Hieronymo*, Marburg-Leipzig 1868. — La liste des témoins donnée par Tischendorf, avec la mention de *fu*, sera reprise telle quelle par beaucoup d'auteurs; voir, par exemple, P. Schanz (*Lucas*, 1883); A. Harnack, *Marcion* (cf. *supra*, n. 17) ²1924, 247*.

[25] *Notes on Select Readings*, 71.

[26] J. Wordsworth, H. J. White, *Novum Testamentum Domini nostri Iesu Christi latine*, vol. 1, Oxford 1889-1898, 477.

[27] *Appendix. I. Notes on Select Readings*, 147. (Voir cependant n. 38).

[28] *Beiträge zur Geschichte des Diatessaron im Abendland* (cf. *supra*, n. 23), 1919,

et autres[29] souligneront la concordance entre le *Fuldensis* et la traduction arabe, à laquelle s'ajouteront encore les traductions néerlandaises et italiennes.[30] D'où l'indication très complète de Jeremias: Tat[arab fuld ned ven tos].[31]

Sans doute, la reconstruction du texte de Tatien à partir de témoins indirects et lointains laissera toujours des sceptiques,[32] mais il est plus important pour nous de noter que si des critiques comme H. J. VOGELS et J. JEREMIAS donnent tant de poids au Diatessaron, ce n'est pas parce qu'ils prétendent y trouver le texte primitif de l'évangile de Luc. Les deux défendent l'authenticité de Lc. xxiv 12. Selon VOGELS (et H. VON SODEN), c'est précisément Tatien qui est responsable pour l'omission du verset dans la Vetus Latina (et éventuellement dans la Vetus Syra).[33] Pour J. JEREMIAS, l'omission est

---

82-83. L'absence de Lc xxiv 12 y est encore signalée dans une autre harmonie latine, celle du *Cod. lat. Mon.* 11025: "unsere Harmonie bietet Lk. 24, 9-35 in fortlaufenden Text ohne die Einschaltungen aus Mk. 16, 10.11.12, die sich in F und Ar finden, aber der Vers 12 fehlt hier wie dort" (p. 83). Voir aussi *Evangelium Palatinum. Studien zur ältesten Geschichte der lateinischen Evangelienübersetzung* (NTA 12/3), München 1926, 91: Tat[ar] Tat[lat] (cf. 101).

[29] Un exemple: J. M. HEER, *Neue griechisch-saïdische Evangelienfragmente*, dans *OrChr* 2 (1912), 1-47, 21, n. 1: "*fuld* geht mit Joh. 20, 6-8, ebenso *Tatian arab*". Voir aussi l'apparat de la Synopse de A. HUCK ([8]1934): *fu Tat*.

[30] Cf. H. J. VOGELS, *Evangelium Colbertinum* (BBB, 5), Bonn 1953, 178: "Seit 1913 sind nun einige neue Tatianformen bekannt geworden, die unsere Kenntnis um ein Beträchtliches erweitert haben. Vor allem das Blatt aus Dura-Europos, das uns zum erstmal ein Stück griechischen Diatessarontextes zeigte (*1935*), dann die von Bergsma (*1895-1898*) und Plooij (*1929-1938*) veröffentlichten niederländischen Texte, ferner die von Todesco und Vaccari edierten italienischen Harmonien in venetianischer und toskanischer Mundart (*1938*), endlich das von Messina entdeckte, aus dem Syrischen ins Persische übertragene Diatessaron (*1951*)".

[31] *Die Abendmahlsworte Jesu* (cf. *supra*, n. 1), 143. Parmi les éditions du N.T., celles de NESTLE(-ALAND), SOUTER et KILPATRICK ne font pas mention du Diatessaron. Par contre, le Diatessaron (ou Tat) est signalé par VON SODEN, VOGELS, BOVER et *GNT*. MERK, depuis 1933, avait d'abord *Ta* (encore en [3]1938), puis la référence avait disparu ([5]1944, [6]1948, [7]1951), et finalement elle devient très précise *Ta³* (= arab ital neerl) ([8]1957; = [9]1964).

[32] On pourrait faire valoir qu'il s'agit ici non pas de la forme du texte mais d'un phénomène plus saisissable, la présence ou l'absence d'une petite section. Toutefois, l'omission de Lc. xxiv 12 devient d'une certaine façon inévitable pour tout auteur d'une harmonie évangélique, indépendamment de l'exemple de Tatien (voir n. 36).

[33] Voir surtout *Beiträge zur Geschichte des Diatessarons im Abendland* (cf. *supra*, n. 23), 1921, 81-84: "durch Tatian verursacht" (*o.c.*, 62); "ein völlig befriedigende Erklärung dafür ( ), woher die auffällige Tatsache stammt, dass dieser Vers (in der Vetus Syra und) bei fünf wichtigen Altlateinern fehlt" (*o.c.*, 84). — L'auteur signale à la page 82 qu'en 1911 il avait encore admis l'inauthenticité du verset, sur la foi des éditeurs du texte, TISCHENDORF, B. WEISS, WESTCOTT-HORT e.a.; cf. *Die altsyrischen Evangelien in ihrem Verhältnis zu Tatians Diatessaron* (BSt(F) 16/5), Freiburg 1911, 138. Il est d'autre part curieux de constater que quelqu'un qui loue von Soden "der den

une des variantes harmonisantes qui caractérisent le texte de l'évangile que Tatien avait trouvé à Rome (ca 150-172).[34] Sans entrer dans cette discussion, on peut faire remarquer que, dans une harmonie évangélique, l'omission de Lc. xxiv 12 n'a rien d'étonnant. Nous avons déjà vu la réaction d'Eusèbe devant le problème de Jn. xx 3-10 et Lc. xxiv 12.[35] Pour l'auteur d'une harmonie qui n'a pas recours à cette solution des deux visites au tombeau, Jn. xx 3-10 et Lc. xxiv 12 racontent un même événement. Mais lorsque Jn. xx 3-10 et Lc. xxiv 12 doivent s'intégrer dans un seul récit harmonistique, n'est-il pas normal que "in a Harmony the verse (*Lc. xxiv 12*) is naturally swallowed up into the fuller narrative from S. John"?[36] Il faut en conclure que l'omission de Lc. xxiv 12 dans le Diatessaron ne peut nous renseigner sur le texte évangélique utilisé par Tatien.

Par contre, on peut se demander si le Diatessaron ne suppose pas d'une manière ou d'une autre le verset lucanien. On pourrait songer à des réminiscences du vocabulaire lucanien dans le récit "johannique".[37] L'ordre des péricopes est peut-être une indication plus contrôlable. La succession de Lc. xxiv 11 et 12, incrédulité des disciples et visite au tombeau, a été ressentie par beaucoup d'exégètes comme une difficulté réelle dans le texte de Luc. La difficulté n'est pas moindre lorsqu'il s'agit de "Pierre et l'autre disciple". Et pourtant,

---

Vers von seinen Klammern befreit hat" (*o.c.*, 82, n. 1) et imprime d'abord le verset sans crochets (1920; ²1922), le met de nouveau entre "Klammer" dans la troisième édition de 1949! Voir aussi *Handbuch* (cf. *supra*, n. 14), 156.

[34] *Die Abendmahlsworte Jesu* (cf. *supra*, n. 2), 141: contre H. VON SODEN (*Die Schriften*, I/2, Berlin 1907, 1535-1648); il renvoie à F. C. BURKITT et A. JÜLICHER (*ib.*, n. 3). — Sur Marcion (et sy) comme témoins de l'omission dans le texte "romain" (*o.c.*, 143), cf. *infra*.

[35] Cf. *supra*, n. 19 (Eusèbe); 22 (Ambroise).

[36] F. C. BURKITT, *Evangelion da-Mepharreshe* II, Cambridge 1904, 231.

[37] Il est plus que probable que μόνα appartient au texte du verset lucanien; sur l'omission en ℵ*A sa et les doutes de K. P. G. CURTIS, voir J. MUDDIMAN, *o.c.* (cf. *supra*, n. 3) spéc. 543, n. 5. Dans Jn. xx 5 et 6, μόνα n'est attesté que très rarement et s'explique sans doute par l'influence de Lc. xxiv 12 (voir l'apparat de VON SODEN). Le Diatessaron de Liège semble le traduire en Jn. xx 5 par "so sach hi dat lijnwaet liggen *daer besiden*"; (comp. les autres Diatessarons néerlandais ou allemands: Haaren, Cambridge; Zürich, München; cf. *Das Leben Jesu*, éd. C. GERHARDT, Leiden 1970, 166: "dar bi siten"). Est-ce une réminiscence du texte lucanien, ὀθόνια μόνα entendu comme "les linges (gisant) séparément", ou est-ce une paraphrase du traducteur du texte de Jean? Le sens du texte de Lc est que Pierre "ne voit que les linges" (c.-à-d. il ne voit pas le corps de Jésus); cf. F. NEIRYNCK *a.c.* (cf. *supra*, n. 3), 550 et 553. La *Harmonie* de CLERICUS (cf. n. 38) traduit ainsi: "videt quidem lintea, quibus cadaver Jesu involutum fuerat, sed praeterea nihil"; Eusèbe introduit ce sens dans le récit de Jean: καὶ τὰ ὀθόνια εἶδον μόνα, τὸ δὲ σῶμα οὐδαμοῦ (PG 22, col. 989; cf. *supra*, n. 19).

c'est à cet endroit que les harmonies néerlandaises (Liège, Stuttgart, Haaren) situent le récit de Jn. xx 2-10:[38] est-ce un indice que l'auteur du Diatessaron y lisait effectivement le verset 12?

3. *Marcion*

Marcion comme témoin de l'omission apparaît pour la première fois dans la seizième édition de NESTLE en 1936. Depuis lors, le nom de Marcion a une place dans l'apparat critique des éditions ultérieures de NESTLE(-ALAND), et de la *Synopsis* de K. ALAND, dans l'édition de MERK (à partir de [5]1944), KILPATRICK ([2]1958) et *GNT* (1966).[39] On peut facilement retrouver l'origine de cette mention. E. NESTLE l'indique dans l'introduction de son édition de 1936: "Nur die Anführungen aus Marcion hat Prof. SCHMIEDEL nach HARNACKS Ausgabe desselben nachzuprüfen die Freundlichkeit gehabt".[40] En effet, l'omission "marcionite" est signalée dans la seconde édition de *Marcion: Das Evangelium vom fremden Gott* (1924).[41] L'indication est reprise par H. J. VOGELS dans un ouvrage de 1926.[42]

---

[38] En ce qui concerne l'ordre des péricopes qui font suite à Mt. xxviii 1-8 (par. Mc. xvi 1-8; Lc. xxiv 1-8; Jn. xx 1), on peut distingueur deux groupes parmi les témoins du Diatessaron. Le Codex Fuldensis et le Diatessaron arabe, vénétien et toscan présentent l'ordre suivant:

a) Jn. xx 2-10.11-17
b) Mt. xxviii 11-15
c) Jn. xx 18
d) Mt. xxviii 9-10
e) Lc. xxiv 9-11; par. Mc. xvi 10-11.

Le Diatessaron de Stuttgart (éd. J. BERGSMA, Leiden 1898), de Liège (éd. C. C. DE BRUIN, Leiden 1970) et de Haaren (éd. C. C. DE BRUIN, Leiden 1970) ont un ordre différent: *d-e-a-c-b*, c.-à-d. (après Mt. xxviii 1-8) Mt. xxviii 9-10; Lc. xxiv 9-11 (par. Mc. xvi 10-11); Jn. xx 2-18; Mt. xxviii 11-15. Le même ordre est attesté par le Diatessaron perse (éd. G. MESSINA, Roma 1951). — Il est à noter que la suite de Lc. xxiv 9-11 et Jn. xx 2 ss., avec la juxtaposition de Lc. xxiv 12a/Jn. xx 3; Lc. xxiv 12b/Jn. xx 5; Lc. xxiv 12c/Jn. xx 10, se retrouve dans une présentation synoptique chez J. CLERICUS, *Harmonia Evangelica*, Amsterdam 1699, 482-484.

[39] Voir aussi l'étude déjà cité de J. JEREMIAS (*o.c.*, 143), le commentaire de W. GRUNDMANN (1961, 439), les notes de critique textuelle publiées par R. V. G. TASKER à propos de NEB (1964, 424), l'article de K. P. G. CURTIS (1971, 515) et diverses autres études (J. A. BAILEY, 1963; H. ZIMMERMANN, [3]1970; B. LINDARS, 1972, etc.). Par contre, Marcion n'est pas cité par BOVER, ni par VOGELS ([3]1949; voir cependant n. 42).

[40] *Novum Testamentum Graece*, [16]1936, 20*.

[41] A. HARNACK, *Marcion* (cf. *supra*, n. 17), [2]1924, 247* (cf. 238*). L'auteur admet une influence marcionite dans les cas suivants: Lc. v 39; ix 54 ss.; xxii 43-44; xxiii 2a.b; xxiii 34; xxiv 12; xxiv 40. — Déjà dans la première édition (1921), HARNACK présente cette liste mais encore sans la mention de Lc. xxiv 12 (229*, cf. 220*). Peu de temps après (à la séance de l'Académie du 2 mars 1922), il fait état de l'omission marcionite: "dieser Vers ist echt. *Weil ihn Marcion gestrichen hat*,

Quelle est, selon les critiques, la valeur de ce témoignage? D'après
HARNACK, il s'agit d'une omission intentionnelle: "von M(arcion)
gestrichen, der den Petrus hier nicht wünschte",[43] et K. ALAND vient
encore de répéter cette explication: "Die besondere Herausstellung
des Petrus war ihm zuwider".[44] E. C. BLACKMAN suggère une raison
supplémentaire: "Tendentious omission of Marcion not only because,
as Harnack suggests, he did not like to believe Peter was at the tomb,
but possibly also because of the implication that clothes provided
evidence of the Resurrection".[45] Pour J. JEREMIAS, par contre, l'omission est un des cas où la combinaison de "D it (vet-syr) Marc"
témoigne du texte que Marcion a trouvé à Rome vers 140.[46]

Mais avant de disputer sur l'origine de l'omission il faut savoir
s'il y a omission. Je ne peux m'empêcher de citer ici l'observation
faite par ZAHN en 1892: "Man hat sich im allgemeinen der Erkenntnis
nicht verschliessen können, dass aus dem Schweigen eines Tertullianus
und eines Epiphanius an sich weder folge, dass ein Stück unseres Lc.
bei Mrc. gefehlt habe, noch auch dass es in abweichender oder gleich-
lautender Gestalt vorhanden gewesen sei. Trotzdem hat man nicht
aufgehört, den Text auch solcher Stellen, über welche wir aus den
Quellen einfach nichts wissen, zum Theil bis aufs Wort festzustellen...".[47] Sur Lc. xxiv 12 le silence de Tertullien et Épiphane
est complet, et lorsque HARNACK a proposé l'omission marcionite,
il l'a fait sans donner la moindre justification.[48]

---

bietet ihn auch ein beträchtlicher Teil der abendländischer Überlieferung nicht"; cf.
*Die Verklärungsgeschichte Jesu, der Bericht des Paulus (I Kor. 15,3ff.) und die beiden
Christusvisionen des Petrus* (SPAW.PH) Berlin 1922, 62-80, spéc. 69, n. 3. En 1923
il publie une liste de *addenda* à la première édition qui comprend la référence à
Lc. xxiv 12; cf. *Neue Studien zu Marcion* (TU 44/4), Berlin 1923, 32-33.

[42] *Evangelium Palatinum* (cf. *supra*, n. 28), 1926, 91 (voir aussi 96). Plus tard,
VOGELS est plus réticent: cf. *supra*, n. 39; voir également *Handbuch*, [2]1955, 45.

[43] *O.c.*, 247*.

[44] Cf. *supra*, n. 3: dans *NTS*, 206; = *Studien*, 168.

[45] E. C. BLACKMAN, *Marcion and His Influence*, London, 1948, 138. L'auteur y
donne la liste des témoins latins de l'omission et veut corriger HARNACK: "not f,
as Harnack says". Mais le manuscrit cité par HARNACK était le *fu*(ldensis)!

[46] *Die Abendmahlsworte Jesu* (cf. *supra*, n. 2), 139. L'auteur signale les huit
exceptions admises par HARNACK (cf. *supra*, n. 41), mais il ne veut y voir des
variantes de tendance marcionite; il se réfère à A. POTT, dans E. PREUSCHEN, A. POTT,
Tatians Diatessaron aus dem Arabischen übersetzt, Heidelberg 1926, 13-19, spéc. 17-18.

[47] *Geschichte des neutestamentlichen Kanons* II, Erlangen-Leipzig 1892, 451; voir
la reconstruction du texte, *o.c.*, 493.

[48] Il se contente de noter le silence des témoins: "bei M. nicht nachzuweisen"
(*loc. cit.*).

4. *Les versions syriaques*

La Syriaque curetonienne, publiée en 1858, est citée comme témoin du verset lucanien par TISCHENDORF ([7]1859, [8]1869) et WESTCOTT-HORT (1881), et ce témoignage sera confirmé par celui de la Syriaque sinaïtique, publiée en 1894. En 1896, F. GRAEFE note qu'en Lc. xxiv 12 les deux versions écrivent "Simon" au lieu de "Pierre", "was in einer syrischen Übersetzung ganz erklärlich ist".[49] Mais la même année, la seconde édition de WESTCOTT-HORT paraît et, dans les *Supplementary Notes*, F. C. BURKITT signale que Lc. xxiv 12 forme la fin d'un paragraphe en syr[s] tandis qu'il est le début d'un paragraphe en syr[c] : "possibly therefore it is a later addition to the version".[50] On trouve la suggestion de BURKITT rapportée par VOGELS en 1919,[51] et dans l'édition de A. SOUTER, la vieille syriaque rejoint les témoins de l'omission : "S (vt.)?".[52]

Toutefois, cette divergence entre syr[c] et syr[s], dans la division des sections, n'a rien d'exceptionnel. Ce n'est pas la seule différence dans le contexte de Lc. xxiv 12 (syr[c] : xxiii 50-xxiv 11 ; xxiv 12-17.18-24.25-35 ; syr[s] : xxiv 1-12.13-24.25-35), et BURKITT lui-même est revenu sur la question pour dire que les deux systèmes de division sont tellement différents qu'on peut admettre qu'ils se sont développés indépendamment.[53] Dans *Evangelion da-Mepharreshe* (1904), il fait appel à un autre argument : en xxiv 12 Πέτρος n'est pas traduit par *Kepha* comme partout ailleurs dans l'évangile de Luc, mais par *Simon*, ce qui pourrait être un indice que le verset a été interpolé dans

---

[49] F. GRAEFE, Textkritische Bemerkungen zu den drei Schlusskapiteln des Lukas-evangeliums, *ThStKr* 69 (1896) 245-281, 269. Cf. *infra*, n. 54-57.

[50] *Notes on Variant Readings*, 147.

[51] *Beiträge zur Geschichte des Diatessaron* (cf. *supra*, n. 23), 82 : "Wenn sich die Vermutung Burkitts bestätigt, dass auch die Vetus Syra zuerst den Vers ausgelassen hat, ..."; cf. *o.c.*, 83 : "das Fehlen derselben in der Vetus Latina, bzw. im lateinisch-syrischen Text". Voir aussi *o.c.*, 84 (cf. *supra*, n. 33).

[52] A. SOUTER, *Novum Testamentum Graece* (cf. *supra*, n. 16). C'est sans doute par inadvertance qu'on peut écrire : "Lk xxiv. 6, 12, 36, 40, 51, 52. Both sy[s] and sy[c] have the same omissions as D and the Old Latin"; cf. V. TAYLOR, *The Text of the New Testament. A Short Introduction*, London [2]1965, 32 ; et encore, à propos de Lc. xxiv 12 : "omis par D it sy ..." (B. RIGAUX, *Dieu l'a ressuscité*, Gembloux 1973, 221, n. 69).

[53] *Evangelion da-Mepharreshe* (cf. *supra*, n. 36), 37-38. L'auteur réagit contre Mrs LEWIS qui souligna l'accord entre les deux manuscrits et montre les différences en Mt. ii-vi. Il conclut : "These grave divergences suggest that the systems of paragraph division in *S* and *C* may have been developed quite independently" (*o.c.*, 38). BURKITT ne se réfère pas de manière explicite à Lc. xxiv 12, mais l'argument n'est plus retenu lorsqu'il parle de l'interpolation (*o.c.*, 231) ; cf. *infra*, n. 54.

syr^{c.s.}[54] L'argument est repris tel quel par J. JEREMIAS.[55] A. MERX avait déjà répondu que l'emploi de Simon indique plutôt que le verset n'a pas été interpolé d'après Jn. xx 2-10 où les manuscrits grecs lisent Simon Pierre (v. 2), Pierre (v. 3), Pierre (v. 4) et Simon Pierre (v. 6).[56] D'après cet auteur, Lc. xxiv 12 appartient au texte original de Luc et l'interpolation serait à chercher au v. 34.[57] On est en droit de se demander si, par l'élimination du v. 34, MERX n'enlève pas du texte lucanien l'élément qui peut avoir suggéré au traducteur du v. 12 l'emploi de *Simon* au lieu de *Kepha*: ὤφθη Σίμωνι.[58]

Certains auteurs signalent également la version harkléenne comme témoin de l'omission,[59] mais cette opinion prend son origine dans une erreur de lecture de l'abréviation employée pour la syro-palestinienne.[60]

La version syro-palestinienne apparaît pour la première fois dans l'apparat critique d'une édition du N.T. en 1796, dans la seconde édition de GRIESBACH. L'indication donnée par GRIESBACH: "om. Syr. hieros. (extat in margine)", sera reprise par D. SCHULZ (³1827) et

---

[54] *Ibid.*, 231. D'après BURKITT, Lc. xxiv 12 n'est pas authentique (voir aussi *o.c.*, 229 et 96). D'autre part, dans syr^{c.s.}, le verset doit venir directement du grec (la Peshitta en diffère et le Diatessaron est exclu). — À noter la formulation prudente de l'auteur: "makes it conceivable that we are here dealing with an interpolation" (*ibid.*). Il s'exprime de manière plus hésitante *o.c.*, 96: "At the same time the hypothesis that *S* and *C* are here themselves interpolated, and that the verse forms no part of the original *Ev. da-Mepharreshe*, raises serious difficulties. The translator may possibly have been influenced by the four-fold occurrence of 'Simon' in the parallel passage Joh. xx 3-10".

[55] *Die Abendmahlsworte Jesu* (cf. *supra*, n. 2), 143, n. 2: "das deutet auf nachträgliche Einfügung des Verses".

[56] A. MERX, *Die vier kanonischen Evangelien nach ihrem ältesten bekannten Texte*, II/2 *Die Evangelien des Markus und Lukas*, Berlin 1905, 519-522, spéc. 519.

[57] *Ibid.*, 520. La tension entre les versets 34 et 12 ("Dieser Zusatz ist aber mit 24 12 unvereinbar, ( ) Vs. 12 leugnet eine solche Erscheinung") doit expliquer l'omission 'latine' (*o.c.*, 522).

[58] Très tôt on fera le rapprochement entre Lc. xxiv 12 et xxiv 34 et 1 Cor. xv 5; voir Eusèbe, PG 22, col. 989 (cf. *supra*, n. 15): Κεφᾶς δὲ αὐτὸς ἦν Σίμων ὁ καὶ Πέτρος!

[59] A. PLUMMER, *The Gospel according to S. Luke*, Edinburgh ⁴1901, 568: "Syr-Harcl.* omits at the beginning of one lection"; J. SCHMITT, *Le récit de la résurrection dans l'évangile de Luc*, RevSR 25 (1951) 119-137, 219-242, spéc. 221: "la version syriaque harkléenne"; K. P. G. CURTIS, *Luke xxiv. 12* (cf. *supra*, n. 4), 1971, 515: "the Harclean Syriac".

[60] La version syro-palestinienne (syr^{pal}) fut appelée *Hierosolymitana* par J. G. C. ADLER (p. 140), sur une proposition de J. D. MICHAELIS (cf. *Orientalische und Exegetische Bibliothek*, Frankfurt 1782, t. 19, 126, note). On comprend la confusion avec syr^h (harkléenne) quand on voit les abréviations utilisées: Syr^{hieros} (GRIESBACH), syr^{hier} (SCHULZ), syr^{hr} (TISCHENDORF), syr.hr. (WESTCOTT-HORT), Hrs (MERX), Sh (ZAHN), syⁱ (VAGANAY), sy^h (VOGELS, *Evangelium Palatinum*, 91).

Tischendorf ([5]1849). Dans les commentaires, elle reçoit une forme
plus brève encore: "om. Syr. hier." (De Wette, [3]1846; Meyer, [4]1864).
Cela nous éloigne beaucoup de la collation exacte que J. G. C. Adler
en avait présentée en 1789: "Hic versus in margine additus est:
incipit enim pericope v. 13. Adest autem in alia pericope, quae hoc
versu 12 terminatur".[61] Tischendorf s'en rapproche de nouveau en
[7]1859 et, de manière plus précise encore, en [8]1869.[62] Omission du
verset au début d'une péricope d'un Évangéliaire: "probably by
accident", écrit Hort,[63] et pour d'autres c'est un témoin à négliger
puisque le verset est attesté ailleurs dans le même manuscrit.[64]
Von Soden, Souter, Vogels, Merk, Bover et Kilpatrick ne le men-
tionnent plus dans l'apparat de leur édition. En 1966, on le trouve
de nouveau dans GNT: "syr[pal mss]". K. Aland parle également, sans
préciser, de "ein Teil der Handschriften von syr[pal]".[65]

Le pluriel renvoie sans doute aux trois manuscrits publiés en 1899
par A. S. Lewis,[66] celui du Vatican (A), connu déjà par les éditions
antérieures, et les deux manuscrits du Sinaï, découverts en 1892 et
1893 (B et C).[67] Le verset est attesté par les trois manuscrits à
la fin de la lectio 152: Lc. xxiv 1-12.[68] Dans l'édition de Lewis,
la lectio 3 est intitulée "Lc. xxiv 12-35" et la liste des variantes

---

[61] J. G. C. Adler, Novi Testamenti Versiones syriacae Simplex, Philoxeniana et
Hierosolymitana, Copenhagen 1789, 135-202, spéc. 185.

[62] Editio octava, 723: "syr[hr•6] (lectio incipit v. 13, sed additur vel potius praemittitur
in margine v. 12. Contra [412] ad finem lectionis quae v. 1 incipit in ipso textu* legitur
versus.)" — Une nouvelle édition de l'Évangéliaire, avec traduction latine, avait été
publiée en 1861 et 1864 par F. Miniscalchi Erizzo (2 vol., Verona).

[63] Notes on Variant Readings, 71. Repris p.e. par Plummer: "perhaps accidentally"
(cf. supra, n. 59).

[64] F. H. A. Scrivener, A Plain Introduction (cf. supra, n. 20), 555, n. 2; F. Graefe,
Textkritische Anmerkungen (cf. n. 49), 268; A. Merx, Die vier kanonischen Evangelien
(cf. n. 56), 519; J. M. Heer, dans Oriens Christianus (cf. n. 29), 21, n. 1; T. Zahn,
Lukas (cf. n. 23), 714, n. 46. Le témoignage est cité par Wordsworth-White,
Harnack (Marcion, [2]1924, 247*), Vogels (Evangelium Palatinum, 1926, 91).

[65] Cf. supra, n. 3: dans NTS 12, 206; = Studien, 168.

[66] A. S. Lewis, M. D. Gibson, The Palestinian Syriac Lectionary of the Gospels,
re-edited from two Sinai MSS. and from P. de Lagarde's edition of the "Evangeliarium
Hierosolymitanum", London 1899. L'édition imprime le texte de B et signale les
variantes de A et C. Cf. P. de Lagarde, Bibliothecae Syriacae, Göttingen 1892, 257-404:
Evangeliarium Hierosolymitanum. Comp. aussi n. 61 et 62. — Les manuscrits sont
datés: A en 1030, B en 1104 et C en 1118.

[67] Je n'ai pas connaissance d'autres manuscrits témoins de Lc. xxiv 12. Pour
une liste complète des éditions voir C. Perrot, Un fragment christo-palestinien découvert
à Khirbet Mird (Act., X, 28-29; 32-41), RB 70 (1963), 506-555, 510, n. 8 (sur les
manuscrits, cf. a.c., 550 ss.).

[68] The Palestinian Syriac Lectionary, 219. Cf. supra, n. 62 (lectio 152 = lectio 412).

signale que le verset 12 fait défaut en B et C.[69] Cette présentation
est à compléter par le renseignement que dans A le verset n'est pas
de la *prima manus*.[70] En outre, la question est à poser s'il est permis
de parler d'omission.[71] N'est-il pas une présentation plus objective
de suivre le texte de A*, B et C et de considérer l'addition marginale
du v. 12 dans A pour ce qu'elle est: un ajout à la lecture originale
de Lc. xxiv 13-35?

L'addition marginale du v. 12 peut s'expliquer par le besoin de
conformité au Synaxaire officiel de l'Église byzantine. Lc. xxiv 12-35
y est en effet la lecture du mardi de Pâques et la cinquième des
lectures matinales du dimanche (la quatrième est Lc. xxiv 1-12).[72]
Mais la possibilité que, dans le texte de l'Évangéliaire syro-palestinien,
le v. 12 ne faisait pas partie de cette *lectio* ne peut pas être exclue,
car nous savons trop peu sur l'origine de cet Évangéliaire[73] et,
d'autre part, nous savons trop sur la diversité liturgique de l'Église
ancienne.[74] Les plus anciens lectionnaires syriaque,[75] arménien[76] et

---

[69] *Ibid.*, LII: "B + C wanting"; cf. 4 (texte).

[70] Voir P. DE LAGARDE, *o.c.*, 357: "comma integrum > A, + manus non nimis recens in margine. interpretis nostri non esse scio". Cf. *supra*, n. 62 (*lectio* 3 = *lectio* 6).

[71] Il est d'usage de parler d'omission depuis GRIESBACH qui traduit ainsi le renseignement donné par ADLER: "Hic versus in margine additus est ..." (cf. *supra*, n. 61).

[72] F. H. A. SCRIVENER, *A Plain Introduction* (cf. *supra*, n. 20), 78-84: Synaxarion, spéc. 78 (le mardi de Pâques) et 83 (les lectures du dimanche); C. R. GREGORY, *Textkritik des Neuen Testaments* I, Leipzig 1900, 343-364: Synaxarion, spéc. 364; S. BEISSEL, *Entstehung der Perikopen des Römischen Messbuches. Zur Geschichte der Evangelienbücher in der ersten Hälfte des Mittelalters*, Freiburg 1907, 13 et 22 (d'après des mss. grecs), 32-33 (mss. syriaques). Voir aussi E. C. COLWELL, *Description of Four Lectionary MSS*, dans E. C. COLWELL, D. W. RIDDLE, *Studies in the Lectionary Text of the Greek New Testament*, Vol. I. *Prolegomena to the Study of the Lectionary Text of the Gospels*, Chicago 1933, 85 et 127; et le catalogue des mss. syriaques de la Bodleian Library (éd. R. PAYNE SMITH, Oxford 1864): col. 127, n° 38, un lectionnaire melchite. — D'après J. W. BURGON la pratique liturgique pourrait expliquer l'omission de Lc. xxiv 12: "it is only because that verse was claimed both as the *conclusion* of the iv[th] and also as the *beginning* of the vth Gospel of the Resurrection so that the liturgical note (ἀρχή) stands at the beginning, –τέλος at the end of it. Accordingly D is kept in countenance here only by the Jerusalem Lectionary and some copies of the old Latin". Cf. J. W. BURGON, *The Last Twelve Verses of the Gospel according to S. Mark*, Oxford-London 1871, 222.

[73] Cf. C. PERROT, *Un fragment christo-palestinien* (cf. *supra*, n. 67), 547-549 (sur l'origine ancienne de la version).

[74] Il faut nuancer maintenant l'affirmation de SCRIVENER: "All the information we can gather favours the notion that there was no great difference between the calendar of Church-lessons in earlier and later ages"; cf. *o.c.* (*supra*, n. 72), 73.

[75] F. C. BURKITT, The Early Syriac Lectionary System, *PBA* 10 (London 1921-23) 10, 33 (= 310, 333): dans le ms. Brit. Mus. Add. 14528, Lc. xxiv 1-12 (Pâques) et

géorgien[77] ont tous une division des péricopes de Lc. xxiv qui est identique à celle de l'Évangéliaire syro-palestinien (A*, B, C): Lc. xxiv 1-12 et 13-35.

Un mot encore sur la *lectio* de Lc xxiv 12-35, introduite dans le ms. A de l'Évangéliaire par l'addition marginale du v. 12. Comme dans les Synaxaires byzantins, le verset fait ainsi partie de deux lectures, xxiv 1-12 et xxiv 12-35, ce qui correspond à la division des paragraphes que nous avons constatée dans syr[s] (v. 12/13) et syr[c] (v. 11/12). La traduction de Πέτρος par Simon est un autre point de contact entre la variante marginale de syr[pal] et syr[c, s].[78] À ce propos nous avons suggéré une influence de ὤφθη Σίμωνι (v. 34). Cette explication prend un relief particulier s'il est permis de la rapprocher de l'opinion d'Origène sur l'identité du compagnon de Cléophas. Il le nomme Simon,[79] et l'objection de LAGRANGE: "Si Simon

xxiv 13 ss. (mardi). — A. BAUMSTARK, *Festbrevier und Kirchenjahr der syrischen Jakobiten* (SGKA III/3-5), Paderborn 1910, 248, n. 1, et 250. Voir aussi le codex de Rabbula (S. BEISSEL, *o.c.* [cf. n. 72] 37: Lc. xxiv 13 ss. la lecture du lundi) et plusieurs témoins occidentaux (*ibid.*, 63, 77, 80, 86, 90, 93, 99, 113, 125, 151: Lc. xxiv 13 ss. y est la lecture du lundi, mardi ou mercredi).

[76] F. C. CONYBEARE, *Rituale Armenorum*, Oxford 1905, 516-527: "The Old Armenian Lectionary"; 523 (Lc. xxiv 1-12.13-35.36-40: le lundi, mardi et mercredi de Pâques); A. RENOUX, *Le Codex arménien Jérusalem 121*, t. 2 (PO 36, fasc. 2, n° 168), Turnhout 1971, 315 et 317 (le ms. J a xxiii 50-xxiv 12 au lieu de xxiv 1-12). Cf. A. RENOUX, Un manuscrit du lectionnaire arménien de Jérusalem (cod. Jérus. arm. 121), *Muséon* 74 (1961), 361-385, 378; 75 (1962), 385-398 (addenda et corrigenda). Il s'agit du "vieux lectionnaire arménien du Ve siècle" (*ibid.*).

[77] M. TARCHNISCHVILI, *Le grand lectionnaire de l'Église de Jérusalem* (*V-VIIIe siècle*) (CSCO, 188-189), Louvain 1959, t. 2, 116 et 118: Lc. xxiv 13-35 (le jour de Pâques et le mercredi); 117: Lc. xxiii 54-xxiv 12 (le lundi); cf. *idem*, Zwei georgische Lektionar-fragmente aus dem 5. und 8. Jahrhundert, *Muséon* 73 (1960), 261-296, spéc. 267-268; G. GARITTE, Un index géorgien des lectures évangéliques selon l'ancien rite de Jérusalem, *Muséon* 85 (1972) 337-398, 359-360 et 385.

[78] Par contre, la traduction est *Kepha* dans la *lectio* 152 (Lc. xxiv 1-12) d'après les mss. A, B, C. La variante *Simon* de la *lectio* 3 est notée par LEWIS, sans signaler qu'il s'agit d'une addition (p. LII). L'apparat de VON SODEN la mentionne également et il la présente tout simplement comme la leçon de *pa*, en accord avec *sy*. — Pour une présentation correcte, voir F. GRAEFE, *Textkritische Bemerkungen a.c.* (cf. *supra*, n. 49), 269.

[79] ORIGÈNE, *Contra Celsum*, II, 62.68 (PG 11, col. 893, 901). Cf. *Comm. in Ioannem* I, 5 (7). 8 (10) (PG 14, col. 34.40); *Hom. in Jeremiam* 19, 8.9 (PG 13, col. 521). H. GROTIUS (*Annotationes in N.T.*) explique aussi le nom donné par Ambroise, Amaon (Ammaon), comme une déformation de Siméon; voir aussi T. ZAHN, *Forschungen zur Geschichte des neutestamentlichen Kanons*, vol. 6, Leipzig 1900, 350-351, n. 2. La conjecture, proposée par GROTIUS comme explication de l'origine de l'opinion d'Origène, a été trouvée par après comme leçon variante du codex Bezae: λέγοντες (au lieu de λέγοντας) au v. 34. (VON SODEN signale comme témoins de λέγοντες D 1071 et aussi "pa?", mais ne s'explique pas sur le témoin syro-palestinien). — L'opinion

(*Le compagnon de Cléophas*) est Pierre, pourquoi ne pas l'avoir nommé dès le début?",[80] perd son objet lorsqu'on lit le v. 34 dans le contexte d'une péricope qui commence avec le v. 12 sur Simon (Pierre).

Concluons. Dans l'apparat de *Greek New Testament*, "syr[pal mss] Marcion Diatessaron Eusebius[1/2]" devraient être supprimés comme témoins de l'omission de Lc xxiv 12.[81] En effet, on peut difficilement retenir tout ce qui, au cours de deux siècles de critique textuelle, a été ajouté à l'indication donnée par WETTSTEIN: "D Codices *Latini*", si ce n'est la précision qu'il s'agit des manuscrits *a b (d) e l r*[1].[82] Le verset est attesté par *aur e f ff*[2] et, au moins pour le dernier témoin, il est exclu d'y voir une interpolation à partir de la Vulgate.[83]

---

d'Origène est citée par beaucoup d'auteurs, parfois avec respect (MALDONATUS: "Si antiquitate res dubia finitur, Origenes vincet"), mais en général pour être rejetée. Elle a été reprise par J. LIGHTFOOT (*Horae Hebraicae et Talmudicae*, 1658-78, éd. R. GANDELL, Oxford, t. 3, 1869, 218) et par A. RESCH, *Agrapha. Aussercanonische Evangelienfragmente* (TU 5/4), Leipzig 1889, 422-426; *Aussercanonische Paralleltexte zu den Evangelien. II. Paralleltexte zu Lucas* (TU 10/3), Leipzig 1895, 767-771. — Dans *The Historical Evidence for the Resurrection of Jesus Christ* (Crown Theological Library, 21), London-New York 1907, 98-103, K. LAKE discute aussi la variante λέγοντες du codex Bezae: "this reading seems to be implied by Origen, who frequently states that the companion of Cleopas was Simon. This reading has therefore quite good authority, especially as it may be represented both by Latin and Syriac MSS. It is, however, a question which is probably insoluble whether the reading in the nominative (λέγοντες) produced the tradition as to Simon, or the tradition produced the reading: whichever came first would inevitably give rise to the other" (p. 98-99). Pour le problème qui nous occupe (l'existence d'une péricope qui commence au v. 12), il suffit de savoir que cette exégèse a été répandue. LAKE lui-même n'admet pas l'originalité du v. 34 (cf. MERX), mais il suggère encore une autre ligne d'interprétation qui elle aussi pourrait justifier l'existence d'une péricope de xxiv 12-35: (dans l'hypothèse de l'authenticité du v. 12, et avec la leçon λέγοντας au v. 34) "it would be possible to think that the meaning is that in the light of the experience of Cleopas the disciples saw that St Peter's visit to the grave was the equivalent of an appearance" (*o.c.* 101-102).

[80] M.-J. LAGRANGE, *Évangile selon saint Luc*, Paris 1921, 611. L'observation qu'il ne s'agit pas de Simon-Pierre mais d'un autre Simon a été faite mainte fois; voir déjà Cyrille d'Alexandrie: καὶ ὁ μετὰ Κλέοπα ὁ Σίμων ἦν, οὐχ ὁ Πέτρος οὐδὲ ὁ ἀπὸ Κανᾶ, ἀλλ' ἕτερος τῶν ἑβδομήκοντα (PG 72, col. 944).

[81] Dans la liste des témoins donnée par JEREMIAS *o.c.* (cf. *supra*, n. 2), 143: "(sy) Marc Tat[arab fuld ned ven tos]". Voir aussi R. MAHONEY, *Two Disciples at the Tomb. The Background and Message of John 20, 1-10* (Theologie und Wirklichkeit, 6), Bern-Frankfurt 1974, 44.

[82] Voir dans les commentaires anciens: *D codd it* (B. WEISS, dans Meyer, [6]1878, 589; H. J. HOLTZMANN, [3]1901, 421; E. KLOSTERMANN, 1919, 601); *D mss. lat.* (A. LOISY, *Luc*, 1924, 571).

[83] Cf. H. J. VOGELS, *Beiträge* (*supra*, n. 23), 1919, 83-84: "nur der Text in *ff*[2] weist darauf hin, dass der Vers auch vor Hieronymus im Abendland nicht ganz unbekannt war". Pour lui, les manuscrits *c f*, "die hier Vulgatafassung einsetzen", sont des témoins indirects de l'omission (*o.c.*, 83). Voir aussi *Evangelium Palatinum*

Le *Corbeiensis* rejoint les manuscrits témoins de l'omission en Lc. xxiv
3.6.9.36.40.51.52.53, mais il contient xxiv 12, d'ailleurs dans une
traduction qui est très fidèle au texte grec:[84]
Petrus autem surgens cucurrit ad monumentum et

(*ff²*) *aspiciens* vid*et*	(*vg*) *procumbens* vid*it*
linteamina posita *sola*	linteamina (sola) posit*a*
et abiit *apud semetipsum*	et abiit *secum*
mirans factum.	mirans *quod* factum *fuerat*.

En raison de ce témoignage de *ff²* et de celui de syr^{c,s} (et après
ce qui a été dit sur les faux témoins de l'omission, Marcion et
Tatien), on ne peut parler d'omission *occidentale* que dans un sens
très restreint.[85]

(cf. *supra*, n. 28), 1926, 54-55: "die in *e* fehlenden Verse 24, 12.40.51b (sind) offenbar
im Colbertinus nach der vg aufgefüllt"; *Evangelium Colbertinum* (cf. *supra*, n. 30),
1953, 10 (sur Lc. xxiv 3.12.40.43.51.52 dans *c*): "Die Lücken sind mit vg aufgefüllt".
— Signalons encore que le texte de *q*, qui a la leçon longue en xxiv 3.6.9.40.51.52.53,
est lacuneux à partir du v. 12 (xxiv 12-39). Dans *e*, d'autre part, l'influence du texte
de *ff²* prend fin avec le v. 12 (xxii 23-xxiv 11: "eine Überdeckung durch einen ff-Text";
cf. H. J. VOGELS, *Evangelium Palatinum*, 44-53).

[84] H. J. VOGELS considère le texte de *ff²* comme la *Vorlage* latine de la Vulgate
et il énumère comme "corrections" de Jérôme: procumbens, vid*it*, om. sola(?), secum,
quod factum fuerat; cf. *Vulgatastudien. Die Evangelien der Vulgata untersucht auf ihre
lateinische und griechische Vorlage* (NTA 14/2-3), Münster 1928, 276. Sur *ff²* voir
aussi *Evangelium Colbertinum*, 10-16.

[85] Comp. A. T. ROBERTSON, *Studies in the Text of the New Testament*, London
1926, 86: "the omission is purely Western geographically. ( ) has only partial support
from the Western documents".

THE AUTHOR OF THE ARABIC DIATESSARON

T. BAARDA

The Arabic Diatessaron [1] has not received due attention in the period of twenty-five years between 1951 and 1976 which is the occasion for this jubilee volume.[2] As a matter of fact, the decline of interest in this text is, to a certain extent at least, easily understood, if one takes into account the fact that new discoveries (viz. the Persian Harmony and the Syriac text of Ephraem's commentary on the Diatessaron) attracted the attention of students in the field of Diatessaron research.

In the middle of this period, 1963-1964, I made several studies on the Arabic form of the Diatessaron which for several reasons have not been made ready for publication. The present article dealing with the authorship of the Arabic Diatessaron was one of these studies. My lack of expertise in Christian Arabic literature has not prevented me from making a firm conclusion, because I indulged the hope that my verdict will provoke a more skillful treatment of the question.

The first manuscript of the Arabic Diatessaron that became known to the scholarly world, *Vat.Arabo 14*, usually designated as Ms. A, did not mention the name of the translator.[3] It was Ms. B, *Vat.*

---

[1] For the status questionis cf. a.o. C. PETERS, *Das Diatessaron Tatians* (OrChrA 123), Roma 1939, ch. II (19-29).

[2] Besides the second edition of P. E. KAHLE, *The Cairo Geniza*, Oxford 1959, ch. III C, 15-17 (297-313), the most important articles to be mentioned here are written by A. J. B. HIGGENS (see below par. 9): The Persian Gospel Harmony as a Witness to Tatian's Diatessaron, *JThS* NS 3 (1952), where due attention is given to the Arabic harmony; The Persian and Arabic Gospel Harmonies, *Studia Evangelica* (TU 73), Berlin 1959, 793-810; Tatian's Diatessaron and the Arabic and Persian Harmonies, in: *Studies in New Testament Language and Text*, Essays in Honour of George D. Kilpatrick, Leiden 1976, 246-261. Cf. also T. BAARDA, An Archaic Element in the Arabic Diatessaron? (T^A xlvi 18 = John xv 2), *NT* 17 (1975), 152-155.

[3] Ms. A was already known to J. S. ASSEMANI, *Bibliotheca Orientalis Clementino-Vaticano*, I, Roma 1719; J. C. ZAHN, Ist Ammon oder Tatian Verfasser des ins Lateinische, Altfränkische und Arabische übersetzten Evangelienharmonie? ... in: (C. A. G. KEIL / H. G. TZSCHIRNER), *Analekten für das Studium der exegetischen und systematischen Theologie* II: 1, Leipzig 1814, 165-210, esp. 184f.; J. C. ZAHN, *Tatian's Evangelien-Harmonie* (unpublished), Beilage Nro. A (with the first and last folium in the transcription of J. D. Åkerblad and in the translation of E. F. K. Rosenmüller); A. MAI, *Scriptorum Veterum Nova Collectio* e Vaticanis codicibus edita, IV, Roma 1831

Borg.Arabo 250, a manuscript presented to the Pope in 1886 A.D.,[4] which turned out to have preserved the name of a famous man to whom the translation is ascribed. Whether this communication was a reliable one or not, that became the question.

A. A SHORT SURVEY OF THE HISTORY OF RESEARCH

1. *The Name of the Translator*

In the preamble of Ms. B we read the following words:[5]

ونقله من السرياني الي العربي القس الفاضل العالم
ابو الفرج عبد الله بن الطيب رضي الله عنه

"The excellent, learned priest 'Abū'l-Faraǧ 'Abdū'llāh ibn aṭ-Ṭayyib (may God be pleased with him) translated it from Syriac into Arabic". And similarly, we read in the colophon:[6]

نقله القس الخير العالم ابو الفرج عبد الله ابن الطيب
رضى الله عنه من السرياني العربي

"The eminent, learned priest 'Abū'l-Faraǧ 'Abdū'llāh ibn aṭ-Ṭayyib (may God be pleased with him) translated it from Syriac into Arabic".

If reliable, both statements would be very important for establishing the date of the Arabic translation of the Syriac harmony.

("Codices Arabici"), 14 (cf. 6); Th. ZAHN, *Tatians Diatessaron*, FGNK 1, Erlangen 1881, 294-298. A. CIASCA, De Tatiani Diatessaron Arabica Versione, in: J. B. PITRA, *Analecta Sacra Spicilegio solesmensi parata* IV (= J. P. P. MARTIN, *Patres Antenicaeni...* ex codicibus orientalibus), Paris 1883, 465-488, was the first scholar who gave a sufficient description of the manuscript; cf. also A. CIASCA, *Tatiani Evangeliorum Harmoniae Arabice*, Roma 1888, vi-vii.

[4] Ms. B has been described in A. CIASCA, *o.c.*, v-xiv.

[5] A. CIASCA, *o.c.*, ۱-: 4-5 (preamble): in his text, Ciasca has printed the reading of Ms. B الطبيب which should be changed into الطيب (cf. A. CIASCA, *o.c.*, xi nota *a*; this note has become somewhat obscure, because he wrote *prioris* where *alterius* was meant). The observation of A.-S. MARMARDJI, *Diatessaron de Tatien*, Beirut 1935, 2 *in apparatu*, that both Ms. A and Ms. B wrote الطيب is apparently wrong, as Ms. A does not contain any such communication in its preamble. Ms. E (see §6), Ms. O (see §7) and Ms. S (see §5) have the right reading; Ms. S omits the ornamental attributes الفاضل العالم.

[6] A. CIASCA, *o.c.*, ۲۱۰: 2-3; A.-S. MARMARDJI, *o.c.*, 536; L. CHEIKHO, نسخ عربية قديمة في المشرق من الانجيل الطاهر, *Al-Machriq* IV (1901), ۹v — ۱۰۹, esp. ۱۰۱, suggested the emendation الخبير "skilled" instead of the textual word الخير "good", "eminent", but I don't see any reason to follow this conjecture.

2. 'Abū'l Faraġ 'Abdū'llāh ibn aṭ-Ṭayyib

The presbyter whom the manuscript adorns with such predicates as learned, excellent and eminent, 'Abū'l Faraġ 'Abdū'llah ibn aṭ-Ṭayyib, was a prominent person within the Nestorian church of his time, being a secretary of the Patriarch Elias I of Bagdad.[7] Among his many works the exegetical writings are highly praised because of their immense importance for the Arabic exegetical literature in the oriental church.[8] Being a gifted exegete,[9] he wrote at least two large exegetical works. A *scholia* commentary on the whole Scripture, entitled *Paradise of Christianity* (فردوس النّصرانية), is perhaps the more famous one.[10] The other work, which was written earlier, consists of a commentary on the Gospels.[11] Interestingly enough, the author mentions in his prologue to the latter work the meagre interest of lay people *and* clergy in the "divine sciences" as an occasion for his commentary: he intentionally wrote it in Arabic, because this had become the language that was commonly used, whereas the Syriac language was on the decline among the people of his church.[12] If 'Abū'l Faraġ really translated the Syriac Diatessaron into Arabic, these reasons given in the prologue of the commentary could have been equally valid for the translation of the Gospel harmony.

However, a difficulty with regard to the connection of 'Abū'l Faraġ with the Diatessaron had to be faced. Already A. CIASCA[13] noted the fact that among the works ascribed to him by Grīgōr bar 'Ebrāyā and 'Abū'l Barakāt[14] the Diatessaron is not found. But CIASCA could point to the fact that their bibliographies are not presented as being

---

[7] Cf. G. GRAF, *Geschichte der christlichen arabischen Literatur* II, Città del Vaticano 1947, 160-176, where an extensive and detailed description of his person and of his works is given; see also G. GRAF, Exegetische Schriften zum Neuen Testament in arabischer Sprache bis zum 14.Jahrhundert, *BZ* 21 (1933), 22-40; 161-169, esp. 24-32 (= II:2). See further S. EURINGER, *Die Überlieferung der Arabischen Übersetzung des Diatessarons* (BSt XVII:2), Freiburg i. Breisgau 1912, 10-19; A.-S. MARMARDJI, *o.c.*, lxxxviif.; P. E. KAHLE, *The Cairo Geniza*, Oxford 1947, 223ff. (²1959, 309f.); J. C. SANDERS, *Inleiding op het Genesiskommentaar van de Nestoriaan Ibn aṭ-Ṭaiyib*, Leiden 1963, ch. I ("De Schrijver"), 12-18 and *passim*.

[8] G. GRAF, *a.c.*, 24.

[9] G. GRAF, *a.c.*, 32; J. C. SANDERS, *o.c.*, 14-17 (cf. ch. IV-VI, VIII).

[10] G. GRAF, *a.c.*, 30-32; *Geschichte* II, 162-164. A sample of its text is found in A.-S. MARMARDJI, *o.c.*, xcvii-xcviii.

[11] G. GRAF, *a.c.*, 25-30; *o.c.* II, 166-169. Cf. A.-S. MARMARDJI, *o.c.*, xcviii-c.

[12] G. GRAF, *a.c.*, 27:25-30 (cf. 26:25ff.).

[13] A. CIASCA, *o.c.*, xii.

[14] A. CIASCA, *o.c.*, xii, n. *c*.

complete. Moreover, two works of this author which are extant in manuscript do not occur in their lists so that, we may conclude, they are in fact incomplete. Consequently, there was as yet no reason to deny the authorship of 'Abū'l Farağ attested in the newly found manuscript.[15] In addition, E. SELLIN thought that the authorship could be demonstrated by a Leyden manuscript in which the commentary on Matthew of 'Abū'l Farağ was contained.[16]

If 'Abū'l Farağ ibn aṭ-Ṭayyib († 1043 A.D.) were the translator, this would suggest that the translation of the Syriac Diatessaron into Arabic was performed in the first half of the *eleventh* century.

3. *First Doubts regarding the Authorship*

In his useful introduction to the Arabic harmony, H. W. HOGG speaks in a way which betrays his intense doubt with regard to the authorship. He says, indeed, that "the inferiority of parts of the translation, and entire absence of any confirmatory evidence, hardly suffice to refute this assertion",[17] namely that of Ms. B concerning the author, but meanwhile he points out that, in the Gospel commentary, 'Abū'l Farağ refers to the readings of the Diatessaron in a "remarkably impersonal" way "for one who had made or was to make a translation of it".[18] Moreover, he states, the Borgian manuscript (= Ms. B) is a late witness "and although it most probably preserves a genuine tradition as to the author of our work (N. B. HOGG means 'Tatian' who was also mentioned in the preamble and colophon of the manuscript) its statement need not therefore necessarily be correct in every point".[19] It is interesting, then, to read somewhat later about "the author or the authors of the Arabic translation".[20] It is evident that HOGG, be it with due reserve, was the first scholar

---

[15] A. CIASCA, *o.c.*, xiii: "Cum ergo in nostro codice praecitata versio apertissime tribuatur Abulpharagio Ben-at-Tîb, nulla ratio est, donec alia in contrarium afferantur, cur eidem abiudicari debeat".

[16] E. SELLIN, *Der Text des von A. Ciasca herausgegebenen arabischen Diatessaron* (FGNK IV), Erlangen 1891 (= 225-246), 243ff. One may question, of course, whether the five instances brought forward by SELLIN are really as convincing as he suggested.

[17] H. W. HOGG, *The Diatessaron of Tatian*, in: A. MENZIES, *Ante-Nicene Christian Library*, Additional Volume, Edinburgh 1897, 35-141 (= idem, *idem*, in: A. MENZIES, *The Ante-Nicene Fathers* X, Grand Rapids [5]1969), 36, under §7, The Origin of the Arabic Text; as a sample of this inferiority Mt xxvii 54 (T[A] lii 11) is referred to *ibidem*, n. 12.

[18] H. W. HOGG, *o.c.*, 36, n. 13.

[19] H. W. HOGG, *o.c.*, 36.

[20] H. W. HOGG, *o.c.*, 40.

who doubted the reliability of the communications in Ms. B. He did so in 1895 A.D., and soon his doubt seemed to be justified by the finding of the Beirut fragments.[21]

4. The Beirut Fragments and the Problem of Authorship

In his discussions of the Beirut fragments, L. CHEIKHO came to the conclusion that the Arabic version actually could not have been the work of 'Abū'l-Farağ ibn aṭ-Ṭayyib. For in these fragments a colophon was preserved which appeared to be much longer than those known from Mss. A and B, and which, what was still more interesting, differed considerably from each of them. This colophon was contained both in the second fragment (recto, from line 9 onwards, and verso) and in the third one (recto). In his letter of August 17, 1897, which was presented to the congress of orientalists at Paris,[22] CHEIKHO had copied this colophon and had also included photographs of it, but the latter were not published along with his letter in the Journal Asiatique of that year. They can, however, be found in an article of CHEIKHO published in Mašriq in 1901, which includes another transcription of the colophon that, in some minor points at least, differs from his earlier one.[23]

The manuscript to which the fragments originally belonged must be dated ca. 1331/2 A.D. It was the fourth descendant in succession of what is called "a very old manuscript" (نسخة عتيقة جداً),[24] originating from Antioch (مدينة الله).[25] The four copyists, according to

---

[21] I paid some special attention to HOGG because the doubts concerning authorship are always connected with the Beirut fragments and the name of CHEIKHO. HOGG's introduction is dated 21st of December 1895; his translation in the Ante-Nicene Library was not published until two years later, when CHEIKHO's letter was read at the congress of the Orientalists at Paris ("séance du 7 septembre"). There is no reason to think that he heard about it; otherwise he would have added a notice about it. One might ask, whether CIASCA felt some suspicion when saying "donec alia in contrarium afferantur" (see n. 15 above), but if he really did it was but a soft tone of doubt which sounds in these words. The hesitation of HOGG depends mainly upon his uncertainty with regard to the relation of the various works concerning the Gospels ascribed to Ibn aṭ-Ṭayyib, cf. o.c., 37, n. 1; it is regrettable that he did not show any acquaintance with the study of Sellin.

[22] L. CHEIKHO, Lettre au sujet de l'auteur de la version arabe du Diatessaron, JA IX: t. ix (1897), 301-307, esp. 303 ff.

[23] L. CHEIKHO, نسخ, ١٠١.

[24] L. CHEIKHO, Lettre, 306; نسخ, ١٠٢; it is the wording of the fragment.

[25] L. CHEIKHO, ll.cc.; A. BAUMSTARK, in his review of A.-S. MARMARDJI, Diatessaron de Tatien, in OrChr 33 (1936), 235-244, 237, mentions as an alternative interpretation of the Town of God Jerusalem.

CHEIKHO, had written *some time* after one another (كل واحد منهم
دهرًا بعد الآخر).[26]

If these communications of the subscription are really exact, the old copy of Antioch must have been written, again according to CHEIKHO, in the tenth or even in the ninth century; in other words, it must have been prior to 'Abū'l-Farağ ibn aṭ-Ṭayyib, who lived and died in the eleventh century.[27] Now, it can be deduced from the text preserved in the Beirut fragments that this "old copy" represents the same Arabic work which Mss. A and B contain. Consequently, 'Abū'l-Farağ could not have been the translator of this work, the Diatessaron, because it already existed before his time. This conclusion was based mainly on the Beirut colophon, but CHEIKHO found an additional argument in the total absence of information in Christian Arabic literature about any such translation from the hand of 'Abū'l-Farağ.[28]

For some time the observations of CHEIKHO were rather influential.[29]

---

[26] L. CHEIKHO, Lettre, 306 had only stated that the three copyists successively wrote ("trois manuscrits copiés successivement les uns sur les autres"), but in his article نسخ, ١٠٢, he introduces the interval of some time (اً دهرًا).

[27] L. CHEIKHO, Lettre, 306: "nous arrivons très facilement à une copie du Xe ou du IXe siècle ... Cette traduction serait dans ce cas antérieure à celle d'Abou'l-Faradj 'Abdallah Ibn aṭ-Ṭayib publié par Ciasca"; less pronounced is his manner of writing in نسخ, ١٠٢, where he asks "Is it not permitted that we conclude from this expression (viz. the very old copy) that the Arabic translator was anterior to the eleventh century, that is, anterior to 'Abū'l-Farağ ibn aṭ-Ṭayyib?" (افلا يجوز ان نستنتج)
من هذا القول ان الترجمة العربيّة كانت قبل الفرن الحادى عشر اعني قبل ابى الفرج
ابن الطيّب).

[28] L. CHEIKHO, *ll.cc.*; it is especially in his Lettre that he underlines this additional argument. As to CIASCA's solution for this silence he remarks "ce que je lis à ce sujet dans la prologue de Mgr. Ciasca ne me satisfait point".

[29] For some time the thesis of CHEIKHO remained almost unknown, as may appear from the fact that A. HJELT, *Die altsyrische Evangelienübersetzung und Tatians Diatessaron besonders in ihrem gegenseitigen Verhältnis* (FGNK VII:1), Leipzig 1903, 65 n. 1, knew of it only through a short notice in *Revue Biblique* (1897, 639): "Leider hat Cheikho, meines Wissens, seitdem seiner Entdeckung keine weitere Öffentlichkeit gegeben ..."; HJELT has the impression "dass seine oben genannte Vermutung auf ziemlich schwachen Füssen stehen dürfte". — In order to give an illustration of CHEIKHO's influence we limit ourselves to some remarks of A. BAUMSTARK, who spoke of "die problematische Arbeit des Abū'l-Farağ ibn al-Tajjib in arabischer Sprache" (*OrChr* 2 (1902), 160), whereas he uses the word "angeblich" in this connection (*Die christlichen Literaturen des Orients*, I, Leipzig 1911, 55; cf. also *Die christlichen Literaturen*, II, 15, where he says "Vielleicht noch eines etwas älteren Zeit als derjenigen des Abû'l-Farağ ibn aṭ-Ṭajjib ... entstammt die arabische Nachbildung des Tatianischen Diatessaron"). But for BAUMSTARK see also below n. 57. — For a British voice we may refer to M. D. GIBSON, Arabic Christian Literature, *ET* 26 (1914/5), 32: "the Beyrout one has indications of an earlier origin".

A decade later, however, his conclusions were criticised by S. Euringer in a specialised study on the Beirut fragments,[30] which has been praised as a specimen of methodical investigation.[31] Its final result remained rather negative: the colophon did not necessarily exclude the possibility of the authorship attested to by the preamble and colophon of Ms. B.[32] Euringer did not come to a more positive conclusion due to the lack of the necessary material: further research had to be done by others.[33] Meanwhile, most scholars accepted Euringer's conclusion regarding the colophon as if the authorship of 'Abū'l-Farağ were vindicated by it.[34] The matter seemed to have been settled again.

5. New Light from the Sbath Catalogue

In the second tome of his catalogue, published in 1928, father Paul Sbath made a few observations about a new manuscript of the Arabic Diatessaron (Sbath Nr. 1020 which may be listed as Ms. S). In the preamble of this manuscript we find the following words:[35]

---

[30] S. Euringer, Die Überlieferung (see n. 7); he discussed (it was 1912) the Beirut fragments in general (23-31: ch. II), the genealogy indicated by their colophon (32-58: ch. III); the results are summed up in ch. IV (59f.).

[31] "Seine Arbeit darf als das Muster einer mit besonnener Ruhe und methodischer Sicherheit geführten Untersuchung bezeichnet werden", A. Baumstark wrote in his review of Euringer's study (OrChr 12 (1912), 350). The judgment of P. E. Kahle, The Cairo Geniza, 213 ([2]298f.), n. 1 "Euringer tries to prove more (2d ed.: to deduce more from this colophon) than is really possible, and he makes some (2d ed.: very) curious mistakes" seems to be less highpitched, but also Kahle has to acknowledge that "his final result seems to be correct".

[32] S. Euringer, o.c., 60 (after having discussed the rubrics of Ms. B and concluded that the notices of Ms. B did not contain anything improbable, cf. 22), writes "Daraus folgt als Schlussergebnis, dass die Beiruter Fragmente, speziell der Kolophon derselben, die Angabe des Codex Borgianus über Ibn aṭ-Ṭajjib als den Übersetzer des syrischen Diatessaron ins Arabische nicht zu erschüttern vermögen' (cf. 57).

[33] S. Euringer, o.c., 60, "Damit ist aber nur die eine Seite des Problems erledigt. Dagegen harrt die positive Seite desselben, ob Ibn aṭ-Ṭajjib tatsächlich die, oder genauer gesprochen, eine arabische Übersetzung des Diatessaron angefertigt hat, noch immer der methodischen Untersuchung. Es wäre daher wünschenswert, dass das hierzu nötige Material endlich einmal ediert würde".

[34] For example, A. Baumstark who, since the study of Euringer (cf. n. 29, n. 31, see also n. 57), did not show any hesitation with regard to the problem of authorship; see also the approving reviews of Eb. Nestle (ThLBl 33 (1912), 416f.), and G. Wohlenberg, Zu Tatian's Diatessaron, ThLBl 33 (1912), 457-459; cf. E. Preuschen (- A. Pott), Tatians Diatessaron, Heidelberg 1926, 54; C. Peters, Das Diatessaron Tatians (see n. 1), 21; cf. A. J. B. Higgins, Tatian's Diatessaron, Introductory Studies, with a portion of the Arabic Version, (unpublished) Ph. D. thesis, University of Manchester 1945, 53 (but see below, § 9).

[35] P. Sbath, Bibliothèque de Manuscrits Paul Sbath, prêtre Syrien d'Alep, Catalogue t. II, Cairo 1928, 135.

ونقله من السريانى الي العربي
القس ابو الفرج عبد الله بن الطيب

"And the priest 'Abū'l-Farağ 'Abdū'llāh ibn aṭ-Ṭayyib translated it from Syriac into Arabic". It must be admitted that this notice is not as impressive as one might wish. It betrays only that the new manuscript, whose preamble largely agrees with that in Ms. B also in other details, may belong to the same family as Ms. B.[36] As a matter of fact, this does not render the evidence of Ms. S worthless, for, if this manuscript is not a mere copy nor an indirect descendant of Ms. B, it may indicate that the notices in Ms. B were not a peculiarity of only one manuscript but of a whole family of manuscripts. Unfortunately, it is not possible to establish the actual relationship of this manuscript with Ms. B, due to the fact that its contents are not known to us.

More important, however, is another manuscript mentioned by SBATH in the same tome of his catalogue, viz. Nr. 1029.[37] This codex contains also a harmony of the Gospels under the title

كنز الابرار الاخيار بما جمع من كلام الاربعة المبشرين الاطهار

"Treasure of pious and good (things, consisting) of that which was collected from the Words of the four holy Evangelists".[38] It appears from the introduction to this harmony (quoted by SBATH) that its author was a Copt,[39] and there is reason to believe that the time in which the Coptic author lived was not later than the *twelfth* century.[40] His introduction contains some interesting remarks which concern also the question with which we are dealing.

First the author makes the general remark that he had observed in the *Gospel* a repetition (التكرار) of the commandments (الوصايا), the miracles (الايات) and stories (الاخبار). It was clear to him that our Lord did not repeat the words (اقواله) and deeds (افعاله) which were repeated in the texts of the Gospel. Therefore, he says, "I have

---

[36] The wording of John I 1-4a which SBATH gives is too short for a textual determination of the family to which this harmony belongs.

[37] P. SBATH, *o.c.*, 141f.

[38] P. SBATH, *o.c.*, 141.

[39] P. SBATH, *o.c.*, 142 (Arabic text, *ll.* 22f.: the Coptic language (لسان القبطى) is his mother tongue (لغة قومه); see below our text ad n. 42.

[40] P. SBATH, *o.c.*, 143: "L'auteur... vivait probablement au xii⁰ siècle". — A.-S. MARMARDJI, *o.c.*, xc, however, wrongly concluded from it "C'est un codex du xii⁰ siècle", for SBATH expressly states that the manuscript was "transcrit au xvi⁰ siècle".

collected from them *one* Gospel" (جمعت منها انجيلا احدًا).[41] The author then tells us about the procedure which he had followed: he arranged his chapters in the order of Matthew, and inserted in each of them the parallel texts of the other three Gospels. As to the matter proper to each Gospel, he inserted it between the various chapters of Matthew at the place where it belonged. As a base for his harmony he took the chapters or sections of the *Coptic Gospels* (فصول اللسان القبطيّ), and interestingly enough he defends this method by saying that one who depends upon the language of his own nation is right and does nor err (فان من يعتمد على لغة قومه يصيب ولايخطى).[42] He introduced these remarks on his own arrangement of the harmony by saying that he avoided the faults of an earlier attempt of harmonizing (... فأصلحت ذلك جميعه),[43] which he had mentioned previously:[44]

وكان قد تقدمني في ذلك جماعة من الأفاضل من جملتهم
القس الفاضل ابو الفرج بن الطيب المشرقي رحمه الله تعالى.
فلما وقفت على الانجيل الذى جمعه وقابلت به على الاناجيل
المحررة المتفق على صحتها من السرياني والقبطي والرمي
وجدته قد أهمل بعض النصوص الانجيلية وحذفها من الاصل
بالكلية وكرر بعض كلام الانجيليين من غير ضرورة ...

"And a number of excellent (men) have preceded me in this respect (i.e. in collecting *one* Gospel from the four). And to the entire group of them belongs the excellent priest 'Abū'l-Farağ ibn aṭ-Ṭayyib, the Oriental — God who be exalted may have mercy upon him. And after having read the Gospel that he had collected, and after having checked it with the Gospels, which were carefully written and commonly accepted as to their authenticity, in the Syriac, Coptic and Greek languages, I found that he had neglected some texts of the Gospels, and that he had totally cut them out of the original, *and that he had repeated some of the wording of the Evangelists without necessity ...*".[45]

---

[41] P. SBATH, *o.c.*, 142 (Arabic text, *ll.* 8-11); cf. A.-S. MARMARDJI, *o.c.*, xc, where also a French translation has been given.

[42] P. SBATH, *o.c.*, 142 (Arabic text, *ll.* 18-23); cf. A.-S. MARMARDJI, *o.c.*, xci.

[43] P. SBATH, *o.c.*, 142 (Arab. *l.* 17), A.-S. MARMARDJI, *l.c.*

[44] P. SBATH, *o.c.*, 142 (Arab. *ll.* 11-17); A.-S. MARMARDJI, *l.c.*

[45] My translation differs from that of A.-S. MARMARDJI, *o.c.*, xc-xci, only on minor points.

It was on account of these observations that father SBATH based his conclusion: "Cette introduction prouve que le traducteur du Diatessaron est bien le prêtre nestorien Aboul Faraj Ben Ettayieb".[46] This conclusion seemed to be a more positive step towards the evidence of the traditional authorship.

6.   *A new Attack: A.-S. Marmardji*

It was only seven years later that A.-S. MARMARDJI, in the fourth chapter *"Qui est l'auteur de la traduction arabe du Diatessaron?"* of his introduction to the edition of the Arabic Diatessaron,[47] contradicted the conclusion of SBATH. Trying to solve the problem MARMARDJI scrutinized the text itself of the Arabic Diatessaron, and he drew the following conclusions concerning the author of the work:

a. he was a *Syriac* speaking person ("Araméen") in view of the Syriasms,[48]

b. he was a *Nestorian*, in view of his transcription of the name of Jesus: ايَسوع,[49] and

c. he was a native of *Assyria* or *Iraq*, in view of some idioms that point to the region of Mossul or Bagdad, e.g. معتزلة instead of فريسيين "Pharisees".[50]

One would be inclined to think that the result of this investigation was in complete agreement with the data of Mss. B and S, to which now could also be added the testimony of Ms. E, a manuscript that was used by MARMARDJI in establishing his Arabic text:[51]

ونقله من السرياني الى العربي القس الفاضل العالِم
ابو الفرج عبد الله بى الطيّب

---

[46] P. SBATH, *o.c.*, 143; It is interesting to note that G. GRAF, Exegetische Schriften (see n. 7), 24 still wrote "von der immer noch nicht endgültig gelösten Frage... ob Abû'l Farağ der Übersetzer des arabischen Diatessaron ist". It is evident that like other scholars (cf. e.g. P. KAHLE, see n. 31) he was not convinced by EURINGER's argumentation, and that he had not yet taken note of SBATH's Catalogue. GRAF wrote this in 1933; hardly a decade later he presents himself as a defender of the authorship of Ibn aṭ-Ṭayyib (see below).

[47] A.-S. MARMARDJI, *o.c.*, lxxxv-xciii (-cii).

[48] A.-S. MARMARDJI, *o.c.*, lxxxv.

[49] A.-S. MARMARDJI, *o.c.*, lxxxv-lxxxvi.

[50] A.-S. MARMARDJI, *o.c.*, lxxxvi-lxxxvii.

[51] For Ms. E (preamble), cf. A.-S. MARMARDJI, *o.c.*, 2; the colophon of Ms. E (A.-S. MARMARDJI, *o.c.*, 536) deviates from that of Ms. B in that it contains not any of the names found in the colophon of the latter manuscript.

In fact, 'Abū'l-Farağ ibn aṭ-Ṭayyib was a *Nestorian* priest, who was familiar with the *Syriac* language, whose origin was connected with *Assyria* or *Iraq*, and who, as a secretary of Elias I the Patriarch, apparently lived at Bagdad. MARMARDJI, however, was not willing to accept the identification. He attributed the manuscript tradition to a personal and biased conjecture of an early copyist, who therefore cannot be accepted as a reliable witness in this historical problem. The *pur sang* historicians, as a matter of fact, did not ascribe a harmonistic work to Ibn aṭ-Ṭayyib. And whoever the author of the Arabic Diatessaron may have been, he was by no means the erudite author that, as we know, Ibn aṭ-Ṭayyib must have been,[52] for he was apparently an author unskilled in Arabic literary language, a beginner, an ignorant debutant, as appears from the many flaws and errors that are found in this Arabic harmony. Therefore, it must have been the work of some unknown author who was for some reason subsequently connected with the famous Ibn aṭ-Ṭayyib.[53]

In this connection MARMARDJI gets talking about the harmony preserved in Sbath Ms. 1029, which we have mentioned in the preceding paragraph.[54] From its introduction (as far as we know it from the extracts given in the catalogue of SBATH) MARMARDJI concludes that the harmony which the Coptic author attributes to Ibn aṭ-Ṭayyib was not a translation but a new *collection* (MARMARDJI lays stress on جمعه), a new piece of work which had nothing to do with Tatian's harmony.[55]

The verdict of MARMARDJI met with approval in many reviews,[56] but also with decided contradiction on the part of one of the leading Diatessaron scholars of that time, A. BAUMSTARK.[57] It was clear that a new quest was necessary.

---

[52] A.-S. MARMARDJI, *o.c.*, lxxxviii.

[53] A.-S. MARMARDJI, *o.c.*, lxxxix.

[54] A.-S. MARMARDJI, *o.c.*, lxxxix-xciii.

[55] A.-S. MARMARDJI, *o.c.*, xcii: the verb جمع is used instead of نقل. He also argues that the unknown author had examined the text of Ibn aṭ-Ṭayyib closely (he renders وقفت علي with "j'eus vu de près"; in my translation "I read"), but did not say anything about Tatian and his Diatessaron.

[56] Cf. e.g. *JTS* 1937, 76 (MARGOLIOUTH); *RB* 1937, 127 (BENOÎT); see also the article of A. F. J. BEESTON, *The Arabic Version of Tatian's Diatessaron*, *JRAS* 1939, 608-610, 610.

[57] A. BAUMSTARK, Review of A.-S. MARMARDJI, *Diatessaron de Tatien*, in *OrChr* 33 (1936), 235-244, esp. 242f. Cf. C. PETERS, *Das Diatessaron Tatians*, 22. BAUMSTARK gave an acute criticism of MARMARDJI's book; it is unfortunate that so many keen observations of this learned scholar are hidden in reviews, where they are easily overlooked by later students.

7. *The Contribution of the Oxford Manuscript*

The discovery of a new manuscript in the Bodleian Library gave
rise to new discussions on the problem of authorship. A. F. L. Beeston
announced the presence of this manuscript in the library in 1939,
four years after the publication of Marmardji's text.[58] It appeared
that the usual attribution of the translation (نقله من السريانى الي العربي
القس) ...) to ʾAbū'l-Farağ ibn aṭ-Ṭayyib was present both in the
preamble[59] and in the colophon[60] of this manuscript (which is now
designated as Ms. O), in a wording that was in agreement with that
of Ms. B. The interesting point of these notices in this late (nine-
teenth century) manuscript was, however, that they had most probably
been transcribed from the exemplar from which the whole manuscript
had been copied: this manuscript, according to a communication of
the copyist in the colophon, was of much older date, for it was
written in the handwriting of the so-called Aulād al-ʿAssal in the
year 1107 A.D.[61] This would imply that the attribution of the Arabic
harmony to the famous Ibn aṭ-Ṭayyib was already current in the
early twelfth century. Even if the conjecture of Beeston is valid that
instead of 1107 a later date, namely 1197 A.D., would be possible,[62]
the testimony of Ms. O remains important. Even Beeston has to
admit that, although he personally is inclined to follow Marmardji
in his denial of the authorship of ʾAbū'l-Farağ ibn aṭ-Ṭayyib: "What
seems to me ... probable is simply that the real translator, whoever
he was, attempted to give currency to his work by passing it off as
the work of the well-known savant".[63]

Two other scholars took their starting-point in this newly found
Oxford manuscript in trying to solve the difficult question of authorship: P. E. Kahle and A. J. B. Higgins.

8. *The Theory of P. E. Kahle*

Kahle[64] agreed with the literary argument of Marmardji: in fact,
the text of the Arabic Diatessaron is beneath the linguistic and

---

[58] A. F. L. Beeston, *a.c.*, 608 ff.

[59] A. F. L. Beeston, *a.c.*, 610.

[60] Cf. A. J. B. Higgins, *The Arabic Version of Tatian's Diatessaron*, JTS 45 (1944),
187-199, 188.

[61] A. F. L. Beeston, *a.c.*, 609; A. J. B. Higgins, *a.c.*, 187 f.

[62] A. F. L. Beeston, *a.c.*, 609.

[63] A. F. L. Beeston, *a.c.*, 610.

[64] P. E. Kahle, *The Cairo Geniza* (see n. 7); the lectures were held in 1941 and
for the first time published in 1947.

stylistic abilities of the *classic* author Abū'l-Farağ ibn aṭ-Ṭayyib. Therefore the negative conclusion MARMARDJI drew from this fact was, in KAHLE's view, fully justified.[65] The only problem that remains is, why did his name come to be associated with the Arabic translation of the Diatessaron, and it is Ms. O that provides the solution. This late text (A.D. 1806) had been copied from a very old exemplar (A.D. 1107). The manuscript consists, generally speaking, of three parts: a Gospel introduction, an exposition of Christian Faith, the Gospel harmony.[66] The outer appearance of this late copy, KAHLE says, does remind us of the *Qurān*. Especially the decorations in the beginning of the first and third parts resemble those of the first and second Sura's. And even the entry of the second part has the modest ornamentation which has its parallels in copies of the Qurān.[67] Kahle does not doubt that, in all these points, Ms. O is a true copy of its exemplar of the year 1107. Why was it that the Aulād al-ʿAssāl, to whom this early manuscript should be ascribed, decorated their copy in this way? They no doubt did so in order to make a deep impression on their Muslim readers.[68] The purpose of the twelfth century text was to answer (explicitly in the second treatise) some questions posed by a prominent Muslim[69] — KAHLE suggests Al-Malik al-Afḍal.[70] These questions were based on the severe criticism of Christian principles in a recent work (1101 A.D.) of the famous Muslim author Al-Ghazālî.[71] The Aulād al-ʿAssāl (or perhaps Ibn al-ʿAssāl[72] who was mentioned as the author of at least the second tract) decorated the text not only with beautiful colours but also with illustrious names. So Ibn al-ʿAssāl "was given a number of epithets so that he may be regarded as a great authority".[73] For the same reason the Gospel harmony, which was added as the third text, was furnished with an impressive authority by connecting it with the name of a prominent scholar Ibn aṭ-Ṭayyib, who deserved the more consideration, as he was known to have been an expositor of the Gospels and a translator

---

[65] P. E. KAHLE, *o.c.*, 225 (²311).
[66] P. E. KAHLE, *o.c.*, 215 (²301).
[67] P. E. KAHLE, *o.c.*, 226 (²312), cf. 215 (²301).
[68] P. E. KAHLE, *o.c.*, 218 (²304), cf. 226 (²312).
[69] P. E. KAHLE, *o.c.*, 216 (²302), cf. 226 (²311).
[70] P. E. KAHLE, *o.c.*, 218 (²304).
[71] P. E. KAHLE, *o.c.*, 216-218 (²302-304).
[72] P. E. KAHLE, *o.c.*, 218-221 (²304-307).
[73] P. E. KAHLE, *o.c.*, 226 (²312).

of at least some of them. In this way the Aulād al-ʿAssāl tried to supply their apologetic work with the greatest authority.[74]

In reality Abū'l-Faraǧ ibn aṭ-Ṭayyib had no hand in the Arabic Diatessaron. The only thing to be said about it was that it had once been translated into Arabic from Syriac and that the Arabic text had been brought into Egypt from Mesopotamia.[75]

9. The Theory of A. J. B. Higgins

HIGGINS[76] started his investigation of the Oxford manuscript from a suggestion once made by KAHLE in the correspondance between them,[77] but he followed a different line. Comparing the various and different colophons of Mss. B, E and O, he found that these were merely recensions of "one original colophon".[78] This being the case, Ms. O turned out to be of great importance, for it preserved a statement which had apparently been omitted in the other copies, and which seemed to be the key for a completely new insight in the problem of authorship. To the usual notice about Ibn aṭ-Ṭayyib and Īsā ibn ʿAlî the following words were added in Ms. O (fol. 287: 5-6):[79]

.كتب هذا على ما هو عليه من غير
.تصنع في النقل لكن حفظ الاوامر

Higgins translates these words, "And this man wrote on the basis of what was before him without any modification in the translation, but kept the words". This translation asks for some explanation. Who was *this man*? And further, is HIGGINS' interpretation of the word *naql* (an ambivalent word meaning *translation*[80] as well as

---

[74] P. E. KAHLE, *l.c.* - cf. *o.c.* 223f. (²309f.) for the great authority which Ibn aṭ-Ṭayyib held among Muslims.

[75] P. E. KAHLE, *o.c.*, 227 (²312).

[76] A. J. B. HIGGINS, The Arabic Version (see n. 60); *Tatian's Diatessaron* (see n. 34); a Summary of the latter study (Ph. D. thesis, Manchester 1945) appeared in *JMUEOS* 24 (1942-1945, published in 1947), 28-32.

[77] A. J. B. HIGGINS, *Tatian's Diatessaron*, 51, n. 1; The Arabic Version, 190, n. 1: "This suggestion was first made to me by Prof. P. Kahle in 1941 in 1941 ...". It is not clear to me to which suggestion HIGGINS is referring, that of the twofold recension within the tradition *or* that of the authorship of Īsā ibn ʿAlî. As far as the work of KAHLE allows us to speak of it, the former possibility seems more probable.

[78] A. J. B. HIGGINS, *o.c.*, 49; *a.c.*, 188.

[79] A. J. B. HIGGINS, *o.c.*, 49; *a.c.*, 189. Compare what Higgins says on page 51 of his thesis about these lines: "The misunderstanding of the Ibn aṭ-Ṭayyib's function has been due to the loss of the sentence which has now been recovered in O".

[80] A. J. B. HIGGINS, *o.c.*, 50, refers to the colophon of Ms. O where, in accordance with that of Ms. B, Ibn aṭ-Ṭayyib has been said to have *translated* (fol. 287ᵛ, *l.* 3: نقله) the Diatessaron into Arabic; cf. *a.c.*, 189.

transcription/copy)[81] correct? But if one takes it for granted that his rendering was accurate, then one is faced with the following startling conclusions: *this man* who *wrote* was no one else than Īsā ibn ʿAlī, or, in other words, Īsā ibn ʿAlī did not accurately *transcribe* some (Syriac) manuscript of the Diatessaron, but made a faithful Arabic *version* on the basis of a Syriac text. But if Īsā ibn ʿAlī really were the translator of the Arabic harmony, then Ibn aṭ-Ṭayyib can no longer be held responsible for that version. Therefore, he must have been a revisor of an Arabic Diatessaron existing since the ninth century.[82]

An independent investigation of the manuscripts led HIGGINS to the conclusion that the translation of Īsā ibn ʿAlī could still be found in Mss. B-E-O, whereas the revision of Ibn aṭ-Ṭayyib was represented by Mss. A-C.[83] It was the impression of HIGGINS that the *translator* (Īsā ibn ʿAlī) still worked on a Diatessaron text of the Old Syriac type, which he faithfully preserved in his Arabic text, and in addition that the *revisor* (Ibn aṭ-Ṭayyib) of this rather archaic Arabic version evidently intended to accommodate it to the current Pešiṭta text.[84]

We need not enter into the question of the specific character of the two distinct groups BEO-AC now, for the matter deserves a separate investigation.[85] The only question to be dealt with here is, whether the additional ("original"?) line in the colophon of Ms. O really proves that the Arabic Diatessaron originated "not in the early eleventh century, but c. A.D. 850".[86] HIGGINS' theory was a challenge.

---

[81] For this meaning A. J. B. HIGGINS, *o.c.*, refers to the same colophon, fol. 288ʳ, *l.* 9; for the text implied, cf. A. F. L. BEESTON, *a.c.*, 609; A. J. B. HIGGINS, *a.c.*, 188 (cf. 189), where this line is found: واما النسخة الذى نقل منها هذا الكتاب "And as to the manuscript from which this book has been copied". It is clear that نقل cannot have but one meaning here.

[82] A. J. B. HIGGINS, *o.c.*, 8,13,50; *a.c.*, 189 ("The implication is that Ibn aṭ-Ṭayyib ..., in his translation, has made modifications and changes").

[83] A. J. B. HIGGINS, *o.c.*, 51; *a.c.*, 190 (n. 1), 193. — Immediately the question arises, why the very group B-E-O which then has nothing to do with Ibn aṭ-Ṭayyib in preamble and colophon contains the attribution of the translation to him, whereas the group A-C does not have the name of the revisor who was responsible for the text of this group. HIGGINS himself has seen this difficulty, but the way in which he tries to argue his position (*o.c.*, 52; *a.c.*, 109f.) is not convincing.

[84] A. J. B. HIGGINS, *o.c.*, 50f., 57f.

[85] I hope to be able to publish another study prepared in 1963/4 on "The two Recensions of the Arabic Diatessaron" fairly soon, in which I deal with the evaluation of the two groups by KAHLE and HIGGINS.

[86] A. J. B. HIGGINS, *o.c.*, 58; *a.c.*, 193.

10. *1947*

In 1947 HIGGINS' theory was met with two criticisms with regard to his translation and interpretation of the line in question. Firstly, P. E. KAHLE gave the following translation of the passage, "And he (the copyist) copied this as it was, not rearranging (anything) in the copy, but observing the orders...".[87] It is very likely that the addition of *the copyist* represents KAHLE's negative reaction to HIGGINS' interpretation.[88] A second criticism was put forward by G. GRAF.[89] He proposed to read the line as follows: "And this was written according to what is proper without finery in the translation, but with observation of the orders...".[90] In spite of differences in their translations, both scholars agree in connecting the statement of the colophon with the copyist, and they rightly do so. In the *Summary* of his thesis which was published in the same year, HIGGINS gave evidence of a change of mind. In an additional note he wrote: "subsequent consideration has made it necessary to disconnect the name of Īsā ibn ʿAlî from the origin of TA, for the words from the colophon of O...refer to the scribe, who did his copying without any rearrangement".[91] However, this does not mean that for that reason HIGGINS is now inclined to accept the manuscript statements concerning the authorship of Abū'l Faraǧ ibn aṭ-Ṭayyib. On the contrary: "it is ... very probable that the origin of TA has hitherto been assigned by scholars to too late a date, and that the ninth century or the early part of the tenth is nearer the truth".[92]

---

[87] P. E. KAHLE, *o.c.*, 222 (²308).

[88] P. E. KAHLE, *o.c.*, 228, n. 1, tells us that he had discussed some of the problems with HIGGINS in 1944, and he adds, "Further studies brought me to new results, and some alterations in his Introductory remarks will therefore be necessary". It seems probable that the difficulty of these words was among the matters discussed by them.

[89] G. GRAF, *Geschichte* II (see n. 7), 169, n. 2 deals with the theory of HIGGINS, and he concludes that his attempt "muss als misslungen gelten".

[90] G. GRAF, *o.c.*, 170 (= 169, n. 2): "Und geschrieben wurde dieses, wie es sich gehört (... wörtlich: gemäss das wozu Pflicht ist), ohne Ausschmückung in der Übersetzung, vielmehr mit Beobachtung der (empfangenen) Befehle".

[91] A. J. B. HIGGINS, *Summary*, 30, n. 1; HIGGINS followed KAHLE when in his translation of the additional line of Ms. O he now uses the words *copying* and *rearrangement* instead of *translation* and *modification*. A. J. B. HIGGINS, *Summary*, 30, n. 1; HIGGINS must have been impressed by KAHLE's criticism (see n. 88), for he has evidently accepted the translation of this scholar, when using *copying* and *rearrangement*, cf. text ad n. 87.

[92] *Ibidem*. HIGGINS refers to the date of Saadya, the translator of the Hebrew bible in that connection.

Epilogue I

In the course of this survey we found several objections against the reliability of the statement in manuscript B and its allies. These objections raised by such competent scholars as CHEIKHO, MARMARDJI, KAHLE and HIGGINS, probably deserve a more profound treatment than I am able to give in this study. It is, however, our purpose to demonstrate that not all the arguments adduced by them are conclusive with regard to their common refusal to accept the authorship of Ibn aṭ-Ṭayyib.

B. SHORT STUDIES INTO THE PROBLEM OF AUTHORSHIP

11. *The Antiquity of the testimony*

The first manuscript known of the Arabic Diatessaron, Ms. A, is usually dated in the *twelfth* century. The second manuscript, Ms. B, which for the first time revealed the name of Abū'l Farağ ibn aṭ-Ṭayyib, was of a later date, probably the *fourteenth* century.[93] It is obvious that the opinion could easily take form that the mention of the translator in the latter manuscript was a late invention by some scribe or editor, the more so, because the discovery of the Beirut fragments revealed the existence of another manuscript, Ms. C, without the name of the translator.[94] As a matter of fact, this manuscript was of a rather late date (scil. July 20, 1332).[95] but the pedigree of this manuscript was impressive in that it had no less than three chains between the last copyist and "the old manuscript of Antioch".[96]

We have seen that CHEIKHO's argument drawn from these Beirut fragments, namely, that the existence of the Arabic version of the Arabic Diatessaron antedates the time of Ibn aṭ-Ṭayyib,[97] was not as valid as he would have wished. Subsequent study[98] made it sufficiently clear that the very old copy of Antioch,[99] which the

---

[93] P. E. KAHLE, *o.c.*, 212, 214 (²298, 300) dates them 13th/14th century (Ms. A) and 16th century (Ms. B).

[94] Cf. §4.

[95] Cf. S. EURINGER, *Die Überlieferung*, 32f.

[96] Cf. §4, ad n. 24-25.

[97] L. CHEIKHO, Lettre, 306; نسخ, ١ . ٢ (cf. §4).

[98] S. EURINGER, *o.c.*, 60 and *passim*; cf. n. 30, 32 above.

[99] S. EURINGER, *o.c.*, 57, reminds us of the fact that "very old" is a comparative notion among orientals (I would add: and not only among them).

colophon mentions as the first antecedent of the manuscript could easily be dated *after* Ibn aṭ-Ṭayyib.[100]

Moreover, it seems to me that we are not certain which copyist was the first to speak of "very old". Was it really, as scholars tacitly seem to assume, the judgment of the man who wrote his copy directly from the Antiochian exemplar, bishop Yūsāb? Or was it the a posteriori conclusion of the last copyist, the writer of the Beirut colophon, Abū'l Barakāt, on account of the long list of copyists he had to mention in it?

It is obvious that manuscripts *without* the name of the translator were circulating at a very early stage: Ms. A was written in the twelfth century, Ms. C in 1332 A.D., the ancestors of Ms. C in the thirteenth century, whereas the very old copy of Antioch was possibly brought into circulation in the twelfth (or: eleventh?) century. The question is, whether the addition of the name is found in later manuscripts only. One of the reasons for H. W. Hogg's hesitation concerning authorship was exactly the fact that Ms. B was *a rather late witness*.[101] Marmardji, then, stated that it was the personal opinion of a copyist in Ms. B.[102] However, his own Ms. E (which he took as the basis for his edition) could have shown him that this "personal opinion" was not exclusively preserved in Ms. B. Was it perhaps for that reason that he afterwards spoke of an "opinion populaire dont certains copistes se servaient"?[103] Later discoveries gave evidence of the fact that it was the tradition of a whole family of manuscripts.[104] As a matter of fact, these allies of Ms. B were surprisingly young, Ms. E 1795 A.D., Ms. S 1797 A.D., Ms. T 18th century[105] and Ms. O even 1806 A.D. The most recent of these manuscripts, however, has ascertained the fact that this tradition concerning the translator must have existed in the *early twelfth* century.[106]

As to its date, the B-family seems not inferior to that of A. This conclusion is corroborated by the fact that a Coptic harmonist of

---

[100] S. Euringer, *o.c.*, 55f., dates the copyist mentioned before the ultimate "very old copy" ca. 1235 A.D., that is two centuries after Ibn aṭ-Ṭayyib († 1043), which would leave enough room for the "very old copy".

[101] H. W. Hogg, *The Diatessaron of Tatian*, 36 (see above §3).

[102] A.-S. Marmardji, *Diatessaron de Tatien*, lxxxviii.

[103] A.-S. Marmardji, *o.c.*, lxxxix.

[104] Cf. §5 (n. 35), §6 (n. 51), §7 (n. 59-60).

[105] Ms. T = Sbath 1280 (P. Sbath, *Catalogue* III, 92).

[106] Cf. §7 (n. 61); cf. §8; but see also §7 ad n. 62.

the twelfth century refers to a harmony written by Abū'l Farağ ibn aṭ-Ṭayyib, which he had at his disposal when he made his own harmonistic endeavour.[107] In the twelfth century this name was already connected with an Arabic Gospel harmony.[108]

Consequently, one cannot simply make the *omission* in the A-family outweigh the *addition* in the B-family on account of the date only. One should explain why precisely this communication was *added* in the latter group or *left out* in the former.

If it was an addition, can it be explained as being occasioned by a personal opinion of some early copyist or by a popular opinion current among Coptic copyists? If so, it would be necessary to answer the question, which was the origin of this opinion. There is no unanimity about that. Did the Aulād al-ʿAssāl, as P. KAHLE is inclined to believe, introduce the name of the famous philosopher, jurist and physician Ibn aṭ-Ṭayyib into their copy of the harmony in order to give more authority to their apologetical work.[109] But is it by all means necessary to assume that they added the name *only* with the purpose of impressing Muslim readers? Is the possibility excluded that they found the name already in the copy which they used as their exemplar for their production? The second explanation which we found was that of BEESTON: the unknown author of the Arabic harmony "attempted to give currency to his work by passing it off as the work of the well-known savant".[110] It is clear that if one assumes the latter solution, it remains to be explained how it could be omitted in the A-family.

If mention of the translator was omitted in the A-family, how can the omission be explained? We have seen that the antecedent of Ms. C originated in Antioch. It has been suggested that Ms. A was also of Antiochian origin.[111] It is not impossible that the A-form of the Arabic Diatessaron was introduced *from* the Nestorian region of Bagdad *into* Coptic Egypt *through* the Monophysitic area of Antioch. Is it not possible that a Monophysitic clerk who admired the enterprise of the Nestorian scholar Ibn aṭ-Ṭayyib (the translation of the Syriac harmony into Arabic) and therefore copied it, but when having finished his transcription did not find the liberty to do justice to

---

[107] Cf. § 5 (n. 44); see below § 13.
[108] Versus A.-S. MARMARDJI, *o.c.*, xcii; see §6 (n. 55).
[109] Cf. §8.
[110] Cf. §7 (A. F. L. BEESTON, *a.c.*, 610).
[111] Cf. P. E. KAHLE, *o.c.*, 213 (²313), under 3.

the names of the renowned Nestorian scholars mentioned in the preamble and colophon. This would not be very surprising. We have the example of the Monophysitic Dionysiōs bar Ṣalībī († 1171), who lived not so much later than the times in which the Antiochian antecedent of Ms. C should be dated. In his preface, this exegete acknowledges his indebtedness to earlier exegetes like Mar Ephraem, Mar John Chrysostom, Mar Cyril, Mōšē bar Kepha and Yohanan of Dārā,[112] that is, apart from the "neutral" first two fathers, only Monophysitic scholars. In fact, however, it appears that he was much more dependent upon the Nestorian exegete Īšōʿdāḏ of Merw whom he did not mention.[113] Can it be that in those times[114] the schism was (still?) felt so deeply in these northern regions that it was not thought advisable to refer to Īšōʿdāḏ or Ibn aṭ-Ṭayyib as authorities on whom one was dependent? Is it also possible that in more southern countries, where contacts between the two parties were less close, the situation was a different one, so that the Monophysitic Coptic Aulād al-ʿAssāl did not object to the Nestorian names in preamble and colophon, when they were collecting materials for their apologetical work on behalf of the prominent Muslim,[115] but willingly left them there as recommendations, because they knew that these names were in high esteem in Muslim circles. Thus the *omission* of the translator's name in the one family of manuscripts and its *preservation* in the other may be explained.

12. *Ibn aṭ-Ṭayyib in the Bibliographies*

H. W. Hogg called attention to the impersonal way in which Ibn aṭ-Ṭayyib referred to the Diatessaron in his commentary on the Gospel.[116] I could not verify this, but it is clear from the remarks of A. Hjelt[117] and D. S. Margoliouth[118] that in this commentary he referred to a Tatianic reading of Mt iii 4 without mentioning

---

[112] I. Sedláček, J.-B. Chabot, *Dionysii bar Ṣalibi Commentarii in Evangelia* I, 1, Paris 1906, 3.

[113] J. R. Harris, "Introduction" in M. D. Gibson, *The Commentaries of Isho'dad of Merv* I, Cambridge 1911, xxxf.

[114] J. C. J. Sanders, *Inleiding op het Genesiskommentaar van de Nestoriaan Ibn Aṭ-Taiyib*, Leiden 1963, 17 speaks of good relations between Jacobites and Nestorians in the days of Grīgōr bar ʿEbrāyā about hundred years later.

[115] If Kahle's assumption is correct.

[116] H. W. Hogg, *o.c.*, 36, n. 13.

[117] A. Hjelt, *Die altsyrische Evangelienübersetzung*, 68.

[118] D. S. Margoliouth, review of A.-S. Marmardji's edition, *JTS* 38 (1937), 76-79, 76.

Tatian or his Diatessaron. It is evident that this does not mean that he did not translate the Diatessaron. It is most likely that he found that interesting notice about the variant reading in Mt iii 4 in the commentary of Īšōʿdāḏ of Merw, where it was actually connected with the Diatessaron.[119] But he consciously omitted any reference to that harmony, since he had not found that variant reading in the Syriac copy of the Diatessaron that was at his disposal.[120]

One might also refer to the Introduction to his commentary on Genesis, where (in the last period of his life)[120] Ibn aṭ-Ṭayyib enumerated the works previously written by him: here also the translation of the Diatessaron is left out of consideration.[122] But again, this does not mean that he did not perform such a translation. The list of works in that Introduction is apparently not complete,[123] and one should be careful in using the argument from silence. The fact that Ibn aṭ-Ṭayyib did not mention the Diatessaron in these cases is not a decisive argument against the authorship of the Arabic harmony.

More impressive an argument seemed to be the fact that others did not mention his connection with the Diatessaron. Even though A. Ciasca had given the reason why there is no mention of the Diatessaron in the scholarly bibliographies of Bar ʿEbrāyā and Abū'l Barakāt,[124] L. Cheikho and A.-S. Marmardji were not at all convinced by his explanation.[125] Nevertheless, the argument of Ciasca was maintained by S. Euringer.[126]

Euringer also made the suggestion that it was not absolutely certain that Bar ʿEbrāyā did not have the Diatessaron in mind when he wrote of Ibn aṭ-Ṭayyib "This (man) *interpreted* (ܦܫܩ) both Testaments in the Arabic language, also the books of Aristotle".[127]

---

[119] M. D. Gibson, *The Commentaries of Ishoʿdad of Merv* II, Cambridge 1911, 39.

[120] Cf. A. Hjelt, *loc. cit.*

[121] Cf. J. C. J. Sanders, *Inleiding*, 7; *idem, Ibn aṭ-Ṭaiyib, Commentaire sur la Genèse* (CSCO 274; Arab 24), Louvain 1967, 1.

[122] Cf. J. C. J. Sanders, *Inleiding*, 6; *Commentaire*, 2.

[123] Cf. J. C. J. Sanders, *Inleiding*, 7 ff.

[124] Cf. §2 (n. 13-15).

[125] Cf. n. 28; A.-S. Marmardji, *o.c.*, lxxxviii.

[126] S. Euringer, *o.c.*, 17.

[127] For the text, cf. S. Euringer, *o.c.*, 11 f., 17. — For the commentary on the Old and New Testament see above ad n. 10; for his interest in Aristotle, cf. M. Kellerman (- Rost), *Ein pseudoaristotelischer Traktat über die Tügend*, Edition und Übersetzung der arabischen Fassungen des Abū Qurra und des Ibn aṭ-Ṭayyib, Erlangen-Nürnberg 1975, 14 f.

The verb *interpret* in Syriac means *explain, expound* as well as *translate*. EURINGER suggested that a possible ambivalent use of the word in this remark should not be excluded: it could mean *he translated*, and Bar ʿEbrāyā might have included the Arabic Diatessaron among the translation activity of Ibn aṭ-Ṭayyib.[128] This suggestion is not convincing; it is quite understandable that it has been neglected in subsequent research.

The omission of the Diatessaron in the bibliography of Ibn aṭ-Ṭayyib published by Abū'l Barakāt was another argument against the authorship. It seems enticing now to identify this famous author with the last copyist mentioned in the colophon of the Beirut fragments who wrote in the year 1332 A.D.[129] The famous Copt lived between 1274 and 1363.[130] So he could have been the copyist of Ms. C. If this were true, the argument from silence would not hold. Ms. C does not mention Ibn aṭ-Ṭayyib, because it belongs to the family of manuscripts which did not contain the name of the author.[131] Therefore, if Abū'l Barakāt had copied the Diatessaron he would not have connected it with the name Ibn aṭ-Ṭayyib, and consequently he would not have attributed this work to that author in the bibliography. However, it is not certain that the last copyist of Ms. C's colophon and the author of the bibliography were one and the same person.[132]

MARMARDJI does not enter into the complicated details of these problems. He merely claims that the "personal opinion" of the unlettered copyist of the Arabic Diatessaron who added the name does not weigh as heavily as does the argument which can be drawn from the silence of professional historians. And to those who would wish to diminish the value of the absence of the Diatessaron in these bibliographies, MARMARDJI says: "Nous pouvons répondre avec autant et même plus de raison: ce n'est ni par oublie ni par ignorance,

---

[128] S. EURINGER, *o.c.*, 17, "Es ist durchaus nicht ausgeschlossen, dass Barhebraeus hier nicht bloss an die Kommentar des Ibn aṭ-Ṭayyib, sondern auch an seine Übersetzung des Diatessaron gedacht hat".

[129] S. EURINGER, *o.c.*, 32 (ad 1), cf. 59.

[130] S. EURINGER, *o.c.*, 34.

[131] The last characters found in the colophon of Ms. C (fol 3a) are ... الرا; these were, according to CHEIKHO, remnants of the word الراهب "the monk"; S. EURINGER, *o.c.*, 58f.: "Es wäre denkbar, dass nach dem [هب]الرا der Name des Ibn aṭ-Ṭayyib gestanden hat. Ich gebe diese Vermuthungen mit aller erforderlichen Reserve". I think that this reservation is quite necessary, as we know that Ibn aṭ-Ṭayyib is mentioned "priest" (القس), not "monk" in the colophons/preambles of B, E, O and S.

[132] S. EURINGER, *o.c.*, 36, 59: it may have been an uncle of Abū'l Barakāt ibn Kibr: Abū'l Barakāt ibn Abī'l-Kibr.

mais simplement parce que cette œuvre n'était nullement la sienne qu'ils ne l'ont pas mentionnée".[133]

13. *The Author of the "new harmony" and Ibn aṭ-Ṭayyib*

MARMARDJI's assured conviction with respect to the contribution of the bibliographies to the problem of authorship raises the question whether the observations of the anonymous Coptic author who composed a "new harmony" (according the data given in the *Catalogue* of father SBATH under Ms. 1029)[134] might fill up the gap of the bibliographies: this author acknowledged Ibn aṭ-Ṭayyib as the author of an Arabic harmony. MARMARDJI entertained a high esteem for this unknown Coptic author, since the fragments of his work found in Sbath's catalogue make evident that he was a good scholar who knew many languages: this put him in a position to judge, the more so because he saw the harmony of Ibn aṭ-Ṭayyib with his own eyes. His authority, therefore, should be estimated much higher than the authority of those poor and ignorant copyists of the Arabic Diatessaron.[135]

As a matter of fact, MARMARDJI continued, the harmony which the Coptic author attributed to Ibn aṭ-Ṭayyib is not a translation, but a fresh, independent work: the Copt used the verb جمع "*he collected*", not نقل "*he translated*", to indicate the activity of Ibn aṭ-Ṭayyib. Consequently, there must have been a harmonistic patchwork of the Gospels under the name of Ibn aṭ-Ṭayib which was to be dissociated from any tradition about an Arabic translation of the Diatessaron of Tatian. But if one must assume such an independent harmony (as MARMARDJI wants us to assume), one would lose the right to appeal to the silence of historians concerning a translation of the Syriac Diatessaron on his part, as MARMARDJI did. For their silence would be as deep in the latter as in the former case: they do not mention *any* harmony, either independent or translated. Strangely enough, MARMARDJI did not realize this inconsistency.[136]

But can we be sure that the harmonies attributed to Ibn aṭ-Ṭayyib by both the Coptic author and the preambles of Mss. B-E-O-S were really identical? It must be admitted that no certainty can as yet be

---

[133] A.-S. MARMARDJI, *o.c.*, lxxxviii.

[134] Cf. §5 (ad n. 44-45).

[135] A.-S. MARMARDJI, *o.c.*, xciii, "... incomparablement supérieure ...".

[136] See for this inconsistency also A. F. L. BEESTON, *a.c.*, 610, and A. BAUMSTARK, *a.c.*, 243.

reached on the basis of the data at hand now. There are, however, a few problems in the text of the Coptic author (as far as we know that text from the catalogue of father SBATH) that deserve further attention.

First of all, the Coptic author mentions of his predecessors only Ibn aṭ-Ṭayyib by name. He does not say that *all* these predecessors had compiled an *Arabic* harmony, as MARMARDJI has suggested.[137] He only says that they *collected* all the words and deeds of our Lord *in one* Gospel.[138] It is not improbable that he had in mind the usual traditions concerning the *Diatessarons* of Tatian and Ammonius;[139] he might even have thought of the Canons of Eusebius.[140] It is most probable that he did not know anything more exact about these works: the work of his predecessor whom he mentioned by name seems to have been the only harmony which he was acquainted with, because only of this work does he say that he had accurately studied it.

Secondly, it cannot even be said that the Coptic author explicitly speaks of this latter harmony as an *Arabic* work, but that this was the case is implied by the fact that he has compared that work with the Gospels that were held to be "authentic", that is, the Gospels written in Syriac, Coptic and Greek: these languages sufficiently proved authenticity, for they were the more archaic languages of the Bible which were gradually superseded by Arabic. It was because the harmony of Ibn aṭ-Ṭayyib was written in the latter language that the Coptic author decided to compare it with Greek, Coptic and Syriac Gospels.

Thirdly, we do not know much about the contents of the harmony of Ibn aṭ-Ṭayyib which the Coptic author had studied before performing his own task[141]. From the few remarks in the text which father SBATH quoted from the manuscript it is only clear that the harmony of Ibn aṭ-Ṭayyib did not include certain Gospel passages which had a place in the original Gospels: he had neglected them and wholly

---

[137] Versus A.-S. MARMARDJI, *o.c.*, xcii, "à ses yeux, Ibn aṭ-Ṭayyib, comme les devanciers et comme lui, n'est rien qu'un auteur d'une harmonie des Évangiles en langue Arabe".

[138] Cf. § 5 (ad n. 44-45).

[139] In Syriac-speaking regions the names of Tatian and Ammonius are mentioned by more than one author, cf. A. HJELT, *Die altsyrische Evangelienübersetzung* (see n. 29), 23, 30, 34, 36, 37f., 39f., 43, 46, 47f.

[140] Cf. A. HJELT, *o.c.*, 39, 43; another name is Elias of Salamia, *ibid.*, 41f.

[141] A.-S. MARMARDJI, *o.c.*, xci, speaks of an "examen approfondi" (cf. xcii: "puisqu'il ... l'examine à fond").

cut them out of the originals. On the other hand he had unnecessarily repeated some of the wordings of the Evangelists.[142] These faults (and perhaps others mentioned in the portion that has been left out by father SBATH in his quotation) were "corrected" in the *new* harmony of the Coptic author.[143] It is true that these general statements fit with what we have in the Arabic Diatessaron usually connected with Ibn aṭ-Ṭayyib: besides omissions (the most striking being the genealogy of Jesus[144] and the pericopa adulterae)[145] there are also several repetitions.[146] Hence we may say that these facts do not contradict the statements of the Coptic author, and so it remains possible that the two texts (the Arabic Diatessaron which we have *and* the harmony that the Coptic author knew) are one and the same.

Fourthly, the question arises why our Coptic author did mention *neither* the title Diatessaron *nor* the name Tatian, which were found in the preamble and/or colophon of Ibn aṭ-Ṭayyib's work.[147] At first sight the answer to this question seems to be that the copy which was at his disposal did not contain these names: "Es genügt zur Erklärung dieser Sachlage die — kaum allzu gewagte — Annahme, dass ihm T^A in einem Exemplar vorlag, das in Titel und Kolophon zwar den Urheber des vorliegenden arabischen Textes nannte, von Tatian aber und deshalb auch von einem syrischen Vorlage dieses Textes nicht redete".[148] This explanation of A. BAUMSTARK was subsequently repeated by A. J. B. HIGGINS, who for that could refer to Ms. O in which the two names were actually missing in the colophon[149] — but I must notice the fact that I found them in the

---

[142] Cf. § 5.

[143] "I have corrected all these" (فأصلحت ذلك جميعه), that is, I have collected with a sounder method than my predecessor — does that mean that the Coptic author is altogether independent of Ibn aṭ-Ṭayyib's work? It would be a fine thing if we could examine the result of the Coptic author's enterprise, but when will the manuscript be published?

[144] The genealogies are not found at their proper place in the manuscripts B, E and O, which bear the name of Ibn aṭ-Ṭayyib.

[145] This section is not found in the Arabic Diatessaron in agreement with Syriac tradition (Sy^{s.c.p} contra Sy^{pal} Sy^h); it is found in some Coptic texts (Cop^{boh mss}).

[146] Cf. S. LYONNET, *Les origines de la version arménienne et le Diatessaron*, Roma 1950, 200.

[147] This was one of the arguments adduced against identification by A.-S. MARMARDJI, *o.c.*, xci, "L'auteur semble n'avoir nullement connaissance de Tatien, ni de son Diatessaron".

[148] A. BAUMSTARK, *a.c.*, 243.

[149] A. J. B. HIGGINS, *o.c.*, 58, n. 3.

preamble of that manuscript.[150]. One might also consider the possibility
that his mentioning of several predecessors (among whom Ibn aṭ-Ṭayyib
was mentioned by name) was prompted by the fact that preamble
and colophon of the manuscript used by him contained the name
of Tatian as the author of the Diatessaron, and in addition the name
of ʿĪsā ibn ʿAlī as the author of the Syriac copy on which Ibn aṭ-Ṭayyib
had based his Arabic translation.

Fifthly, it is necessary to say a few words about the fact that
the author speaks of Ibn aṭ-Ṭayyib's activity as *collecting* (جمع)
instead of *translating* (نقل), which made MARMARDJI think that Ibn
aṭ-Ṭayyib's work was an independent harmony that had nothing to
do with the translation from Syriac into Arabic which we have in
the extant manuscripts. It does not seem to me that the word جمع
can bear the burden of MARMARDJI's conclusion. The Coptic author
intentionally took as a basis for his own "harmony" the *Coptic*
Gospels, because "one who depends upon the language of his own
nation is right and does not err":[151] he wrote an *Arabic* harmony,
for which he used *Coptic* Gospels. Did he perhaps see a parallel
on this score between his own harmony and that of Ibn aṭ-Ṭayyib?
The latter, living in a region where Syriac Gospel texts had been
and still were current, would naturally have relied on *Syriac* texts
in order to produce an *Arabic* harmony. Therefore, he was not
surprised to read in preamble or colophon that it was *translated* from
Syriac into Arabic. However, his own work was not restricted to
translating, but it was above all *collecting*. Has the parallel which
he found between Ibn aṭ-Ṭayyib and himself (Arabic harmonies based
on texts in national tongues) given him occasion to use instead of
نقل the verb جمع which was the most appropriate word to denote his
own activity?[152]

In conclusion, the data of Sbath 1029 do not necessarily support
the distrustful views of MARMARDJI.[153] The view of father SBATH that

---

[150] Ms. O (= Bodleian Library, Ms. Arab. e 163), fol. 141 f.

[151] Cf. § 5, ad n. 42.

[152] We may refer to the "editor" of the flemish Diatessaron, who, although he
apparently worked on a Latin model which he *translated* from Latin into Dutch,
characterized his own work as a new *collection*: "... it is difficult work, among these
discordances which the Evangelists appear to have between them, to glear and collect
and put together a continuous narrative ..." (C. C. DE BRUIN, *Diatessaron Leodiense*,
Leiden 1970, 3; translation of A. J. BARNOUW).

[153] Was there a moment of hesitation, when MARMARDJI wrote (*o.c.*, xcii, n. 1)
"Nous croyons — *si nous comprenons bien l'arabe* — que ces conclusions découlent
clairement et logiquement de ce document".

the "introduction" of the Coptic author might prove the authorship
of Ibn aṭ-Ṭayyib has not been refuted by MARMARDJI's conclusions.[154]
But the defense of that authorship requires further substantial argumentation.

14. The Inferiority of the Translation

H. W. HOGG was the first scholar who drew attention to "the
inferiority of" at least "parts of the translation",[155] but he refused
to draw conclusions from it. A.-S. MARMARDJI made it the main
argument in his contestation of the authorship of Ibn aṭ-Ṭayyib,[156]
and several scholars were apparently imposed by his argument.[157]

The translation was so incorrect and unclassical, MARMARDJI said,
that the scholarly author of so many classical Arabic writings could
not have been the translator.[158] If one would maintain that Ibn
aṭ-Ṭayyib had written the Arabic Diatessaron, it would be necessary
to assume that

a. Ibn aṭ-Ṭayyib did not know much of the Arabic language — an
    assumption refuted by the facts, or
b. Ibn aṭ-Ṭayyib deliberately performed a bad translation — which
    would be unworthy of a scholar of his repute, or
c. Ibn aṭ-Ṭayyib actually made a perfect translation which has after-
    wards been corrupted by copyists — it is clear that MARMARDJI
    does not wish to deny the deteriorating influence of later scribes,[159]
    but this influence is not a sufficient explanation of the condition
    in which the text now is.[160]

Therefore, it seems quite clear that it was not this famous scholar
who made this translation, but some unknown and unskilled author.
In order to illustrate his view that the Arabic text was appallingly

---

[154] See § 5 (n. 46).

[155] H. W. HOGG, o.c., 36.

[156] A.-S. MARMARDJI, o.c., lxxxviii f., xciii.

[157] Cf. A. F. L. BEESTON, a.c., 609; D. S. MARGOLIOUTH, a.c., 76.78; P. E. KAHLE, o.c., 275 (²311).

[158] A.-S. MARMARDJI, o.c., lxxxviii, "Les choses paraissant si claires pour nous, comment pourrions-nous déterminer à attribuer cette piètre traduction à un homme que l'histoire nous présente comme illustre savant qui a écrit de nombreux ouvrages dont la plupart en arabe".

[159] Cf. A.-S. MARMARDJI, o.c., lxxxix (cf. also A. J. B. HIGGINS, o.c., 59, "... cor-rupted by ill-educated scribes").

[160] A.-S. MARMARDJI, o.c., xiii, "Ses défauts ne tiennent plus de l'ignorance des copistes ou des variantes des manuscrits, mais plutôt de l'insuffisance de l'auteur même de la traduction".

inferior, MARMARDJI gave several examples from the text which he had established, among which we find violations against the rules of Arabic grammar ("fautes de grammaire"),[161] infringements of classical usage ("fautes de contre-sens"),[162] and above all the unlimited use of Syriac words and expressions ("syriacismes").[163] He collected specimina of each kind of errors in brief lists, and subjoined to them another, longer list in alphabetical order of some more important and rather consistent errors.[164] As a contrast to these *syllabi errorum* MARMARDJI presented his readers with specimina of authentic writings of Ibn aṭ-Ṭayyib[165] and of some of his contemporaries who wrote classical Arabic.[166] At first sight it seems a real problem that MAR-MARDJI has touched upon when discovering so many deviations from classical Arabic, but the question which we have to face is whether he has interpreted them properly: are they really to be ascribed to the ignorance or incompetence of the translator? or is there another explanation of the "inferiority" of the translation?

a. When MARMARDJI repeatedly speaks of the ignorance and incompetence of the translator, he compares some of the "crying" mistakes of the author with the usual errors made by beginners in their themes and translations.[167] He does not consider the possibility of Ibn aṭ-Ṭayyib being a *débutant* when he undertook this translation. Why should we always attribute works to the acme of an author's career? Their literary activity may well have started before their flourishing period. Therefore, if Ibn aṭ-Ṭayyib has really written "classical" works later in his lifetime, we are not obliged to apply the classical rules as a standard in order to deny his authorship of the Arabic Diatessaron.

b. Did Ibn aṭ-Ṭayyib, however, write "classical" Arabic? A.-S. MAR-MARDJI[168] and also P. E. KAHLE[169] have stated that his Arabic was *good*, or even *excellent*. But what may have been the reason for the famous Muslim author Ibn Sīnā (Avicenna) to say that his Arabic

---

[161] A.-S. MARMARDJI, *o.c.*, xiii-xv (§ 2).

[162] A.-S. MARMARDJI, *o.c.*, xv-xviii (§ 3).

[163] A.-S. MARMARDJI, *o.c.*, xviii-xix (§ 4).

[164] A.-S. MARMARDJI, *o.c.*, xx-xxiv (§ 5).

[165] A.-S. MARMARDJI, *o.c.*, xciii-c (Spécimens des écrits d'Ibn aṭ-Ṭayyib).

[166] A.-S. MARMARDJI, *o.c.*, c-cii (Barhébraeus, Elias III, Saʿadya, Mūsā ibn Maymūn).

[167] A.-S. MARMARDJI, *o.c.*, xv (§ 3), "Cette faute est celle que les débutants commettent dans leur thèmes et versions".

[168] A.-S. MARMARDJI, *o.c.*, lxxxix.

[169] P. KAHLE, *o.c.*, 224 (but see below n. 179).

language was not pure (فصيح, "sprachrein").[170] It is not very probable
that Ibn Sīnā had in mind the Christian works of Ibn aṭ-Ṭayyib;
he must have thought of the philosophical or medical works which
were meant also for Muslim students and scholars.[171] Of course,
one should not lay too much stress on Ibn Sīnā's judgment, which
was not shared by every scholar.[172] It partly may have been due to
the usual jealousy of contemporaries, as Al-Bahaiqi has suggested.[173]
On the other hand, one should not too easily dismiss such criticism
which may have been prompted by the actual reading of texts of
Ibn aṭ-Ṭayyib. In this connection, it is interesting to read what the
famous Christian scholar Grīgōr bar 'Ebrāyā has said about the
linguistic ability of Ibn aṭ-Ṭayyib, "I think that he was weak in
Syriac language, for I have found errors everywhere in his commentaries".[174] These commentaries were written in Arabic, but the expert
in Syriac (and Arabic) Bar 'Ebrāyā was seems to have discovered
misinterpretations of the Syriac books which Ibn aṭ-Ṭayyib had
commented upon. It seems to me that the testimonies of Ibn Sīnā
and Bar 'Ebrāyā prove that the works of Ibn aṭ-Ṭayyib did not
always meet the requirements of "classical" Arabic and of good
translation. The question is again, whether it is possible to apply
"classical" standards to his works, as MARMARDJI did in his evaluation
of the Arabic Diatessaron.[175]
c. The language of Ibn aṭ-Ṭayyib may be reckoned to what has
been characterized as *Middle Arabic*,[176] the language or should we
say the group of dialects in which Classical Arabic had developed
in the various regions and cultures over which the Islam had gained
authority. Whereas Muslim authors often maintained the ideal of

---

[170] Cf. W. HOENERBACH, O. SPIES, *Ibn aṭ-Ṭaiyib. Fiqh an-Naṣrāniya, Das Recht der
Christenheit* I (CSCO 162; Arab 17; tr.), Louvain 1956, iv. who refer for this
judgment to 'Alī b. Zaid al Baihaqi († 1169), *Tatimmat Ṣiwān al-Ḥikma* (ed. MUHAMMAD
SHAFI', Lahore 1935, 27-32).

[171] Cf. P. E. KAHLE, *o.c.*, ²310; J. C. J. SANDERS, *Inleiding*, 30.

[172] W. HOENERBACH, O. SPIES, *loc. cit.*, refer to Ibn Miskawaih. — For the discussion
between Ibn Sīnā and Ibn aṭ-Ṭayyib, cf. H. Z. ÜLKEN, *Les opuscules d'Ibn Sīnā*,
Ankara 1953 (cf. O. SPIES, *WI* N.S. 4 (1956), 221).

[173] W. HOENERBACH, O. SPIES, *o.c.*, iv.

[174] Cf. S. EURINGER, *o.c.*, 11f. (with a reference to BEDJAN's edition of Bar Hebraeus'
Chronicon Syriacum, 1890, 226f.).

[175] A.-S. MARMARDJI, *o.c.*, xiii, "nous nous en tenons aux règles raisonnablement
admises par tout le monde".

[176] Cf. J. BLAU, *A Grammar of Christian Arabic* I-II-III (CSCO 267, 276, 279),
Louvain 1966-1967, esp. I, 19ff.

Classical Arabic, Jewish and Christian authors more easily gave way to vulgarisms, to non-classical idiom and vocabulary. The influences of living speeches such as Hebrew and Aramaic (Syriac) made themselves felt in the Jewish and Christian communities where Arabic gradually gained ground.

d. The Christian works of Ibn aṭ-Ṭayyib, as far as they have been edited, confirm this state of affairs. They betray the conditions of a Syriac-speaking church, the Christian community of Bagdad, within an Arabic-writing Muslim world. This is true for Ibn aṭ-Ṭayyib's *Fiqh an-Naṣrānīya* (published by W. HOENERBACH and O. SPIES)[177] as well as for his *Fardaus an-Naṣrānīya* (as far as it can be deduced from the commentary on Genesis published by J. C. J. SANDERS).[178] From these works it became clear that the famous scholar did not write the excellent Arabic which KAHLE had praised in 1947. In 1959, KAHLE acknowledged "the well-founded judgment about the quality of this Arabic", given by HOENERBACH and SPIES, "with which I entirely agree"; he denied that his earlier verdict had been his own opinion.[179]

e. Nevertheless, it is a remarkable thing to see that, although he changed his view with respect to the quality of Ibn aṭ-Ṭayyib's language, he still maintained MARMARDJI's opinion that the author was "an able stylist who could write very well classical Arabic".[180] It is equally surprising to read how SANDERS, who is fully alive to the peculiar character of the author's idiom and vocabulary in the commentary on Genesis[181] and consequently asks attention for the importance of his *œuvre* for our knowledge of the specific, Christian form of Middle Arabic,[182] is still inclined to refuse to accept Ibn Sīnā's criticism:[183] the fact that, as a secretary to the Patriarch Elias bar

---

[177] Cf. W. HOENERBACH, O. SPIES, *Ibn aṭ-Ṭaiyib, Fiqh an-Naṣrānīya, Das Recht der Christenheit* II (CSCO 161; Arab 16; txt), Louvain 1956, vi, "Der Text weist deutliche Spuren einer Übersetzungsliteratur aus dem syrischen auf, so dass er sprachlich nicht auf der Höhe jener Werke Ibn aṭ-Ṭaiyibs steht, deren *excellent Arabic* P. Kahle hervorhebt".

[178] J. C. J. SANDERS, *o.c.*, 30.

[179] P. E. KAHLE, *The Cairo Geniza*, Oxford ²1959, ix, "When I wrote... of the *excellent* Arabic... this was simply an allusion to what Marmardji had written and did not represent my own opinion".

[180] P. E. KAHLE, *o.c.*, 311.

[181] J. C. J. SANDERS, *o.c.*, 30-38.

[182] J. C. J. SANDERS, *o.c.*, 78ff., esp. 85f.

[183] J. C. J. SANDERS, *o.c.*, 12, asks "what is the gist of this reproach?", but he does not explicitly answer that question.

Šīnāyā, Ibn aṭ-Ṭayyib was helpful in the ultimate redaction of the latter's work on "the Mastership of the Christians in Grammar, Lexicography and Rhetorics" etc., presupposes that he had reached a high perfection in the use of cultural language.[184] Therefore, SANDERS suggests that a difference may have existed between Ibn aṭ-Ṭayyib's *Christian Arabic* writings for the Christian community (in which Syriac influences are visible) *and* his other works (medical and philosophical) meant for both Christians and Muslims and therefore written in *Classical Arabic*.[185] This may be true, but as long as his medical, philosophical and apologetic writings have not carefully been studied in this respect,[186] it seems too early to make this distinction.

f. The Syriacizing tendency of biblical translations is quite natural in an environment in which Syriac was the language of liturgy and of the scriptural lessons. If a translation slavishly follows the original text it need not be the product of ignorance, but it may be the result of a respectable principle of translation. If I am allowed to illustrate this with a modern example: MARMARDJI himself, who in his criticism of the Syriacizing character of the harmony declares this phenomenon to be the inevitable result of "une traduction servilement littérale" (apparently a pejorative designation in that connection),[187] says of his own translation of the Arabic harmony text "nous n'avons pas hésité à employer des tournures qui ne sont pas tout à fait conformes à la grammaire ni au génie de la langue française".[188] Of course, MARMARDJI had his reasons: the book was not meant for the general public, but for the experts. It is very probable that the author of the Arabic Diatessaron had his own reasons to do so: he closely followed the Syriac text of the harmony with an opposite purpose, namely to reach the general public familiar

---

[184] J. C. J. SANDERS, *o.c.*, 13; *Ibn aṭ-Ṭaiyib, Commentaire sur la Genèse* (CSCO 275, Arab. 25; tr.), Louvain 1967, i.

[185] J. C. J. SANDERS, *Ibn aṭ-Ṭaiyib, Commentaire*, i, "Les critiques formulées à ce sujet par des Juifs et des Musulmans visent, ce semble, son œuvre écrite en arabe chrétien, où l'influence du syriaque est manifeste". — Is it very probable that these critics had read these works? It is more likely that Jews and Muslims were interested in his medical and philosophical works.

[186] Unfortunately, M. KELLERMAN, *Ein pseudoaristotelischer Traktat* (cf. n. 127), 14 ff., 26, does not enter into the linguistic problems of the Arabic text.

[187] A.-S. MARMARDJI, *o.c.*, xviii.

[188] A.-S. MARMARDJI, *o.c.*, xxxvii.

with the Syriac Bible, and not the experts.[189] To those for whom
he translated, this work was a venerable document even in its form
of language. Therefore he was more or less compelled to keep the
Syriac flavour of his exemplar, as far as Arabic grammar and
vocabulary permitted to do so in the view of a man who knew both
languages, who lived in a period when the transition from Syriac
to Arabic has already made progress in the Christian community of
his region, and who could not consult such modern handbooks of
Classical Arabic as MARMARDJI knew. Genuine literary works cannot
be compared with translations, especially when these are translations
of Sacred Writings. Essays and commentaries permit their author
great freedom, a translation keeps him under restraint: not only
the unconscious factor of his own acquaintance with (or his piety
towards) the standing texts known by heart, viz. the Syriac harmony
or at least the Pešiṭta Gospels, but most likely also the conscious
factor of adopting the principle of an exact, slavish rendering for
the believers must have influenced the result.

g.   In our view, this Syriacizing aspect of the text explains the majority
of "errors" which MARMARDJI has discovered. When, in his *third* list,
MARMARDJI deals with the "Syriacisms"[190] he touches the essential
point of the matter, in spite of the fact that he mentions it "une
autre particularité défectueuse de ce texte arabe".[191] As a matter
of fact, Syriacisms concern not merely one peculiarity among others,
but the basic trend in form and structure of the language in the
harmony. Naturally, there may also be faults in that text that cannot
be explained with this key. Therefore, it will remain an object of
intensive study to determine which of the faults go back to the
translator and which to the copyists who may not always have
understood the Syriacizing text, since they partly lived in other regions
where Syriac text and speech were not current. Such an investigation
requires not only a careful collation of all the extant manuscripts
now known (in order to establish the original text of the harmony),

---

[189] Cf. also A. BAUMSTARK, *a.c.*, 243, who supposes that the eventual discrepancy
between the Arabic Diatessaron and the writings of Ibn aṭ-Ṭayyib may be explained
by the fact "dass dem hervorragenden Gelehrten gerade darangelegen gewesen wäre,
in seiner Arabischen Wiedergaben mit möglichster Treue seine Vorlage wiederzuspiegeln,
die er naturgemäss auch in ihrer gegebenen Gestalt ohne weiteres dem ehrwürdigen
Werke des christlichen Altertums gleichsetzte".

[190] A.-S. MARMARDJI, *o.c.*, xviii-xix.

[191] A.-S. MARMARDJI, *o.c.*, xviii.

but also a good deal of ingenuity in tracing the causes of corruption in the textual history of the harmony.[192] The possibility is not excluded that someone who has a profound knowledge both of Syriac and Middle Arabic would arrive at a more nuanced judgment than MARMARDJI did when he proclaimed the "inferiority" of the Arabic Diatessaron. In order to substantiate this expectation we want to make a few remarks about some of the "errors" noticed by MAR-MARDJI.

15. *Syriac Influence in the Arabic Harmony: Grammar*

The list of "grammatical errors" which MARMARDJI gave contains several instances of Syriac influence. In two cases MARMARDJI himself noticed two anomalies under Syriac influence, namely

a. the fact that the translator has used the imperfect tense where in Arabic a iussive form would have been normal,[193] and

b. the fact that the translator sometimes has used the positive form of an adjective (with من) instead of the comparative form.[194]

But Syriac influence may be assumed in other instances mentioned by MARMARDJI:

1. The author used ل where classical Arabic requires the accusative. MARMARDJI criticizes the wording of T^A xiii 38[195]

$$\text{وخبّر ليوحنا تلاميذه}$$

"and they told John, scil. his disciples", but this is an exact rendering of Syriac ܘܐܬܟܪܙ ܠܝܘܚܢܢ ܬܠܡܝܕܘܗܝ (Sy^{s.p}). The translator would not have felt himself wrong in this slavish rendering, as it was a characteristic feature of Middle Arabic (in Aramaic or Syriac-speaking regions).[196] Therefore, MARMARDJI is also wrong when he criticizes this idiomatic phenomenon elsewhere, e.g. in T^A xliv 35 (Lk. xxii 8) where Jesus is said to have sent his two disciples *Peter and John* (للصفا وليوحنا = ܠܟܐܦܐ ܘܠܝܘܚܢܢ). MARMARDJI wants this to be corrected into الصفا ويوحنا (acc.).[197] It is noteworthy that

---

[192] See for example the ingenuity of H. W. HOGG (below ad n. 225).

[193] A.-S. MARMARDJI, *o.c.*, xiv (under d.) — for this phenomenon, cf. J. BLAU, *o.c.*, II, 270ff. (Middle Arabic).

[194] A.-S. MARMARDJI, *o.c.*, xiv (under f.) — cf. J. BLAU, *o.c.*, I, 234ff. (Middle Arabic).

[195] A.-S. MARMARDJI, *o.c.*, xiv (under b.); the reference to T^A xiii 10 is wrong: read xiii 38 (MARMARDJI's translation "Et les disciples de Jean l'informèrent de ..." is misleading.

[196] Cf. J. BLAU, *o.c.*, II, 413ff.

[197] A.-S. MARMARDJI, *o.c.*, 425 app.

already L. CHEIKHO, in his edition of the Beirut fragments of this passage (the name of John is illegible) objected to the reading للصفنا which he printed in his text: he added — within brackets — that one should read الصفنا, as the manuscript reading was a "locution syriaque".[198] However, there is no necessity for correcting this "error".

2. In the story of Jesus' baptism we are told (T^A iv 37; Lk. iii 22) that the Holy Spirit *descended*: the Arabic text has the feminine form نزلت, instead of the masculine form نزل.[199] MARMARDJI condemns this as a grammatical mistake. He should have taken into consideration that the Syriac reads ܚܘܣܬܐ ... ܪܘܚܐ ܕܩܘܕܫܐ (Sy^{s.p}).[200] In Syriac the Holy Spirit is often treated as feminine in gender, and therefore a feminine verbal form is required. This is important, for it may help in establishing the text: in T^A i 36 (= Lk. i 35) the words "the Holy Spirit will come" should be read ܪܘܚܐ = روح القدس تاتي ܕܩܘܕܫܐ ܬܐܬܐ in accordance with Ms. A (= fem.), against the text of both CIASCA and MARMARDJI who followed Mss. B and E: ياتي (masc.).[201] In these two cases one cannot even say that the translator has violated classical usage, for the word روح is both feminine and masculine in Arabic.[202] Here it was apparently MARMARDJI's own Church Arabic that became the standard.

3. In the story of Jesus' withdrawal to Bethany (Mt. xxi 17 parr.) the expression هو واثنا عَشَّرتهُ "He and *his Twelve*" occurs (T^A xxxii 22), at least in Ms. A which has been adopted as textual basis by A. CIASCA at this point.[203] MARMARDJI criticizes this wording as an "emploi anormal de l'annexion et du relatif" which proves that the translator had not been equal to his task (although he himself adopted a different text in his edition هو واثنا عشريه of Ms. E).[204] MARMARDJI suggests that the correct rendering would have been ثلا ميذه الاثنا عشر

---

[198] L. CHEIKHO,

[199] Cf. A.-S. MARMARDJI, *o.c.*, xiv (under c.).

[200] A.-S. MARMARDJI, *o.c.*, 37 (where also the Syriac text is printed in the apparatus).

[201] A. CIASCA, *o.c.*, ܚ seems right in attributing the feminine reading to Ms. A (see app.) contra A.-S. MARMARDJI, *o.c.*, 8 (app.).

[202] Cf. J. BLAU, *o.c.*, I, 204.

[203] A. CIASCA, *o.c.*, ١٢٢: 1; Ms. B differs from Ms. A in having اثنى عشرية (cf. Ms. E in text ad n. 204).

[204] A.-S. MARMARDJI, *o.c.*, xv (under m.); MARMARDJI criticizes the reading of Ms. A (= CIASCA's text) as the translator's text; but if this is the translator's original wording, why does he not assume this as the reading of his own text of the Diatessaron? (*o.c.*, 306).

(lit. "his disciples-the-twelve"),[205] whereas the reading اثنا عشرته was condemned as being against the grammatical rules. The origin of the wording is found in Mk. xi 11, where μετὰ τῶν δώδεκα is the original text.[206] The Syriac versions (Sy^{s,p}) have rendered the words with ܥܡ ܬܪܥܣܪ. In one Pešiṭṭā manuscript, Codex Dawkinsianus III of Oxford, we read a different expression ܥܡ ܬܪܥܣܪ̈ܬܗ.[207] The words اثنا عشرته which MARMARDJI has censured in the Arabic harmony, are in my view an appropriate but unclassical reproduction of this Syriac expression ܬܪܥܣܪ̈ܬܗ: the translator has almost exactly transliterated the Syriac word of the Syriac harmony, retaining the ending ـܬܗ with his Arabic equivalent ending in ـته.

This conclusion may shed some light upon the second passage to which MARMARDJI refers in the list of grammatical errors, T^A xvi 19 (= Lk. viii 1). MARMARDJI criticizes the textual reading اثنا عشرية and wants to replace it by الاثنا عشر.[208] The reading which MARMARDJI criticizes appears in CIASCA's edition without any variation in the apparatus criticus;[209] according to MARMARDJI,[210] it was the reading of Ms. E. This would suggest that it was the common reading of all the manuscripts that are collated (Mss. A-B-E). To our surprise, MARMARDJI does not follow the manuscript evidence here but adopts the reading اثنا عشريه, which he subsequently critizes as "un syriacisme qui va, à la fois, contre le génie et la grammaire arabes"[211] and which therefore has to be corrected into the non-existing reading تلاميذه الاثنا عشر "his disciples-the-twelve".[212] All these considerations fall to the ground, if we assume that the author of the Arabic Diatessaron wrote اثنا عشرته = ܬܪܥܣܪ̈ܬܗ (Sy^{s,c,p}), again a more or less slavish transliteration of the Syriac Vorlage.[213]

---

[205] This rendering is actually found in T^A xii 42, where it does not reflect Lk. ix 1 (τοὺς δώδεκα = Sy^{s,p} ܬܪܥܣܪ̈), but Mt. x 1 (τοὺς δώδεκα μαθητάς), and in T^A xxx 40, where it does not represent Mk. x 32/Mt. xx 17/Lk. xviii 31 (τοὺς δώδεκα), but the varia lectio of Mt. xx 17 (τοὺς δώδεκα μαθητάς, B C W φ 118 209 pm Lat Sy^p Sah ...).

[206] Varia lectio: add. μαθητῶν D it.

[207] Ph. E. PUSEY, G. H. GWILLIAM, Tetraevangelium Sanctum iuxta simplicem Syrorum versionem, Oxford 1901, 269 app.

[208] A.-S. MARMARDJI, o.c., xv (under m. – second example).

[209] A. CIASCA, o.c., ٦٣.

[210] A.-S. MARMARDJI, o.c., 152 (app. on p. 153).

[211] He uses the symbol ⋇.

[212] A.-S. MARMARDJI, o.c., 153 app. (cf. n. 205 in text).

[213] The same reasoning may be applied to T^A xx 7 (John vi 68), where the original reading must have been لاثني عشرته.

It would be tempting to weigh all the examples given in MAR-
MARDJI's first list of "errors", but for reasons of space we have limited
ourselves to these instances. It is clear that unclassical elements are
present in the Arabic harmony, but they are partly to be attributed
to the language shift in Middle Arabic (i.c. Christian Arabic of
Baghdad),[214] partly to direct Syriac influence.[215]

16. *Syriac Influence in the Arabic Harmony: Vocabulary*

In his second list ("fautes de contre-sens") MARMARDJI's objections
are mainly concerned with the vocabulary of the author. Here again,
it must be said at the outfit, it is unjustified to weigh each of
the author's words on the "classical" balance. At this point, MAR-
MARDJI's procedure has already been criticized by D. S. MARGOLIOUTH:
"... what is less pardonable is the evident desire to poke fun at the
Arabic translator by giving his words senses which he did not intend
them to have".[216]

It seems to me that if one wishes to censure the "vocabulary"
of the Arabic harmony, one should first fulfil the conditions under
which a fair criticism can be levelled against the responsible author:
a. a first prerequisite would be the making of a concordance of all
the words in (the manuscripts of) the Arabic Diatessaron together
with their possible Syriac equivalents; b. a second task would be
to perform lexicographical studies into the works of Ibn aṭ-Ṭayyib[217]
and of his contemporaries in Baghdad or in Mesopotamia throughout;
c. a third requirement would be the constant consultation of Syriac-

---

[214] We may mention here some examples given by MARMARDJI, *o.c.*, xiiiff.,
under *a.* plural verb instead of classical singular (before subject in plural): J. BLAU,
o.c., II, 275 (§177); under *d.* imperfect instead of iussive forms: J. BLAU, *o.c.*, II,
271f. (§172); under *e.* imperfect indic. plur. with ending -*û* instead of -*ûn*: J. BLAU, *o.c.*,
II, 260ff. (§171); under *i.* neglect of difference in cases: J. BLAU, *o.c.*, II, 317ff.
(§215ff.) etc.

[215] Among the instances given by MARMARDJI as "errors" I would reckon to this
group, besides *d-f* already signalized by MARMARDJI himself, also *a* (see n. 214);
cf. also *h.* the confusion of different broken plurals (perhaps also a feature of Middle
Arabic?): MARMARDJI refers to T^A xxxiii 39 (= Mt. xxi 32) where instead of الزوانى
"harlots", الزناة "whoremasters" is found, possibly under influence of Syriac fem.
plur. ܐܬܢܙ (Arab. -*āt(u)*, Syr. -*āṯā*).

[216] Cf. also his ironical words "this form of humour of which Prof. Marmardji is
clearly a master ..." (*a.c.*, 78).

[217] Compare the short glossaries in W. HOENERBACH, O. SPIES, *Ibn aṭ-Ṭaiyib, Fiqh
an-Naṣrānīya* (CSCO 167, Arab. 18), Louvain 1957, 201-214 ("Glossar"); J. C. J.
SANDERS, *Ibn aṭ-Ṭaiyib, Commentaire sur la Genèse* (CSCO 274; Arab. 24), Louvain
1967, 103f. ("Vocabulaire d'Arabe chrétien").

Arabic lexicons that were written before and in the lifetime of
Ibn aṭ-Ṭayyib.[218] Such inquiries would present us with a sounder
basis to form an opinion about the quality of the Arabic language
in the harmony than the insufficient florilegium that MARMARDJI
offered to his readers in order to substantiate his condemnation.
It is not the place here for a lengthy criticism of his evidence,
but three instances may suffice to show how MARMARDJI sometimes
discovered "errors" by error:

1. T^A liii 58 = Lk. xxiv 32: Instead of the original reading καιομένη,
the Arabic harmony reads ثقيلا "heavy". This is at least the reading
of Ms. A (cf. Ms. B: كاثقيلا),[219] which has rightly been adopted as
the harmony's text by CIASCA.[220] MARMARDJI has in his text a
different wording, namely يتقلا (apparently based on Ms. E),[221] which
in his view is a grammatical error for يتقلّي "roasted", which in its
turn is the wrong word for "burning" (καιομένη): the translator
apparently chose the wrong expression, for he should have chosen
the impf. verb يتقد or participle متقد "burning".[222] However, it is
quite evident that Ms. A has preserved the original Arabic harmony
text: ثقيلا is an exact rendering of ܝܩܝܪ, which is the wording found
in all Syriac versions (Sy[s.c.p]).[223] The Arabic translator is not to blame
at this point.

2. T^A xv 35 = Lk. x 19: This is another instance in which
MARMARDJI accuses the translator of having used a wrong word.
CIASCA's text,[224] based on Mss. A-B, presents us with the wording
"and the whole جنس (γένος) of the enemy": جنس has been translated
with *genus* (CIASCA), *race* (HOGG), *Art* (PREUSCHEN). This is not,

---

[218] I think of the lexicographical activities in the ninth and tenth centuries, e.g.
Ḥunain ibn Isḥāq, Íšô' b. 'Alî, Abū'l Ḥasan b. Bahlul), but also of the work written
by Elias b. Šînāyā († 1049), *Kitāb at-Targumān fī ta'līm luġat as-suryān*. Cf. A. BAUM-
STARK, *Geschichte der syrischen Literatur*, Bonn 1922, 227ff., 231f., 241f., and 287;
G. GRAF, *Geschichte der christlichen Arabischen Literatur*, II, Città del Vaticano 1947,
177ff., 187f.

[219] The reading of Ms. B confirms that of Ms. A. Is it a copyist's error, by which
the word ثقيلا is contaminated with -ك of the preceding كان?

[220] A. CIASCA, *o.c.*, ٢ . ٤.

[221] A.-S. MARMARDJI, *o.c.*, 517 (cf. xv).

[222] A.-S. MARMARDJI, *o.c.*, 517 (impf.), xv (ptc.).

[223] The reading ܝܩܝܪ "heavy" is found in the Syriac codices examined by PUSEY
and GWILLIAM, and therefore it is rightly the text of their edition. Some of the older
editions (SCHAAF, GUTBIR) have ܝܩܕ = καιομένη. For the Harqlaya/Philoxeniana
cf. H. GRESSMANN, Studien zum Syrischen Tetraevangelium, *ZNW* 5 (1904), 250f.

[224] A. CIASCA, *o.c.*, ٦ ١.

however, a peculiar reading of the *original* Diatessaron, but purely
a scribal error — as H. W. Hogg has already observed in his annotations.[225] If the Arabic word were punctuated in a different way,
viz. جيش instead of جنس, the matter would be explained: the word
جيش means "army" which is a *possible* rendering of Syriac ܚܝܠܐ
(1. power, strength, 2. army, military force).[226] The reading جيش turned
out to have been preserved by Ms. E, the manuscript on which
Marmardji based his text.[227] But even here Marmardji is not
satisfied with the rendering of the translator. In his view, the underlying
ܚܝܠܐ means, above all, *power, strength*,[228] which, again according
to Marmardji, is apparently the meaning of the word in Lk. x 19:
"mais notre traducteur, malgré le titre de *savant* qui lui est decerné
par les copistes, eut, le premier, le grand tort de rendre, dans ce cas
présent, ܚܝܠܐ par جيش *armée* et non par قوّة, *vertu, force*".[229] It is
this latter word that Marmardji wants to propose as the right word
to read. All these considerations, however, are unnecessary: the wording
of the Arabic author represents in no way a case of mistranslation.
In the commentary of Dionysios bar Salībī, for example, the words
ܟܠܗ ܚܝܠܗ ܕܒܥܠܕܒܒܐ (= πᾶσαν τὴν δύναμιν τοῦ ἐχθροῦ) are
paraphrased with ܣܛܢܐ ܘܚܝܠܘܬܗ "Satan and (his) hosts".[230]
This interpretation of ܚܝܠܐ as "army" has a long history in Syriac
exegesis.[231] There is no reason to find fault with the author at this point.

   3. T^A xxv 42 = Mt. xix 12: Another rendering on account of
which the translator of the harmony is severely criticized by Marmardji is مؤمنون for "eunuchs".[232] The Syriac word ܡܗܝܡܢܐ

---

[225] H. W. Hogg, *o.c.*, 67, n. 9, "This is a clerical error for forces"; cf. A.-S. Marmardji, *o.c.*, xvi, "une faute de copiste".

[226] Cf. H. W. Hogg, *loc. cit.*

[227] A.-S. Marmardji, *o.c.*, 146.

[228] A.-S. Marmardji, *o.c.*, xvi ("signifie, de plus, *vertu, force*").

[229] A.-S. Marmardji, *o.c.*, xvii; 146 app.

[230] A. Vaschalde, *Dionysius bar Salībī, Commentarii in Evangelia* II:1 (CSCO 95;
Syr. 47; txt.), Louvain 1953, 331:2.5.

[231] Aphrahat, *Demonstratio* VI:17 (ed. J. Parisot, *Patrologia Syriaca* I:I, Paris
1894, 305f.), writes "And our Lord said again to his disciples: Look, I have given
to you the power to tread upon the ܚܝܠܐ of the Enemy — The Scriptures reveal
that he has a ܚܝܠܐ and also ministers...". In that connection, Aphrahat speaks
of a waging of war between God and Satan. This interpretation of ܚܝܠܐ (= δύναμις)
is in accordance with the Greek patristic exegesis, cf. Clement of Alexandria's
paraphrase of Lk x 19 ... κυριεύειν τε καὶ δαιμόνων καὶ τῆς τοῦ ἀντικειμένου
στρατιᾶς (Strom. IV.6.26).

[232] A.-S. Marmardji, *o.c.*, xvi, 246.

means both "faithful, believer, Christian" and "eunuch".[233] In Mt. xix
12 the word εὐνοῦχοι (4×) has aptly been rendered with ܡܗܝܡܢܐ.
The Arabic word مؤمن, however, does not mean "eunuch", it only
means "faithful" or "believer". The correct word is خصي (plur.
خصيان).[234] "Or, notre brave traducteur emploie, partout où revient
ce terme, مومنين pour خصيان", MARMARDJI laments.[235]

At first sight, MARMARDJI's case seems strong. But I wish to draw
the attention to a passage in one of Ibn aṭ-Ṭayyib's works, namely
his commentary on Genesis, which might illustrate that this translator
(if he were also the translator of the harmony) *could* have used
the term مؤمن as an equivalent to ܡܗܝܡܢܐ "eunuch". Ibn
aṭ-Ṭayyib writes in his comment on Gen. xxxix 1:[236]

The Midianites sold him (viz. Joseph) to Potiphar, the faithful one
(الثقة), the chief of the court of Pharao, according to the Greek,
and, according the Syrian, the chief of the guard.

والمؤمن هاهنا	And the *mū'man* (means) here the one
يريد به الثقة	to whom confidence has been shown
لا الخصي	— not the castrated one,
ففي ذلك الوقت	for in that time
لم يعرف خصي	castrated persons were unknown.

From this passage one might possibly conclude that in the time and
environment of Ibn aṭ-Ṭayyib مؤمن = ܡܗܝܡܢܐ *could* be interpreted as "castrated, eunuch".[237] Therefore, Ibn aṭ-Ṭayyib avoided
translating ܡܗܝܡܢܐ with المؤمن, but chose the unambiguous
rendering الثقة "trustworthy". If I am right, MARMARDJI's evidence

---

[233] Of course, the meaning "eunuch" is secondary: one who is faithful and
trustworthy becomes one who becomes entrusted with power: chamberlain, minister,
steward, and consequently (in the court of a monarch) eunuch.

[234] This is the usual equivalent in Syriac/Arabic lexicons, cf. R. PAYNE SMITH,
Thesaurus Syriacus I, Oxford 1879, 233f. (ܐܡܢ) and II, Oxford 1901, 2743f. (ܫܠܡ).

[235] A.-S. MARMARDJI, o.c., xvi – N.B. "partout où revient ce terme" is somewhat
exaggerated, since the term occurs only in Mt xix 12 (cf. Acts viii 27).

[236] J. C. J. SANDERS, *Ibn aṭ-Ṭaiyib, Commentaire sur la Genèse* (txt), 91:2-5. It is
an extract from Iso'dad of Merw, cf. J. M. VOSTÉ, C. VAN DEN EYNDE, *Commentaire
d'Išo'dad de Merv sur l'Ancien Testament* I (CSCO 126, Syr. 67), Louvain 1950,
202:5-10 (cf. also A. SCHER, *Theodorus bar Kōni, Liber Scholiorum*, I (CSCO 55,
Syr. 19), 185:13-14). The last remark, namely that there were no eunuchs in that time,
is apparently based on the fact that Potiphar was married.

[237] Cf. also G. MESSINA, *Diatessaron Persiano*, Roma 1951, 213 n. 1, for a similar
phenomenon in the Persian harmony.

against identifying the author with Ibn aṭ-Ṭayyib might become an
argument in favour of that identification.[238]

These three instances may suffice to show that the vocabulary of
the Arabic harmony is not an argument with which one can make
great play in the question of authorship.

17. *The additional Line in Ms. O and the language of the Harmony*

A few words need to be said about the remarkable line that
HIGGINS had discovered in the Oxford manuscript.[239] We have seen
that its wording has not the impact that HIGGINS gave to it,[240]
but still it deserves our attention. First of all, it seems certain that
the line has to be connected with the following words "... on the 8th of
Tobah, in the year of the Martyrs 1522 – 25th of Shawwāl A.H. 1220".[241]
What did the late copyist mean when he added the words of the
additional line?

1. كتب — هذا these words present us with a difficulty. If one
wishes to translate the verbal form in the active sense (*kataba*),
"he wrote", the question has to be answered who was the subject.
Against KAHLE's solution (the copyist) must be said that the name
of the copyist Antūnī Saʿd occurs only some lines below; it is,
therefore, less probable that he is the subject here. It is quite understandable that HIGGINS sought the subject in هذا "this" (= this man,
namely the man just mentioned, Īsāʿ ibn ʿAlī). However, this solution
turned out to be wrong: the communication about Ibn ʿAlī cannot
be brought into accord with that about this man. Therefore no other
possibility is left than the one GRAF chose: we have to read the
passive form *kutiba*, and consequently to take هذا as its subject:
"And this has been written", viz. either *this* whole book (the codex),
cf. fol. 288ʳ, line 9, or rather *this* fourfold Gospel, cf. fol. 287ᵛ, line 1
(هذا الانجيل الرباعى).

2. على ما هو عليه — although we did agree with GRAF under 1,
we do not accept his interpretation of these words; he rendered
the expression عليه in such a way that it contains the notion of an

[238] The fact that Ibn aṭ-Ṭayyib worked on a Syriac text here (the commentary of
Išôʿdāḏ) does not diminish the value of Ibn aṭ-Ṭayyib's notice; this would have been
the case, if Ibn aṭ-Ṭayyib had rendered the Syriac word ܗܝܡܢܘܬܐ with مؤمن,
but he did not do so, apparently because he wished to avoid the ambiguity of مؤمن
in the Christian Middle Arabic of Baghdad or Mesopotamia.

[239] See above §9, where the line in question is found.

[240] See above §10 (the criticism of P. KAHLE and G. GRAF).

[241] Cf. P. KAHLE, *o.c.*, ²308; the date is January A.D. 1806.

obligation: "according to what is proper".[242] This would fit better, if one should adopt *kataba* instead of *kutiba* (the latter reading is the one we have adopted in agreement with GRAF!). The meaning of the words, therefore, is rather "in the state wherein it was" (cf. Qurān III 173 عَلَى مَا أَنتُمْ عَلَيْه), cf. "as it was" (KAHLE) or "on the basis of what was before him" (HIGGINS). My translation, if it is right, presupposes that the text which the scribe had before him as his *exemplar* might easily invite someone to make corrections or emendations.

3. تصنع — "modification" (HIGGINS), "rearrangement" (KAHLE) or "Ausschmuckung" (GRAF)? The word seems to imply a kind of mannerism or artificiality, and this is apparently what GRAF wished to express. "This was written in the state wherein it was *without mannerism*": the copyist had not yielded to his desire to emend the text which he was copying. All the Syriacizing aspects of the text, which were in a certain sense foreign to the Coptic scribe, were preserved in the text, even though their correction might have seemed natural.

4. في نقل — the word نقل (noun or infinitive) should be rendered with" (in the) copy" (KAHLE) or "(in) copying"; certainly not with "translation". HIGGINS could use only this latter rendering for his thesis, but I do not understand why GRAF has rendered it thus.

5. حفظ الاوامر — HIGGINS' rendering "kept the words" is wrong. The word امر (certainly with the plural اوامر) means "order". The word حفظ (KAHLE: "observing"; GRAF: "with observation of") is in accordance with *kutiba* (see 1) a passive form: "(but) the orders were observed". Does this mean that the scribe observed the general rules which scribes have to take into consideration when they are copying manuscripts. I would suppose that the scribe of 1806 A.D. was aware of the strangeness of the Arabic text but did not give way to his desire for corrections or embellishments (see 3), because he was instructed to transcribe the text in the state wherein it was (see 2). The reason for that instruction may have been out of respect for the famous name of Ibn aṭ-Ṭayyib that was connected with this text. This is precisely the difference between this scribe of 1806 and the scholar of 1935: the latter could not believe that Ibn aṭ-Ṭayyib

---

[242] In this case عليه (GRAF does not render the pronoun) has been interpreted thus "(according to what is) *upon him as an obligation*", the pronoun referring to the subject of *kataba*, "*he* wrote".

was responsible for this text, and consequently proposed so many corrections and embellishments.

Epilogue II

In our first epilogue we held out a prospect of demonstrating that not all the arguments adduced by CHEIKHO, MARMARDJI, KAHLE and HIGGINS were conclusive with respect to the problem of authorship. The unwillingness of these scholars to accept the reliability of the notices found in the manuscripts of the B-family was perhaps understandable, but the preceding paragraphs may have shown the reader that their scepticism was not founded on indisputable "facts". There is no decisive proof for the thesis that the testimony of Ms. B and its allies is a later invention. Why would the Coptic Aulad al-'Assāl, when composing their large (apologetical?) work, have included in it also this linguistically somewhat "impure" harmony text, if it had not been their strong conviction that the name of the famous (Nestorian) philosopher and physician was rightly connected with it? The question is not *how* he translated, but *that* he translated the Syriac harmony into Arabic.[243] To that fact the very preambles and

---

[243] I have left out a discussion of the differences between this translation and another Gospel translation connected with the name of Ibn aṭ-Ṭayyib. H. W. HOGG, *o.c.*, 37, n. 1 (cf. also D. S. MARGOLIOUTH, *a.c.*, 76) pointed to the fact that, apart from the version of the harmony, there was another version of the Gospels (at least, of Matthew and John) attributed to him. One of the famous Aulād al-'Assāl, namely Al-As'ad Abū'l-Faraǧ Hībatallāh ibn al-'Assāl (cf. G. GRAF, *Geschichte* I, 151.162), tells us in the preface of his own recension of the Gospel text that he made use also of the Gospel of Matthew and that of John in the translation of Ibn aṭ-Ṭayyib. We also know of a Gospel text which is interwoven in his commentary on the four Gospels (Y. MANQURIYŪS, *Tafsīr al-Mašriqī* I, Cairo 1908; specimens in A.-S. MAR-MARDJI, *o.c.*, xcviii-c). Which were the mutual relations between these texts? The question is whether Ibn al-'Assāl referred to the text of the Gospels in the commentary. But why did he then make use of Matthew and John only? Or could he lay hands only on these two parts? Or is there another explanation? We should remember that the Arabic harmony translated by Ibn aṭ-Ṭayyib consists grosso modo of two parts, Matthew (Mark/Luke) and John. Did Ibn al-'Assāl have in mind the text of the commentary or that of the Diatessaron? Or was there a third text? Another question is whether the Gospel text in Ibn aṭ-Ṭayyib's commentary was his own translation or a text that already existed before Ibn aṭ-Ṭayyib (cf. A. BAUMSTARK, *a.c.*, 242); if it was not his translation it cannot be compared with the Arabic harmony in order to demonstrate that the latter could not be the work of Ibn aṭ-Ṭayyib (contra MARMARDJI's procedure); if it was really the work of Ibn aṭ-Ṭayyib it must said that the text in the commentary is not written in the classical Arabic which MARMARDJI wished to find in it: I found several Syriacisms and a good deal of Middle Arabic in this text as well.

colophons with his name (I heartily agree with BAUMSTARK [244] and GRAF [245] at this point) may bear witness, as they mention not only the translator of the *Arabic* text, but also the copyist of the *Syriac* exemplar on which the translation was based.

As long as there is no decisive proof to the contrary the name of the translator should be none else than

'Abū'l Farağ 'Abdū'llāh ibn aṭ-Ṭayyib.

---

[244] A. BAUMSTARK, *a.c.*, 243, "Entscheidend wird aber für die Urheberschaft Ibn aṭ-Ṭajjibs am Tᴬ und damit für dessen Identität mit dem von Kopisten genannten Werke immer die Tatsache bleiben, dass der Kolophon von B an dem Ḥunain-Schüler Īšā b. 'Alī den Schreiber sogar der vom Übersetzer zugrunde gelegten Hs. der syrischen Vorlage kennt".

[245] G. GRAF, *Geschichte* I, 153, "Diese doppelte bestimmte Angabe mit dem Namen des Übersetzer und dem des Schreibers seiner Vorlage, welche letztere Bemerkung nur vom Übersetzer selbst herrühren kann, macht die Einwände gegen Ibn aṭ-Ṭayyibs Urheberschaft ... hinfällig".

JEREMIAS HOELZLIN:
EDITOR OF THE "TEXTUS RECEPTUS" PRINTED
BY THE ELZEVIERS LEIDEN 1633*

H. J. DE JONGE

In the critical apparatus of recent editions of NESTLE-ALAND about two hundred conjectures have been included, with ninety odd names of authors.[1] The abbreviation *cj* has been added to these names where a radical alteration of the traditional spelling is concerned. Otherwise, if only matters of orthography, accentuation, breathing, and so on, are involved only the name is given. The question whether it is correct to designate readings of the latter category as conjectures, can be left out of consideration here, and attention called to a slight but conspicuous irregularity in the series of 'authors' mentioned. Those enjoying the honour of having their conjectures mentioned in NESTLE-ALAND are with one exception editors, critics or commentators of the New Testament. Only one of the names which one encounters in NESTLE is not that of a scholar, but of a printer and publisher: ELZEVIER. This name occurs in the apparatus on Matthew viii 18, John ix 21 and Acts xx 30, in all instances without *cj*.

The reason why no editor's name has been added to the readings concerned, but instead that of a printing and publishing-house, is obvious. The person whom the printers entrusted with the superintendence of their editions of the Greek Testament, is wholly unknown. To put it in the words of Eberhard NESTLE: "Welche Gelehrten sie (die Buchhändler Elzevir) an der Hand hatten — wenn man hier überhaupt noch von Gelehrten reden darf — ist unbekannt".[2]

As the Elzevier text as printed in 1624 and 1633 became the generally received text for centuries (it was in the preface to the

---

* I am grateful to Professor J. SMIT SIBINGA of Amsterdam who read the typescript of this article and helped me with several pertinent comments and suggestions. Hoelzlin's signature has been reproduced after the original at Oxford, Bodleian Library, MS. Rawl. Lett., 84E f. 83r. (Hoelzlin to G. J. Vossius, 25 July 1630), by kind permission of the Bodleian Library, Oxford. See p. 126.

[1] *Novum Testamentum Graece* cum apparatu critico curavit Eberhard NESTLE, novis curis elaboraverunt Erwin NESTLE et Kurt ALAND, Stuttgart 1963[25], 67*.

[2] Eb. NESTLE, *Einführung in das Griechische Neue Testament*, Göttingen 1909[3], 14.

second edition that it was styled the *textus nunc ab omnibus receptus*: hence the designation Textus Receptus), many authors since the seventeenth century have paid attention to the problem of the editorship of these editions. In 1971 I was fortunate in finding documentary proof of Daniel HEINSIUS' responsibility for the preface to the 1633 edition, reprinted in that of 1641. Starting from this new evidence I argued that Heinsius was also highly likely to have been the editor of the 1633 text, seeing *inter alia* that he also wrote a panegyric on the New Testament to be printed among the preliminaries to Elzevier 1633 and was engaged in a commentary on the New Testament at the time.[3] The evidence adduced in support of the supposition of Heinsius' editorship, though not conclusive, was persuasive enough to cause Professor KÜMMEL to state that the preface as well as the text of the Elzevier edition of 1633 had been proved to be due to Heinsius.[4]

Plausible as the assumption that Heinsius was the editor of Elzevier 1633 was, it was not corroborated by a comparison of the Elzevier text with the Greek manuscript of the Gospels which Heinsius possessed and occasionally consulted, now MS. Vatic. Reg. gr. 79 = minuscule *155*. This codex which Heinsius considered, or at least praised as "antiquissimus", turned out to have played no part in establishing the text of the Elzevier Greek Testament of 1633.[5] This means that either Heinsius did not esteem it worth while to examine an old manuscript in editing the Elzevier text, or that he did not officiate as its editor at all. It is the purpose of the present contribution to show that the latter is the case.

The hitherto unnoticed testimony of Cloppenburg

In the years 1631 to 1635 a very lively correspondence took place between a minister of the Reformed Church at The Brill (Den Briel, situated at the mouth of the river Maas) of the name of Johannes CLOPPENBURG, and one of Leiden's outstanding biblical scholars of the day, Louis DE DIEU, likewise a reformed minister.[6] In their

---

[3] H. J. DE JONGE, *Daniel Heinsius and the Textus Receptus of the New Testament*, Leiden 1971. For a review see *WThJ* 35 (1973), 356-357 (L. P. DILG).

[4] W. G. KÜMMEL, *Einleitung in das Neue Testament* (17. Auflage der Einleitung in das N.T. von P. FEINE und J. BEHM), Heidelberg 1973, 480.

[5] "The 'Manuscriptus Evangeliorum Antiquissimus' of Daniel Heinsius (Vatic. Reg. gr. 79)", *NTS* 21 (1974-5), 286-294.

[6] On Cloppenburg, see A. J. VAN DER AA, *Biographisch Woordenboek der Neder-landen...*, Nieuwe Uitg. 3 (Haarlem 1858), 483-487; J. P. DE BIE and J. LOOSJES (ed.),

letters the two men discussed sundry exegetical questions, most of
them concerning the New Testament. Excerpts from their letters were
published under the title "Biblical Delights from The Brill: J. Cloppenburg's conversations on topics of sacred criticism carried on by
letter with Louis de Dieu", *Deliciae Biblicae Brielenses: Joh. Clop-
penburgi Collationes Criticae Sacrae per Epistolas cum Ludovico de
Dieu*.[7] The opuscule was deemed important enough to be incorporated
in the *Critici Sacri*, that 17th-century Pantheon of exegetes.[8]

In a letter of 1 October 1632 CLOPPENBURG drew De Dieu's attention
to a grammatical difficulty in Matthew xxiv 15 ὅταν οὖν ἴδητε τὸ
βδέλυγμα τῆς ἐρημώσεως... ἑστὼς ἐν τόπῳ ἁγίῳ and Mark xiii 14
ὅταν δὲ ἴδητε τὸ βδέλυγμα τῆς ἐρημώσεως... ἑστὼς ὅπου οὐ δεῖ
(Textus Receptus). Cloppenburg pointed out that a number of editions,
among them that of Elzevier, i.e. the first Elzevier edition of 1624,
rightly read ἑστὼς, in conformity with the rule of ancient grammarians
who taught that the perfect participle of ἵστημι was ἑστώς in masculine
as well as in neuter.[9] The point was, however, that other editions

Biographisch Woordenboek van Protestantsche Godgeleerden in Nederland II, 's-Gravenhage 1920, 106-122; Chr. SEPP, *Het Godgeleerd Onderwijs in Nederland gedurende de
16ᵉ en 17ᵉ eeuw* II, Leiden 1874, see Index. On Louis de Dieu, see G. H. M. POSTHUMUS
MEYJES, *Geschiedenis van het Waalse College te Leiden*, Leiden 1975, 78-97, and
the chapter "The Study of the New Testament", in: Th. H. LUNSINGH SCHEURLEER
(and others, edd.), *Leiden University in the Seventeenth Century. An Exchange of Learning*,
Leiden 1975, 64-109, esp. 72-74.

[7] An edition "Bremae 1632" is referred to in DE BIE and LOOSJES (cf. n. 6),
but as the *Deliciae* contains fragments of letters dated in 1633, 1634 and 1635 one
may doubt whether such an edition has existed. Neither in any Dutch public library,
nor in the British Museum, nor in the Bibliothèque nationale at Paris, is a copy of
an edition printed in 1632 to be found. The earliest edition known to me is that in
CLOPPENBURG's *Opuscula tria ab ultima autoris opera*: nempe Enarratio in LIII. Cap.
Esajae. Disputationes duae, I. De Deitate Filii Dei, II. De Christo Servatore. Delitiae
Biblicae Brielenses ..., Franeker 1652 (I used a copy in the Royal Library at The Hague).
The *Deliciae* was reprinted in CLOPPENBURG's *Theologica Opera Omnia* I, Franeker
1684, 306-354.

[8] London 1660, IX, 3968-4004; reprints of the *Critici Sacri* appeared at Frankfurt
in 1695, and at Amsterdam in 1698. In the Amsterdam edition the *Deliciae* is in
vol. VIII, 1427-1460.

[9] CLOPPENBURG's latter observation is strikingly pertinent. His fellow ministers of
today may wish to be reminded that the grammarians Herodian (2nd century A.D.)
and Choeroboscus (4th-5th century A.D.) indeed preferred the form ἑστώς for the
neuter to the form ἑστός. Cf. R. KÜHNER - F. BLASS, *Ausführliche Grammatik der
griechischen Sprache* I, 2, Hannover 1892, 236: "Das Neutrum müsste aus ἑστα-ός
kontrahiert ἑστώς lauten, und diese Form haben auch oft die Hdschr., aber in der
Regel bieten die besten Hdschr. die Form ἑστός, so ἑστός Plat. Parm [etc. ...].
Diese Form muss zur Unterscheidung von der Maskulinform gebildet sein, indem
sie sich der Analogie von λελυκός angeschlossen hat. [...] Herodian indes (Lentz I, 351)

read ἑστός. Hence Cloppenburg's question to De Dieu whether the reading ἑστός had to be considered as a mistake. At the same time he suggested that De Dieu should bring the question to the notice of Jeremias HOELZLIN, until recently Cloppenburg's fellow-townsman as Rector of the Latin School at The Brill but now Professor of Greek at Leiden, so that he could clear up the problem in the Greek grammar he was preparing, and could choose with discernment the most preferable reading when correcting the new edition at which he was labouring at the Elzevier press, as Cloppenburg had learned from the sometime Leiden Professor of Divinity Andreas Rivetus.

The cardinal part of CLOPPENBURG's letter runs in his own words as follows:

"Poteris super hoc [the fact that some editions read ἑστός, others ἑστώς] monere D. Holtzlinum; ut hoc enucleet in Graeca quam parat Grammatica, si ante non observavit; & eligat cum judicio quod potius videbitur in correctione novae editionis, in qua ipsum ad praelum Elzevirianum laborare indicavit D. Rivetus".

On 18 October 1632 DE DIEU replied that he had passed on Cloppenburg's observations on ἑστός and ἑστώς to Hoelzlin and that the latter would take them into account, at least — as De Dieu added — in his grammar. The restriction did not mean that Hoelzlin was unwilling to consider Cloppenburg's observations in establishing the text of Elzevier 1633, but either that the sheets of Matthew and Mark had already passed through the press when he received Cloppenburg's suggestion, or that he simply agreed with Cloppenburg that the readings ἑστώς as given in Elzevier 1624 had to be preferred to ἑστός and that, as a result, he did not have to introduce changes into the text of the places referred to by Cloppenburg.

DE DIEU's own words are:

"Quod de ἑστός pro ἑστώς Matth. xxiv 15. Marc. xiii 14. diligentia tua observasti, mihique arridet, communicavi cum D. Holtzlino; qui gratias tibi eo nomine mecum agit, ejusque rationem, saltem in sua Grammatica habiturum promisit".

From the passage quoted from Cloppenburg's letter it becomes clear that the editor employed by the Elzeviers to prepare their second edition of the Greek Testament for the press, was none other than the Leiden Professor of Greek, Jeremias HOELZLIN.

---

scheint auch im Neutrum nur ἑστώς, βεβώς u.s.w. zu kennen". LIDDELL-SCOTT[9], s.v. ἵστημι: "neut. ἑστός [...], -ώς freq. v.l. [...], preferred by Choerob. in Theod. 2.313".

Obviously Hoelzlin's task did not consist merely in correcting the printing errors, which the first Elzevier edition of 1624 contained in spite of Hugo GROTIUS' testimonial to the contrary.[10] Hoelzlin was also free to evaluate variant readings — though presumably only such as figured in printed editions of the 16th century — and to choose the readings which seemed most acceptable to him. This at least is the presupposition of Cloppenburg's words "eligat cum judicio quod potius videbitur". Furthermore it is apparent from the present tense of the infinitive "laborare", that Cloppenburg, at the moment of writing, assumed Hoelzlin to be at work on the revision of the Elzevier text.

As to the source to which Cloppenburg owed his information about the editor of Elzevier 1633, his words "indicavit Rivetus" presumably mean that Rivet had informed him by letter. Several letters exchanged between Rivet and Cloppenburg have been preserved,[11] but the letter in which Rivet mentioned Hoelzlin's editorial responsibility for the Elzevier edition of 1633 is not to be found.[12]

Jeremias Hoelzlin (1583-1641)

Jeremias Hoelzlin, Professor of Greek at Leiden from 1632 to 1641, is not among this University's most celebrated professors of the 17th century, his fame being eclipsed by that of his contemporaries and colleagues Daniel Heinsius, Salmasius, Golius and De Dieu. A brief biographical note may therefore be thought not out of place.[13]

---

[10] GROTIUS averred that the Elzevier edition of 1624 had been printed so carefully, "ut ne quidem in minimo accentu peccatum sit". He regarded this edition as being free from all printing errors: "omnibus plane mendis typographicis carere". See "The Study of the New Testament" (cf. n. 6), 93.

[11] See P. DIBON, E. ESTOURGIE and H. BOTS, Inventaire de la correspondance d'André Rivet (1595-1650) (AIHI 43), The Hague 1971.

[12] Dr. J. A. H. BOTS of Nijmegen kindly informs me that the letter in question does not occur among Rivetus' letters located after the completion of the Inventaire of 1971 (see n. 11). Neither is the letter to be found in the Public Record Office (Rijksarchief) at Arnhem where the archives of Harderwijk University are kept, or in the Provincial Library at Leeuwarden which manages the inheritance of Franeker University. Cloppenburg was appointed Professor of Divinity in Harderwijk in 1641 and in Franeker in 1644.

[13] See also C. G. JÖCHER, Allgemeines Gelehrten-Lexicon II, Leipzig 1750, 1642; G. A. WILL, Nürnbergisches Gelehrten-Lexicon II, Nürnberg and Altdorf 1756, 150-153; VAN DER AA, op. cit. (n. 6), VIII, 863-864; P. C. MOLHUYSEN, Bronnen tot de Geschiedenis der Leidsche Universiteit II, 's-Gravenhage 1916, Index. Three letters from Hoelzlin to Vossius have been published in P. COLOMESIUS (ed.), Gerardi Joannis Vossii et clarorum virorum ad eum epistolae, London 1690. These three letters plus two others to

Hoelzlin was born in Nuremberg in 1583. He received a classical education at Augsburg and matriculated in 1600 at the University of Altdorf near Nuremberg. Here he specialized in Greek philosophy and proceeded to the degree of Master of Philosophy in 1609.[14] He had already held for some time the place of "Ephorus" or "Inspector alumnorum Reipublicae Noribergensis in Academia Altorfina". In 1611 he was appointed Rector of St. Martin's School at Amberg in the Upper Palatinate (North Bavaria), later Conrector of the Electoral Gymnasium or Paedagogeum in the same town. When the danger of war became more serious, he departed for Bremen. For some time he was Rector of the Gymnasium at Hamm in Westphalia, but in 1630 he decided to take refuge in the Netherlands. Gerard Vossius, the then Professor of History, Eloquence and Greek at Leiden, had given him hopes of a career in more tranquil and favourable circumstances than were to be had in Germany, ruined as it was by the religious wars. In August 1630 Hoelzlin and his wife (they had no children) arrived in Leiden, and the 16th of that month he was enrolled in the University.[15] At the same time, if not earlier, they went over to the Reformed Church.

From August 1630 to April 1631 Hoelzlin lived as a private citizen at Leiden. He published a Latin translation of the Psalms in hexameters, which he dedicated to the Curators of the University, and to which Heinsius, among others, contributed a laudatory poem.[16]

Vossius are now among the Rawlinson Letters in the Bodleian Library, vol. 84 E. A letter from Vossius to Hoelzlin is preserved in the same collection, vol. 82; Vossius' draft of a letter from the Leiden Senate to the Magistrate of The Brill to recommend Hoelzlin for the Rectorship of the Latin School of that town, is in vol. 84 A. I am most grateful to Dr. C. S. M. RADEMAKER of Amsterdam, who was kind enough to permit me to consult copies of these and other documents concerning Hoelzlin in the Institute of Neophilology and Neo-Latin in the University of Amsterdam.

[14] The congratulatory poems which he received on this occasion were published in a volume entitled *Congratulatio Clarissimorum Virorum, nec non Amicorum, facta Jeremiae Hoelzlin Noribergensi, cum illi Magisterii Philosophici honos tribueretur in Academia Altorphina, prid. KL. Iulii Anno MDCIX*, Altorf 1609, a copy of which I consulted in the Library of Amsterdam University.

[15] W. N. DU RIEU, *Album Studiosorum Academiae Lugduno Batavae MDLXXV-MDCCCLXXV*, 's-Gravenhage 1875, 229, *sub* 16 August 1630. J. J. WOLTJER in his article "Foreign Professors" in: Th. H. LUNSINGH SCHEURLEER (and others edd.), *Leiden University ... An Exchange ...*, 465, wrongly mentions Hoelzlin's activities at Middelburg and The Brill in 1631 as his "first Dutch reference", instead of his enrolment at Leiden in 1630.

[16] *Davidis Regis et Prophetae Psalmorum Paraphrasis epica nova*, Leiden 1630. The Bibliotheca Thysiana at Leiden preserves a copy with Hoelzlin's autograph presentation inscription addressed to Antonius Thysius, merchant at Amsterdam.

In April 1631 Hoelzlin moved to Middelburg, where he had been appointed teacher at the Latin School,[17] but within three months he took his leave, this time for The Brill, where in August 1631 he became Rector of the Latin School, at the recommendation of Vossius and the Leiden Senate. In November followed his appointment to the professoriate of Greek at Leiden, which had fallen vacant by Vossius' acceptance of a chair of History at Amsterdam. In the spring of 1632 Hoelzlin returned to Leiden.

After the summer-holidays, in September 1632, Hoelzlin took up his office by delivering an inaugural address entitled *De Graecae linguae praestantia*[18] (see Appendix II). He chose Pindar's Odes as the subject of his lectures, and (as we learned from Cloppenburg) contemplated writing a Greek grammar. This grammar came to nothing; probably Hoelzlin soon gave up his plan, for not later than spring 1633 he was engaged in a project to which he devoted the rest of his life: the edition, translation and annotation of Apollonius of Rhodes. Seven years later, a week before his death, he completed the manuscript, assisted by his relative Georg A. Richter, who also took on the burden of indexing the book and preparing it for publication and seeing it through the press.[19] Hoelzlin himself died, 46 or 47 years old, on 25 January 1641, Louis de Dieu by his side. He was buried in St. Pancras' Church. The funeral oration was delivered by Antonius Thysius Jr, Extraordinary Professor of Poetry and Public Law.[20]

The Chair of Greek and the teaching of New Testament Greek at Leiden

It may be observed that, after all, Hoelzlin's editorial responsibility of Elzevier 1633 is not in the least to be wondered at, in view of the relationship that existed between the Chair of Greek and the

---

[17] J. G. VOEGLER, *Geschiedenis van het Middelburgsche Gymnasium*. Tweede-Vierde Tijdvak, 1574-1894, in: *Archief Zeeuwsch Genootschap der Wetenschappen* VII, Middelburg 1894, 389-390.

[18] Published at Leiden in 1632. A copy is in Paris, Bibliothèque nationale.

[19] This edition, published by the Leiden Elzeviers in 1641, caused David Ruhnkenius to speak of Hoelzlin as "hominum, qui sunt, fuerunt, et erunt futilissimus"; G. L. MAHNE (ed.), *Epistolae mutuae duumvirorum clarissimorum, Davidis Ruhnkenii et Lud. Casp. Valckenaerii*, Vlissingae 1832, p. 18. That the edition was not entirely without merit may appear from the critical apparatus to the text edited by R. C. SEATON in 1900, published and repeatedly republished by the Clarendon Press in the Scriptorum Classicorum Bibliotheca Oxoniensis. Cf. RUHNKE, *Ep. cr. II in Callim.*, 1751, 68.

[20] Antonii THYSII Ic. *Oratio Funebris, in Obitum Clarissimi Doctissimique Viri, Ieremiae Hoeslini* (sic), *Graecae linguae in Batavorum Academia Professoris dignissimi*, Leiden 1641. A copy is in Leeuwarden, Provincial Library.

teaching of New Testament Greek in Leiden University during the 17th, 18th, and 19th centuries. From 1625 theological students who wished to be admitted to the ministry in the province of South Holland had to sit an examination in which among other things they were obliged to submit a testimonial from the Professor of Greek to the effect that they had acquired an adequate knowledge of that language to be able to read the original text of the Greek Testament.[21] From about 1625 to 1815 it was, consequently, one of the tasks of the Leiden Professor of Greek, to teach New Testament Greek for undergraduates of the Faculty of Divinity. Lecture notes on the New Testament by several Leiden hellenists, among them Jacob Gronovius, Petrus Burmannus, Tiberius Hemsterhuis, David Ruhn-kenius, Lodewijk C. Valckenaer,[22] Joan Luzac, and Daniel Wytten-bach, have been preserved.[23]

From 1815 the student who wished to become a theologian, had to be Bachelor of Arts and was obliged, as far as Greek was concerned, to attend lectures of the Professor of Greek, not in New Testament Greek, but in classical Greek. The famous Cobet (1846-1884) taught prospective theologians Greek and did so in lectures on Homer's Iliad![24]

In the 17th century, however, students of theology were only obliged to submit a testimonial from the Professor of Greek as to their

---

[21] Cf. "The Study of the New Testament" (see n. 6), 67-8, and C. Sepp, *Proeve eener Pragmatische Geschiedenis der Theologie in Nederland, 1787-1858*, Amsterdam 1860[2], 82: "Weleer [from 1625 to 1815] gaf de professor, die de Grieksche taal onderwees, collegie over de kritiek en exegese des N.T.; Wyttenbach deed het, knorrende over het onzuiver dialect des N.T., anderen op minder knorrigen toon, toch altijd bloot als eene literarische taak, of (...) zoo wat dogmatiserende; één enkele slechts kennen wij uit dit tijdvak, wiens werk in eere verdient te blijven. Ik bedoel Lodewijk Caspar Valckenaer (etc.)".

[22] This is the Valckenaer mentioned in NESTLE-ALAND *ad* Luke xix 38, and in n. 21 above.

[23] In a considerable number of note-books preserved in Leiden University Library.

[24] "Tijdens de Propaedeutische Examens las Z.H.G. met de literatoren en theologen het begin van de Ilias", thus the *Almanak van het Leidsche Studentencorps voor 1876*, 225, in an account of Cobet's lectures. A similar account of Cobet's "collegie over de Grieksche taal... voor litteratoren en Theologanten" appeared in the *Leidsche Studenten-Almanak voor 1860*, 175. SEPP, too, pointed out that Cobet "in onze dagen ... door propaedeutische studien den aanstaanden theoloog grammatiesch-kritiesch vormt" (*Proeve*, see n. 21, 1860[2], 98; 1867[3], 208). See also H. Oort, "Herinneringen van een theologant van voor zeventig jaar", in: *Pallas Leidensis*, Leiden 1925, 70. Like his predecessor Hoelzlin (si magna licet componere parvis), COBET prepared an edition of the Greek Testament, in collaboration with A. KUENEN: Ἡ καινὴ διαθήκη. *Novum Testamentum ad fidem Codicis Vaticani*, Leiden (Brill) 1860. For one of Cobet's conjectures see Nestle-Aland, *ad* Hebr. xi 4.

proficiency in New Testament Greek and as a result this subject formed part of this professor's teaching responsibility. When in 1632 the professoriate in Greek was entrusted to Hoelzlin, he was no doubt bound to give inter alia lectures in which the Greek New Testament was read cursorily and its text grammatically expounded. Now the Elzeviers did not possess the required scholarship to undertake the editing of a Greek text. Accordingly, it stands to reason that when planning a new edition of their Greek Testament, as University Printers they appealed to Professor Hoelzlin who was already involved in reading New Testament Greek to students and for whose lectures the new, inexpensive pocket-edition would become the obvious textbook.[25]

Hoelzlin's share in Elzevier 1633

We must now answer the question to what extent the editorial hand of Hoelzlin extended to the text as published by the Elzeviers in 1633. Fortunately, the material on which this answer has to be based has been made available in an admirable way by H. C. HOSKIER in his full collation of Elzevier 1624 with Elzevier 1633.[26] It should only be borne in mind that while both editions were passing through the press alterations were made in each after certain copies had been struck off.[27] As a result, HOSKIER signalized at least ten variants and alterations in places where my copies do not differ.

Typographical errors

In the first place then it is clear that the text which Hoelzlin handed in at the Elzevier Press was — as was to be expected — a revised copy of the edition of 1624. This appears from the fact that a number of misprints peculiar to the edition of 1624 were retained in that of 1633. In Rom. vii 2, for instance, both editions read ἐὰν δὲ ἀποθάνῃ ὁ ἀνήρ, κατήργηται ἀπὸ τοῦ ἄνδρος instead of ... κατήργηται ἀπὸ τοῦ νόμου τοῦ ἄνδρος. In Rom. xiii 5 both read διὸ ἀνάγκη προτάσσεσθαι instead of ... ὑποτάσσεσθαι, and in Luke xvii 19 both have σέκωκέ for σέσωκέ.

---

[25] On the character of the Elzevier Greek Testaments as editions "in usum tironum", see "The Study of the New Testament", 90.

[26] A Full Account and Collation of the Greek Cursive Cod. Ev. 604, London 1890, 'Appendix C'.

[27] See H. C. HOSKIER, "The Elzevir New Testaments of 1624 and 1633", JTS 12 (1911), 454-456, in reply to Eb. NESTLE, "Some Points in the History of the Textus Receptus of the New Testament", JTS 11 (1910), 564-568.

But this much credit at least must go to Hoelzlin, that some of the worst misprints of 1624 were amended in 1633. Thus the reading ἐπιλαβομένου in Hebr. viii 9 was corrected to ἐπιλαβομένου μου. It testifies to the care with which the text was revised that Κυρίῳ in Acts xxv 26, wrongly spelled with a capital in 1624, was changed into κυρίῳ in 1633, and that the misprint ἀποφανισθέντες of 1624 was corrected to ἀπορφανισθέντες (1 Thess. ii 17). Excluding all matters of breathing, iota subscript, accent, *nu paragogicum* and punctuation, at least 14 typographical errors of Elzevier 1624 were corrected in 1633.[28] On the other hand, if the same restriction is made, at least 25 new typographical errors crept into the text of 1633.[29] Whether these new misprints are to be attributed to Hoelzlin can not be established as long as we do not know whether the proofs were read by a reader of the press or by Hoelzlin himself. Cloppenburg's account of Hoelzlin's work "ad praelum Elzevirianum" suggests that Hoelzlin was indeed charged with the correction of proofs.

Breathings

HOSKIER's evaluation of the divergences between Elzevier 1624 and 1633 is indeed not in the least as trustworthy as his collation of these editions. This appears, for example, from an examination of his analysis of the differences between 1624 and 1633 in the matter of rough and soft breathings. According to Hoskier, the 1633 edition changes a breathing for the worse in 30 cases by comparison with 1624. Upon closer inspection 10 of these 30 cases prove to be changes of the soft breathing of αὐτοῦ, αὐτῷ etc. into the rough breathing of αὑτοῦ, αὑτῷ etc. in sentences in which the pronoun refers to the subject. A simple illustration can be found in 2 Peter iii 15: Παῦλος κατὰ τὴν αυτῷ δοθεῖσαν σοφίαν ἔγραψεν.... In this sentence 1624 has αὐτῷ, 1633 reads αὑτῷ, in Hoskier's view a change for the worse. He does not seem to have perceived that, in dealing with the breathing of αυτ-, 17th-century editors had other conventions

---

[28] HOSKIER listed 21 typographical errors peculiar to the edition of 1624, but 8 of these can be left out of consideration. In fact in 6 instances registered by Hoskier as misprints, my copy of 1624 has no error whatsoever (2 Cor. ix 1; Phil. iii 21; 1 Peter iii 19; Acts ii 31; Rev. iv 10; ix 7). In one case the reading of 1624 is not so much a misprint, but rather an intentional change introduced by the unknown editor of 1624 (Rom. xi 31 ἡμετέρῳ for ὑμ-). In another case the misprint of 1624 concerns only the catch-syllable.

[29] HOSKIER (p. 24) listed 36 new misprints in 1633, but for various reasons 11 instances must be struck off his list, most of them because they are not misprints but intentional alterations of the text attributable to an editorial hand.

than those of the 19th century, as they had also with regard to accentuation, e.g. in the use of the grave accent on the ultimate syllable before punctuation marks. It should have been a warning to him that in counting the errors common to both editions, he had found no less than 644 instances in which the rough breathing of αυτ- occurs 'incorrectly' for the soft, whereas he never noticed in either edition a soft breathing for a rough one. This result should have made him suspicious as to the criteria according to which he judged the use of breathings.

The truth is that wherever the pronoun αυτοῦ etc. refers to the subject of the sentence (corresponding to *suum* etc., *sui, sibi,* or *se* in Latin) 16th and 17th-century editors felt free to use the form αὐτοῦ etc. with rough breathing. Thus also in Matth. xxiii 37, Ἰερουσαλὴμ, Ἰερουσαλὴμ, ἡ ἀποκτείνουσα τοὺς προφήτας, καὶ λιθοβολοῦσα τοὺς ἀπεσταλμένους πρὸς αυτήν, where recent editors like GRIESBACH, COBET, TISCHENDORF, WESTCOTT and HORT, BALJON, VON SODEN, NESTLE-ALAND and the editors of *The Greek New Testament* read αὐτήν, whereas earlier editors like ERASMUS, ROBERT STEPHEN, BEZA, and the editors employed by the Elzeviers, among them HOELZLIN, preferred to read αὑτήν. The latter reading was also approved by Georg PASOR, the author of the first grammar of New Testament Greek ever written (Groningen 1655).[30] As late as the 18th century, Christian STOCKIUS of Jena, who also wrote a grammar of the Greek New Testament, consistently used the aspirated forms in quoting passages like Ἔβλεψεν τὴν ταπείνωσιν τῆς δούλης αὑτοῦ (Luke i 48), Κατὰ τὸν αὑτοῦ ἔλεον ἔσωσεν ἡμᾶς (Tit. iii 5), Ἦν δὲ Ἰωάννης ἐνδεδυμένος ... ζώνην δερματίνην περὶ τὴν ὀσφὺν αὑτοῦ (Mark i 6).[31] In such cases αυτοῦ was obviously taken to be the contracted form of the reflexive pronoun as it was known from Attic tragedy and oratory.

Only in the 19th century was the form αὑτοῦ etc. banished from the New Testament. The learned Friedrich BLEEK went so far as to aver that the authors of the New Testament writings had not

---

[30] On G. PASOR, Professor of Greek at Franeker University from 1626 to his death in 1637, see Gerhard DELLING, in *NT* 18 (1976), 213-240. His *Grammatica graeca sacra Novi Testamenti* was edited only eighteen years after his death, in Groningen 1655, by his son Matthias PASOR, Professor of Theology at Groningen University. That Pasor accepted the reading αὑτήν in Matth. xxiii 37 appears from his *Manuale Graecarum Vocum Novi Testamenti* (cf. n. 35), *s.v.* Ἑαυτοῦ, "Matth. xxiii 37. πρὸς αὑτὴν *ad te*".

[31] Chr. STOCKIUS, *Interpres Graecus Novi Testamenti*, Jena 1726³, 31, 32, 349.

known the reflexive pronoun in its contracted form at all.[32] HORT, in his 'Notes on Orthography' added to his and WESTCOTT's edition (in which the aspirated form has been introduced only twenty odd times), showed that there are good reasons not to reject αὐτοῦ etc. completely, but to use it very sparingly.[33] 17th-century editors, however, were not yet aware of these reasons. Consequently, HOSKIER was wrong in condemning the use of αὐτοῦ etc. in cases in which it refers to the subject of the sentence, as well as in denoting alterations from αὐτοῦ into αὑτοῦ in such cases as "changes for the worse". Of the 30 cases in which, according to Hoskier, the breathing was changed for the worse in 1633, 10 reflect rather editorial attempts at improvement of the text.

At two places Hoskier's copies of 1624 and 1633 left him in doubt as to whether the breathings had been changed there; the answer must be in the negative. Thus there remain 18 cases in which a breathing as printed in 1624 was changed for the worse in 1633; in all these cases the change is owing to a misprint.

On the other hand, Hoskier counted 23 cases in which the breathing was changed for the better. For 18 cases this turns out to be correct, either in the sense that a misprint of 1624 was corrected, or that a breathing was changed on purpose, though not in all cases according to clear principles. Added to the 10 intentional changes mentioned above, they make 28 cases in which, by contemporary standards, the editor of 1633 corrected the Elzevier text. As the number of new misprints in the matter of breathings amounted to 18, the useful effect of the editor's labours was as many as 10 corrections.

iota subscript

As regards the iota subscript, the editor of 1633 corrected 9 plain mistakes occurring in the 1624 edition. In 6 other cases the change was a correction only by the grammatical standards of the time (e.g. 1 Peter iii 4: πραέος 1624, πρᾳέος 1633) or was intended as a correction though either grammarians of Hoelzlin's time, or modern critics could have accepted the reading of 1624 (e.g. Acts viii 33: ἤρθη 1624, *approbante Pasore*, ἤρθη 1633. James v 15: κἂν 1624,

---

[32] F. BLEEK, *Der Brief an die Hebräer*, 2. Abt., Berlin 1836, 66-69.

[33] B. F. WESTCOTT, F. J. A. HORT, *The New Testament in the Original Greek*, II, Cambridge and London 1882, Appendix, 144-145. On the whole matter see G. B. WINER, *Grammatik des Ntl. Sprachidioms*, Leipzig 1855, § 22. 5; J. H. MOULTON, *Einleitung in die Sprache des N.T.*, Deutsche Ausgabe, Heidelberg 1911, 139-140; A. T. ROBERTSON, *A Grammar of the Greek New Testament*, Nashville, 4th ed., preface dated 1923, 226, 287.

approbantibus recentioribus, κἀν 1633 *approbante Pasore*). Curiously enough, Hoskier stated that he could not regard the change of ᾮ (dative of the relative pronoun) into ᾯ as an amelioration. But it is difficult to see what the addition of the iota in such a case is, if it is not an amelioration, and in any case it is an attempt at an amelioration. The editor of 1633 introduced this change 7 times. In sum the second Elzevier edition corrected the iota subscript in 22 places. As a result of misprints it changed in 6 places for the worse. Consequently, the editor of 1633 can claim an advancement of 16 corrections.

Accentuation

Although Grotius is reported to have contended that Elzevier 1624 had been printed with such care "ut ne quidem in minimo accentu peccatum sit",[34] the editor of 1633 found 34 places in which the accentuation had to be corrected.[35]

Now in 10 out of these 34 places the accent of 1624 cannot be regarded as wrong without comment. As every student of the New Testament knows, one of the rules for the use of enclitics is that after a paroxytone a monosyllabic enclitic takes no accent. Yet, Elzevier 1624 reads ἔχον τὶ (Luke xi 36), λέγῃ τὶς (James ii 14) and ἵνα τὶς (1 John ii 27). In 1633 these passages were corrected in accordance with the rule just mentioned: ἔχον τι, λέγῃ τις, ἵνα τις. This does not mean, however, that the editor of 1624 erred in these places. In a discussion of the rule in question in his ever useful *Libellus de Graecis Novi Testamenti accentibus*[36] (§ 122), Georg Pasor pointed out: "Quidam hîc τὶς τὶ excipiunt". So the accentuation of τὶ and τὶς in the places under consideration is certainly not an indication that the editor of 1624 was not proficient in the writing of Greek accents. The same is true, for instance, for a change like ἑστᾶναι (Acts xii 14) into ἑστάναι; the former reading was approved by Pasor as the perfect infinitive of ἵστημι, whereas he described the latter form (as occurring in I Cor. x 12) as the present infinitive

---

[34] Cf. n. 10.

[35] Hoskier, *o.c.*, 21, listed 35 such cases, but I exclude 1 Cor. i 18, where the change of ἐστι, at the end of the verse, into ἐστί is not a correction but a deterioration.

[36] The *Libellus* is an appendix to Pasor's *Manuale graecarum vocum Novi Testamenti*, Herborn [1]1624, reprinted, inter alia, at Leiden (Elzevier) 1640, and at Amsterdam (Janssonius) 1656; the *Libellus* also occurs in the *Grammatica* (1655), 696 ff.

of ἕστημι = ἵστημι.[37] Similarly, the 1624 edition has the acute accent on μού in Rom. i 9 Μάρτυς γάρ μού ἐστιν ὁ Θεός, according to the rule that when two or more enclitics follow one another, all of them take an acute accent except the last one which takes no accent; but the 1633 edition reads μου ἐστιν, according to the exceptive clause which Pasor added to his treatment of the rule just mentioned: "(§ 128) Excipe μοῦ, σοῦ, οὔ, μοὶ, etc.". Although this change, too, is clearly meant as a correction, one cannot regard the reading μού ἐστιν of 1624 as faulty: Nestle-Aland, for instance, follows 1624 against 1633 in this place.

Nevertheless the editor of 1633 has tried to correct the accentuation of 1624 at 34 places.[38] In 10 cases the accentuation of 1633 is definitely worse than in 1624,[39] a positive result of 24 corrections.

Nu paragogicum

The 1633 edition adds the wanting *nu* in 2 cases, but omits it once where it is necessary, which leaves 1633 one to the good on this count.[40]

Punctuation

Hoskier recorded 233 places in which the 1624 edition varies from that of 1633 in punctuation. In 6 of these[41] my copy of 1624 proves not to differ from that of 1633. I found two cases not listed by Hoskier: Luke xiii 4, where 1624 has a comma after ὀκτώ which was omitted in 1633, and Acts xx 29, where 1624 equally has a comma, after ὑμᾶς, which was not taken over in 1633.

In my opinion, 96 of the 229 alterations which were introduced in the text of 1633 in the matter of punctuation and could be verified in my copies, are changes for the worse. In 115 instances, however, the change is an amelioration, or at least it is clearly recognizable as an attempt at correction, the effect of which is

---

[37] *Manuale*, s.v. ἵστημι. *Lexicon*, Herborn [4]1632, 370. *Grammatica*, 189.

[38] Hoskier, *o.c.*, 21, counted 35 corrections of accents, but the alteration of ἐστί into ἐστί in 1 Cor. i 18 is not a correction but definitely a deterioration.

[39] Hoskier, *o.c.*, 21, registered 12 changes for the worse. By the criteria of the time, however, παντὸς in Acts x 2 cannot be regarded as worse than παντός. Nor can I agree with Hoskier that διὰ τί in Rev. xvii 7 is worse than διατί. Further, in Rev. vii 2 my copy of 1633 does not differ from that of 1624. To the remaining 9 cases one should add the change in 1 Cor. i 18, which Hoskier wrongly classed among the ameliorations, cf. n. 35.

[40] Thus Hoskier 21, to whose statement I have nothing to add.

[41] In Rom. i 14; iii 1; v 18; vii 9; viii 28 my copy of 1624 reads exactly what Hoskier's copy of 1633 has. In Rev. xiii 4 my copy of 1633 reads what Hoskier noted from his copy of 1624.

justifiable. The remaining 18 cases cannot be classed under either of these categories.

The final result is meagre, but there is a slight advancement of 19 corrections, and in any case I cannot possibly agree with HOSKIER that as far as punctuation is concerned, 1633 is less correct than 1624 three times over.[42]

Result

From the preceding analysis it may be seen that the 1633 edition is certainly not less correctly printed as a whole than the previous edition. Two things should be taken into account. First, that in several respects the editor of 1633 followed principles different from, but not worse than those of his predecessor. Second, that often a change of 1633 which was obviously meant as an improvement resulted in a reading, notation, or punctuation for which there is certainly a good case, although the reading of 1624 is just as acceptable. Such cases, in which 1624 is as good as 1633 but in which the editor of 1633 can be seen to have altered the text with the intention of ameliorating it, — such cases can deservedly be counted as changes for the better. In fact, these changes originated as corrections, and cannot be said to fall short of their claim to present a correct text.

All in all, then, the edition of 1633 proves to improve that of 1624

> 10 times in the matter of breathings;
> 16 times in the matter of iota subscript;
> 24 times in the matter of accents;
> once   in the matter of *nu paragogicum*;
> 19 times in the matter of punctuation.

in sum   70 times.

As 1633 has 11 typographical errors more than 1624, the editorial exertions spent on the second Elzevier edition may be said to have finally resulted in 59 corrections. It is true that there remains a considerable number of errors common to both editions, but for reasons explained above HOSKIER erred in reckoning among these all 644 cases in which the Elzevier text has a rough breathing with αὐτός and its cases, whereas HOSKIER would have preferred a soft breathing. And at any rate, the errors common to the editions of 1624 and 1633 do not alter the fact that on the whole the edition of 1633 is somewhat more correctly printed than that of 1624.

---

[42] P. 23.

This progress in the quality of the Elzevier text is at least partly
owing to the man whom CLOPPENBURG indicated as responsible for
the 'correctio novae editionis': Jeremias HOELZLIN.

Real variant readings of 1633 as compared with 1624

Leaving aside all ordinary typographical errors, insignificant orthographical variants and less important matters of punctuation, one
finds the following 26 real variant readings in which the second
Elzevier edition edited by HOELZLIN varies from the first.

	1624	1633
1. Matthew x 19	λαλήσητε	λαλήσετε
2. Mark iii 10	αὐτῷ	αὐτοῦ
3. Mark iv 18	οὗτοί εἰσιν²	om.
4. Mark viii 24	ὅτι et ὁρῶ	om.
5. Mark ix 30	ἵνα τις	τίς ἵνα
6. Luke xi 33	κρυπτήν	κρυπτόν
7. Luke xii 20	ἄφρων	ἄφρον
8. John iii 6	γεγενημένον (bis)	γεγεννημένον (bis)
9. John iv 8	Οἱ - ἀγοράσωσι	versus totus uncinis in-cluditur
10. John iv 14	γενήσεται	γεννήσεται
11. John iv 21	ὅτι (ante ἔρχεται)	ὅτε
12. John v 2	κολυμβήθρα (nomin.)	καλυμβήθρᾳ (dat.)
13. John xx 15	ἀρῶ (coni. aor., teste Pasore)	ἀρῶ (fut.)
14. Acts v 28	τούτῳ	τούτου
15. Acts xvii 18	τῶν Στωϊκῶν	Στωϊκῶν
16. Acts xxvii 13	ἄσσον (adv.)	Ἄσσον (nomen propr. geogr.)
17. Rom. vi 4	εἰς θάνατον (in quibus-dam tantum exem-plaribus, vide infra; alia ut 1633)	εἰς τὸν θάνατον
18. Rom. xi 31	ἡμετέρῳ	ὑμετέρῳ
19. 1 Cor. ix 2	ἀποστολῆς	ἐπιστολῆς
20. 2 Cor. vi 16	ἐν αὐτοῖς	καὶ αὐτοῖς (vitium ty-pothetae?)
21. Col. i 7	ὑμῶν (post ὑπέρ)	ἡμῶν
22. Col. iv 7	ὑμῖν	ἡμῖν
23. 2 Tim. i 12	παραθήκην	παρακαταθήκην

24. Hebr. ix 12	εὑρόμενος	εὑράμενος (*in quibus-dam exemplaribus, vide infra*)
25. 2 Peter i 1	σωτῆρος ἡμῶν	σωτῆρος
26. Rev. xvi 5	ὅσιος	ἐσόμενος

Several of these variants, e.g. those numbered 1, 7, 8, 10, 12, 13, and 16, would justly be considered as mere orthographical variants without any significance if they were found in manuscripts. In a printed edition, however, the change from λαλήσητε to λαλήσετε in Matthew x 19 may be an indication that the editor definitely preferred a future indicative to an aorist subjunctive. The same applies to the alteration in John xx 15, from ἀρῶ to ἀρῶ. Such changes do not merely concern mood and tense. Indeed, the editor may purposely have replaced a deliberative and a hortatory subjunctive by a simple future. Similarly, in manuscripts γεγενημένον and γεγεν-νημένον, or ἄφρων and ἄφρον are mere orthographical variants rather than real variant readings. But when the editor of a revised edition changes the one reading into the other, he deliberately expresses his preference for a certain verb or for a distinct form of the vocative.

Further it should be noticed that the reading εἰς θάνατον in Rom. vi 4 occurs only in certain copies of the 1624 edition (e.g. that which belonged to HOSKIER), while other copies (including that of Eb. NESTLE,[43] now in the library of Westminster and Cheshunt Colleges, Cambridge, and mine) read εἰς τὸν θάνατον. In Hebr. ix 12 certain copies of the 1633 edition (among them those of SCRIVENER and NESTLE, one of HOSKIER's two copies of 1633, and mine) read εὑράμενος, while other copies of the same edition (including the other of HOSKIER's two copies) read εὑρόμενος. As was stated above, the text of 1633, like that of 1624, was altered while still in the press, so that different issues of the same edition can be distinguished.

The Origin of the Real Variant Readings

An examination of the 26 real variant readings as to their origin, seems to lead to surprisingly clear conclusions.

---

[43] See his article referred to in n. 27. I am grateful to Professor J. C. O'NEILL of Cambridge who kindly informed me by letter of 22 September 1975 that Eb. NESTLE's copies of Elzevier 1624 and 1633, with the readings reported by Nestle in *JTS* 11 (1910), 564-8, are still in the possession of the library of Westminster and Cheshunt Colleges.

15 of the 26 variants (*viz.* 3, 4, 6, 7, 8, 9, 12, 13, 16, 17, 18, 23, 24, 25, and 26) appear to occur in certain, for each of them different combinations of earlier printed editions. In the first appendix to this article these readings have been listed each with its support from previous editions. As the old standard editions like those of ERASMUS, Robert STEPHEN and BEZA, have been reprinted numerous times in unauthorized and pirated editions, it is impossible to establish with certainty from which particular edition the variants which Elzevier 1633 derived from earlier editions were taken. Theoretically the possibility cannot be ruled out that the 15 variants in question derive from 15 different editions. But in this context the most simple hypothesis is perhaps the most preferable. To find all 15 variants, then, the editor of 1633 needed to consult only two earlier editions:

1. Robert STEPHEN's folio edition of 1550;
2. Henry STEPHEN's 16mo edition of Geneva 1587.[44]

As 13 of the 15 variants deriving from the printed text tradition are to be found in the 1587 edition of Henry Stephen, HOELZLIN probably did little more than collate Elzevier 1624 with Stephen 1587, from which he picked now and than a reading which he liked. The value of these variants need not be discussed in detail. They can all be explained in terms of grammatical, stylistic or logical simplification of the text, except perhaps the correction of εὑρόμενος into εὑράμενος in Hebr. ix 12 which may simply have been introduced on account of its occurring in an authoritative edition. — The alteration in the text of Rom. vi 4 dates from 1624 rather than from 1633.

The 11 variants not attested by earlier editions can be divided into two clearly distinguishable categories: those resulting from a mistake on the part of the compositor, and those due to the initiative of the editor.

What makes it easy to ascribe 6 variants (*viz.* 1, 2, 11, 14, 15, and 21) to the inaccuracy of the compositor, is that they reflect,

---

[44] In 3 of the 13 variant readings which Elzevier 1633 has in common with Henry Stephen's second edition (Geneva 1587), Stephen's first edition (*ib.*, 1576) agrees with Elzevier 1624 against Elzevier 1633, viz. in Mark viii 24, 2 Peter i 1 and Rev. xvi 5 (cf. Appendix I). The edition with which Hoelzlin collated Elzevier 1624 was, therefore, Stephen 1587[2] rather than Stephen 1576[1]. Probably Henry Stephen's readings adopted in Elzevier 1633 do not derive either from the reprint of Stephen 1587[2] which appeared at London in the same year, as this reprint reads ὅτι ὡς δένδρα in Mark viii 24, whereas the reading ὅτι ὡς δένδρα ὁρῶ of Elzevier 1624 was changed into ὡς δένδρα in 1633. Of Henry Stephen's edition of 1576 I consulted a copy in the National Library at Paris (A 6294), no copy being available in the Netherlands or Belgium.

with striking consistency, a specific type of transcriptional corruption. That is, in all these cases the compositor replaced the final or initial letters of a word by the final or initial letters which the same word had somewhat further in the same verse. Thus, for instance, λαλήσητε in Matthew x 19 bécame λαλήσετε because that was the form in which the word returned at the end of the verse. Similarly αὐτῷ was changed into αὐτοῦ, ὅτι into ὅτε, τούτῳ into τούτου and ὑμῶν into ἡμῶν owing to the words αὐτοῦ, ὅτε, τούτου, and ἡμῶν occurring at a short distance in the same verses. The type of *parablepsis* which is concerned here is remarkable in that it did not result in ordinary haplographies, but the more fatal because the readings thus introduced by the compositor made perfect sense, so that they were not detected or corrected by the man who did the proof-reading. Related to this group of readings is the omission of τῶν in Acts xvii 18 (variant no. 15), probably due to the fact that the same word occurs also at the beginning of the verse.

Probably two other changes (viz. 5, and 20) have equally to be ascribed to the compositor. The transposition of ἵνα and τὶς in Mark ix 30 seems to be best accounted for as the result of a misunderstanding. Presumably Hoelzlin had marked in the copy destined for the press that the accent on τὶς had to be removed, as he was found to have done at several other places. For some reason or another the sign was misunderstood by the compositor and taken to be an indication that ἵνα and τὶς had to be transposed. — In 2 Cor. vi 16 the preposition ἐν was replaced by καί. The obvious explanation is that the compositor in seeking the type of the ligature for ἐν from the fount, mistakenly took a type of the ligature for καί. When entering this curious reading in his text-critical apparatus, TISCHENDORF rightly noted that Elzevier 1633 read καὶ αὐτοῖς instead of ἐν αὐτοῖς "per incuriam": he could have added "operarum".

None of the 8 readings for which the compositor of the Elzevier press can be held responsible, had ever been printed in an earlier edition. But it is worth noting that there is respectable manuscript evidence for the readings 1, 15, and 21. For the latter two readings the support from manuscripts became so important that ὑπὲρ ἡμῶν in Col. i 7 was adopted in the editions of GRIESBACH, LACHMANN and TREGELLES, and that τῶν in Acts xvii 18 was omitted by TISCHENDORF, WESTCOTT and HORT, WEISS, VON SODEN and *The Greek New Testament*. What was once a compositor's error is now part of the critical text.

Finally there remain 3 readings (viz. 10, 19, and 22) which do not derive from any earlier edition, nor belong to the compositor's errors of the type discussed above. These readings are best explained as alterations which HOELZLIN made when skimming the text of 1624 with a view to the new edition. At these places he seems to have altered the text at the first glance, feeling that, on the face of it, there was something wrong with it. Thus he blundered into a reading like ἐπιστολῆς in 1 Cor. ix 2, where 1624 correctly had ἀποστολῆς. True, there is some scarce manuscript evidence for ἐπιστολῆς, *inter alia* from the famous Leicester Codex (minuscule 69) and from the little less famous manuscript written by Erasmus' friend James Faber of Deventer,[45] now in the library of Amsterdam University (minuscule 90). But there is no reason to suppose that Hoelzlin had any acquaintance with these manuscripts. More likely he introduced the variant ἐπιστολῆς on his own authority. The same applies to the other 2 readings which he corrected at haphazard. As to the intrinsic value of his 3 corrections, they can only be considered as plain deteriorations.

Epilogue and Conclusions

The reader may have wondered why nothing has been said so far on the three readings which, as was stated in the beginning of this article, are attributed to "Elzevier" in the apparatus of NESTLE-ALAND. The reason is that these readings are not peculiar to the Elzevier text as edited by HOELZLIN in 1633; they already occur in Elzevier 1624. Still they give some cause for comment. One of the rules according to which the apparatus of Nestle was established, is that wherever the "Urheber" of a reading would be mentioned, the reading would be supplied with the name of, if possible, the earliest author.[46] Now three readings have been supplied with the name "Elzevier". In reality, however, these three readings all occur for the first time in much earlier editions: αὐτόν (in Matthew viii 18) in ERASMUS' second edition of 1519, αὐτοῦ (in John ix 21) in his third edition of 1522, and αὐτῶν (in Acts xx 30) in Robert STEPHEN's edition of 1546. The attribution of readings to the rightful *auctores* is indeed not the strongest side of NESTLE-ALAND. Thus GRIESBACH

---

[45] WETTSTEIN's information on Faber (*Prolegomena*, 56-7) can be supplemented with the material published by P. S. ALLEN, *Opus Epistolarum Des. Erasmi Roterodami*, I, Oxford 1906, 385-388, and IV, xxi.

[46] NESTLE-ALAND, *o.c.* (n. 1), 11* and 67*.

is quoted for a reading in Hebr. xii 3 which figures already in STEPHEN 1546. And the suggestion to read πόρνων (masculine) instead of πορνῶν (feminine) in Rev. xvii 5 is likewise attributed to GRIESBACH, although the reading πόρνων was already defended by Joseph SCALIGER in 1591, from whose correspondence it was published by Johannes DRUSIUS in 1612 and by a (still) unknown editor in 1619.[47] But enough. The preceding pages may be summarized as follows.

1. Although the preface to the second Elzevier edition of the Greek Testament (Leiden 1633) was written by Daniel HEINSIUS, Jeremias HOELZLIN was the editor of its Greek text.

2. As Professor of Greek at Leiden, HOELZLIN had the teaching responsibility for New Testament Greek; it is quite comprehensible, therefore, that it was he whom the University Printers[48] entrusted with the editorship of their new edition of the Greek Testament.

3. HOSKIER's analysis of the differences between the first and the second Elzevier edition does not deserve the same confidence as his collation of these editions. He wrongly did not take into account that 17th-century rules for the use of breathings and accents were different from those of the 19th century.

4. In spite of HOSKIER's affirmation to the contrary, the second Elzevier edition is not less correctly printed as a whole than the first.

5. Of the 26 real variant readings in which the 1633 edition differs from that of 1624, 15 have been taken from earlier editions;

---

[47] J. DRUSIUS, *Annotationum in totum Jesu Christi Testamentum sive Praeteritorum libri X*, Franeker 1612, ad Rev. xvii 5; also in *Critici sacri, ad locum*. Jos. SCALIGER, "Notae in locos aliquot difficiliores", posthumously published in *Novum Iesu Christi D.N. Testamentum*, Geneva 1619 and with a new title-page 1620, 11, republished in London 1622 and 1633, and Leiden 1633; also in the *Critici sacri, ad locum*.

[48] Many writers on the subject (e.g. SCRIVENER, DARLOW-MOULE, GROENEN, WIKENHAUSER-SCHMID, JÜLICHER, CULLMANN, METZGER, MANSON-ROWLEY, J. FINEGAN, and L. Paul DILG) speak of the Elzeviers as "brothers". However, Bonaventura and Abraham who published the 1633 edition (not that of 1624, as FINEGAN claims) were not brothers, but uncle and nephew respectively. Isaac, the publisher of the 1624 edition, was a brother of Abraham, so likewise a nephew of Bonaventura. Reference may be made to A. WILLEMS, *Les Elzevier*, Brussels-Paris-The Hague 1880. In Professor METZGER's introduction to *A Textual Commentary on the Greek New Testament*, 1971[1], xxiii, the term *Textus Receptus* should now be attributed to Daniel Heinsius, not to "the Elzevir brothers". Further the Elzeviers should no longer be called "brothers, who were printers in Leiden and later in Amsterdam": Abraham and Bonaventura, were not brothers, nor did they become printers at Amsterdam. The sentence *Textum ergo habes ...* should be provided with its correct punctuation, and its translation should be changed from "Therefore you now have the text received by all" into "Therefore you have the text now received by all".

8 are attributable to the compositor; and 3 are innovations of
HOELZLIN.

6. HOELZLIN's part in the edition of the Elzevier text of 1633 mainly
   consisted in:
   a. collating Elzevier 1624 with Henry Stephen's 16mo edition of
      Geneva 1587;
   b. occasionally consulting some other edition, principally Robert
      Stephen's folio edition of 1550 or his 16mo edition of 1551,
      or a reprint of either of these;
   c. replacing 13 readings of Elzevier 1624 by readings found in
      the edition he collated, and 2 readings by such as he found
      in the editions he consulted;
   d. correcting typographical errors of 1624, and altering breathings,
      accents, and so on;
   e. and presumably in reading the proofs; if this was really his
      responsibility, he overlooked 25 fresh misprints.

7. The three readings ascribed to Elzevier in NESTLE-ALAND should
   be attributed to ERASMUS and Robert STEPHEN. Πόρνων in Rev. xvii 5
   should be attributed to J. SCALIGER instead of to GRIESBACH;
   αὐτόν in Hebr. xii 3 should be attributed, not to GRIESBACH,
   but to Robert STEPHEN.

APPENDIX I

*The fifteen variant readings of Elzevier 1633 as compared
with Elzevier 1624 with their support from previous editions*

	1624	1633
3. Mark iv 18	οὗτοί εἰσιν[2]	] *om.*, Complutensis; editio Froschaueri, Tiguri 1547; Henrici Stephani 1576 et 1587; Bezae 1580 in-8vo; editio Whittakeri ab Elzeviriis impressa 1633.
4. Mark viii 24	ὅτι *et* ὁρῶ	] *om.*, Complutensis; editiones Bezae 1582 et 1588 in-folio; Vignonii 1587; Polyglotta Antwerpiensis; editiones Plantinianae 1573, 1574, 1583, 1584;

Henrici Stephani 1587 (contra 1576); editio Plantino-Moreta 1606-10; editiones Plantino-Raphelengianae 1591, 1601, 1612, 1613; Commeliniana 1599; Roverianae 1609, 1619; Crispini 1612, 1622; Stoerii 1627; Jansonii Amstelodami 1632.

6. Luke xi 33 κρυπτήν] κρυπτόν, omnes editiones Erasmi; Aldina; Colinaei; Bogardi (1543); minores Rob. Stephani 1549, 1551; omnes Bezae; Henrici Stephani 1576 et 1587; Stoerii 1625.

7. Luke xii 20 ἄφρων] ἄφρον, Complutensis; Aldina; Henrici Stephani 1576 et 1587; Bezae 1588.

8. John iii 6 γεγενημένον (bis)] γεγεννημένον (bis), Complutensis; omnes Erasmi; Aldina; Colinaei; minores Rob. Stephani 1546, '49 et '51, eiusdemque editio in-folio 1550; omnes Bezae; Henrici Stephani 1576 et 1587; Harsyanae 1600 et 1611; Stoerii 1625.

9. John iv 8 Οἱ - ἀγοράσωσι] uncinis includunt editiones Henrici Stephani 1576 et 1587; Bezae 1580 in-8vo; Harsyanae 1600 et 1611; Stoerii 1625.

12. John v 2 κολυμβήθρα] κολυμβήθρᾳ, Aldina; Henrici Stephani 1576 et 1587; Harsyanae 1600 et (?) 1611.

13. John xx 15 ἀρῶ] ἀρῶ, Roberti Stephani 1550; Roberti Stephani jun. Parisiensis 1568; Vignonii 1587; Henrici Stephani 1576 (contra 1587); Bezae 1580 et 1588; Harsyanae 1600 et 1611; Stoerii 1625.

16. Acts xxvii 13 ἄσσον] Ἄσσον, Roberti Stephani editiones 1550 et 1551.

17. Rom. vi 4 εἰς θάνατον] εἰς τὸν θάνατον, omnes editiones ante 1624.

18. Rom. xi 31 ἡμετέρῳ] ὑμετέρῳ, omnes editiones ante 1624.

23. 2 Tim. i 12 παραθήκην] παρακαταθήκην, Complutensis; omnes Erasmi; Aldina; Colinaei; Polyglotta Antwerpiensis; Henrici Stephani 1576 et 1587; Bezae 1580; Harsyanae 1600 et 1611; Stoerii 1625; editio Whittakeri ab Elzeviriis impressa 1633.

24. Hebr. ix 12 εὑρόμενος] εὑράμενος, Complutensis; Colinaei; omnes Roberti Stephani; omnes Bezae; Henrici Stephani 1576 et 1587; Harsyanae 1600 et 1611; Stoerii 1625.

25. 2 Peter i 1 σωτῆρος ἡμῶν] σωτῆρος, Complutensis, omnes Erasmi; Aldina; Colinaei; omnes Roberti Stephani; Henrici Stephani 1587 (contra 1576).

26. Rev. xvi 5 ὅσιος] ἐσόμενος, Bezae editiones in-folio 1582, 1588, 1598; Henrici Stephani 1587 (contra 1576).

From this collation it may be seen that thirteen of the fifteen variant readings in Elzevier 1633 may be derived from Henry Stephen's second edition (Geneva, 1587). Only the variants numbered 13. and 16. must come from another source, possibly Robert Stephen's folio edition of 1550.

APPENDIX II

Hoelzlin on the Greek language and the New Testament

Three excerpts from *De graecae linguae praestantia et quadam directius faciliusque percipiendae via oratio ab Jeremia Hoelzlin habita, IV/Non. Septembr. anno 1632,* Lugduni Batavorum, ex officina B. et A. Elzeviriorum, 1632 (Paris, National Library, X 4563).

P. 4: "Spiritus Sanctus novioris pacti libros non alio sermone conscribi voluerit".

P. 5-6: "sola lingua Graeca etiamnum nobis Evangelii libros porrigit, hoc est, Petro Apostolo interprete, verba vitae aeternae suppeditat ...".

P. 13: Hoelzlin remarks that within the Greek language as a whole one can distinguish between a *lingua communis* in which dialogues, history and speeches have been written, and a *lingua poetica.* The *lingua communis* was used, e.g., by Lucian and Isocrates: "A quibus Novi Testamenti scriptores secludi nolim. Etsi enim illi elegantissimè loquuntur, etsi horum oratio Hebraismis abundat; tamen quia initio verborum copulationem requiro rectam magis quam venustam, idcirco indigenas illorum hellenismos, prout debeo, admiror, horum caelestem veritatem amplector, utrorumque ad intelligendum pronitatem tironibus prodesse aio".

ADDITIONAL NOTE TO FOOTNOTE 44

After the manuscript of this article had been completed, Professor A. M. T. WELKEN-HUYSEN of Louvain kindly informed the writer that, contrary to what has been remarked in n. 44, a copy of H. Stephen's *Novum Testamentum* of 1576 is preserved in the Royal Library at Brussels. This copy (class-mark II.23079) was found to be entered in the catalogue under the word *Diathèkè*, transcribed from the Greek title of the book: Ἡ Καινὴ Διαθήκη.

PROBLEME UND IMPULSE DER
NEUTESTAMENTLICHEN APOKALYPTIK

P. L. SCHOONHEIM

"Ratlos vor der Apokalyptik", so hat Klaus Koch geschrieben.[1] Wir lassen beiseite was dieser Autor mit seiner Schrift beabsichtigte; "ratlos" ist hier nämlich eine allgemeine Andeutung der Situation, in die die Theologie des Neuen Testaments schon seit vielen Jahren geraten ist. Die Auslegungen und theologische Einsichten anlässlich apokalyptischer Aussagen im Neuen Testament sind meistens nicht befriedigend. Die zeitbedingte Form dieser Apokalyptik verursacht Probleme und gibt andererseits Impulse.

Man könnte eine lange Geschichte schreiben über die vielen Lösungen der für unsere Generation rätselhaften Apokalyptik. Eine der bekannten und vielfach benützten Lösungen ist die Unterscheidung Apokalyptik und Eschatologie.[2] Andere qualifizieren die Apokalyptik als ein fremdes Element in der Zukunftsschau Jesu und der ersten Christen.[3] Dem-

---

[1] Angeführt durch Alexander SAND, Zur Frage nach dem "Sitz im Leben" der apokalyptischen Texte des Neuen Testaments, *NTS* 18 (1971-1972), 167.

[2] Im allgemeinen gibt es im Sprachgebrauch der verschiedenen Forscher keinen deutlichen Unterschied zwischen Eschatologie und Apokalyptik. Hier sei gewiesen auf L. GOPPELT, Apokalyptik und Typologie bei Paulus, *TLZ* 89 (Mai 1964), 321-343. Er schreibt u.a.: "Die Apokalyptik lieferte wichtige Interpretamente, um die Erscheinung Jesu und ihre Wirkung zu deuten. Sie bringt z.B. in das Urkerygma den Begriff "Auferstehung" ein, und Paulus versteht die Auferstehung Jesu tatsächlich im apokalyptischen Sinne als Anfang der eschatologischen Erweckung der Toten zu einem neuen leibhaften Leben (1 Kor. xv 20-28)" (327-328). Und später (342): "Jesu Auferstehung und die Sammlung der Gemeinde könnten für Paulus deshalb eschatologische Vorgänge sein, weil sie für ihn Teile eines bereits einsetzenden eschatologischen Dramas wären". — R. BULTMANN (*Apophoreta*, Festschrift für Ernst Haenchen, Berlin 1964, 64) unterscheidet: "Die Eschatologie ist die Vorstellung vom Ende der Welt; eine Vorstellung, die als solche kein konkretes Bild vom Endgeschehen zu enthalten braucht, die sogar das Ende nicht als ein chronologisch fixiertes zu denken braucht. Die Apokalyptik dagegen ist eine bestimmte Konkretisierung der eschatologischen Vorstellung. Sie entwirft Bilder vom Endgeschehen, und sie fixiert das Ende chronologisch". Paul SCHÜTZ, Parusia, *Hoffnung und Prophetie*, Hamburg 1963, bestreitet die Unterscheidung (491): "Selbst in der christlichen Theologie ist heute ein Hoffnungsbegriff möglich, der es dem Glauben anrechnet, zwar zu wissen, DASS er hoffe, nicht aber WAS er hoffe. Anders beim biblischen Menschen. Da manifestierte sich das 'Dass' eben gerade am 'Was' seiner Hoffnung".

[3] John A. T. ROBINSON, *Jesus and His Coming*, The Emergence of a Doctrine, New York 1957 (In einer zusammenfassenden Bemerkung bei Bruce VAWTER C.M.,

gegenüber wird die Apokalyptik, im Rahmen der christlichen Zeugnisse, die Mutter aller christlichen Theologie genannt.[4] Auch hat man keine einheitliche Meinung über den Einfluss der Apokalyptik auf die frühchristliche Theologie.[5] Es gibt tiefgreifende Versuche, um so genau wie möglich die ursprünglichen und die späteren christlichen Elemente, in einem Kapitel wie Markus 13, festzustellen.[6] Bekannt sind die Forschungen der jüdischen Apokalyptik.[7] In moderner Zeit sind in der Philosophie und auf dem praktischen Gebiet der Wirtschaft die Zukunftsplanungen entstanden.[8] Auch damit hat man bei der Auslegung der neutestamentlichen Apokalyptik in irgendeiner Weise zu rechnen.

And He shall Come Again with Glory, *AnBib*, 17-18 (1961), 145). ROBINSON geht nicht so weit, dass er Jesus die Eschatologie untersagt, wohl ist die Parusie eine Hineininterpretierung der Gemeinde und er fasst die "realized Eschatology" als die authentische Eschatologie Jesu auf. Von einer anderen Seite her spricht Rudolph PESCH, *Naherwartungen, Tradition und Redaktion in Markus 13* (KBANT), Düsseldorf 1968. Dieser entdeckt in Markus 13 eine Widerlegung der falschen Apokalyptik. Damit liegt in diesem Kapitel eine Form einer legitimen christlichen Zukunftserwartung vor. T. F. GLASSON meint in seinem Buch, *The second Advent*, 1947, dass alle Evangeliumaussagen bezüglich der Wiederkunft Christi an dem Gerichtstage sekundär sind. So H. H. ROWLEY, *Apokalyptik, ihre Form und Bedeutung zur biblischen Zeit*, Einsiedeln - Zürich - Köln 1965, Exkurs 136-137: Die Wiederkunft Christi.

[4] E. KÄSEMANN, Die Anfänge christlicher Theologie, *ZThK* 57 (1960), 179: "Die Apokalyptik ist — da man die Predigt Jesu nicht eigentlich als Theologie bezeichnen kann — die Mutter aller christlichen Theologie gewesen". Bestritten ist diese Auffassung von G. EBELING, Der Grund christlicher Theologie, *ZThK* 58 (1961) und von R. BULTMANN, *a.c.*, 69. Dieser formuliert: "... kann man m.E. wohl sagen, dass die Eschatologie die Mutter der urchristlichen Theologie ist, nicht aber, dass es die Apokalyptik ist".

[5] H. D. BETZ, Das Verständnis der Apokalyptik in der Theologie der Pannenberg-Gruppe, *ZThK* 65 (1968), 259, entlehnt von W. PANNENBERG, *Offenbarung als Geschichte*, Göttingen 1965, 50, die Aussage: «Jesus von Nazareth ist kein Rabbi gewesen, sondern Apokalyptiker". Andererseits sagt G. EBELING, *a.c.*, 228, *Anm.* 1: "Es bleibt die Frage, ob ... nicht eher ... die christliche Theologie ihren Ursprung hätte in der Überwindung der Apokalyptik".

[6] Hervorragend ist hierbei R. PESCH, *Nahererwartungen* (Vgl. Anm. 3).

[7] Neben den bekannten Werken von E. SCHÜRER (1909), W. BOUSSET und H. GRESSMANN (1926), P. VOLZ (1934), können genannt werden: H. H. ROWLEY, *Jewish Apocalyptic and the Dead Sea Scrolls*, London 1957, und: Ch. GUIGNEBERT, *Le monde juif vers le temps de Jésus*, Paris 1935, ²1969.

[8] W. D. MARSCH, *Zukunft*, in: *Themen der Theologie* (hrsg. W. J. SCHULTZ), Bd 2, Stuttgart 1969, handelt im zweiten Teil seines Werkes über philosophisch — politische und futurologisch — technische Aspekte der Geschichte. Eine spezielle Abhandlung dieses Themas liegt von Wilhelm KAMLAH vor: *Utopie, Eschatologie, Geschichtsteleologie, Kritische Untersuchungen zum futuristischen Denken der Neuzeit* (BIH 461), Mannheim - Wien - Zürich 1969.

1. Apokalyptik: Enthüllung - Verhüllung

Die Apokalyptik ist so vielseitig und die Apokalyptikforschungen sind so detailreich, dass es unmöglich (geworden) ist, die vielen Themen unter einem einzigen Gesichtspunkt zu ordnen. Eigentlich sind es viele Rätsel, die uns zur Auslegung vorgelegt werden. Manchmal muss festgestellt werden, dass mit allzu einfachen Mitteln und Methoden die apokalyptische Botschaft der Bibel verkündigt wird. Viele Prediger und Ausleger fragen nicht: "Was steht da?" oder: "Warum steht das da so?". Mit anderen Worten: die Hintergründe und der Einfluss der Umwelt, die Geschichte der Tradition, die Entwicklung der christlichen Theologie werden nicht ernst genommen. Im Gottesdienst ist es schwierig, analysierende und kritische Diskussionen zu führen, denn die Hörer der Predigt kommen unvorbereitet in die Kirche. Möglicherweise liegt darin eine Ursache, dass die eigentlichen Fragen der Menschen von heute in der Kirche nicht aufgeworfen werden. Die allgemeine Verlegenheit in kirchlichen Kreisen diesen Fragen gegenüber, wird besonders auf dem Gebiet der Apokalyptik mit viel Schärfe deutlich. Nur sehr wenige Gemeindeglieder wissen von Entstehung, Überlieferung und Entwicklung des Evangeliums. Dass die kritische Bibelwissenschaft nicht nur negative sondern auch positive Seiten hat,[9] ist vielen von ihnen unbekannt. Die biblische Botschaft will verstanden werden. Die moderne Fragestellung und die theologischen Möglichkeiten dieser Zeit sollen dabei nicht verschwiegen werden. Dies gilt in verstärktem Masze für die Apokalyptik. Es gibt wahrscheinlich kein Gebiet, wo die Ganzheit der zentralen Fragen der Theologie so in den Vordergrund gerückt werden wie bei der Apokalyptik: Gottes Herrschaft und Gottes Reich, unsere Zukunft, Christologie,[10] Deutung der Geschichte im Lichte der Bibel, moderne Zukunftsplanung im technischen und ökonomischen Verfahren.[11]

---

[9] Zum Beispiele die Textanalyse der formgeschichtlichen Methode und die Studien zur Theologie der Evangelienbücher des Neuen Testaments.

[10] Auf den engen Zusammenhang zwischen Apokalyptik und Christologie, in der Urchristenheit, weist G. EBELING hin: a.c., 240. Er merkt aber an, dass "die von der Apokalyptik bereitgestellte Wirklichkeitsinterpretation nur begrenzt und nicht auf die Dauer die Sprache der Christologie bestimmen konnte". Er akzentuiert: "Der Grund ... (Gott und Geschichte zusammenzudenken). ... ist nicht die Apokalyptik, sondern die Erscheinung Jesus". Siehe auch: "Eschatologie ist primär Christologie", bei W. KRECK, *Die Zukunft des Gekommenen, Grundprobleme der Eschatologie*, München 1961, 83 und 117.

[11] Die oben angeführten (Anm. 8) Werke von W. D. MARSCH und W. KAMLAH.

Dazu kommt, dass die Apokalyptik, obwohl Enthüllung damit gemeint ist, vielmehr verhüllend wirkt. Vielleicht kann man sagen, dass unser Sprechen über Gott, auch wenn wir seine biblischen Namen und seine biblischen Eigenschaften nennen, mehr verhüllend als enthüllend ist. Wer Gott sagt, deutet ein Mysterium an. Wer Apokalyptik zu verstehen versucht, hat mit der verborgenen Zukunft und der rätselhaften Geschichte vor uns zu tun. Es ist ein Merkmal der biblischen Apokalyptik, dass nicht alle Deutungen und Bilder erklärt werden können.

Die Ereignisse einer bestimmten Zeit geben manchmal Anlass, um ein aktuelles Bild der neutestamentlichen Apokalyptik zu schaffen. So hat ANDREWS [12] Endgeschichte und Zeitgeschichte — die Jahre 1914-1918 — miteinander verbunden. Er hat eine einheitliche und lesenswerte Beschreibung der dramatischen und theologischen Grundgedanken der christlichen Apokalyptik hervorgebracht. Hat ANDREWS aber die Enthüllung der Apokalyptik dargeboten? Unsere Antwort ist: Nein. Die neutestamentliche Apokalyptik akzentuiert nicht (so sehr) die Zeitgeschichte. In Markus 13 geht es um den entscheidenden Tag und um Wachsamkeit. Zweitens ist es die Frage, ob man die Apokalyptik des Neuen Testaments in die begrenzte Apokalyptik des damaligen Judentums einordnen darf, oder ob diese Apokalyptik im weiteren Sinne als prophetischer Blick in die allumfassende Zukunft Gottes verstanden werden muss.

Im Zusammenhang damit können die Probleme der christlichen Bearbeitung der mit zeitgeschichtlichen Ereignissen der damaligen Welt verbundenen apokalyptischen Predigt ins Auge gefasst werden. Sind die Elemente der Evangelium-Tradition als echte und ursprüngliche Überlieferung anzunehmen? Man denke hierbei an: Zerstörung Jerusalems, Naherwartung der Parusie Jesu, das (unmittelbar) bevorstehende Weltende! Welche Erwartungen können Jesus selbst zugeschrieben werden? Bekanntlich werden einerseits die Aussagen Jesu als "echte" Worte verteidigt,[13] andererseits ist die Überzeugung, dass unsere Evangeliumsbeschreibungen und die Apostelgeschichte deutliche

---

[12] H. T. ANDREWS, The Message of Jewish Apocalyptic for Modern Times, *Exp* 14 (1917), 58-71.

[13] In den Werken von W. G. KÜMMEL und O. CULLMANN. — Aug. STROBEL, *Die apokalyptische Sendung Jesu*, Rothenburg 1962, ist der Meinung, dass Jesus in seinen Aussagen über den kommenden Menschensohn sich selbst bezeichnet hat. Die Wiederkunft aber will STROBEL auffassen im Sinne "eintreten, erscheinen". Die buchstäbliche Bedeutung "Wiederkunft" ist nach seiner Auffassung eine spätere moderne Auslegung.

Spuren der "Gemeindetheologie" zeigen, sowohl in der evangelischen als in der katholischen Theologie, stärker geworden.[14] Eine Entscheidung für die eine oder die andere Meinung oder Variationen der genannten Einsichten haben aber nicht die Kraft allgemeiner Gültigkeit. Alle sind im Grunde Theorien und Konstruktionen. Ebensogut ist die Verleugnung der neutestamentlichen Apokalyptik durch Unechtserklärung aller betreffenden Aussagen noch immer möglich.[15]

Vielleicht ist dies ein Zeichen, dass die Schwierigkeiten mit der Apokalyptik in irgendeiner Weise überwunden werden müssen. Die Versuche, nicht so sehr eine harmonische Einheit des christlichen Zukunftsbildes zu präsentieren, sondern eine kritische und zugleich theologische Lösung zu finden, sind andererseits Anregungen für die Exegese der neutestamentlichen Apokalyptik.

2. *Apokalyptik: Prophetie, Eschatologie, Mythologisierung*

Die biblischen Propheten haben einen weiten Blick. Demgegenüber hat man den Eindruck, dass bei den Apokalyptikern eine Verengung der Zukunftsschau eingetreten ist. Sie richten ihr Zeugnis meistens auf eine bestimmte Entwicklung der Geschichte und schematisieren die Ereignisse. Sie geben konkrete Beschreibungen und stellen Berechnungen an. VON RAD will dann auch keine unmittelbare Verbindung zwischen Apokalyptik und Prophetie legen.[16] Die Apokalyptiker sprechen von wahrnehmbaren Vorzeichen der Endereignisse.[17] Damit hängt zusammen, dass sie die Endkatastrophen und die Reinigung der Welt vom Bösen durch Gottes Gericht in der nahen Zukunft erwarten. Der Apokalyptiker ist gespannt. Der Termin, der noch aussteht, ist kurz. MICHAELIS meint, dass die Naherwartung im Evangelium nicht ursprünglich christlich ist oder auf Jesus selbst zurück-

---

[14] E. KÄSEMANN, H. CONZELMANN. — Von katholischer Seite: Wilh. THÜSING, *Erhöhungsvorstellung und Parusie-erwartung in der ältesten nachösterlichen Christologie*, Stuttgart 1969. Vergleiche Gerh. LOHFINK, *Die Himmelfahrt Jesu, Untersuchungen zu den Himmelfahrts- und Erhöhungstexten bei Lukas* (StANT, 26), München 1971.

[15] A. FEUILLET legt den Anfang der neuen Zeit in das Osterereignis: "le siècle futur ... fait ici son entrée". Parousia, in Matt. 24, wird durch ihn nicht verbunden mit der Endzeit sondern mit dem Gericht Israels: A. FEUILLET, Le sens du mot Parousia dans l'évangile de Matthieu, in: *The Background of the N.T. and its Eschatology* (ed. W. D. DAVIES and D. DAUBE) in Honour of Ch. H. Dodd, Cambridge 1956, 261-280.

[16] Gerh. VON RAD, *Theologie des Alten Testaments* II, München 1960, 314, hat die tiefe Verschiedenheit von Prophetie und Apokalyptik herausgearbeitet. Er sagt (316): "... entscheidend ist u.E. die Unvereinbarkeit des Geschichtsverständnisses der Apokalyptik mit dem der Propheten". So Gerh. EBELING, *a.c.*, 232.

[17] Diese Kennzeichnung der Apokalyptik beleuchtet Fr. MUSSNER, Wann kommt das Reich Gottes?, *BZ* 6 (1962), in Beziehung auf Luk xvii 20b-21.

geführt werden kann. Erst nachher sei die Erwartung der Welterneuerung innerhalb der damaligen Generation der jüdischen Apokalyptik entnommen.[18] Dies könnte für die Auslegung der apokalyptischen Kapitel des Neuen Testaments wichtige Konsequenzen
haben.

Andererseits kann mit Recht behauptet werden,[19] dass die Ankün-
digung der Parusie Jesu in den Evangelienbeschreibungen eine christliche Überzeugung ist. Sein "Kommen" ist eine "reelle Erscheinung".
Im Vergleich mit der jüdischen Erwartung des kommenden Menschensohnes bedeutet die christliche Hoffnung eine neue Version. Die Frage
bleibt, ob die Gemeinde diese Parusieerwartung konstruiert hat, oder
dass Jesus selbst schon die Erhöhung des Menschensohnes als seine
bevorstehende Wiederkunft angekündigt hat. Im allgemeinen ist es
immer schwierig, um genau festzustellen, wo sich ein völlig neuer
Gebrauch einer Vokabel vorfindet. Es gibt bekanntlich viele Formen,
wenn ein Ausdruck in eine ganz andere oder in eine verwandte
Gedankenwelt übernommen wird. Dass zwischen Judentum und Christentum viele Verbindungen in der Terminologie und in fundamentalen
Glaubensvorstellungen vorhanden sind, ist keine Frage. Dennoch
ändert sich bei Übernahme einer Vokabel die ursprüngliche Bedeutung.
Durch die neue Anwendung werden zentrale oder nebensächliche
Elemente des Ausdrucks verschoben oder umgebogen. Die Akzente
werden verlegt. Allerdings ist der Inhalt nicht ohne weiteres übernommen. So kann man, sei es etwa einseitig, folgenden Unterschied
machen. Die jüdische Apokalyptik erwartet die Veränderung dieser
Welt, die christliche Apokalyptik erwartet die Erscheinung Jesu Christi
in aller Pracht und Herrlichkeit. Diese Hoffnung steht im Zusammenhang mit den grossen Heilstatsachen, Kreuztod und Auferstehung

---

[18] Vgl. W. MICHAELIS, Kennen die Synoptiker eine Verzögerung der Parusie?, in:
Synoptische Studien (Festschrift für Wickenhauser), München 1953. Siehe Otto KNOCH,
Die eschatologische Frage, ihre Entwicklung und ihr gegenwärtiger Stand; Versuch
einer knappen Übersicht, *BZ* 6 (1962), 112-120. KNOCH stellt u.a. neben die Ansichten
von MICHAELIS diejenigen von KÜMMEL und CULLMANN. W. G. KÜMMEL, *Verheissung*
und *Erfüllung* (AThANT 6), Zürich ³1956, findet in den Aussagen Jesu über die
Zukunft die Naherwartung zum Ausdruck gebracht. O. CULLMANN (*Christus und die
Zeit*, Zürich ²1948) hat — so urteilt Knoch — eine konstruktive Beantwortung der
eschatologischen Frage gegeben, indem sowohl das "schon jetzt" als das "noch nicht"
in Christo anwesend ist. Bei den damaligen Juden gibt es aber diese Spannung nicht.
[19] Argumente hierfür gibt z.B. Aug. STROBEL, *Die apokalyptische Sendung Jesu*,
Rothenburg 1962, 24-25. Da wird u.a. hingewiesen auf Ed. SCHWEIZER, Der Menschensohn. Zur eschatologischen Erwartung Jesu, *ZNW* 50 (1959), 185ff., 205ff.

Jesu. O. CULLMANN [20] hat darauf hingewiesen: "Jesus ist gekommen und wird noch einmal (wieder)kommen. Schon jetzt ist der Glaube im Kreuz und Auferstehung fest gegründet, aber die Vollendung liegt noch in der Zukunft". Diese tiefgehende prinzipielle Umsetzung kennt die jüdische Apokalyptik nicht. Da findet man, wie bei den alttestamentlichen Propheten, eine Hoffnung auf eine neue Welt vom heutigen hoffnungslosen Zustand heraus. Man kann dies als ein Pessimismus der Apokalyptiker auffassen.[21] Diese Welt geht zugrunde, das Böse wird stärker, und die Gottlosen bekommen alle Gewalt. Auch im Neuen Testament finden wir solche Gedanken, z.B. der Antichrist und die kosmischen Katastrophen, wie sie im letzten Buch der Bibel ausgemalt werden. Andererseits sind die Ankündigungen im Kapitel 13 des Markusevangeliums nicht nur pessimistisch geprägt. Die Christen werden zu Wachsamkeit aufgerufen. Lukas xxi 28 ist gerade die Umkehrung einer negativen und pessimistischen Erwartung.[22] Man wird aufgefordert, die Häupter zu erheben; die Erlösung naht!

Es gibt also, wie bei den alttestamentlichen Propheten, zwei Seiten. Die Propheten predigen Urteil. Der Tag Jahwes bedeutet Gericht. Zugleich predigen sie Trost, Gnade und Hilfe. Die Welt und die Gesellschaft werden erneuert.

Die neutestamentliche Apokalyptik hat vieles gemeinsam mit der positiven Zukunftshoffnung der Propheten. Das Gericht schliesst Heil und Aussicht auf Erneuerung von Welt und Kosmos ein. Dem jüdischen Apokalyptiker kann man die prophetischen Merkmale nicht absprechen. Sein Blick ist aber begrenzter durch zeitliche und nationale

---

[20] CULLMANN, o.c., (Anm. 18). — Vergleiche U. WILCKENS, Die Bekehrung des Paulus als religionsgeschichtliches Problem, *ZThK* 56 (1959), 287-293. Zusammenfassend sagt L. GOPPELT, Apokalyptik und Typologie bei Paulus, *TLZ* 89 (Mai 1964), 325, bezüglich U. Wilckens u.a.: "Jesu Tod und Auferstehung, die Gegenwart der Gemeinde und das zukünftige Gericht wurden in der hellenistischen Kirche als apokalyptisches Endgeschehen in eins gesehen".

[21] Die christliche Eschatologie lässt sich nicht mit dem Pessimismus der jüdischen Apokalyptik vereinigen. Die Eschatologie hat eine positive Bedeutung ("productive Significance") für die soziale Ethik der Christen. So A. N. WILDER, Eschatology and Social Ethics, in: *The Background of the NT and its Eschatology* (sehe Anm. 15), 509-536.

[22] Paul SCHÜTZ, *Freiheit, Hoffnung, Prophetie*, Hamburg 1963, 491, schreibt in apodiktischer Weise: "War es nicht so, dass die Hoffnung auf "den neuen Himmel und die neue Erde" der mächtigste Impuls der urchristlichen Gemeinden war?". Verschleiert — wie mehrmals in diesem mit Weitläufigkeit geschriebenen Buch ist der Satz, 514: "Parusie heisst: Anwesenheit. Das im Ursprung Gültige ist nicht nur in der "Vergangenheit" gültig. Nur die Zukunft rettet die Gültigkeit des Ursprungs".

Erwartungen. Diese Einengung zeigt sich auch bei mehreren alttestamentlichen Propheten. Andere gehen darüber hinaus. Bei ihnen
sind Perspektiven auf eine Zukunft vorhanden, die alle Völker und
die ganze Schöpfung umfasst. In den neutestamentlichen apokalyptischen Zeugnissen wird diese universale Anschauung weiter ausgebaut.
Einmal sollen Sünde und Tod völlig überwunden sein. Damit ist
eine Enderwartung erreicht, die sowohl bei den alttestamentlichen
Propheten als in der jüdischen Apokalyptik nur in Ansätzen zu finden
ist.

Ein anderer Gesichtspunkt der Apokalyptik im Zusammenhang
mit der Prophetie ist die Bildersprache. Kann man die Bildersprache
von der apokalyptischen Predigt abschälen, so dass die jüdische,
beziehungsweise christliche Eschatologie übrigbleibt? Dies ist sehr
zweifelhaft, weil Bild und Botschaft sich so eng verschlingen. Im
Unterschied zu den Gleichnissen im Evangelium geht es in der
Apokalyptik nicht nur um Verkündigungsformen, die das bessere
Verständnis einer schwer zu fassenden Predigt fördern. Bekanntlich
hat man in der Apokalyptik mehr die inhaltliche Zukunftserwartung
herausgelesen, das Was der jüdischen oder christlichen Hoffnung.
Dagegen spricht dann die Eschatologie mehr formell ohne Bilder und
ohne konkrete Ausmalung der kommenden Ereignisse über Gottes
künftiges Handeln.[23] Auch dieser Unterschied ist aber unhaltbar.
Apokalyptik gebraucht die Bildersprache nicht nur als Hilfsmittel.
Überdies kann man nicht exakt festellen, wo die Apokalyptik endet
und die Eschatologie anfängt und umgekehrt. Die alttestamentlichen
Propheten bringen manchmal ihre eschatologische Botschaft in bild-
hafter Sprache. Damit sind sie noch keine Bildpropheten, denn das

---

[23] R. BULTMANN, in: *Festschrift Haenchen*, 64: "Die Eschatologie ist die Vorstellung
vom Ende der Welt; eine Vorstellung, die als solche kein konkretes Bild vom Endgeschehen zu enthalten braucht, ..., u.s.w., siehe oben Anm. 2. Dagegen KAMLAH,
Utopie, Eschatologie, Geschichtsteleologie, 30: "Die dem Christentum so eigentümliche
enthusiastische Hoffnung ist an die mythische Sprache, in der sie zuerst und
dann durch die Jahrhunderte ausgedrückt wurde, gebunden und wird durch ent-
mythisierende Auslegung ausgelöscht". Kamlah spricht bewusst von entmythisierend
und nicht von entmythologisierend, wie üblicherweise seit Bultmann *o.c.*, 29). W. STAERK,
Der eschatologische Mythos in der altchristlichen Kirche, *ZNW* 35 (1936), 83-95.
Er handelt (90-95: II Die Rekapitulationstheorie des Irenaeus), über den Sieg Jesu
als Sooter, als zweiter vollendeter Adam. Dieser überwindet den Teufel und führt den
gefallenen Menschen in den Urstand der Schöpfung zurück. Der Sootermythos steht
in Verbindung mit der mythischen Weltzeitalterlehre. Staerk behält also den Mythos
bei, er spricht nicht von der Eschatologie im Sinne Bultmanns, aber er deutet sogar
den betreffenden Mythos als eschatologisch, nicht als apokalyptisch.

Wort ist bei ihnen Zentrum ihrer Arbeit. Ebensowenig sind die Apokalyptiker nur Zeugen mit Hilfe eindrucksvoller Bilder, denn das Wort ist auch bei ihnen ein wesentlicher Teil ihrer Zukunftspredigt. Anlässlich der Bildersprache kann die Frage einer möglichen Entmythologisierung der Apokalyptik gestellt werden. A. SAND[24] beantwortet diese Frage bejahend. Er ist der Meinung, dass man Apokalyptik als Mythologisierung, als Entgeschichtlichung der Eschatologie charakterisieren kann. Diese mythologische Deutung der Geschichte tritt hervor, wenn nationale Umwälzungen oder Naturkatastrophen menschliches "Selbstverständnis" bedrohen. Sie können aufgefasst werden als endgeschichtliche Ereignisse, die das Ende der Welt ankündigen und einleiten, sagt A. SAND. Diese "mythologische" Kennzeichnung der Apokalyptik macht es möglich, die Endereignisse — Ende der Geschichte, Anfang des Reiches Gottes — und die grossen Geschehnisse in der Vergangenheit — Schöpfung, Sintflut — miteinander zu verbinden. Wie es am Anfang der Welt war, so wird es an ihrem Ende wieder sein. In dieser Hinsicht lässt es sich vertreten, auch Tatsachen wie den Exodus Israels, die Erscheinung Gottes auf dem Berge Sinai, den Tod und die Auferstehung Jesu im Rahmen der Apokalyptik, als "mythologisch" zu bezeichnen. In diesen historischen apokalyptischen Ereignissen wird der Gang der Weltgeschichte durchbrochen.

Es sei noch darauf hingewiesen, dass die moderne Terminologie sich nicht deckt mit der biblischen Vorstellungswelt. So kann man z.B. nicht reden vom transzendenten oder supernaturalen Charakter der Apokalyptik. Bekanntlich sind in der biblischen Weltanschauung Himmel und Erde, Gott und Menschen nicht so weit voneinander entfernt wie in der Gedankenwelt und in den Glaubensvorstellungen des heutigen Menschen. Was wir Mythologie nennen können, ist in der Bibel Geschichte und umgekehrt. Die historische Welt steht mitsamt Urgeschichte und Endgeschichte unter der Gewalt Gottes. Nicht nur zeitlich aber auch räumlich gehören ihm Himmel und Erde. H. BRAUN[25] zeigt, wie wenig vom Evangelium in der heutigen Form

---

[24] A. SAND, *Zur Frage nach dem "Sitz im Leben" der apokalyptischen Texte des Neuen Testaments*, NTS 18 (1971-1972) 167-177, weist hin auf die Verbindung der Naherwartung mit der Apokalyptik einerseits und der Erwartung in weiterliegender Zukunft mit der Eschatologie anderseits. SAND stimmt der Meinung von Stanley Brice FROST in dem Punkte zu, dass Apokalyptik charakterisiert werden kann als "Mythologisierung, als Entgeschichtlichung der Eschatologie" (in: *Old Testament Apokalyptic. Its Origins and its Growth*, London 1952, 33).

[25] *ZThK* 59 (1962), 16-31: Das AT im NT.

übrigbleibt, wenn alles, was in mythologischer Form hinzugefügt wäre, entfallen würde.

Bleibt dennoch die Frage, wie wir uns mit dieser, mit der Botschaft der Propheten und Apostel unlösbar verbundenen Apokalyptik oder, wenn man will, den apokalyptisch-mythologischen Vorstellungen abfinden können. Darauf soll in Abschnitt drei später noch eingegangen werden.

3. *Planung und Erwartung*

Der heutige Mensch hat, individuell und als Teilhaber an einer technisch-manupilierbaren Welt, mehr als jemals die Möglichkeit sich selbst eine Zukunft zu bauen. Es geht dabei um Entscheidungen, die den heutigen und kommenden Generationen Heil oder Unheil bringen können.

Wie verhält sich nun diese grossartige und zugleich ängstigende Möglichkeit der Planung zu der biblischen Erwartung? Im Rahmen der Apokalyptik kann man sagen: Verwirklicht Gott sein Reich und vollführt er sein Gericht oder bauen Menschen ihre eigene neue Welt und liegt die Verwüstung der Erde und der Menschheit in ihrer Hand? Der christliche Glaube kann aufgrund biblischer Aussagen antworten: Und dennoch hat Gott das letzte Wort. Sein Reich kommt, welche Planungen mit positiven oder negativen Erfolgen die Menschen ausdenken und ausführen können. Aber diese Überzeugung soll geprüft werden.

W. KAMLAH[26] hat tiefgehend gehandelt über christliche und säkulare Zukunftsgedanken. Seine Gesichtspunkte, in einfacher und fragmentarischer Weise zusammengefasst, sind folgende: der christliche Glaube mit eschatologischer Erwartung in Abhängigkeit von Gott steht der Vernunft und einer mit menschlichen Kräften zu verwirklichenden Utopie gegenüber. Seit LUTHER[27] ist eine Spannung sichtbar geworden zwischen der christlichen Erwartung einer nur durch Gott zu verwirklichenden neuen Welt und der Einsicht der Aufklärung, dass wir Menschen selbst für eine bessere Zukunft zu sorgen haben. KAMLAH ist der Meinung: "Was auch immer von der bisherigen theologischen Interpretation der neutestamentlichen Verkündigung zu halten ist, sie läuft auch im günstigsten Fall allein auf Existenzwahrheit und Individualethik (im formelhaft angegebenen Sinne) hinaus — und

---

[26] KAMLAH, *o.c.*, 30-32.
[27] KAMLAH, *o.c.*, 33-34.

das ist wahrlich nicht wenig! Zur Neuordnung unserer politischen,
sozialen, wirtschaftlichen Institutionen hingegen bedürfen wir nach
wie vor der Philosophie, d.h. wir bedürfen der Anknüpfung an die
Tradition nicht allein des biblischen, sondern auch des griechischen
Denkens".[28]

W. D. MARSCH[29] sagt, dass die Eschatologie, im Gegensatz zur
Philosophie, die Zukunft hinter das Rationelle und Sichtbare verlegt.
Die christliche Eschatologie gibt "Aussicht auf eine nachgeschichtliche
Vollendung des Daseins". Dennoch will MARSCH diese unbestimmte
Zukunft mit der auf kurze Frist orientierten Teleologie verbinden.
Diese Planung der Zukunft gibt zwar keine Sicherheit, aber diese
zeitliche Zukunft ist auch nicht das Eigentliche und das Letzte für
den Menschen. "Der Mensch muss notwendig auf ein wenn auch
fernes und geschichtlich nicht einlösbares Ziel hindenken und handeln,
um für die näheren und nächsten Zukünfte gewappnet zu sein".

MARSCH hat auch die Hauptgedanken E. BLOCHS erwähnt. So führt
er von ihm den Satz an: "Die Paradiesschlange hat den Menschen
gesagt: Ihr werdet sein wie Gott, und dies ist auch endlich die
einzige Frohbotschaft des christlichen Heils". Ebenso von BLOCH ist
die Aussage: "Wo Hoffnung ist, ist Religion".[30] Das ineinander
Verweben von christlicher Erwartung und säkularer Planung findet
man auch schon in einer Forderung Alb. SCHWEITZERS. Er hält den
Christen vor, dass sie den Auftrag bekommen haben, das Reich
Gottes zu realisieren. Wenn das nicht geschieht, ist, nach SCHWEITZER,
der Untergang der Welt unvermeidlich.[31] Jeder Versuch in irgendeiner
Form eine Verbindung zwischen gläubiger und hoffnungsreicher Erwartung mit aktiv-menschlicher Planung zu konstruieren bleibt unbe-
friedigend. KAMLAH hat, wie oben schon angeführt ist, eine mögliche
Lösung der seit LUTHER und der Aufklärung herrschenden Gegensätze
des Denkens in den Vordergrund gestellt. Diese rationale Akzen-

---

[28] *O.c.*, 34. Vergleiche R. BULTMANN, in: *Apophoreta*, 69, "... die Theologie und
das Geschichtsbild des Paulus stammen nicht aus der Apokalyptik, sondern aus der
Anthropologie, nämlich ein Verständnis der menschlichen Existenz. ... da die Vollendung
der Weltherrschaft Christi in der Besiegung des Todes besteht, ist die Frage, wem
sie gehört, letzlich eine Frage der Anthropologie. Paulus dankt Gott, der UNS den
Sieg gibt (1 Kor. xv 57)".
[29] W. D. MARSCH, *Zukunft*, in: *Themen der Theologie* (hrsg. H. Jürgen SCHULTZ)
Bd 2, Stuttgart (1969), 13 und 76.
[30] E. BLOCH, *Prinzip Hoffnung*, 1959; angeführt bei MARSCH, *Zukunft*, 65.
[31] Alb. SCHWEITZER, *Aus meinem Leben und Denken*, 131 (und in: *Theol. Umschau*,
Febr. 1953). Bei H. SCHUSTER, Die konsequente Eschatologie in der Interpretation
des Neven Testaments kritisch betrachtet, in: *ZNW* 47 (1956), 23-24.

tuierung hat aber zu tun mit dem seit alters bekannten Gegensatz zwischen Vernunft und Glaube. Ein Ausgleich dieser beiden ist nicht möglich, denn die Vernunft stellt sich gegen den Glauben, weckt Zweifel an Stützpunkten des Glaubens, will dem Sinn für Realität gerecht werden. Andererseits neigt der Glaube zur Verschleierung der Kritik und verwischt die Folgerungen der konsequenten Vernunft. Für die Apokalyptik bewirkt eine vernunft-orientierte Beurteilung der dramatischen Beschreibung der Endereignisse, dass sie als unwesenhafte Erwartung oder als Äusserung einer vergangenen Gedankenwelt herabgesetzt werden.

Die meisten Bibelexegeten, Prediger und Forscher gehen den Weg der Vernunft nicht zu Ende. Damit würde auch die Vernunft die Alleinherrschaft bekommen und vom Glauben wenig oder nichts übrigbleiben. Dagegen hat man versucht, dem Glauben einen grösseren oder kleineren Raum neben der Vernunft zu geben. Umgekehrt haben viele für die Vernunft mehr oder weniger Platz reserviert, ohne dem Glauben schaden zu wollen. So sind viele problematische Bestandteile der Apokalyptik dennoch in heutigen Glaubensvorstellungen akzeptiert oder in moderne Gedankensysteme eingefügt.

In einer unvollständigen Reihe aufgezählt, gibt es u.a. die folgenden Gesichtspunkte:

a. Man hat soviel Ehrfurcht vor der biblischen Apokalyptik, dass ihre Welt und Zeit überragenden Aussagen ohnehin buchstäblich im Glauben angenommen werden.

b. Die bunte Ausmalung der Zukunft und die fremdartige Bildersprache werden nach Form und Inhalt unterschieden. Zentral wird gestellt, dass die Apokalyptiker eine von Gott her zu verwirklichende neue Welt ankündigen. Die Mittel dazu sind im Vergleich mit der alle menschlichen Wörter und Bilder übersteigenden Botschaft nebensächlich.

c. Die schematisierende Geschichtsauffassung der Apokalyptik ist irritierend. Es gibt einen Anfang der Welt in der Zeit — nämlich die Schöpfung — und das Ende der Geschichte — Gericht und Reich Gottes. Diese Aspekte werden stark beleuchtet. Man gewinnt jedoch den Eindruck, dass die Apokalyptik nur die Zukunft ins Auge fassen will und die Gegenwart und die Vergangenheit vernachlässigt. Hier ist aber eine Möglichkeit zu harmonisieren vorhanden. Die gespannte Zukunftserwartung soll nach dem Zeugnis der Apokalyptiker eine Anregung sein, den biblischen Geboten in diesem irdischen Zeit- und Lebensraum genau zu gehörchen. Zugleich wissen sie sich frei von der Schuldenlast der Vergangenheit, da sie hoffen, von der Verurteilung im letzten Gericht gerettet zu werden.

d. Die apokalyptische Zukunftshoffnung hängt aufs engste zusammen mit der bestimmten Glaubensüberzeugung eines einzelnen oder einer Gruppe. Es ist begreiflich, dass andere Gläubige oder die Kirchen im allgemeinen gar nicht oder nicht völlig über die so prägnanten Vorstellungen der Endzeit sich einigen können. In der christlichen Lehre und in der Verkündigung der Prediger sind die apokalyptischen Erwartungen dann auch meistens Randbemerkungen geworden. Forscher haben sich ebenfalls von der apokalyptischen Zukunftsschau distanziert. Nur individuelle Gläubige und Sondergruppen haben die apokalyptische Enderwartung gepredigt. Vielleicht war die Apokalyptik sowohl bei Juden als Christen vor und in den ersten Jahrhunderten auch schon Sache der einzelnen und der strenggläubigen Kreise.

e. Die Apokalyptiker bringen manchmal Unruhe und Schrecken. Nun lässt sich Glaube — im Sinne von Zuversicht und Vertrauen — schwerlich mit Angst um Errettung zusammenfügen. Auch dies war für viele Menschen Ursache, die Apokalyptik zu meiden. Wenn aber die Stimme des Zukunftschauers als Warnruf zu uns kommt, gibt es eine Parallele mit dem Weckruf derjenigen, die an die Menschheit einen Appell richten, unsere Welt nicht einer drohenden Vernichtung zu überlassen. Obwohl die Bilder und die Predigt der Apokalyptiker ängstigend sind, letztlich geht es auch bei ihnen um Rettung der Schöpfung und Welterneuerung. Die Apokalypsen in der Synopse gehören zum Evangelium!

f. Den rationalen Einwänden gegen die Apokalyptik ist am schwierigsten zu begegnen. Die subjektiven Zeugnisse der Apokalyptiker sind nicht akzeptabel für die objektiven Massstäbe der neuzeitlichen Denkmethoden. Diesen Widerspruch hat man versucht, durch Umdeutungen zu lösen. Die futuristische Eschatologie wurde übersetzt in präsente Eschatologie (DODD). Die kommende Entscheidung im Weltgericht bekam Aktualität als existentielle Entscheidung, und die Essenz der apokalyptischen Enderwartungen hat man durch Entmythologisierung auszuscheiden versucht (BULTMANN). Noch andere damit zusammenhängende Arbeitsformen u.a. auf dem Gebiet der Textforschung und der theologischen Strukturen in den Schriften des Neuen Testaments könnten genannt werden. Hier sei noch die Auffassung GOPPELTS angeführt. Er sagt:[32] "Die Apokalyptik gibt wieder

---

[32] L. GOPPELT, *Apokalyptik und Typologie bei Paulus*, TLZ 89 (Mai 1954), 321-344, 343.

mehr die weltanschaulichen Umrisse, vor allem die universale Schau, und die Ausdrucksmittel an die Hand, die Typologie aber die zentrale theologische Linie. Paulus geht im Grunde nicht wie die Apokalyptik von einem geschichtstheologischen Bild der Menschheitsgeschichte aus, sondern entwirft mit Hilfe der Typologie Bilder der Erwählungs-geschichte (Röm iv; Gal iii).

g. W. KAMLAH gehört zu denjenigen, die radikal-kritisch keinen Kompromiss und keine der oben angeführten Lösungen für annehmbar halten. In dem Kapitel[33] "Ursprung und Versagen der Neuzeit und ihrer Vernunft" heisst es: "Heute bedarf es der kritischen Destruk-tion, der definitiven "Entmythisierung" des traditionellen teleolo-gischen Zeitalterdenkens, des christlichen so gut wie des neuzeitlichen".

In Bezug auf die Gedanken R. BULTMANNS schreibt KAMLAH: "Wenn Theologen heute den entmythisierten Glauben als den eigentlichen und ursprünglichen christlichen Glauben darstellen, so täuschen sie sich selbst und ihre Hörer und Leser darüber hinweg, dass sie diesen Glauben nicht durch Interpretation unverändert bewahrt, sondern durch eine rationale, kritische Interpretation verändert haben — mit gutem Recht, wie mir scheint — und dass diese Veränderung ein-schneidender ist als alle Veränderungen, durch die hindurch die christliche Verkündigung schon immer bewahrt und überliefert wurde". Auch sagt KAMLAH: "Wenn wir Menschen selbst für die Bedingungen unseres Lebens, für bessere Institutionen, für unsere Zukunft zu sorgen haben, dann können wir menschliche Eigenmächtigkeit nicht mehr in genau der gleichen Weise wie Paulus oder Luther verstehen.... Anders ausgedrückt: Die rationale Interpretation der "urchristlichen" Ver-kündigung, durch die erst das "Christentum" als geschichtlich dauernde Religion entstanden ist, bedarf der Erneuerung und Ergänzung".[34]

Diese Zitate, mit denen nur ein kleiner Teil der Gedankengänge KAMLAHS angedeutet ist, genügen um zu zeigen, dass von den kritischen Fragestellungen jedoch eine positive Wirkung ausgehen kann. Die Erneuerung und Ergänzung, die KAMLAH fordert, ist symptomatisch für viele in dieser Zeit, die eine Antwort auf Fragen des Glaubens und der Existenz verlangen. Denn es geht hier im Grunde nicht nur um Detailprobleme. Die Zukunftserwartungen haben, mehr als man sich in früheren Generationen bewusst sein konnte, oder bewusst sein

---

[33] W. KAMLAH, *Utopie, Eschatologie, Geschichtsteleologie*, 103.
[34] W. KAMLAH, *o.c.*, 30-31, 34-35.

wollte, eine tiefgehende funktionelle Bedeutung. Die Zukunftsfrage ist Fundamentalfrage, Lebensfrage, Gottesfrage.

h. Im Neuen Testament formt die Apokalyptik einen sich weit ausdehnenden Boden für die Heilsverkündigung. Die Apokalyptik in diesem Sinne ist nicht beschränkt auf Beschreibungen kommender Endereignisse. Auferstehung der Toten, Neuschöpfung der Erde, völlige Überwindung des Bösen sind darin mitbegriffen. Die Wundertaten Jesu, seine Auferstehung und Himmelfahrt sind ebensogut wie seine Wiederkunft in den Rahmen der apokalyptischen Vorstellungswelt einzureihen. Diese Erweiterung hat Konsequenzen für die Theologie im allgemeinen und für die neutestamentliche Auslegungsarbeit im Besonderen. Das Feld der Untersuchungen und der exegetischen Erfolge wird damit vergrössert, aber die Zentralfragen — Gottesglaube, Hoffnung, Sinngebung des Lebens und der Geschichte — treten unausweichlich vor uns hin. Hat Kamlah recht, dass Entmythologisierung nicht zureicht, um die viel umfassenderen Fragen in dieser Zeit zu bewältigen? Sind radikalere Methoden und Auffassungen notwendig geworden?

Futurologie, Teleologie, die Möglichkeiten seine Zukunft weitgehend selbst zu bauen, und die damit zusammenhängenden rationalen Weltanschauungen und Denkarten dieser Zeit, können nicht ohne weiteres abgelehnt oder übergangen werden.

Wir müssen abwarten, was realisierbar ist, sowohl auf dem Gebiet der Bibelauslegung als im Rahmen der modernen Zukunftsplanung. HAUPT[35] hat gesagt: "Die Schwierigkeit der hier vorliegenden Probleme ist so gross, dass die Arbeit daran wohl für jeden eine Schule in der Bescheidenheit wird". Achtzig Jahre sind vergangen seit diese Bemerkung niedergeschrieben ist. Die Schwierigkeiten sind nicht geringer geworden.

Erstens ist die Welt der Apokalyptik für die Menschen dieser Zeit unverständlicher geworden. Dennoch hat die Erforschung der jüdischen und christlichen Glaubensvorstellungen und die bessere Kenntnis der heidnischen mythologischen Religionen ans Licht gebracht, welche Hoffnungen und Ängste angesichts der Zukunft vor zweitausend Jahren in den antiken Menschen lebten. Aber diese Kenntnis hat für den heutigen Menschen keine direkte aktuelle Bedeutung.

Zweitens ist die Frage nach dem Charakter und der speziellen

---

[35] E. HAUPT, *Die eschatologischen Aussagen Jesu in den synoptischen Evangelien*, Berlin 1895, III.

Bedeutung der biblischen Zukunftserwartung nicht zum Schweigen gekommen. Es gibt hauptsächlich zwei Standpunkte. Einerseits wird noch immer hervorgehoben, dass die Bibelaussagen unveränderlich sind und im Wechsel der Jahrhunderte ihre Kraft und Bedeutung nicht verlieren. Andererseits kann man akzentuieren, dass in neunzehn Jahrhunderten Entwicklungen und Veränderungen im Vergleich mit der Zeit vor zweitausend Jahren eingetreten sind. Sowohl das Festhalten an einem Status quo der christlichen Glaubens- und Hoffnungswelt als auch die Meinung, dass alle Überzeugungen und Erwartungen, auch die auf biblischer Basis, fortwährend in Bewegung sind, stossen auf Widerspruch.

Drittens erhebt sich die Frage, wo die Grenzen der Glaubens- und Hoffnungsgewissheit liegen. Oder mit anderen Worten: können Bild und Sache in der Apokalyptik, sowohl in der neutestamentlichen Theologie, in wissenschaftlichen Abhandlungen als auch in der Praxis und Weltanschauung der heutigen Christen objektiv unterschieden werden? Persönliche religiöse Grundauffassungen und Erfahrungen sind dabei wichtig und dürfen nicht als nebensächliche, subjektive Meinung herabgesetzt werden. Denn immer sind die sogenannten objektiven Einsichten von tiefgehenden, nicht mit vernunftmässigen Mitteln festzustellenden Faktoren mitbestimmt. So haben die Apokalyptiker geschrieben, und so sind auch die vielen früheren und gegenwärtigen Auslegungen dieser Verkündigung zustande gekommen. Auf dem Gebiet der heutigen Philosophie, in theoretischen Disziplinen und in der technischen, sozialen und politischen Praxis finden sich manche methodischen Formen und kritische Hinweise für die theologische Wissenschaft. Die Zukunftsfragen in der Welt und in der Kirche haben mindestens Berührungspunkte. Säkulare und konfessionelle Weltanschauungen, direkt oder indirekt hervorgehend aus den grossen Weltreligionen, das Ersehnen nach einer besseren Zukunft überall in der Welt und gleichzeitig die Hoffnungslosigkeit — hat man auf lange Sicht noch Hoffnung, braucht man noch Hoffnung? Hinzu kommt die revolutionäre Bewegung der jungen Völker[36] für

---

[36] Eine merkwürdige theologische Stimme aus Süd Amerika kommt zu uns in dem Markus-Kommentar von Fernando BELO, *Lecture matérialiste de l'Évangile de Marc*; Récit - Pratique - Idéologie, Paris 1974. Das Buch ist den Ermordeten in den lateinamerikanischen Ländern und in Afrika gewidmet. "Aux frères du Brásil et du Chili. Dans un même contexte de féroce et sanglante répression il y a dix-neuf siècles, a été écrit l'évangile de Marc. En mémoire aussi des Noirs massacrés en Afrique australe. Répression et massacres selon la bonne tradition de l'Occident, sont le fait des gens qui souvent se disent chrétiens. Surpême méconnaisance de l'Évangile,

Gleichberechtigung und Freiheit. Aber dies alles ist ein Programm, das nur in umfangreicher und sorgfältiger Zusammenarbeit angefasst werden kann. Die Theologie, die weiteren Forschungen der neutestamentlichen Apokalyptik eingeschlossen, kann dazu einen bescheidenen Beitrag einbringen. Möge diese inhaltlich unzulängliche Auseinandersetzung trotzdem hierzu einen wirksamen Impuls geben.

---

aveuglement sans retour". Das Buch gibt, wie jeder wissenschaftlicher Kommentar, exegetische Information, manchmal in origineller Weise. Wie ein roter Faden finden sich jedesmal Verbindungen aus der Zeit Jesu — zum Beispiele anknüpfend an die Zeloten — mit revolutionären Gruppen und Guerillas in unserer Welt. Frappant ist die Bemerkung (356) "...la théologie n'est elle pas la matrice même du discours occidental logocentrique, discours idéaliste par excellence au regard du matérialiste historique?".

FROM CREATION TO NOAH IN
THE SECOND DREAM-VISION OF THE ETHIOPIC HENOCH

A. F. J. KLIJN

In the chapters lxxxiii to xc of 1 Henoch we find two dream-visions of which the first one (lxxxiii-lxxxiv) deals with the flood and the second (lxxxv-xc) gives an historical survey from the creation of the world until the coming of the Messiah.[1] This history is described in a symbolical way, animals taking the place of men. The history from the creation to the flood is given in lxxxv 1 to lxxxix 9. From the data in ch. xc scholars usually date this vision during the Maccabaean era, hesitating between the period before the death of Judas in 160/1 and the time of John Hyrcanus between 135 and 105.[2]

Long ago R. H. CHARLES considered this part "the most interesting fragment of the Book of Enoch".[3] He wrote that in general the allegory "is based on the O.T., but some mythical elements from later Jewish exegesis are incorporated".[4] These elements will be considered in this article. The existence of these in Henoch shows that

---

[1] This vision was known to the writer of the *Book of Jubilees*, cf. iv 19: "And what was and what will be he (scil. Henoch) saw in a vision of his sleep, as it will happen to the children of men throughout their generations until the day of judgment ...".

[2] G. BEER, in: E. KAUTZSCH, Die Apokryphen und Pseudepigraphen, Tübingen 1921, II, 230, suggested John Hyrcanus; R. H. CHARLES, in: R. H. CHARLES, *The Apocrypha and Pseudepigrapha*, 170-171, suggested the time before the death of Judas, also in R. H. CHARLES, *The Book of Enoch or 1 Henoch*, Oxford 1912, 180 and R. H. CHARLES, *Eschatology*, New York 1963 (repr. of 1913[2]), 220, followed by BOUSSET-GRESSMANN, *Die Religion des Judentums...* 1926[3], 12; E. SCHÜRER, *Geschichte des jüd. Volkes* III 1909[4], 278: "im Drittel des zweiten Jahrhunderts vor Christo". Cf. also more recent literature: C. P. VAN ANDEL, *De Structuur van de Henoch-traditie en het Nieuwe Testament*, Utrecht 1955, 26-30, 28: "tijdens de hogepriester Menelaos 173-167"; O. PLÖGER, *Henochbücher*, in: *R.G.G.*[3] III, 222-225, 223: Judas the Maccabee or John Hyrcanus; O. EISSFELDT, *Einleitung in das Alte Testament*, Tübingen 1964[3], 838.839, gives the same opinion but adds Alexander Jannaeus (103-70), cf. C. C. TORREY, Alexander Jannaeus and the Archangel Michael, *VT* 4 (1954), 208-211; A. S. V. D. WOUDE, in: Th. C. VRIEZEN, *Literatuur van Oud-Israel*, Wassenaar 1973, 345, repeats EISSFELDT's opinion, and H. C. C. CAVALLIN, *Life after Death*, *CB.NT* 7:1 (Lund 1974), 40: "This vision is an allegory of contemporary Jewish history, Hellenistic oppression and Macabaean revolution".

[3] CHARLES, *Eschatology*, 220.

[4] CHARLES, in: *The Apocrypha and Pseudepigrapha*, 250.

we are dealing with a wide-spread and ancient haggadic tradition.

First we shall give the text so far it is relevant to the subject and add some remarks.[5]

lxxxv 3 Before I (Henoch) took thy mother Edna, I saw in a vision on my bed, and behold a bull came forth from the earth, and that bull was white; and after it came forth a heifer, and along with this (latter) came forth two bulls, one of them black and the other red. 4 And that black bull gored the red one and pursued him over the earth, and thereupon I could no longer see that red bull. 5. But that black bull grew and that heifer went with him, and I saw that many oxen proceeded from him which resembled and followed him. 6. And that cow, that first one, went from the presence of that first bull in order to seek that red one, but found him not, and lamented with a great lamentation over him and sought him. 7. And I looked till that first bull came to her and quietened her, and from that time onward she cried no more. 8. And after that she bore another white bull, and after him she bore many bulls and black cows. 9. And I saw in my sleep that white bull likewise grow and become a great white bull, and from him proceeded many white bulls, and they resembled him. 10. And they began to beget many white bulls, which resembled them, one following the other, (even) many.

lxxxvi 1 And again I saw with mine eyes as I slept, and I saw the heaven above, and behold a star fell from heaven, and it arose and ate and pastured amongst those oxen. 2. And after that I saw the large and the black oxen, and behold they all changed their stalls and pastures and their cattle, and began to live with each other. 3. And again I saw in the vision, and looked towards heaven, and behold I saw many stars descend and cast themselves down from heaven to that first star, and they became bulls amongst those cattle and pastured with them. 4. And I looked at them and saw, and behold they all let out their privy members, like horses, and began to cover the cows of the oxen, and they all became pregnant and bare elephants, camels and asses...

In chapters lxxxvii and lxxxviii it is said that the archangels descend from heaven to bind the stars and to cast them into an abyss.

lxxxix 1 And one of those four (scil. archangels) went to that white bull and instructed him in a secret, without his being terrified: he was born a bull and became a man, and built himself a great vessel and dwelt thereon; and three bulls dwelt with him in that vessel...

After the flood the story continues:

9 But that white bull which had become a man came out of that vessel, and the three bulls with him, and one of those three was white like that bull, and one of them was red as blood, and one black: and that white bull departed from them.

---

[5] The translation has been taken from the edition of CHARLES in *Apocrypha and Pseudepigrapha*, 250 ff. I thank Dr. B. JONGELING in Groningen for checking Charles' translation and giving valuable information not only about the Ethiopic text, but also about the rest of this article.

In 10. it is said that these brothers "began to bring forth beasts of the field ... and among them was born a white bull".

At the end of this vision in xc 37 we read:

And I saw that a white bull was born, with large horns, and all the beasts of the field and all the birds of the air feared him ... 38. And I saw till all their generations were transformed, and they all became white bulls...

The historical survey deals with the generation of mankind but leaves out the creation of the world, paradise and Adam's fall.

Some details require our attention. Adam is called a bull who "came forth from the earth" (lxxxv 3). The word bull is *lāhm* in Ethiopic. Eve who came forth after it is called a heifer, *tā'wā* with the addition "female" in Ethiopic. Nothing is said about the birth of the two bulls (some mss.: other young bulls) who came forth along with this heifer. It is not said that they are sons of Adam. Later when the red bull was killed by the black one only "that cow", viz. Eve or the heifer, went to look for her son. Also the red and black bull are called *tā'wā*.

In lxxxv 4 it is said that Cain killed Abel.

In lxxxv 5 we read that the black bull became adult. The second part of the sentence is not clear. Litterally it is said: "and with him came that (or: the, or: a) heifer" (the same word as in vs. 3). At first sight this heifer seems to be identical with the one mentioned in vs. 3, viz. Eve, which could mean that Cain and Eve begot "many oxen" (again *lāhm*).[6] But in the light of vs. 6 speaking about "that cow" (*'egwàlt* with the addition "female") we may assume that the author speaks about two different females, viz. Cain's wife in vs. 5 and Eve in vs. 6, without saying whence Cain's wife came.

In lxxxv 6 we read about a lamentation which is not mentioned in the Hebrew text.

---

[6] The idea that Eve and Cain had sexual intercouse is available in an old midrash, viz. Gen. R. XXII 7, see *Midrash Rabbah* I, *Genesis* I (ed. H. FREEDMAN), London and Bournemouth 1951, 187: "... Cain rose up against his brother Abel, etc. Judah b. Rabbi said: 'Their quarrel was about the first Eve ...' ", cf. V. APTOWITZER, *Kain und Abel in der Agada* (VAKMF 1), Wien u. Leipzig 1922, 22-28. The idea is also available in the Manichaean tradition according to the Fihrist, cf. G. FLÜGEL, *Mani*, Leipzig 1862, 91: "Alsdann kehrte der Archon zu seiner Tochter Hawwâ zurück und beschlief sie mit der Geilheit, die ihm innewohnt, dass sie einen Sohn gebar hässlich von Ansehen und röthlich, mit Namen Kâin, der röthliche Mann. Dieser Sohn beschlief darauf seine Mutter und sie gebar einen weissen Sohn, mit Namen Hâbîl der weisse Mann. Hierauf beschlief Kâin nochmals seine Mutter, so dass sie zwei Mädchen gebar ...".

In lxxxv 7 we read about Adam and Eve in the same sentence for the first time. And it is from this meeting that in vs. 8 it is said that "another white bull" (*lāhm*) is born, viz. Seth.[7] After that many bulls (*lāhm*) and black cows (*ᵉgwàlt*) are born.

lxxxv 9 deals with the generation of Seth and his descendents who are "white bulls". In this verse we find a different word for bull, *sōr*, twice and *lāhm* again in the plural.

In lxxxv 10 we find *lāhm* again in the plural. Here again reference is made to the generation of Seth.

In lxxxvi 1 we find the story of Genesis 6 about the "sons of God". In this case we first read about one star falling from heaven and later about "many stars" (vs. 3). The star pastured amonst "those oxen" (*lāhm* in the plural) with which obviously are meant the oxen mentioned in lxxxv 5, viz. the children of Cain.

In lxxxvi 4 we read about the birth of elephants, camels and asses with which the "giants" of Genesis 6,4 can be identified.

In lxxxix 1 we read again about a white bull (*lāhm*) in whom we recognize Noah. The three bulls, white, red and black, are Shem, Ham and Japheth. In lxxxix 10 is spoken of Abraham, again a white bull (*lāhm*).

The vision ends with the coming of the Messiah, a white bull (*lāhm*) who transformed all who belong to him into white bulls (*lāhm* in the plural).

In this vision there figure two or three generations. From Eve originated two sons, one of whom was killed by his brother. A black generation remains, to be distinguished from a white generation, represented by Seth, the son of Adam and Eve. The black generation was corrupted by the "stars" while a representative of the white generation, Noah, is saved. This generation is next represented by Abraham and finally by the Messiah who rallies his own around him after he had transformed them into white bulls.

In the following we shall point out some of the parallels between the contents of this vision and Jewish haggadic material.

In lxxxiii 3 it is said about Adam that "a bull came forth from the earth..." which not only refers to Gen. iii 19 but also shows close resemblance with Gen. R. XXII 2: "In the past, Adam was created from the ground, and Eve from Adam...".[8]

---

[7] Some mss.: "a pair of white oxen" in place of "another white bull".
[8] FREEDMAN, *o.c.*, 181.

We have already shown that Cain and Abel are supposed to be children of Eve, but not of Adam. This idea we often meet in both Jewish and gnostic literature. In the *Vita Adae et Evae* we undoubtedly have a traditiom that Cain and Abel are not Adam's sons. It is said that Eve goes to the West after their expulsion from paradise "while she had in the womb offspring of three months old" (xviii 1-3). With Michael's help she received a son who was shining (*lucidus*). Next Eve conceived again and Abel is born. Finally we read: "And thereafter Adam knew his wife and he begat a son and called his name Seth". These are the words of Gen. iv 25 without the word "again". The fact that Cain was *lucidus* shows that he was a son of a superhuman being as shown by passages in 1 Henoch and the Apocryphon of Genesis.[9]

In Gen. R. XXIV 6 we read that in the first 130 years of Adam's and Eve's life, viz. before the birth of Seth, both Adam and Eve had intercourse with demons, male and female. This is explained from Gen. v 1 which deals with the genealogy of Adam in which is only spoken of Seth and his descendants.[10] Eve having had intercourse with demons is a wide-spread idea which is found several times in the Babylonian Talmud.[11] Here Zohar is even more explicit saying that at the birth of Cain and Abel it is said "*she* bore" (cf. Gen. iv 1 and 2) but after the birth of Seth "*he* begat in his own likeness after his image" (Gen. v 3).[12]

We also meet the idea that Cain is the son of Sammael but that Abel is Adam's son. We may refer to Ps. Jon. Gen. iv 1:

---

[9] See 1 Henoch 106 5-6: when Noah is born Lamech says that he has begotten a strange son οὐχ ὅμοιον τοῖς ἀνθρώποις ἀλλὰ τοῖς τέκνοις τῶν ἀγγέλων τοῦ οὐρανοῦ... The same story also in *Genesis Apocryphon* (ed. N. AVIGAD), Jerusalem 1950, 40, c. II. In *Apoc. Mosis* I 3 Eve gave birth to two sons τὸν Διάφωτον τὸν καλούμενον Κάϊν καὶ τὸν Ἀμιλαβὲς τὸν καλούμενον Ἀβελ. The name Διαφωτος (also spelt Ἀδιάφωτος) is not quite clear but certainly hints at the idea of Cain being "shining", cf. Also *The Zohar* I, *Bereshith* 37a (ed. J. ABELSON), London and Bournemouth 1949, 138: "For Cain was born from Samael and his aspect was not like that of other human beings, and all who came from his stock were called 'sons of God'". See also *Apocryphon of John* II (ed. M. KRAUSE-P. LABIB), 10, 34-36: "...Kain, den die Menschengeschlechter 'die Sonne' nennen", which can also be found in the *Gospel of the Egyptians*, III 58, 15-17 (ed. A. BÖHLIG, F. WISSE and P. LABIB), in: *Nag Hammadi Studies* IV, Leiden 1975, 124.

[10] FREEDMAN, *o.c.*, 203.

[11] Cf. b. Shabb, 146a (ed. GOLDSCHMIDT I, 898); b. Jabmuth 103b (IV, 683) and b. Ab. Zara 22b (IX, 503): "Als nämlich die Schlange der Hava beiwohnte impfte sie ihr eine Unflat ein...".

[12] ABELSON, *o.c.*, 55a, 174.

"And Adam was aware that Eve his wife had conceived from Sammael the angel, and she became pregnant and bore Cain, and he was like those on high, and not like those below; and he said, 'I have acquired a man, the angel of the Lord'".[13] The words "And Adam was aware..." are clear as soon as we look at the passage in Pirkê de Rabbi Eliezer XXI: "(Sammael) riding on the serpent came to her, and she conceived; afterwards Adam came to her, and she conceived Abel, as it is said, 'And Adam knew Eve his wife' (Gen. iv 1). What is the meaning of 'knew'? (He knew) that she had conceived. And she saw his likeness that it was not of earthly beings but of heavenly beings, and she prophesied and said: 'I have gotten a man with the Lord'".[14]

This means that Cain and Abel were twins but Cain was Sammael's son and Abel Adam's. We meet this idea also in Zohar 54a: "R. Eliezer said: 'When the serpent injected his impurity into Eve, she absorbed it, and so when Adam had intercourse with her she bore two sons — one from the impure side and one from the side of Adam; ...'".[15]

In christian literature we do not find much of this tradition, though the *Protevangelium Jacobi* seems to hint at this idea saying that Joseph lamented that the same happened to him as to Adam in the past who was praying when the serpent happened to meet Eve alone.[16]

In gnostic literature the tradition occurs often. The earliest exemple is Ps.-Tertullian writing about the Sethians, though the statement is not very clear. He might be writing about the creation of Cain and Abel by angels.[17] The Sethian book called *Allogeneis*, however, undoubtedly refers to the archons who desired to have intercourse

---

[13] See J. BOWKER, *The Targums and Rabbinic Literature*, Cambridge 1969, 132, cf. v 1, *o.c.*, 142: "For before that time (scil. that Adam begat Seth) Eve had borne Cain who was not from him (scil. Adam) and did not resemble him...".

[14] See *Pirke de Rabbi Eliezer* (ed. G. FRIEDLANDER), London - New York 1916, 150-151.

[15] ABELSON, *o.c.*, 172.

[16] Ed. M. TESTUZ, in: *Papyrus Bodmer V* (B Bod), Zürich 1958, 83. See also Tertullian, *De patientia* 5, 15 (ed. J. W. Ph. BORLEFFS) in: SCP IV, 's-Gravenhage 1948, 25-26: *Nam statim illa (scil. Eva) semine diaboli concepta malitiae fecunditate irae filium procreavit*.

[17] Ps. Tertullianus, *Adversus omnes haereses* (ed. A. KROYMANN) in: CSEL 47, Vienna... 218, 2: *huius perversitatis (scil.* the sect of the Sethians) *doctrina haec est: duos homines ab angelis constitutos, Cain et Abel*. Epiphanius, *Panarion*, 39.2.1, rewrote this passage: γεγενῆσθαι ἐξ ὑπαρχῆς εὐθὺς δύο ἀνθρώπους καὶ ἐκ τῶν δύο εἶναι τὸν Κάϊν καὶ τὸν Ἄβελ, ...

with Eve.[18] The *Archontici* mentioned by Epiphanius taught that the devil had intercourse with Eve and begat Cain and Abel.[19] In the gnostic "Untitled Work" we read that the first archon had intercourse with Eve after which Abel was born. Later she gave birth to the "other sons" who were children of "the seven powers and their angels".[20] Finally we may refer to the Apocryphon of John according to which the first archon is the father of Eloim, viz. Cain, and Jave, viz. Abel, and the Gospel of Philip which says that Cain is "the son of the serpent".[21]

The dream-vision refers to Cain's wife of whose origin nothing is said. In Jewish sources we meet two traditions. According to the first, Adam and Eve received a number of sons and daughters successively, and according to the second a number of twins were born.[22]

The former tradition stems from the Book of Jubilees. Successively are born Cain, Abel, their sister Âwân,[23] Seth and their sister Âzûrâ.[24] Cain married Âwân[25] and Seth Âzûrâ.[26] The tradition is known to Epiphanius[27] and Syncellus.[28] Malalas writes that Cain

---

[18] See H.-C. PUECH, Fragments retrouvés de L'"Apocalypse d'Allogène", in: *Mélanges Franz Cumont*, Bruxelles 1936, II, 935-962, who discovered fragments of this Sethian book in the writings of Theodor bar Konai, Agapius of Menbidj and Gregorius bar Hebraeus.

[19] Epiphanius, *Panarion*, 40.5.3.

[20] See *Die Koptisch-Gnostische Schrift ohne Titel aus Codex II von Nag Hammadi* (ed. A. BÖHLIG u. P. LABIB), Berlin 1962, 164, 33 - 165, 18. This writing is related with the *Hypostasis of the Archons*, where in 137, 18-31 is spoken of the intercourse of Eve with the Archons and in 139, 11-14 about the birth of Cain and Abel without clearly stating that they are the offspring of the archons, see R. A. BULLARD, *The Hypostasis of the Archons*, Berlin 1970, 92.

[21] *Apocryphon of John* (ed. M. KRAUSE - P. LABIB), II 24, 15-18 (see also IV, 37, 27-38, 11): "Und der Erste Archôn befleckte sie (scil. Eve), und er zeugte mit ihr zwei Söhne...: Elôim und Jave...", 24-25: "Diese aber rief er mit dem Namen: 'Kain und Abel'", and *The Gospel of Philip* 109, 7-8 (ed. R. McL. WILSON), New York and Evanston 1962, 105-106.

[22] According to Philo, *de posteritate Caini* 34, Cain had no sisters.

[23] *Jubil.* iv 1.

[24] *Jubil.* iv 7-8.

[25] *Jubil.* iv 9.

[26] *Jubil.* iv 11. In iv 10 it is said that Adam and Eve had also nine other sons. In *Vita Adae et Evae* xxiv, we read that Adam and Eve "begat thirty sons and thirty daughters", also in *Apocalypsis Mosis* iv 1.

[27] Epiphanius, *Panarion*, 39.6.4, writes Ἀζουρα and Σαυή.

[28] Syncellus (ed. G. DINDORF), in: CSHB, Bonn 1829, 14-15, writes about the birth of Cain, Abel, Ἀσουάμ, with whom Cain married, and *o.c.*, 16-17, of Seth and Ἀζουρα with whom Seth married.

married Azoura and Seth Asouan[29] and this tradition is found in all later Byzantine chronographers.

Ps.-Jonathan explains the word וַתֹּסֶף in Gen. iv 2 as an indication that Eve bore twins: "And she went on to bear from Adam, her husband, his twin sister and Abel".[30] This is stated even more explicitly in Pirkê de Rabbi Eliezer: "Rabbi Miasha said: 'Cain was born, and his wife, his twinsister, with him". And it goes on: "Rabbi Joseph said: 'Cain and Abel were twins, as it is said: 'And she conceived and bore (with) Cain' (Gen. iv 1). At that hour she had an additional capacity for child-bearing (as it is said), 'And she continued to bear his brother Abel'" (ibid. 2).[31]

This kind of haggadic tradition resulted in remarks such as the one in Gen. R. XXI 2: "R. Joshua b. Karhah said: 'Only two entered the bed, and seven left it: Cain and his twin sister, Abel and his two twin sisters'".[32]

The idea that Cain and Abel had twin-sisters occurs also in the Cave of Treasures where we read that Cain's sister was called ܠܒܘܕܐ and Abel's ܩܠܝܡܐ. Adam wished Cain to marry Abel's twin-sister but he preferred his own which is the cause of the quarrel between the two brothers.[33]

The idea that Eve lamented Cain's death arises from the play upon the words אבל and הבל. The tradition is already present in Jubil. iv 7: "And Adam and his wife mourned for Abel four weeks of years...". Also Philo knew this tradition, cf. de migr. Abrahami 74: "..."Αβελ — ὄνομα δέ ἐστι τὰ θνητὰ πενθοῦντος καὶ τὰ ἀθάνατα εὐδαιμονί-

---

[29] Malalas (ed. G. Dindorf), in: CSHB..., Bonn 1931, 3.

[30] J. Bowker, o.c., 132.

[31] G. Friedlander, o.c., 152.

[32] H. Freedman, o.c., 180, cf. also b. Sanh. 38b (ed. Goldschmidt VIII, 609): "...in der achten (Stunde) legten sie (scil. Adam and Eve) sich ins Bett zu zweien und verliessen es zu vieren" and Aboth de Rabbi Nathan (ed. J. Goldin), New Haven 1955, 13: "On that day two lay down together and four arose. R. Judah b. Bathyra says: On that day two lay down together and seven arose". See L. Ginzberg, Die Haggada bei den Kirchenväter und in der apokryphischer Literatur, MGWJ 13 (1899), 225, n. 3: "Die zweite Zwillingsschwester im Midr. hat ihr Dasein dem doppelten את, welches bei der Geburt Habels steht, zu verdanken".

[33] The Book of the Cave of Treasures (ed. E. A. W. Budge), London 1927, 69-70, taken over by A. Dillmann, Das christliche Adambuch des Morgenlandes, JBW 5 (1852/53), 67, cf. 70, and Eutychius (PG 111, 910 C), who writes that Cain married Azura and Abel Owain quae Graece Laphura, which shows the influence of the Book of Jubilees, and The Book of the Bee (ed. E. A. W. Budge), Anecdota Oxoniensia, Oxford 1886, 25.

ζοντος. For the rest we find this idea in Syriac writings connected with the Cave of Treasures only[34] and in the *onomastica*.[35]

It is said in Henoch that a star descended and afterwards many more (lxxxvi 1 and 3). This hints at the story in Genesis vi. It strikes us that stars are mentioned since Gen. vi 2 speaks about בְּנֵי הָאֱלֹהִים. Henoch obviously follows the tradition we find in Josephus[36] and Philo[37] who rendered the words by angels who on their turn were identified with stars. This can already be found in 1 Henoch where in vi 2 it is said that the angels "lusted after the beautiful daughters of men". Later the fallen angels were bound and cast into darkness (x 4). When Henoch is shown that place he is said: "These are of the number of the *stars* of heaven which have transgressed the commandments of the Lord and are bound here till ten thousand years" (xxi 6). The descent of the angels is connected with stars abandoning their appointed place in heaven. In 1 Henoch xviii 15 we find that the stars transgressed the commandments of the Lord "in the beginning of their rising, because they did not come forth at their appointed times". The same idea we find in the Testament of Naphthali which considered the fall of the angels a change of the order of nature.[38] In Christian literature this was taken over in the instances where reference is made to angels transgressing their τάξις.[39]

It is not quite clear why first only one star descended and later

---

[34] E. A. W. BUDGE, *o.c.*, 71: "And Adam and Eve mourned for Abel one hundred years"; *Book of the Bee*, 27: "Adam and Eve mourned for Abel one hundred years. After this period Seth is born". These hundred years bridge over the difference between the Hebrew text according to which Seth was born in 130 and the LXX according to which Adam was 230 years old. *Adambuch* 74: "Und Adam und Eva blieben in Trauer und vielem Weinen hundert Tage lang". In the Armenian 'Erzählung von den Söhnen Adams Abel und Kain' 10, in: E. PREUSCHEN, *Die apokryphen gnostischen Adamschriften*, Giessen 1900, 36: "Als Adam und Eva die Ermordung Abels erfahren, weinen sie lange Zeit". Contrary to Henoch always both Adam and Eve are mourning.

[35] *Hieronymi interpretationis hebraicorum nominum*, in: P. DE LAGARDE, *Onomastica Sacra*, Hildesheim 1966 (repr.) 27 (2, 18); 61 (31, 15); 93 (60, 17); 112 (77, 26): *Abel luctus*...; *Onomastica Vaticana*, 206 (177, 67); 212 (185, 87): Ἄβελ ἀτμὶς ἢ πένθος ....

[36] Josephus, *Antiquitates* I. 73.

[37] Philo, *de gigantibus* 6, cf. also *Jubil.* iv 15 and see Ph. ALEXANDER, The Targumim and Early Exegesis of the "Sons of God" in Genesis 6, *JJS* 23 (1972), 60-71.

[38] *Testament of Naphthali* 3, 5: Ὁμοίως δὲ καὶ οἱ Ἐγρήγοροι ἐνήλλαξαν τάξιν φύσεως αὐτῶν..., see also Philo, *de gigant.* 6-12.

[39] Papias fr. IV, Justinus, *Apologia* 2.5.3.; Irenaeus, *Epideixis* 10; Athenagoras, *Legatio* 24,4; Clemens Alexandrinus, *Strom.* V I 10 2, Ps-Clementine, *Recognitiones* IV 26, cf. I 29.

the other ones. Ps.-Jon. Gen. vi 4 reads: "Shamhazai and Azael fell
from heaven and were on the earth in those days, and also after that,
when the sons of the great ones came into the daughters of men,
and they bore children of them...", which means that the descent
took place in two stages, but whether this is a meaningful parallel
is doubtful.[40]

The remark that the star takes the form of a bull (lxxxvi 3) may
be compared with passages where it is said that the fallen angels
became men, like Testament of Reuben.[41] Also in Pirḳê de Rabbi
Eliezer XXII it is said that as a result of their fall "their strength
and stature (became) like that of the sons of man, and their frame
was (made of) clods of dust...".[42] In the Ps.-Clementines we find
the idea, already present in the Book of Jubilees, that the angels
initially descended to help mankind. Later they took on the nature
of men and mingled with the daugthers of men.[43] The tradition
entered into the Apocryphon of John where it is said that the angels
came to the women in the form of "husbands".[44]

In lxxxvi 1 we read that a star fell from heaven and pastured
amongst "those oxen". The stars became bulls (3) and they began
to impregnate the cows of the oxen. Thereupon elephants, camels
and asses are born (4) which are feared by all the oxen (5). With
these oxen are meant those proceeded from the black bull Cain
(lxxxv 5). These oxen were destroyed by the flood together with
the elephants, asses and camels, but "that white bull", Noah, was
saved. We are dealing with a tradition, deviating from the Old Testament, that the "sons of God" only mingled with the Cainites and
that only the Cainites were destroyed. Only the Sethites, the white
bulls, were saved.

Apart from the peculiar and isolated tradition that Cain himself
was killed by the flood[45] we meet the idea of the Cainites being
a generation separated from the Sethites in Gen. R. XXIV 6 referring
to Gen. v 1 about the generation of Adam. It is said: "These are

---

[40] BOWKER, o.c., 251.

[41] Testament of Reuben 5, 6-7: μετασχηματίζοντο γὰρ εἰς ἄνδρα καὶ ἐν τῇ
συνουσίᾳ τῶν ἀνδρῶν αὐτῶν συνεφαίνοντο αὐταῖς.

[42] Ed. FRIEDLANDER, o.c., 160.

[43] Ps.-Clementine, Homilies VIII 12-13.

[44] Apocryphon of John (ed. KRAUSE-LABIB), II 29, 26-30, and the other versions.

[45] Testament of Benjamin 7. It seems that according to Josephus, Antiquitates I 66,
the descendents of Cain were already vanished before Adam's death: "...and inheriting
and imitating one another's vices, each ended worse than the last".

the descendants of Adam, but the earlier ones were not descendants of Adam. Why? because they were destroyed by the flood, for R. Joshua b. Levi said: 'All these names signify chastening...'".[46] In Pirkê de Rabbi Eliezer XXII this is stated more clearly: "Rabbi Simeon said: 'From Seth arose and were descended all the generations of the righteous. From Cain arose and were descended all the generations of the wicked...'", and further: "Rabbi Meir said: 'The generation of Cain went about stark naked, men and women, just like beasts...'. Rabbi said: 'The angels who fell from their holy place in heaven saw the daughters of the generations of Cain walking about naked, with their eyes painted, like harlots, and they went astray after them, and took wives from amongst them, as it is said: 'and the sons of Elohim...'".[47]

In Christian literature the "sons of God" are generally identified with the Sethites.[48] At the beginning they lived separated from the Cainites but some of them mingled with the Cainites. These and their offspring were destroyed in the flood. Only some of the Sethites, like Noah, kept their purity.[49] In gnostic literature we often meet the idea that the Sethites as a whole were saved during the flood. It is this idea which is closely related with Henoch.[50]

From the white bull, Noach, three bulls were born, one white, one red and the last one black. These sons can be compared with Abel, Cain and Seth who were also identified with a red, a black

---

[46] FREEDMAN, o.c., 203-204. Ps.-Jon. Gen. v 3 (ed. BOWKER, o.c., 142) paraphrases: "Eve had borne Cain who was not from him (scil. Adam) and did not resemble him, and Abel was killed at the hands of Cain and Cain was cast out...".

[47] BOWKER, o.c., 158-160, cf. also Testament of Adam III 15 (ed. P. RIESSLER, Altjüdisches Schrifttum, 1088): "Du hast gehört, mein Sohn, dass eine Sintflut kommt die die ganze Erde abwascht wegen der Sünde der Töchter Kains, der, aus Eifersucht auf deine Schwester Lebora, seinen Bruder Abel totschlug", and Zohar 55a (ed. ABELSON, 177-178). See also the difference between the generations of Cain and Seth according to Philo, de posteritate Caini, who, however, draws no historical conclusions.

[48] The first one known to us identifying the "sons of God" with the Sethites was Julius Africanus, quoted by Syncellus (ed. DINDORF, 34-35); see also H. GELZER, Sextus Julius Africanus und die Byzantinische Chronographie, Leipzig 1898, 63-64.

[49] This is the general idea in Greek, Latin and Syriac authors.

[50] Sethians according to Ps.-Tertullian, adversus omnes haereses 2, cf. Epiphanius, Panarion 39 3 1-3; Ps. Hieronymus, Indic. de haeresibus c. IX (ed. F. Oehler, in: CHaer I, Berolini 1856, 290); the same in the gnostic Gospel of the Egyptians III 61, 1-22, cf. IV 72, 10-73, 6, see also Apocalypse of Adam (ed. A. BÖHLIG - P. LABIB), Halle-Wittenberg 1963, 67, 22-70, 9; Apocryphon of John (ed. KRAUSE-LABIB), II 28, 34-29, 12 and parallel versions. We must add that in gnostic tradition the Highest God causes the flood to destroy the Cainites and sometimes the archons to destroy the Sethites.

and a white bull. The idea that the three sons represent three generations can be found in Philo according to whom Shem was good, Ham evil and Japheth indifferent,[51] which was taken over by Ambrosius[52] and can be compared with Hilarius who writes that Ham respresented the pagans, Japheth the people under the law and Shem those justified by grace.[53]

Finally we see that the Messiah is called a white bull who transforms his own into white bulls (xci 37-38). This means that an uninterrupted line runs from Seth, Noah, Abraham to the Messiah and his people.

The idea that the Messiah belongs to the generation of Seth can be found in Gen. R. XXIII 5 referring to Gen. iv 25: "And she called his name Seth: For God hath appointed me another seed, etc. R. Tanhuma said in the name of Samuel Kozith: '[She hinted at] that seed which would arise from another source, viz. the king Messiah'".[54] In later Christian literature this idea re-appears: the meaning of the name Seth is considered to be "ressurrection".[55] But especially the gnostic sect of the Sethians considered Jesus the incarnation of Seth.[56]

We may conclude that 1 Henoch in this part shows many parallels with haggadic material of a much later date. This is of great importance

---

[51] Philo, *Questions and Answers on Genesis* (ed. R. MARCUS, *o.c.*, 55) referring to Gen. v 31.

[52] Ambrosius, *de Noe* 2 (CSEL 32, 414).

[53] Hilarius, *Tractatio Mystica* I 15 (SC 19, 104); see also *Excerpta e Theodoto* 54: ἡ ἄλογος (φύσις) ἧς ἦν Κάιν... ἡ λογικὴ καὶ δικαία ἧς ἦν ῎Αβελ· τρίτη δὲ ἡ πνευματικὴ ἧς ἦν Σήθ, and Irenaeus, *Adversus haereses* I. 7.5; cf. J. S. LEWIS, *A Study of the Interpretation of Noah and the Flood*..., Leiden 1968, 178-180.

[54] FREEDMAN, *o.c.*, 196. The same we find referring to Gen. xix 32 in LI 8 (*o.c.*, 448) and *Ruth Rabba* (ed. A. WÜNSCHE), 58.

[55] Isidorus of Seville, *Questiones in Vetus Testamentum, in Genesim*, in: *PL* 83, c. 228: 'Seth quippe interpretatus "ressurrectio" qui est Christus'. Cf. R.-M. TONNEAU, *Sancti Ephraem Syri in Genesim et in Exodum Commentarii* (CSCO 153), Louvain 1965, 43: 'In Seth autem, qui omnino similis fuit Adae, similitudo Filii figurata est...'.

[56] Ps. Tertullian, *adversus omnes haereses* 2: 'de Christo autem sic sentiunt ut dicant illum tantummodo Seth et pro ipso Seth Christum fuisse'. The same idea in Epiphanius, *Panarion*, 39.3.5, and Filaster (ed. F. HEYLEN, in: CChr.SL IX, Turnhout 1937, *praef*. III 3); Ps. Hieronymus, *Indic. de haeresibus* (OEHLER, *o.c.*, 290) IX; Honorius Augustodunensis, *De haeresibus liber* (OEHLER, *o.c.*, 328) XXXI; Paulus, *De haeresibus liber* (OEHLER, *o.c.*, 315) XIV; Isidorus of Seville, *De haeresibus* (OEHLER, *o.c.*, 305) VI 16; and *Etymol. Lib.* VIII VI 16, in: *PL* 82, 299; Augustinus, *De haeresibus liber* (OEHLER, *o.c.*, 200), XIX, but: *Quidam eos dicunt Sem filium Noe Christum putare*. See also the *Gospel of the Egyptians* (ed. BÖHLIG-WISSE, 146: III 64, 1-3): "...even Jesus the Living one, even he whom the Great Seth has put on" (= IV 75, 17-18).

for the dating of this material with appears at the same time to be of a very early date.

It is not unknown that this material found its way into Christian and gnostic writings.[57] It is, however, striking that in this case Henoch shows some resemblance with gnostic ideas. In the first place we may refer to the idea that the generation of the Sethites remains incorrupted. This is very important in gnostic circles because they represent the righteous people which are destined to be saved. In the second place we see that the Redeemer is not only a member of the generation of Seth but he is also a reincarnation of him.

This again shows that some gnostic ideas appear to have roots in Apocalyptic Jewish tradition.

---

[57] M. KRAUSE, Aussagen über das Alte Testament in z.T. bisher unveröffentlichten gnostischen Texten aus Nag Hammadi, in: *Ex Orbe Religionum, Studia G. Widengren* I, Lugduni Batavorum 1972, 449-456, and B. D. PEARSON, Jewish Haggadic Traditions in the Testimony of Truth from Nag Hammadi (*CG IV, 3*), in: *idem*, 457-470.

MARCUS GNOSTICUS AND THE NEW TESTAMENT:
EUCHARIST AND PROPHECY

J. REILING

Any study of the phenomenon of false prophecy in the first and second century A.D. has to deal with Irenaeus' account of Marcus the Gnostic in the 13th chapter of the first book of his *Adversus Haereses*. In my study of the 11th Mandate of the Shepherd[1] I dealt with some aspects, such as the criteria by which the prophets are judged, the δαίμων πάρεδρος which appears to inspire the prophet, and the state of mind of the women whom Marcus initiated into the mysteries of prophecy. The bizarre phenomenon of the prophet, celebrating the Eucharist, spelling out his symbolisms of words and numbers was not taken into account. In this paper I attempt to investigate Marcus himself and his sacred acts and to determine his place in the history of early Christianity. Firstly, a remark about the sources. The first source, of course, is Irenaeus, *Adv. Haer.* I 13, known to us not only in the Latin translation, but also from Epiphanius, *Panarion* 34. Epiphanius expressly points out that he did not want to duplicate Irenaeus' work, and that therefore he did his utmost to πρὸς ἔπος ἐκθέσθαι the data compiled by him, and this he does faithfully.[2] His text differs on some points from Irenaeus in Latin and I will come back to that whenever it is relevant to our survey.

A further source is Hippolytus *Elenchus* VI 39-41. It must be doubted whether, beside Irenaeus, this is an independent source, certainly with regard to the data about eucharist and prophecy. He summarizes Irenaeus' story and adds some brief comments. At no point does he appear to have had original information about Marcus. In the Greek and the Latin versions, Irenaeus remains our only source.

Before starting out on our journey through the text, some remarks about Marcus himself. Irenaeus introduces him as *alius... ex iis qui sunt apud eos*, and, as appears from the *praefatio*, these are οἱ περὶ Πτολεμαῖον; furthermore, Marcus regarded himself as *emendator magistri*, and this magister is of course Valentinus himself. Elsewhere,

---

[1] J. REILING, *Hermas and Christian Prophecy*, Leiden 1973.
[2] Epiphanius, *Panarion* 36, 1.

he calls himself μήτρα καὶ ἐκδοχεῖον τῆς Κολορβάσου σιγῆς (I 14, 1) but who or what Κολόρβασος is, is not certain. According to Harvey (*ad loc.*) and Hilgenfeldt,[3] he was a pupil of Valentinus. According to others, a.o. Leisegang,[4] the word, supposedly a Hebrew word, means *Tetras*, fourness. All told, a datum from which nothing of substance can be derived with regard to Marcus' life. Concerning time and place of his activity, too, our information is rather slight. Irenaeus relates (13, 5) that he had an affair with the wife of a deacon τῶν ἐν τῇ Ἀσίᾳ τῶν ἡμετέρων who had received him into his house with open arms. Disciples of Marcus pottered about ἐν τοῖς καθ᾽ἡμᾶς κλίμασι τῆς Ῥοδανουσίας, that is the Rhône area (13, 6). Hieronymus reports that Marcus was an Egyptian, and that he introduced his combination of *voluptas* and *scientia* first in Gallia and later in Spain,[5] but no further confirmation can be found for this. From the fact that Irenaeus relates his story in the present tense, Hilgenfeldt[6] concludes that Marcus is his contemporary, but Irenaeus makes use of the present tense in a number of other places as well. Harvey (*ad* 13, 1) believes that Marcus must have been a contemporary of Valentinus. If the truth lies somewhere in between, we can date Marcus' *floruit* at approximately 160-170 A.D.

The report about Marcus and his pupils comprises more than just the eucharist and his performance as a prophet, and it seems expedient to indicate the other things in a few words. Their gnosis is imbued with a curious symbolism of letters, syllables and numbers which, to my knowledge, are not found with other Gnostics. The origin of this symbolism has not yet been explained in a satisfactory way, indeed, it has not yet been thoroughly investigated either. Furthermore, the diversity of traditions and practices of the Marcosians concerning ἀπολύτρωσις, as described in ch. 21, is striking. An ἀπολύτρωσις is necessary for those who have received the perfect gnosis. It can take place in a bridal chamber in the form of a πνευματικὸς γάμος; it can happen in the form of an immersion with various baptismal formulas followed by an anointment with myrrh. Others think baptism superfluous, and anoint the head with a mixture of olive oil and water, and then with myrrh. Still others reject all

---

[3] *Die Ketzergeschichte des Urchristentums*, Darmstadt (repr.) 1963, 369.
[4] *Die Gnosis*, Leipzig (without year), 326.
[5] Hieronymus, *Epistula* 75, 3.
[6] *Loc. cit.*

outward action, for they believe that the ἐπίγνωσις τοῦ ἀρρήτου μεγέθους is itself the τελεία ἀπολύτρωσις.

For our purpose, it is of particular importance to note that no connection is made between these ritual actions and eucharist and prophecy, though, as we shall see, the text of ch. 13 does give occasion to that on some points.

We therefore have reason to assume, for the time being, that with Marcus eucharist and prophecy were a thing apart, and were of secondary importance with regard to his teaching.

The addition to the title of this paper: "and the New Testament" does not, as will probably become clear, serve as a mere embellishment. Eucharist and prophecy are two soundly New Testament subjects, and the fact that Marcus explicitly claims both words for his activities, justifies an effort, after an adequate appraisal in terms of history of religion, to test them, too, on their relationship with the primitive Christian traditions concerning the celebration of eucharist, and the prophets. Leonard FENDT gave his little book *Gnostische Mysterien* the subtitle: *Ein Beitrag zur Geschichte des Christlichen Gottesdienstes*, because, he writes, these mysteries, "muten, trotz allem echten Heidentum, immer wieder an wie alte schwerverständliche Kommentare zum Christlichen Abendmahl".[7] Even though one arrives "selten bis zum festen Kontinent der Historie, man bleibt nur allzuoft auf den Dämmerinseln der Wahrscheinlichkeit, Möglichkeit, Vermutung", it is nevertheless part of the task of the scholar to determine the borderlines between the clear continent and the glimmering islands around it.

1. *Eucharist*

The description of eucharist consists of two parts. First, there is Marcus himself who εὐχαριστεῖ, and then he tells some women to do the same. Both times, he connects the εὐχαριστεῖν with some magical trick. It is striking that the technical term for the celebration of eucharist is used with such emphasis, though Irenaeus modifies it by writing προσποιούμενος εὐχαριστεῖν: he pretended to celebrate the eucharist. It is this very pretension which is important. Marcus wanted what he did to pass for a eucharistic celebration. Εὐχαριστεῖν is used with ποτήρια as object. FOERSTER's translation reads: "gab er vor zu beten", the 'Ante-Nicene Fathers' have "pretending to consecrate". It is questionable whether this latter translation is in

---

[7] München 1922, 3.

keeping with this stage of the development of the eucharist. Neither the New Testament nor the apostolic fathers use εὐχαριστεῖν with an object. In the well-known passage of Justin's *Apology*[8] which describes the eucharist, the participle of the passive aorist occurs with the substantive ἄρτος, but this is immediately preceded by εὐχαριστή-σαντος δὲ τοῦ προεστῶτος καὶ ἐπευφημήσαντος πάντος τοῦ λαοῦ, where εὐχαριστέω clearly means to give thanks. In Latin this meaning is preserved better, because *gratias agere* is used throughout, and that cannot have an object.

The thanksgiving is spoken over ποτήρια οἴνῳ κεκραμένα, cups mixed with wine. Supposedly, this should mean that the cups contained a mixture of wine and something else. It is again in Justin that we find the key to understanding these words: προσφέρεται τῷ προεστῶτι τῶν ἀδελφῶν ἄρτος καὶ ποτήριον ὕδατος καὶ κράματος, a cup with water and mixture,[9] and this is repeated in the next chapter, and explained as ἄρτος προσφέρεται καὶ οἶνος καὶ ὕδωρ.[10] The cups over which Marcus pronounces thanksgiving contain a mixture of water and wine.

An extensive λόγος τῆς ἐπικλήσεως belongs to this thanksgiving. To the present writer's knowledge, Irenaeus is the first to use ἐπί-κλησις in connection with the eucharist. That this was not new to him, may be concluded from the way in which he uses it in IV 18,5: ὁ ἀπὸ τῆς γῆς ἄρτος προσλαβόμενος τὴν ἐπίκλησιν τοῦ θεοῦ οὐκέτι κοινὸς ἄρτος ἐστίν, ἀλλὰ εὐχαριστία ἐκ δύο πραγμάτων συνεστηκυῖα, ἐπιγείου τε καὶ οὐρανίου.

No mention is made of an ἐπίκλησις in Justin's report. The substantive does not occur at all in early Christian literature before Irenaeus. Nor do the instructions of the *Didache* about the celebration of the eucharist know the epiclesis.

The authenticity of the epiclesis in Hippolytus' *Traditio Apostolica*[11] is questioned, and so is the implication of the words. We will not enter into this matter, and abide by the judgment of CONOLLY and CHADWICK, who say that there is no trace in the Latin and Ethiopian texts of "a petition for any action of the Holy Spirit on the oblation

---

[8] *Apologia* lxv 5.
[9] *Ibid.*, lxv 3.
[10] *Ibid.*, lxvii 5. For the mixture of wine and water cf. also Clement of Alexandria, *Paedagogus* I vi 47 (I 118, 6f. STÄHLIN), II ii 20 (I 168, 4f., STÄHLIN).
[11] Cf. Hippolyte, *La Tradition Apostologique* (ed. B. BOTTE), Paris 1968, 53f., Gr. DIX, *The Apostolic Tradition*, London 1968, 9.

itself. The only action of the Holy Spirit which it speaks of or implies has for its object the minds and hearts of the faithful communicants".[12] It is a prayer for the κοινωνία τοῦ πνεύματος. We will come back to the relationship between εὐχαριστία and ἐπίκλησις in due course.

What the content of Marcus' epiclesis was, is not revealed but it is nevertheless clear that he makes it appear as if his words do have effect on the content of the cups: he causes the content to colour alternately purpur and red. Irenaeus does not say how this is effected, but in his introduction he has described Marcus as τὰ ᾽Αναξιλάου παίγνια τῇ τῶν λεγομένων μάγων πανουργίᾳ συμμίξας, someone who combines Anaxilaos' tricks with the craftiness of the so-called magicians.

Pliny, in his *Naturalis Historia*, recounts some of Anaxilaos' curious buffooneries, one of which has something to do with colouring effects: a piece of sulphur is introduced into a cup of wine, and a glowing coal is put underneath; when the cup passes round, the successive small shocks make the sulphur take fire, and cast a *pallorem dirum velut defunctorum* on the faces of those who participate in the celebration.[13] But this is not quite the same thing as making a mixture of wine and water change colour.

Therefore, Hippolytus was not satisfied with this explanation, and returned to his own κατὰ μάγων βίβλος, which has been preserved in *Elenchus* IV 28-42. There he reports that Indian ink added to (burning) incense causes a blood-red flame to blaze up, and that wax mixed with *anchusa* and added to it, creates a sanguineous liquid.[14] This is not an exact parallel either, but it is sufficient to show that the haeresiologists did regard Marcus' eucharist as trickery, but on the other hand saw no reason not to use the word εὐχαριστία. That it had a numinous effect on the spectators is shown by the following passage: it seemed as if ἡ ἀπὸ τῶν ὑπὲρ τὰ ὅλα Χάρις let her blood drip into the cup as a consequence of the epiclesis, so that those present desired to drink the potion, in order to have the Charis κληζομένη (technical term of magic), invoked by the magician, stream into their insides. The image is not entirely consistent, because ἐπομβρέω is said of rain which comes down in torrents, and not of a space which is being filled.[15] Irenaeus does not mention,

---

[12] Cf. Dix, *o.c.*, 1 (Preface to the second edition).
[13] Pliny, *Nat. Hist.*, 35, 175.
[14] *Elenchus*, IV 28, 13.
[15] Cf. LIDDELL-SCOTT, *Greek-English Lexicon*, Oxford 1948, I. 675 s.v.

however, whether the desire of those present was gratified and they received some of the potion. He is primarily interested in Marcus' portrait. The emphatic use of εὐχαριστία and εὐχαριστέω does indicate, though, that a communion took place. Because there is no mention of bread, we might almost speak of a *communio sub una*, but then of the wine only. We shall come back to this.

The question arises: who is this Charis from the world above all things? There is reason to think of the Ennoia, who existed together with τέλειος Αἰὼν πρόων, also called Propator and Buthos, the Ennoia ἣν δὴ καὶ Χάριν καὶ Σιγὴν ὀνομάζουσιν.[16] But we can only see the full scope of this question after having looked at the remainder of the text.

In the second round some women are brought into the ritual, as Marcus tells them to take cups with a mixture of wine and water (ἐκπώματα κεκραμένα) and to give thanks over them, while he acts as chief celebrant. Again this is accompanied by some sleight of hand: first Marcus empties the cup — the story suddenly shifts to the singular, and speaks of one woman and one cup — into a much larger one, but subsequently it turns out that the cup is not only completely filled by the contents of the smaller one, but is even too small; so it overflows. This last point is mentioned only at the end of the story, after Marcus has completed the prayer formula, but it belongs to the first part. Irenaeus does not go into this any further, but Hippolytus explains in great detail how such a τεχνή works: there are φάρμακα which cause an αὔξησις when dissolved in a liquid, especially in οἴνῳ κεκερασμένῳ. Such a φάρμακον had been put into the empty cup beforehand by Marcus. Because the substance was active only for a short time, the wine had to be drunk quickly, and therefore μετὰ σπουδῆς τοῖς παροῦσι προσεδίδου πίνειν, a remarkable *communio sub una*, though now with very fizzy and foaming wine.[17]

Of greater importance is the prayer formula. It is introduced with the words ἐπιλέγων ἅμα οὕτως, without any finite verb. HOLL, in his edition of Epiphanius, supplemented εὐχαριστεῖ but I doubt whether this was used in Irenaeus graece. Possibly, Irenaeus did not write a finite verb, because he was especially interested in the things expressed by the participles: προσενεγκών, μετακενώσας ἐπιλέγων. In any case, that is how Hippolytus interpreted it, for he has turned

---

[16] Iren., *Adversus Haereses*. I.1, 1.
[17] Hipp., *Elenchus* VI 40, 4.

ἐπιλέγων into a finite verb: ἐπέλεγεν οὕτως. Thus, this means that the εὐχαριστία, the prayer of thanksgiving, was said by the woman or women, and that Marcus added something to it.

It is tempting to think of a separate epiclesis, the more so because eucharistia and epiclesis were mentioned side by side before. But what follows is not an actual epiclesis, because it is not addressed directly to God. However, this is primarily determined by the intention and the content of the prayer formula, for they have, as we shall see, more to do with the initiation of the prophetesses than with the eucharist. Precisely for that reason, it is striking that this prayer has a place in the eucharist, and this can only have been the place of the epiclesis. If these suppositions are correct, this is a glimpse of a liturgy in which εὐχαριστία and ἐπίκλησις have not yet merged, as in Hippolytus' *Traditio Apostolica*.

Let us now look at the prayer formula in more detail. The subject is ἡ πρὸ τῶν ὅλων, ἡ ἀνεννόητος καὶ ἄρρητος Χάρις, the same Charis who was invoked in the first epiclesis, now even more reinforced by some epithets favoured by the Gnostics. Furthermore, with πρὸ τῶν ὅλων the emphasis is shifted from space to the primordial beginning. Charis, Sige, Ennoia, Barbelo, all are names for one and the same thing: the female part of the syzygy.[18] FENDT calls Marcus' Charis "nur eine hellenistische Form der Muttergöttin",[19] but that is, to my mind, too general a conclusion: Charis is the gnostic form of the mother-goddess, the magna mater who appears in so many forms and with so many names in the Ancient World. The specific gnostic element lays in the fact that she is part of the primordial syzygy. But the mother goddess always remains a complex figure. For what is desired of her in this prayer is indicated in pneumatic-mystical terms: πληρῶσαι σου τὸν ἔσω ἄνθρωπον καὶ πληθύναι ἐν σοὶ τὴν γνῶσιν αὐτῆς, fill your inner man and multiply the knowledge of her within you. The picture of the fulfilment of the inner man reminds one of the fulfilment with the Holy Spirit, and indeed, in a syncretistic way of thinking, the transition from the mother goddess to the pneuma is not a great step. This is clear in some prayers in the *Acta Thomae*, of which one stands in the context of the celebration of the eucharist.[20] It is an epiclesis with a steadily

---

[18] Cf. FENDT, *o.c.*, 41 and references there.
[19] *Ibid.*
[20] *Acta Thomae*, 49f.: *Acta Apostolorum Apocrypha* (ed. LIPSIUS-BONNET) Darmstadt 1959 (repr.) II 2, 165ff.

reiterated imperative ἔλθε, and the invoked person is adressed, among other things, as ἡ κοινωνία τοῦ ἄρρενος, ἡ ἡσυχία ἡ ἀποκαλύπτουσα τὰ μεγαλεῖα τοῦ πάντος μεγέθους, ἡ ἱερὰ περιστερά, ἡ ἀπόκρυφος μήτηρ, Spirit and mother combined.[21] Partly the same, partly similar words and expressions are found in the baptismal prayer in ch. 27.[22] No wonder then that the same freedom of images is found which already figured in the early Christian idiom: baptism with and outpouring of the Spirit occur together with fulfilment with the Spirit, just as the fulfilment of the inner man is synonymous here with the pouring down of the Charis, who appeared to let her blood drip into the cup. That this fusion of eucharist, Spirit, wine and even blood, however astonishing at first sight, is not unusual, is proved by some passages in the Gospel of Philip. In this gospel, sacramental action and related speculations have a larger place than in any other gnostic document. Some logia refer to the eucharist. We quote logion 100 (= 75, 14-21) according to the translation by GAFFRON in his doctoral thesis of 1969:[23]

"Der Kelch des Gebets enthält Wein, enthält Wasser; er dient als 'Typos' des Blutes über dem gedankt wird, und ist gefüllt mit dem Heiligen Geist. Und der zum ganz vollkommenen Menschen gehörende ist er (sc. der Heilige Geist). Wenn wir diesen (sc. Kelch) trinken, werden wir uns den vollkommenen Menschen nehmen".[24]

The eucharistic terminology is clearly determining in this logion and the whole passage, as GAFFRON remarks, could just as well have been part of a 2nd-century Catholic document. The prayer discussed here must have been an epiclesis, because otherwise the words "filled with the Holy Spirit" are incomprehensible. The cup is τύπος of the blood and filled with the Holy Spirit. GAFFRON calls this: "abbild-liche Anwesendheit einer geistigen Wirklichkeit". In the Gospel of Philip, Spirit and blood are not associated solely through the wine. In logion 23, in an exegesis of John vi 35: "unless you eat the flesh of the Son of Man and drink his blood you can have no life in you", it is said: "Was bedeutet das? Sein Fleisch ist der Logos und sein

---

[21] The Syriac version adds, "come Holy Spirit".

[22] O.c., 142f.

[23] H. G. GAFFRON, Studien zum Koptischen Philippusevangelium unter besonderer Berücksichtigung der Sakramente, Bonn 1969, 174.

[24] Different but less convincing KRAUSE in: W. FOERSTER (ed.), Die Gnosis, Zürich 1971, II, 115: "(Der Kelch) gehört dem ganz vollkommenen Menschen", and SCHENKE (Th.L.Z. 84 (1959), c. 19: "Und der (Geist) des ganz vollkommenen Menschen ist es".

Blut ist der Heilige Geist".[25] This interpretation, as GAFFRON remarks, is "im kirchlichen Christentum bereitet", but that does not alter the fact that we deal here with a typical non-catholic, heterodox explanation. In any case, the elements for a gnostic pneuma-eucharist were available in the margin of the Valentinian gnosis: imbedded in a magic spectacle, as we have encountered it with Marcus, or connected with all sorts of speculations, as in the Gospel of Philip.

The purpose of the gnostic eucharist is fulfilment with the Spirit, which means at the same time fulfilment with the true gnosis. As such, this link is not specifically gnostic. The λόγος γνώσεως (1 Cor. xii 8) is a gift of the Spirit. But in the gnosis, this theme takes on a special meaning. Particularly in Valentinian gnosis, the idea of fulfilment with the Spirit plays an important part. In logion 100 of the Gospel of Philip, which was quoted above, the last two sentences read: "the Holy Spirit belongs together with the perfect man (τέλειος) and through drinking the cup (image of being filled with the Spirit) the perfect man is received". Particularly in the *Epistula Jacobi Apocrypha*, the word group πληροῦν c.s. is of importance, to the extent that the commentators even speak of a key word, equivalent and synonymous with τελειοῦν.[26] In ii 30-35 we read: "No one shall ever enter into the Kingdom if I command him so, but because you, yes you are fulfilled. Give me James and Peter, in order that I may fulfil them". In iii 35: "The Kingdom of God is yours. Therefore I say to you: be fulfilled, and do not leave any place inside you empty". In iv 2-19, a rather heavily damaged page, the command: "be fulfilled", occurs several times, but somewhere in the middle of the page it reads: "be fulfilled with the Spirit". This purpose, which is so crucial, is also served by Marcus' eucharist.

Finally, the question must be asked, what does this eucharist have to do with the tradition of the church in the first and second centuries. We will deal with this question on the basis of Wilhelm BOUSSET's interpretation in his *Hauptprobleme der Gnosis*.[27] In the 7th chapter he discusses the gnostic mysteries. "Das Sakrament der Eucharistie" is dealt with after baptism. In this passage, the celebrations from the Acts of Thomas quoted above are treated, but not Marcus' eucharist. Only when discussing the bridal chamber and the

---

[25] GAFFRON, o.c., 178.
[26] *Epistula Jacobi Apocrypha* (ed. MALININE, PUECH, QUISPEL, TILL, KASSER), Zürich 1967, 41 f.
[27] Göttingen 1907, 316.

related μυσταγωγία of Marcus' followers, as described at the end of Irenaeus' account of Marcus' practices and doctrine, does BOUSSET touch upon this matter. BOUSSET believes that the prayer formula as uttered by Marcus in the eucharist, would actually be more appropriate in the rite of the nuptial chamber. In his opinion, in ch. 13.2 it is only a "Schauwunder" that is related. GAFFRON agrees with this, and says that, of the so-called eucharist, nothing remains but the "Gaukeleien eines bewussten Betrügers".[28] I think that this is not correct. The tenor of the whole account with the emphatic use of εὐχαριστεῖν, ἐπίκλησις and ποτήρια κεκραμένα, points in another direction. The celebration is explicitly meant as a eucharist, and Irenaeus does not deny it either.

Furthermore, to my mind, the prayer formula does not belong to the ἱερὸς γάμος of the bridal chamber at all, but to Charis and the fulfilment of the inner man with Charis. Therefore, in my opinion, the eucharist must be regarded apart from the two miracles which accompany it. They serve to heighten the effect of the eucharist, and not vice-versa.

If we observe, however, the eucharist separately, the connection with the tradition of the church appears to be very slight. As far as I know, there is no information as to a communion with wine alone. Of the early Christian elements, only the cup and thanksgiving are in evidence, and of later developments just the epiclesis. The remainder — apart from the magical tricks — is hellenistic-gnostic. The eucharist was aimed at fulfilment with pneuma and gnosis, the heart's desire of every gnostic.

2. Prophecy

The first sentence of the third paragraph of Irenaeus, *Adv. Haer.* I 13 runs as follows: εἰκὸς δὲ αὐτὸν καὶ δαίμονά τινα πάρεδρον ἔχειν, δι'οὗ αὐτός τε προφητεύειν δοκεῖ, καὶ ὅσας ἀξίας ἡγεῖται μετόχους τῆς χάριτος αὐτοῦ, προφητεύειν ποιεῖ.

In my study on the Eleventh Mandate of the Shepherd of Hermas, I have written about this more extensively, and now a few remarks may suffice here. The mention of the δαίμων πάρεδρος identifies Marcus' prophecy as belonging to the magical divination through an invoked demon who answered questions about the future for the μάντις so that he can communicate the answers to the questioners,

---

[28] *O.c.*, 173.

ὡς ἀφ'ἑαυτοῦ, as if they were his own.[29] His prophesying and that of his followers is equated in what follows (ch. 13.4) with μαντεύεσθαι. The salient point in Marcus' performance as a prophet is that he initiates others in the office of prophecy. The fact that it involves mainly well-to-do ladies, is a spicy detail which might very well be true, but is of no further importance. Marcus wants others to share in his χάρις. In the great Paris magical papyrus a μάγος says to a god twice: δός μοι χάριν,[30] but the context makes clear that the meaning here is rather luck or success, and that is not what we are dealing with. The prophet's χάρις is his χάρισμα, a gift of the Spirit. Paul already calls his apostolic mission χάρις.[31] It is striking that Marcus, after the invocation of the divine figure of the Χάρις who should fulfil the inner man with πνεῦμα and γνῶσις now suddenly speaks of his own χάρις and the question arises: what is the relationship between the two?

In VOELKER's text this is answered clearly: they are identical, for both begin with a capital Χ.[32] In the opening sentence (not printed by Voelker) HOLL, however, has μετόχους τῆς χάριτος. This seems to betray the interpretation that, with the transfer of the prophetic χάρισμα, the Spirit is also conveyed. This distinction seems to me to be rather too subtle, for I fail to see much difference between μετόχους τῆς χάριτος αὐτοῦ and μεταδοῦναι τῆς ἐμῆς Χάριτος. Because the text further on speaks of Charis as a personal being, it seems to me to be obvious that this is the same Charis who was also invoked at the eucharist, the Charis-primordial mother-pneuma. The connection between the eucharist and the prophetic initiation appears to be the fact that the first Charis-communication is intended for the whole community of πνευματικοί, and the second only for those who will be initiated in prophecy, the πνευματικώτατοι. Because Marcus himself is the πνευματικώτατος par excellence, he can say to the woman of his choice μεταδοῦναι σοι θέλω τῆς ἐμῆς Χάριτος. The following sentences are strange and call for attention both separately and as a whole. The first sentence gives an explanation of Marcus' choice: the father of all continually beholds your angel before His face. We are dealing here with the same picture as for

---

[29] J. REILING, o.c., 87-90.

[30] K. PREISENDANZ, *Papyri Graecae Magicae* I, Leipzig 1928, 148 (IV.2436), 176 (IV. 3165).

[31] Cf. e.g. Rom. i 5, xii 3; 1 Cor. iii 10-15.

[32] W. VOELKER, *Quellen zur Geschichte der christlichen Gnosis*, Tübingen 1932, 136f.

instance in Matth. xviii 10: the little ones have their guardian angels
in heaven, who always behold the face of my heavenly father,
a special form of the widespread belief in a personal guardian angel.[33]
The difference is that in Matthew the angels look at God and here
God is said to behold the angel of the chosen woman. This must
be a sign of special favour, even though parallels are lacking.

The relationship between a human being and his angel, according
to some gnostic texts, is such that, on entering the pleroma, the
redeemed human being is united with his angel. This is said in
Irenaeus *Adv. Haer.* III 15, 2: *putat neque in terra se esse, sed
intra Pleroma introïsse et complexum iam angelum suum.* This entering
into the pleroma and the union of the gnostic with his angel is
an anticipation of the eschatological entering of Achamoth into the
pleroma, which takes place when all seed has come to perfection
(τελειωθῇ), and Achamoth receives her as his νυμφίος Soter, so that
a syzygy comes into being of Sophia/Achamoth and σώτηρ; and,
Irenaeus continues, τοῦτο εἶναι νυμφίον καὶ νύμφην, νυμφῶνα δὲ
πᾶν τὸ πλήρωμα. The πνευματικοί who have shed their ψυχή and
have become πνεύματα νοερά, ἀκρατήτως καὶ ἀοράτως ἐντὸς πληρώ-
ματος εἰσελθόντας νύμφας ἀποδοθήσεσθαι τοῖς περὶ τὸν Σωτῆρα
ἀγγέλοις.[34] This extensive quotation may be justified by the fact
that in our text too the words bride, bridegroom and bridal chamber
occur. For the moment, we can understand the clause that the father
looks upon the angel of the *initianda* continually, to mean that the
road to union with the angel is open through the favour of the father.

The sentence which now follows is, to my mind, the most obscure
of the whole passage. In Latin it runs: *locus tuae magnitudinis in
nobis est; oportet nos in unum convenire,* and this is how it is rendered
in the translations. The Greek text lacks the possessive pronoun and
has in the second part δι'ἡμᾶς ἐγκαταστῆσαι, which could mean
something like: to institute or to constitute on our behalf, but that
does not make sense, and the correction in δεῖ ἡμᾶς εἰς τὸ ἓν
καταστῆναι is obvious, even though εἰς τὸ ἓν καταστῆναι is still
a somewhat strange expression.

The true problem, however, lies in ὁ τόπος τοῦ Μεγέθους, the place
of the greatness. Usually for an explanation, Irenaeus, *Adv. Haer.* I 13, 6

---

[33] Cf. H. L. STRACK - P. BILLERBECK, *Kommentar zum Neuen Testament aus Talmud
und Midrasch,* München 1922, on Mt. xviii 10; Acts xii 15 and 1 Cor. xi 10.
[34] Irenaeus, *Adv. Haer.* I.7, 1.

is referred to, where the story is told of the libertine disciples of
Marcus, who have become intangible and invisible to the (earthly)
judge. If he did get hold of them, they said the following prayer,
while approaching him: ὦ πάρεδρε θεοῦ καὶ μυστικῆς πρὸ αἰῶνος
Σιγῆς,ἣν τὰ μεγέθη διαπαντὸς βλέποντα τὸ πρόσωπον τοῦ Πατρός,
O thou who sittest beside God and the mysterious pre-aeonic silence,
through whom the μεγέθη always see the face of the father...[35]
In this light there can be little doubt that the "greatnesses" are
the angels of the redeemed gnostics, genuine guardian angels, for they
must make those in trouble invisible with the help of the invoked.
The mother hears their prayers, puts on their heads the homeric
helmet which makes them invisible, so they can escape the judge.
But what follows is of particular importance to our survey: καὶ
παραχρῆμα ἀνασπάσασα αὐτούς, εἰς τὸν νυμφῶνα εἰσήγαγε, καὶ
ἀπέδωκε τοῖς ἑαυτῶν νυμφίοις, in other words, the salvation from
earthly troubles suddenly turns into an eschatological entry into the
pleroma.

Understood in this light, the expression τόπος τοῦ Μεγέθους may
have the following meaning: the place of the greatness is the (so to
speak) pleromatic presence of the angel-bridegroom.[36] It is clear
that we deal here with the image of the bridal chamber which,
compared to other gnostic systems, plays an important role in Valentinian gnosis. This is confirmed by the rest of Marcus' words to
the *initianda*; they mainly speak for themselves: "receive first from
me and through me the Charis", i.e. Marcus has the Charis at his
disposal, and with his help, the woman can receive it too. He can
make her μέτοχος τῆς Χάριτος αὐτοῦ. This is to be distinguished
from the symbolism of the nuptial chamber, for it is a continuation
of the Charis-eucharist, and, to my mind, directly connected with
the prophetic inspiration which is forthcoming: "Get yourself ready,
as a bride expecting her bridegroom, so that you may become what
I am, and I, what you are" — i.e. the coming together leads to
union and to identification, whereby Marcus is himself the bridegroom
and not just the mystagogue who brings bride and groom together.
But a little further, he is just that: "place the seed of the light

---

[35] The text is not clear, ἣν being difficult to understand. The translation "through
whom" is that of the *The Ante-Nicene Fathers*, vol. I (repr.), Grand Rapids 1973, 335,
and of Foerster, *Die Gnosis* I, 264.

[36] Conceivably, τόπος is to be understood as referring to Hebrew *makōm*, the
"place" as a name of the godhead.

in your bridal chamber" — one might think of a candle or other
illumination which is placed in the bridal chamber — "and take
from me the bridegroom and hold him and be in him", which is
about the same as total union — "behold, the Charis has descended
upon you, open your mouth and prophesy".[37]

So much for Marcus' formulas. Before going on, we note that
there are three questions which need further discussion:

A. The role played by Marcus; is he the mystagogue who brings
bride and groom together in the spiritual nuptial chamber, or is
he a partner in a spiritual ἱερὸς γάμος of a θεῖος ἀνήρ with an
initianda?

B. What dominates: the symbolism of the bridal chamber, or the
prophetic initiation?

C. What, in this context, is the role of the Charis who is transferred
and who descends from above?

To these questions we will come back presently, but first we
continue our investigation of the text.

The woman has not reached the point of daring to prophesy yet,
as Marcus commanded, and therefore he starts again and performs
ἐπικλήσεις τινάς and says: "Open your mouth, say something and
you will prophesy" — an appeal that sounds a little strange to us,
but which betrays insight in the psychology of the charismata — and
then, the breakthrough takes place in the woman. She is excited
(χαυνωθεῖσα)[38] and entangled in Marcus' rhetoric (κεπφωθεῖσα) with
a heated soul, not just from nervous tension, — expressed by a
pounding heartbeat — but also ὑπὸ κενοῦ πνεύματος. She now throws
caution to the winds and dares to say πάντα κενῶς καὶ τολμηρῶς.
This description has several points in common with that of the false
prophet in *Mand.* XI of the Shepherd of Hermas, and can be read
and understood as a portrait *in malam partem* of the ἐνθουσιασμός
of the Pythia. It is the state of mind, ὅταν ἔνθερμος ἡ ψυχὴ
γενομένη καὶ πυρώδης ἀπώσηται τὴν εὐλάβειαν, ἣν ἡ θνητὴ φρόνησις
ἐπάγουσα πολλάκις ἀποστρέφει καὶ κατασβέννυσι τὸν ἐνθουσιασμόν,
when the soul, hot and fiery, throws off the reluctance so often
summoned by common sense and thereby fending off and extinguishing
the ἐνθουσιασμός.[39]

---

[37] Cf. GAFFRON, *o.c.*, 191 ff.
[38] Cf. Eusebius, *Hist. Eccl.* V.16, 8.
[39] Plutarch, *Defectu Oracul.* 432 F.

The rest of paragraph 3 completes the picture: from now on, the woman regards herself as προφῆτις and feels such a strong bond with Marcus that she wants to do something in return, not only in the form of giving money or goods, but also κατὰ τὴν τοῦ σώματος κοινωνίαν, for she wants to experience the union with him once more, ἵνα σὺν αὐτῷ κατέλθῃ εἰς τὸ ἕν.

BOUSSET's interpretation of the eucharistic celebration was already brought up earlier, and we will now have to come back to this. Not only the eucharist, but also the initiation in prophecy are thought by BOUSSET to be closely connected with the sacrament of the bridal chamber which — as Irenaeus reports in *Adv. Haer.* I. 21, 2 — is practiced by pupils of Marcus. According to BOUSSET, the "Berichterstatter", i.e. Irenaeus or possibly his source, did not understand the story in ch. 13 at all, and turned it into a prophetic initiation, including ecstasy. Actually, BOUSSET says, the formulas uttered by Marcus at the eucharist as well as at the initiation belong to the celebration of the sacrament of the bridal chamber. Only the closing formula of the initiation ἄνοιξον τὸ στόμα σου καὶ προφήτευσον is "kaum ursprünglich".[40] REITZENSTEIN does not mention BOUSSET's opinion, but speaks without hesitation of a "Prophetenweihe".[41] Rightly so, I think, though it should be recognized that the terminology of the nuptial chamber is very striking and this must be explained. Against BOUSSET's opinion, three things must be pointed out. First, it is strange that ch. 21, 2 does not refer back at all to our passage, if the same sacrament were discussed. The fact that 21, 2 deals with a sacrament of the Marcosians, and our passage with one of Marcus himself, does not sufficiently explain it. Irenaeus must have regarded it as something different, even though the similarity of the terminologies will not have escaped him. In the second place, deleting the words "open your mouth and prophesy" is rather an emergency solution. Thirdly, it appears from what follows, that Marcus' performance has provoked repercussion and discussion on the very subject of initiation. Other women who resisted Marcus' efforts to initiate them into prophecy as well, have disengaged themselves from his θίασος because they knew perfectly well that the gift of prophecy is not bestowed upon human beings by Marcus, but: οἷς ἂν ὁ θεὸς ἄνωθεν ἐπιπέμψει

[40] BOUSSET, *o.c.* 315f.

[41] R. REITZENSTEIN, *Poimandres*, Darmstadt (repr.) 1966, 220ff.; *Die hellenistischen Mysterienreligionen*, Darmstadt (repr.) 1956, 251.

τὴν χάριν αὐτοῦ, οὗτοι θεόσδοτον ἔχουσι τὴν προφήτειαν, καὶ τότε λαλοῦσιν ἔνθα καὶ ὁπότε θεὸς βούλεται, ἀλλ'οὐχ ὅτε Μάρκος κελεύει.

This sequel would be hard to place if Marcus had not actually initiated people as prophets. Nevertheless, the terminology of the bridal chamber does remain odd, and we must ask ourselves whether a solution can be found for it. In my opinion, this is possible, and an attempt may be made to describe the way towards it.

For this, we return to the three questions formulated above (p. 174). They concern the role of Marcus, the relationship between the bridal chamber and the initiation, and the role of the Charis.

Ultimately, what is needed is clarity with regard to the second question. Therefore, we start with the other two.

To start from the bottom, the combination of the Charis and the bridal chamber is remarkable. Even though our knowledge of the symbolism of the bridal chamber is limited, we can posit that, usually, Charis does not figure in it. Those places in the Gospel of Philip which mention or allude to the bridal chamber,[42] and are therefore discussed by GAFFRON,[43] do not mention anything like an epiclesis, and a κατάβασις of the Charis. So there are two distinct matters: the union of bride and groom, and the descent of the Charis. We have already noted that Charis is the primordial mother and the Holy Spirit combined. Fulfilment with the Spirit, as a consequence of the eucharist, is followed by the descent of the Spirit on the *initianda*. The fulfilment led to an increase of γνῶσις, the descent to prophecy, το λόγος γνώσεως.

However, between the primordial Charis of the eucharistic prayer and the Charis who descends on the prophetess, there is a rather important point of difference: in the second instance, she is also Marcus' χάρις, so to speak his "Geistbesitz", which he wants the woman to share with him. In this communication of the Charis, Marcus himself plays a decisive role, that of the "Geistvermittler". With this conclusion, we are back at the question of the role played by Marcus. This appears to be a double one: on the one hand, he is the one who shares the Spirit with others: λάμβανε ἀπ'ἐμοῦ καὶ δι'ἐμοῦ τὴν χάριν, on the other hand the one who leads the bridegroom, the angel, to the waiting bride: λάβε παρ'ἐμοῦ τὸν νυμφίον; — the one who says δεῖ ἡμᾶς εἰς τὸ ἓν καταστῆναι (which

---

[42] *Gospel of Philip*, log. 31, 55, 60, 61, 67, 122.
[43] *O.c.*, 199-219.

indicates close union), on the one hand: hold him and be held in him; so that you are what I am and I what you are; on the other hand preceding this: prepare yourself as a bride expecting her bridegroom. In short: Marcus is both bridegroom and mystagogue, and that is why the initiation does not result in a mystical anticipation of the eschaton, but in ἐνθουσιασμός and prophecy.

Here we are dealing with a typical example of syncretism, a mixture, of hellenistic and gnostic religiosity. The latter element has been explained sufficiently. Therefore, we add some remarks and parallels to illustrate the hellenistic element.

First, it should be pointed out that after the metaphysical and the mantic prophetic union, ἡ τοῦ σώματος κοινωνία is, so to say, is the logical consequence of such a sensual and intimate spiritual contact. The terminology used by Irenaeus already points in this direction: κατὰ πάντα ἑνοῦσθαι αὐτῷ προθυμουμένη, ἵνα σὺν αὐτῷ κατέλθῃ εἰς τὸ ἕν, which recalls Marcus' saying δεῖ ἡμᾶς εἰς τὸ ἕν καταστῆναι.

Secondly, erotic and mantic ἐνθουσιασμός are closely related: οὐδένα... ἐνθουσιασμὸν ἀνεὺ τῆς ἐρωτικῆς ἐπιπνοίας συμβαίνει γεγενῆσθαι,[44] and that is why the images of a sexual or even marital relationship between a seeress and a deity are numerous.[45] In this way, the Pythia is ἐγκύμων τῆς δαιμονίου δυνάμεως in connection with the ἀτμὸς ἔνθεος which rises up from the crevice.[46] The fact that most probably the crevice never existed, does not alter the significance of the image. It could only originate from the idea of the συνουσία of the deity and the Pythia.[47] The Cumaean Sibyl is plena deo, and Servius relates that the place Cumae had received that name because of the prophecy of a pregnant woman, quae graece ἔγκυος dicitur.[48]

The image, however, was not restricted to either mythology or the relationship between a god and a woman. This becomes clear when we descend to the so-called magical divination, the level on which — according to Irenaeus — Marcus too operated. In the Berlin magical papyrus, the μάγος who sought to win the δαίμων πάρεδρος in order to be able to divine says: ἦκέ μοι, ὁ ἅγιος Ὠρίων... ἀλλοιῶν ζωῇ καθώσπερ ἀνδρὸς ἐπὶ τῆς συνουσίας τὴν σπόραν,

---

[44] Hermeias on Plato's Phaedrus, 105 Ast.
[45] Cf. J. SCHMIDT, art. Heilige Brautschaft, R.A.C. II. 537f.
[46] Longinus, De Subl. 13, 2.
[47] Plut., Pyth. Orac. 405c.
[48] Cf. E. NORDEN, P. Vergilius Maro Aeneis Buch VI, Leipzig 1916, 144ff.

a formula of which the symbolism, but not the exact meaning is clear.[49] In another papyrus, Hermes is invoked with the words: ἔλθε μοι, κύριε Ἑρμῆ, ὡς τὰ βρέφη εἰς τὰς κοιλίας τῶν γυναικῶν, a formula of which both symbolism ànd meaning are clear.[50] What this entering of the deity or demon leads to, is said further on in the same papyrus: σὺ γὰρ ἐγὼ καὶ ἐγὼ σύ, τὸ σὸν ὄνομα ἐμὸν καὶ ἐμὸν τὸ σόν,[51] as another incantation says: εἰσέλθοις τὸν ἔμον νοῦν καὶ τὰς ἔμας φρένας ... σὺ γὰρ εἶ ἐγὼ καὶ σύ. ὃ ἐὰν εἴπω δεῖ γενέσθαι,[52] the same identification which Marcus is after with the woman whom he initiates in prophecy: ἵνα ἔσῃ ὃ ἐγὼ καὶ ἐγὼ ὃ σύ. However, there is one significant difference. In the quoted papyri, it is the μάγος who seeks to win the divine power, as Marcus himself must have done with regard to his own δαίμων πάρεδρος. With regard to the women, he himself acts as a deity who wants to make himself known to others, in the name of the Charis, and with the words of the bridal chamber. He can do this because he claims that ἡ μεγίστη ἀπὸ τῶν ἀοράτων καὶ κατονομάστων τόπων δύναμις is in him, just as it was said of Simon Magus that he was ἡ δύναμις τοῦ θεοῦ ἡ μεγάλη (Acts viii 10), and further because he had "Glück bei den Frauen".

With Simon Magus we are back in the New Testament. The comparison with early Christian tradition cannot render much of a positive nature. According to early Christian criteria, Marcus is a ψευδο-προφήτης plain and simple: his doctrine is false, his prophecies do not come true, his behaviour is morally unsound, and the spirit which inspires him is not from God, but from the devil.[53] From an early Christian point of view, however, it is interesting to note how Marcus' performance invokes the exact opposite of true prophecy, notably in the reaction of the Godfearing women who do not succumb to Marcus' charms. It was mentioned in passing earlier, and it is fitting to repeat the passage, followed by Irenaeus' comment:

"Well aware that the gift of prophecy is not conferred upon humans by Marcus (the magician), but that only those to whom God sends his grace from above possess the divinely bestowed power of prophesying: and then they speak where and when God pleases, and

---

[49] PREISENDANZ, o.c. I 30ff. (vol. I, 4).
[50] O.c. VIII 1ff. (vol. II, 45).
[51] 37f.(.47).
[52] O.c. XIII 791-795 (vol. II, 123).
[53] For these criteria cf. present writer, o.c., 67ff.

not when Marcus orders them to do so". And Irenaeus adds: "For that which commands is greater and of higher authority than that which is commanded, inasmuch as the former rules, while that latter is in a state of subjection. If, then, Marcus, or any one else, does command, — as these are accustomed continually at their feasts to play at drawing lots, and (in accordance with the lot) to command one another to prophesy, giving forth as oracles what is in harmony with their own desires, — it will follow that he who commands is greater and higher authority than the prophetic spirit, though he is but a man, which is impossible". For οὐ θελήματι ἀνθρώπου ἠνέχθη προφήτεια ποτε ἀλλ᾽ὑπὸ πνεύματος ἁγίου φερόμενοι ἐλάλησαν ἀπὸ θεοῦ ἄνθρωποι (2 Peter i 21).

"IN IHREN ZELTEN..."

Bemerkungen zu Codex XIII Nag Hammadi p. 47:14-18
im Hinblick auf Joh. i 14*

J. HELDERMAN

Erfreulicher Weise wurden in letzter Zeit immer mehr Schriften aus den Nag Hammadi Codices zugänglich, vor allem durch die Reihe *The Facsimile Edition of the Nag Hammadi Codices*: Textausgaben oder Übersetzungen (im deutschsprachlichen Raum) des Berliner Arbeitskreises für koptisch-gnostische Schriften, die auf dieser Edition basieren-die Schriften des Codex I (Jung)nicht mitgerechnet.

So wurden 1974 von Yvonne JANSSENS eine Textausgabe, welche sie nur "une première lecture" nennen möchte, der Schrift *Die dreigestaltige Protennoia* aus Codex XIII und vom Berliner Arbeitskreis eine Übersetzung veröffentlicht.[1] Ob man jetzt noch von einem Codex XIII reden sollte, ist nach James M. ROBINSONS Untersuchung zu beweifeln, wurden doch die acht Papyrus-Blätter, auf denen der als einziger *vollständig* erhaltene Text aus Codex XIII, die *Prōtennoia Trimorphos*, geschrieben steht, zwischen der vorderen Einbanddecke und dem Buchblock des Codex VI aufgefunden.[2] In Nachfolge von ROBINSON sollte man tatsächlich nunmehr reden von zwölf Codices und einem vollständig erhaltenen Traktat oder genauer: elf Codices, Fragmente (des Codex XII) und einem vollständig erhaltenen Traktat.[3] In diesem

---

* Herr Prof. Dr. Dr. Martin KRAUSE, Münster, war so freundlich meinen Aufsatz auf gutes Deutsch durchzusehen. Ihm verdanke ich das in Anm. 3 Bemerkte. Für beides sage ich ihm herzlichen Dank!

[1] Y. JANSSENS, Le Codex XIII de Nag Hammadi, *Muséon* 87 (1974), 341-413; "Die dreigestaltige Prōtennoia". Eine gnostische Offenbarungsrede in koptischer Sprache aus dem Fund von Nag Hammadi, *ThLZ* 99 (1974), 731-746. Der Leiter des Arbeitskreises ist bekanntlich Hans-Martin SCHENKE. Federführend für diese Übersetzung war Gesine SCHENKE. Vgl. ebenfalls: Berliner Arbeitskreis, Die Bedeutung der Texte von Nag Hammadi für die moderne Gnosisforschung, in: *Gnosis und N.T.* (Herausg. K.-W. TRÖGER) Berlin (DDR) 1973, 74-76: Protennoia Trimorphos.

[2] James M. ROBINSON, Inside the front cover of Codex VI, in: *Essays on the Nag Hammadi Texts in Honour of Alexander Böhlig* (NHS III), Leiden 1972, 74-87. Auch von Y. JANSSENS in ihrem Aufsatz angeführt (342) und im Vorwort der Facsimile Edition der Codices XI, XII, XIII, Leiden 1973, XV erwähnt.

[3] ROBINSON, *a.c.*, 87. In Codex XIII waren jedoch mindestens zwei Traktate enthalten, von denen von der zweiten, die *Titellosen Schrift*, nur der Anfang erhalten ist,

Zusammenhang möchte ich auf einen interessanten Nebenertrag *koïhologischer* Art[4] des Studiums der Codices aufmerksam machen: bei eingehender Prüfung der Lederhüllen sind z.B. in der Kartonage des Codex VII Brieffragmente (gerichtet an "Vater Pachom") und Genesisfragmente (Genesis xxxii und xlii) ans Licht gekommen.[5] Auch in der von James M. Robinson neulich für das Institute for Antiquity and Christianity in Claremont angekauften Ledereinband von Codex I (Jung) sind Breiffragmente an Pachom gerichtet entdeckt worden![6] Unsere Untersuchung befasst sich mit dem Ursprung und der Bedeutung des Ausdrucks ⲛⲉⲩⲥⲕⲏⲛⲏ = ihre Zelte, in der *Prōtennoia Trimorphos* 47:15. Der Kontext lautet:

```
13   ⲕⲱⲛ ⳣⲁϩⲟⲩⲛ ⲁⲧⲟⲩⲥⲩⲛⲧⲉⲗⲉⲓⲁ ⲡⲙ[ⲁϩ]
14   ⳣⲟⲙⲧ ⲛⲥⲟⲡ ⲁⲉⲓⲟⲩⲟⲛϩⲧ' ⲉⲃⲟⲗ ⲛⲁⲩ [ϩ]ⲛ
15   [ⲛ]ⲉⲩⲥⲕⲏⲛⲏ ⲉⲉⲓⳣⲟⲟⲡ ⲛⲗⲟⲅⲟⲥ ⲁⲩⲱ ⲁⲉⲓ
16   ⲟⲩⲟⲛϩⲧ' ⲉⲃⲟⲗ ϩⲙ ⲡⲉⲓⲛⲉ ⲛⲧⲟⲩϩⲓⲕⲱⲛ ⲁⲩ
17   ⲱ ⲁⲉⲓⲣⲫⲟⲣⲓ ⲛⲧⲟⲩϩⲃⲥⲱ ⲛⲟⲩⲟⲛ ⲛⲓⲙ ⲁⲩ
18   ⲱ ⲁⲉⲓϩⲟⲡⲧ ⲟⲩⲁⲁⲧ ϩⲣⲁⲓ ⲛϩⲏⲧⲟⲩ ⲁⲩⲱ ⲙⲡ[ⲟⲩ] —
```

"Zum drit(te)n Male manifestierte ich mich ihnen (i)n ihren Zelten als Logos. Und ich manifestierte mich in der Gestalt ihres Aussehens. Und ich trug ihres Gewand, eines jeden. Und ich verbarg mich selbst in ihnen".

---

publiziert von A. Böhlig (*Die koptisch-gnostische Schrift ohne Titel*, Berlin 1962, 36 Apparat). Insofern ist die Aussage von J. M. Robinson zu korrigieren.

[4] So möchte ich die Untersuchung der Ledereinbände koptischer Codices nach ⲕⲟⲉⲓϩ (siehe Crum, Coptic Dictionary, 132ᵃ) nennen.

[5] Für die Brieffragmente siehe die "Introduction" im 1. Band der *Facsimile edition of the Nag Hammadi codices*, Leiden 1972, 4. Für die Genesisfragmente: R. Kasser, Fragments du livre biblique de la Genèse, cachés dans la reliure d'un codex gnostique, *Muséon* 85 (1972), 65-89. In diesem Zusammenhang sollte man auch bedenken, dass der Fundort der Codices in der Nähe von Hamra-Dum nicht weit entfernt ist vom ältesten Pachom-Kloster Tabennîsi. Vielleicht sind die "Nag Hammadi"-Schriften dort abgefasst! Vgl. schon damals auf der Tagung über Gnostizismus in Messina 1966 (*Le Origini dello Gnosticismo*-colloquio di Messina 13-18 aprile 1966, Leiden 1967, 78, 553 und 559-560!). Diesbezüglich auch zu beachten: D. W. Young, The milieu of Nag Hammadi: Some historical considerations, *VigChr* 24 (1970), 128. Vor allem jetzt: T. Säve-Söderbergh, Holy Scriptures or Apologetic Documentations? The "Sitz im Leben" of the Nag Hammadi Library, in: "*Les Textes de Nag Hammadi*", colloque du Centre d'Histoire des Religions, Strasbourg, 23-25 octobre 1974, édité par J. E. Ménard (NHS VII), Leiden 1975, 3-14.

[6] Siehe C. Aalders-J. H. Plokker/G. Quispel, Jung, een mens voor deze tijd, Rotterdam 1975, Photoseite 13. Vgl. auch den Beitrag von J. W. B. Barns, Greek and Coptic Papyri from the Covers of the Nag Hammadi Codices in: *Nag Hammadi Studies* VI, Leiden 1975, 9-18.

In ihrem Kommentar beschränkt Y. JANSSENS sich bezüglich des Ausdruckes "ihre Zelte" auf folgende Bemerkung: "cf. Jo., 1, 14: ἐσκήνωσεν ἐν ἡμῖν". (a.c., 409). Wir haben uns im folgenden die Aufgabe gestellt die Legitimität und die Trageweite dieses "confer" zu untersuchen.

Bekanntlich sind Zweck und Bedeutung der Aussage in Joh. i 14 im ganzen des Johannes-Prologs oft diskutierte Fragen. So ist z.B. für Rudolf BULTMANN dieser Vers das Thema des Evangeliums slechthin,[7] während Ernst KÄSEMANN entgegengesetzter Meinung ist.[8] Eine der Schüler KÄSEMANNS, Luise SCHOTTROFF, hat sich in ihrer Habilitationsschrift Der Glaubende und die feindliche Welt[9] selbstverständlich auch mit der Frage bez. Joh. i 14 auseinandergesetzt. Die Verse Joh. i 14 und iii 16 sind für ihre These begreiflicherwiese die schwierigste Stellen.[10] Hartwig THYEN hat in seinem Forschungsbericht und Literaturüberblick die folgende pointierte Frage ventiliert: "Ob man aber i 14 von dem Zwei-Ebenen-Dualismus bzw. von der johanneïschen Theorie der zwei Wirklichkeiten (gemeint ist L. SCHOTTROFFS Umschreibung und Typisierung der Zwei-Ebenen-Theorie, welche dem Johannes spezifisch eigen sein sollte - H.) her interpretieren kann oder nicht vielmehr gerade in der Fleischwerdungsaussage (und anderen Passagen) eine sehr bewusste Korrektur dieser naiven Weltlosigkeit sehen muss, das scheint mir eine der fundamentalsten Fragen der gegenwärtigen Johannesinterpretation zu sein".[11]

Interessanterweise hat der Berliner Arbeitskreis, wenn auch im anderen Zusammenhang aber m.E. aus gleicher Sicht bez. der johanneïschen Kernfragen, auch "einen Schwerpunkt zukünftiger Arbeit" — nämlich an dem neuen Text der Prōtennoia Trimorphos — definiert,[12] und zwar so, dass die dritte Rede der Protennoia für die

---

[7] R. BULTMANN, Das Evangelium des Johannes, Göttingen [10]1964, 43 Anm. 4 und 44.

[8] E. KÄSEMANN, Aufbau und Anliegen des johanneïschen Prologs, in: Exegetische Versuche und Besinnungen II, Göttingen 1964, 155-180. Siehe: Karl Martin FISCHER, Der johanneïsche Christus und der gnostische Erlöser, Überlegungen auf Grund von Joh. 10, in: Karl-Wolfgang TRÖGER, Gnosis und Neues Testament, Berlin 1973, 245-266, 245-249; Bez. der Unstimmigkeit Bultmann-Käsemann, a.c., 245: "eine Kluft, die sich nicht mehr durch Kompromisse überbrücken lässt". Auch C. K. BARRETT, The Prologue of St John's Gospel, London 1971, 8-11 und 27.

[9] Beobachtungen zum gnostischen Dualismus und seiner Bedeutung für Paulus und das Johannesevangelium, Neukirchen-Vluyn 1970.

[10] Kurt RUDOLPH, Gnosis und Gnostizismus, ein Forschungsbericht, ThR 37 (1972), 305 (zum ganzen: 297-308). (Forschungsbericht, ab ThR 34 (1969), 181 ff.).

[11] Hartwig THYEN, Aus der Literatur zum Johannesevangelium, ThR 39 (1974) I, 1-252, 237.

[12] A.c., 734.

Interpretation des Johannes-Prologs von grösster Bedeutung zu sein
scheint, indem man entweder mit dem Berliner Arbeitskreis der
Meinung ist, dass "wie es auf den ersten Blick aussieht, das Licht
mehr von der Prōtennoia auf den Johannes-Prolog fällt als umgekehrt"[13] oder eben nicht. Letzteres trifft zu für Y. JANSSENS.[14] Anders
formuliert: wird der neue Text eine glänzende Bestätigung der längst
vorhandenen Hypothese sein (gemeint ist die "im Wirkungsfeld der
Johannes-Interpretation R. BULTMANNS'-H.) und ... die Substanz der
dritten Rede der Protennoia auf derselben Ebene liegend ... wie das
als Vorlage des Johannes-Prologs erschlossene gnostische Logos-
Lied"[15] ... oder wird auf weiterer Blick die gedachte "glänzende
Bestätigung" ... nicht gefunden werden?

Hierunter wird versucht einen kleinen Beitrag zu der oben genannten
zukünftigen Arbeit an dem neuen Text im Hinblick auf den Johannes-
Prolog zu liefern.

Die dreigestaltige Protennoia: kurzer Umriss

Yvonne JANSSENS kennzeichnet unseren Traktat als eine dreiteilige
Hymne, worin sich die Protennoia, der erste Gedanke des Unsichtbaren
Vaters, in drei Gestalten nämlich als Gedanke, Stimme und Wort auf
drei ebenbürtigen Ebenen offenbart, manifestiert. Die Hymne, "assez
ancienne" sei barbelognostischen Charakters.[16] Der Berliner Arbeitskreis hält als Arbeitshypothese fest, "dass der Text-ungeachtet schwa-
cher oder stärker an seinem Rande auftauchender christlicher Elemente
— in der Substanz ein Dokument der vom Christentum (noch)
unberührten (sethianischen) Gnosis ist".[17]

Der Traktat ist in drei Teile untergliedert, jedesmal mit ⲀⲚⲞⲔ
ⲡⲉ = *Ich bin*, eingeleitet. Und zwar folgendermassen: p. 35-42:3,
(Ich) bin die Prō(tennoia, der Gedanke, der ...; mit dem Titel am
Ende: Die (Re)de von der Prōtennoia. Dann p. 42:4-46:4, Ich bin
die Stimme, die sich manifestierte ... mit vier Buchstaben als Über-
rest des Titels, sehr wahrscheinlich zu ergänzen als (Heimar)menè.
Schliesslich p. 46:5-50:22, Ich bin (der Lo)gos, der ist (oder: der

---

[13] *O.c.*, 733.

[14] *O.c.*, *passim*; explizit in ihrem "Short Paper": "Une source gnostique du Pro-
logue?" am 21.August 1975, Colloquium Biblicum Lovaniense XXVI. Vgl. auch ihr
Aufsatz "L'Apocryphon de Jean", *Muséon* 83 (1970), 53. Der Aufsatz erschien in
Muséon 83 (1970), 157-165; 84 (1971), 43-64 und 403-432.

[15] Berliner Arbeitskreis usw., *a.c.*, 733/734.

[16] *Muséon* 87 (1974), 413.

[17] *A.c.*, 733.

wohnt) ... mit dem Titel: Die Rede von der dritten Epiphanie.
Dann folgt der Gesamttitel: Prōtennoia Trimorphos ⲅ, was bedeutet,
dass der letzte Teil (p. 46:5-50:22) der *dritte* der ganzen Schrift
Protennoia Trimorphos (hiernach PT) war. Der Traktat wird mit
folgendem Charakteristikum abgeschlossen: ⲁⲅⲓⲁ ⲅⲣⲁⲫⲏ ⲡⲁⲧⲣⲟ-
ⲅⲣⲁⲫⲟⲥ ⲉⲛ ⲅⲛⲱⲥⲉⲓ ⲧⲉⲗⲉⲓⲁ = Heilige Schrift vom Vater geschrieben in vollkommener Gnosis.

Protennoia (auch Barbelo genannt p. 38:9) manifestiert sich also
in drei Regionen, damit diese die ihnen je gebührende Rettung
erhalten; dabei wird immerhin schon im I. Teil auf die noch zu
behandelnde Aspekte der Protennoia (als Stimme und Wort) prae-
ludiert. Erstens offenbart sie sich im Pleroma den Aeonen des Lichtes
und zwar in männlicher Gestalt als ⲙⲉⲉⲩⲉ, Gedanke, damit die
Unordnung im Pleroma aufgehoben werde (am klarsten p. 42:23-25
und p. 49:14). Zweitens offenbart sie sich ausserhalb des Pleromas
in der "Zwischenwelt" der Archonten als die folglich in Eva verborgene
ⲁⲣⲟⲟⲩ, Stimme. Ist sie doch gerade diejenige, die mittels des unwis-
senden Archigenetor — des Schöpfers des Menschen — als "Mutter
der Lebenden" den göttlichen Kern, den Samen (p. 36:15, vgl. p. 50:16)
in alle Menschengeschlechter hineinsenkt (die μόρφωσις κατὰ γένεσιν).
So erhalten auch die Pneumatiker ein εἰκών, ein Leib, vgl. p. 42:17-18;
besonders 45:24 und 47:11. Schliesslich kommt die Protennoia dann
als ⲗⲟⲅⲟⲥ, Wort in die Menschenwelt hinein um für ihre Brüder
(p. 47:23 die μόρφωσις κατὰ γνῶσιν,[18] die pneumatische Vollendung, die συντέλεια herzustellen (p. 47:13, vgl. auch das ⲱⲁⲛϯ-
ⲟⲩⲟⲛⲁⲧʼ ⲉⲃⲟⲗ in 47:23 und 49:19: *bis ich mich manifestiere,*
teleologisch!). Zu diesem Zweck kommt sie als Logos, der sich in
den Menschen einhüllend, den Archonten unbekannt weil verborgen,
den Erwählten manifestiert (p. 47:14f.) und durch seinen Ruf weckt
(vgl. schon p. 35:22). Wir begegnen hier dem in den meisten gnostischen Systemen so wichtigen "Täuschungsmotiv": der herabsteigende
Offenbarer täuscht die Archonten.[19] Der gnostische Erlöser jedoch
nimmt die Gestalt des jeweiligen Äons an, so dass die (getäuschten)
Äonen des Kosmos Ihn für einen der Ihrigen halten! Vgl. das
aufschlussreiche ⲁⲱⲥ in 49:15.16: unter den Mächte *als* einer von

---

[18] Vgl. F. M. M. SAGNARD, *La Gnose Valentinienne et le Témoignage de Saint Irénée*,
Paris 1947, 484; J. ZANDEE, Gnostic ideas on the fall and salvation, *Numen* 11 (1964), 59,
und der Kommentar Y. JANSSENS' zur Stelle *a.c.*, 408/409.
[19] Vgl. BULTMANN, *Johanneskommentar* 10 und 39 Anm. 1; Karl Martin FISCHER,
a.c., 258/259 (zu unserer Stelle 47:15f.)

ihnen; unter den Menschensöhnen *als* ein Menschensohn (siehe unsere Stelle!).

Inzwischen kann der Erlöser, kann die Protennoia die Erwählten, ihre Glieder (49:19 ⲙⲉⲗⲟⲥ), nur wecken, wenn sie den Menschen sichtbar ist. Die Protennoia braucht deswegen einen Leib, um die im fleischlichen Leibe Gefangenen erreichen zu können. Mit Recht sagt BULTMANN: "(Der Erlöser) hat sich, um die dämonischen Mächte der Finsternis zu täuschen *und* um die zu rettenden Menschen nicht zu erschrecken, in einen menschlichen Leib verkleidet".[20] Es mutet mich seltsam an, dass der Berliner Arbeitskreis 47:16f. m.E. ohne jeden Grund auf die kosmischen Äonen deutet. Darum wird auch in der Übersetzung ein Wort zugefügt, das der koptische Text gar nicht bietet: "Und ich offenbarte mich (den Mächten)"![21] Es handelt sich hier eben nicht um die Mächte, sondern um die Menschen, die salvandi!

In ihrer Untersuchung hat Y. JANSSENS einleuchtende Übereinstimmungen zwischen der PT und dem Apokryphon des Johannes festgestellt.[22] Auch im Apokryphon des Johannes (im folgenden: AJ) begegnet ein dreimaliges Herabsteigen der Pronoia/Ennoia. Hierbei ist jedoch zu beachten, dass, anders als in der PT, die Aktivität des "Ersten Gedankens" im Pleroma zwar abgemalt wird (z.B. p. 27:14-29; 35:4:[23] die erste Manifestation, die die Mängel der gefallenen Sophia richtig stellen muss p. 47:5), die *schöpferische Aktivität*, wodurch der anfangs bewegunglose Adam den Geist empfängt und sich nun bewegen kann, jedoch als *erste* Manifestation *ausserhalb* des Pleromas im

---

[20] *O.c.*, 10 (43). Vgl. auch Zandee *a.c.*, 52 und 64.

[21] *A.c.*, 743.

[22] *A.c.*, 349-351. Wir zitieren: "Nous retrouvons à peu près tous ces termes (gemeint sind Pro(ten)noia, Bild, Barbelo, Erste Gedanke usw, H.) dans le Cod. XIII. Une telle concordance nous autorise bien à interpréter ces deux traités l'un par l'autre, au moins pour la doctrine, car la présentation littéraire est différente. Pas tellement cependant. ... Les fréquentes similitudes textuelles nous font supposer au moins une source commune à ces ouvrages" (*a.c.*, 349). Es ist erwähnenswert, dass auch im Aufsatz des Berliner Arbeitskreises von sich gegenseitig interpretierenden Texte die Rede ist. Hier bezieht es sich aber auf den Johannes-Prolog und die dritte Rede der PT! Die dritte Offenbarungsrede der Protennoia stelle "in weiten Partien geradezu eine Sachparallele zum Prolog des vierten Evangeliums dar" ... "Die bieden Texte interpretieren sich gegenseitig", *a.c.*, 733. Diese rasch gezogene aus einem bestimmten Denkschema erklärbare Gleichung sollte m.E. jedoch einer ernsten Kritik unterzogen werden. Was sind "Sachparallelen"? Was "Anklänge"? Auch diese Kritik wäre m.E. "Ein Schwerpunkt zukünftiger Arbeit"!

[23] Text: W. C. TILL, *Die gnostischen Schriften des koptischen Papyrus 8502*, Berlin 1955, 78-194 (AJ).

Kosmos dargestellt wird. Das zweite Mal in der Gestalt der Zoè/Eva belehrt die Pronoia Adam (vgl. PT 42:17-18). Das dritte Mal befreit sie die durch ihren Weckruf erwachte Menschen (76:1-5).

Wie bekannt, wird jenes dreimalige Herabsteigen in die Welt eindrucksvoll beschrieben im AJ-Text des Codex II (par. Codex IV: die sog. lange Version) und zwar p. 30:11-31:28.[24] Sehr meinungsvoll II, 31:4-5: "(Pronoia) ich ging hinein in die Mitte ihres Gefängnisses-das ist das Gefängnis des Körpers (σῶμα)..."![25] Übrigens wird in der PT die schöpferische 'bewegende' Aktivität der Protennoia angedeutet in p. 35:2.12; 46:26; 47:21 (die κίνησις, koptisch ⲕⲓⲙ).

Aber nicht nur mit AJ, sondern auch mit anderen wichtigen gnostischen Texte vergleicht Y. JANSSENS m.E. sehr zweckmässig den Inhalt der PT. So unter anderem mit dem "Unbekannten altgnostischen Werk" des Codex Brucianus — in dieser Weise verdient wieder ins Licht gestellt —[26] und dem für die Ursprungsfrage des Gnostizismus so äusserst wichtigen Apokalypse des Adam (Codex V Nag Hammadi).[27] Doch wird das AJ zur Erklärung der PT auch von Y. JANSSENS in ihrem Kommentar jeweils begründet (die "gegenseitige Interpretation"!) angeführt. Das (barbelognostische) AJ — Schrifttum ist m.E. tatsächlich von grösster Bedeutung, nicht nur für das Verständnis der Grundthematik des Gnostizismus überhaupt,[28] sondern auch für das Verständnis des Ursprungs und des Werdeganges des valentinianischen Gnostizismus.[29] In diesem Zusammenhang sollte jedoch

---

[24] Martin KRAUSE/Pahor LABIB, *Die drei Versionen des Apokryphon des Johannes im koptischen Museum zu Alt-Kairo*, Wiesbaden 1962.

[25] Französische Übersetzung der Passage 30:11-31:28 bei Y. JANSSENS, *a.c.*, 351/352. Vgl. auch SCHOTTROFF, *o.c.*, 101, 110-111.

[26] Y. JANSSENS, *a.c.*, 344 und 348; cf. *Muséon* 84 (1971), 46. Ausser der von Y. JANSSENS angeführten Bayneschen Edition des Textes, ist zu verweisen auf die Tillsche (W. C. TILL (Carl SCHMIDT), *Koptisch-Gnostische Schriften* I. Band, Berlin ³1962, 335ff.

[27] James M. ROBINSON, The Coptic Gnostic Library Today, *NTS* 14 (1968), 377 *idem, The Nag Hammadi Codices*. A general introduction to the nature and significance of the Coptic Gnostic Codices from Nag Hammadi, Claremont (U.S.A.) 1974, 7 und 13. Vgl. *ibidem* (2) Notiz über Pachom, oben Anm. 5. George MACRAE, The Apocalypse of Adam Reconsidered, in: *The Society of Biblical Literature One Hundred Eight Annual Meeting, Book of Seminar Papers* (ed. L. C. MCGAUGHY, S.B.L. 1972), 573-579. Bei beiden Genannten, die Apok. Adams als *"Brücke"* zwischen jüdischer Apokalyptik und dem Gnostizismus.

[28] Y. JANSSENS, *a.c.*, *Muséon* 84 (1971), 429.

[29] Vgl. SAGNARD, *o.c.*, 445-446: Irenaeus hätte eine Version des AJ benützt und Valentin und seine Schule(n), hätten AJ-Material verarbeitet, vgl. unter anderen: H.-Ch. PUECH in E. HENNECKE/W. SCHNEEMELCHER, *Neutestamentliche Apokryphen* I,

Frederik WISSES nüchterne und durchaus richtige Beobachtung nicht umgangen werden, dass nämlich Qualifizierungen und Benennungen gnostischer Schulen und Systeme in naïver Nachfolge der altkirchlichen Heresiologen irreführend sind, weil sie das Anliegen und die Eigenart der Gnostiker nicht richtig einschätzten: "The heresiologists appear to have made the mistake of seeing a different sect behind every variant myth".[30] Dabei behalten Klassifizierungen wie Sethianismus und Barbelognostizismus natürlich ihr Recht, wenn umsichtig angewendet.

Da Y. JANSSENS die PT schliesslich noch folgendermassen charakterisiert: "Une doctrine relativement pure encore, où les éléments mythologiques occupent peu de place" — und deswegen auch eine "hymne ... assez ancienne" —,[31] wird wiederum die Frage akut, ob nun das mehr philosophisch frisierte bzw. lehrhafte gnostische System oder Denkschema ursprünglicher jedenfalls zeitlich früher, anzusetzen wäre als das (mehr) mythologische, oder gerade umgekehrt. Die Meinungen ad hoc sind bekanntlich geteilt.[32]

Tübingen [3]1959, 242/243; W. FOERSTER u.A., *Die Gnosis* I Zürich/Stuttgart 1969, 164; G. QUISPEL, *Gnosis als Weltreligion*, Zürich 1951, 11 ff.; *idem*, Origen and the Valentinian Gnosis, VigChr 28 (1974), 42; G. C. STEAD, The Valentinian Myth of Sophia, *JThS* 20 (1969) 76/77; G. MACRAE in *Le Origini* (sehe Anm. 5), 504/505. Die Datierung des AJ ist eine wichtige Frage, besonders aus der Sicht der Beziehung AJ-Valentin! Bekanntlich stellen die AJ-Texte im Berolinensis 8502 und Codex III-Nag Hammadi die kürzere Fassung des AJ dar, die im Codex II und IV Nag Hammadi, die längere (und jüngere) vgl. Martin KRAUSE in *Le Origini*, 61/62 Anm.

[30] Frederik WISSE, The Sethians and the Nag Hammadi Library" in: *Book of Seminar papers* (siehe oben Anm. 27), 607. Namentlich schon in seinem Aufsatz "The Nag Hammadi Library and the Heresiologists", *VigChr* 25 (1971), 209 ff.; 220 ff.

[31] Y. JANSSENS, *a.c.*, 413.

[32] Zum ganzen Problem: H. J. W. DRIJVERS, The origins of gnosticism ... in: *NedThT* 22 (1967/68), 321 ff.; diesbezüglich spez. 333. Für den ersten Standpunkt (das lehrhafte, mehr oder weniger un-mythologische) sei älter, vgl. unter anderen: W. C. TILL, Die Gnosis in Ägypten, *Par Pass* 4 (1949), 230-249; *idem*, Coptic and its Value, *BJRL* 40 (1957), 254/5; H. LANGERBECK, *Aufsätze zur Gnosis*, Göttingen 1967, 167-169; PUECH, *a.c.*, 243. Man könnte diesbezüglich noch darauf hinweisen, dass das "schöpferische Bewegen" (siehe oben S. 187) in der PT ebensowenig "mythologisch" aufgezogen ist. Für den zweiten Standpunkt (das mythologische sei primär), vgl. unter anderen: H. JONAS, *Gnosis und spätantiker Geist* I, Göttingen 1964[3], 359 und 415; II, 1, Göttingen 1966, 20 und 122ff. ("Vom zweiten zum dritten Jhdrt oder: von der mythologischen zur philosophisch-mystischen Gnosis"); H. M. SCHENKE, Hauptprobleme der Gnosis, *Kairos* 7 (1965), 120. Vgl. auch BULTMANN, *o.c.* (sehe Anm. 7), 13. Anders: R. McL. WILSON, Gnostic origins again, *VigChr* 11 (1957), 108/109: ein "Dreistufen-schema": "Gnosticism, originally mythological, became for a period more or less philosophical and then relapsed once more into mythology". Dies scheint auch mir richtig. Vgl. noch Kurt RUDOLPH, *a.c.*, 294 und C. H. DODD, *The Interpretation of the Fourth Gospel*, Cambridge 1953, 128/129.

Bevor wir uns nun der Bedeutung unserer Stelle: PT 47:14-15 zuwenden, scheint es mir angebracht erst *einige Vorbemerkungen sprachlicher Art* zu machen, nicht zuletzt deshalb weil sich im Text: ⲥⲕⲏⲛⲏ als griechisches Lehnwort findet.

Dass hier ein Lehnwort begegnet — dazu dieses statt z.B. des näherliegenden ⲟⲓⲕⲟⲥ — und nicht eines der koptischen Äquivalente, zieht unsere Aufmerksamkeit auf sich. Da es nicht in den Rahmen unserer Untersuchung passt die Frage der griechischen Lehnwörter im Koptischen ausführlich zu erörtern, möge es genügen, unter anderem auf in anderem Zusammenhang von mir dazu Bemerktes zu verweisen.[33] Zwei Punkte jedoch sollten hervorgehoben werden. Erst einmal, dass "ein Übersetzer ins Koptische für ein ihm in seiner griechischen Vorlage begegnendes, von ihm als fremd empfundenes Wort ein sinnverwandtes griechisches Wort einsetzen konnte".[34] Zweitens, dass "die griechischen Wörter nicht erst aus den griechischen Texten bei der Übersetzung ins Koptische eingedrungen sind, sondern dass sie schon in der damals in Ägypten gesprochene Umgangssprache fest verwurzelt waren".[35] Jedenfalls ist auch in der PT der hohe Prozentsatz griechischer Lehnwörter auffallend. Ob man darum wie z.B. hinsichtlich des Tractatus Tripartitus des Codex I (Jung) von einer "version improvisée" reden sollte, bleibe dahingestellt.[36] Die dem griechischen σκηνή eigenen Bedeutungen "Zelt" und "Wohnung" — letztere ist zu betonen[37] — werden normalerweise im Koptischen differenziert: die Hauptäquivalente für "Wohnung, Haus" sind ⲏⲓ und ⲙⲁ ⲛ̄ϣⲱⲡⲉ; für "Zelt" ϩⲃⲱ und ϩⲁϊⲃⲉⲥ, wobei es interessant zu bemerken ist, dass die für σκηνή aus etymologischen Gründen vermutete zugrunde liegende Wurzel *škai-*, Schatten, im koptischen Äquivalent ϩⲁϊⲃⲉⲥ zwar nicht bestätigt, jedoch aber merkwürdigerweise betont wird![38]

Exkurs: σκηνή *in der sahidischen Übersetzung des Neuen Testaments*

Wir geben zuerst die sahidische und bohairische Übersetzung des von uns hier untersuchten Versteiles *Joh. i 14.*

---

[33] Jan HELDERMAN, Anachorese zum Heil. Das Bedeutungsfeld der Anachorese bei Philo und in einigen gnostischen Traktaten von Nag Hammadi, in: *Essays on the Nag Hammadi Texts in honour of Pahor Labib*, (NHS VI) Leiden 1975, 44-45.

[34] HELDERMAN, *a.c.*, 44. Vgl. auch W. C. TILL, *Die Gnostischen Schriften*, 14.

[35] Martin KRAUSE, Die Koptologie im Gefüge der Wissenschaften, *ZÄS* 100 (1974), 116f. Hinsichtlich des Einflusses des "Ägyptischen" vgl. *ThWNT* X, 43!

[36] R. KASSER u.A., *Tractatus Tripartitus*, Pars I De Supernis, Bern 1973, 34 Anm. 4.

[37] MICHAELIS in *ThWNT* VII, 372 und 380 (*s.v.*).

[38] *ThWNT* VII, 369 Anm. 1.

Sah.: ⲁϥⲣⲥⲁⲣⲝ ⲁϥⲟⲩⲱϩ ⲛⲙⲙⲁⲛ ...
Er ward Fleisch, Er wohnte *mit* uns.

Boh.: ⲟⲩⲟϩ ⲡⲓⲥⲁⲭⲓ ⲁϥⲉⲣⲟⲩⲥⲁⲣⲝ
ⲟⲩⲟϩ ⲁϥϣⲱⲡⲓ ⲛϧⲣⲏⲓ ⲛϧⲏⲧⲉⲛ
Und das Wort ward Fleisch und Er wohnte unter uns.[39]

Er ward *Fleisch*.[40]

Es ist bemerkenswert, dass das Sahidische "*mit* uns" hat.[41] Im griechischen N.T. begegnet σκηνή 20mal. An allen Stellen hat die sahidische Übersetzung[42] das Lehnwort ⲥⲕⲏⲛⲏ, mit Ausnahme von Hebr. xi 9, das ϧⲃⲱ hat (Boh. hat ⲥⲕⲏⲛⲏ!). Auch σκῆνος und σκήνωμα (ersteres in 2 Cor. v 1.4; letzteres in Apg. vii 46 und 2 Petr. i 13) werden beide mit ⲙⲁ ⲛϣⲱⲡⲉ übersetzt; das ist aufschlussreich, weil diese Übersetzung zu unserem Befund passt, dass nämlich im Koptischen bei der Wiedergabe des griechischen σκηνή die Bedeutung "Wohnung, Haus" vorherrscht.[43] Das Zeitwort

---

[39] G. W. HORNER, The Coptic version of the N.T. ... Sahidic ... Oxford 1911-1924, *idem*, The Coptic version of the N.T. ... Bohairic ... London 1898-1905.

[40] Er ward σάρξ, *nicht*: er ward ἄνθρωπος oder σῶμα. Dazu richtig COLPE in *ThWNT s.v.* υἱὸς τ.α. (474, Z. 23ff.). Das paradoxe σάρξ ist von grundlegender Bedeutung, weil so das Personhafte des Logos betont werden konnte. Die Auslegung BULTMANNS schillert. Zwar betont auch *ér* die pure, konkrete Menschlichkeit Jesu, andererseits jedoch deutet er die σάρξ auf die Menschengestalt hin, worin der Erlöser sich (ver)kleidete und auf σάρξ als die Gott entgegengesetzte Sphäre (vgl. *o.c.*, 39-43). Der Evglist hätte sich die Sprache der Gnosis angeeignet. "Der Offenbarer ist nichts als ein Mensch" (40). Zum Logos: "... der Logos nicht ein Jemand ist, sondern Gott, sofern er sich offenbart" (40 Anm. 2). BULTMANNS Paradoxie (44) ist deswegen anderer Art. *Der Logos aber wurde eben nicht "ein Mensch" oder "ein Leib", sondern Fleisch*: diese Paradoxie ist das völlig Neue (vgl. nochmals COLPE, *a.c.*, 474 und Ch. DODD, *Interpretation*, 249, 272, 281, 283-285). In Codex I (Jung): "*Evangelium Veritatis*" (ed. M. MALININE u.A., Zürich 1956; Suppl. Zürich 1961) findet man p. 26: 4-8 folgende "Umdeutung" von Joh. i 14. "... der Logos... welcher im Herzen von denen ist, die ihn sprechen — er war nicht nur ein Ruf, sondern er war Leib (ⲥⲱⲙⲁ) geworden — entstand eine grosse Verwirrung usw.": ⲁϥⲣ̄ ⲟⲩⲥⲱⲙⲁ! Hier sieht man die Menschengestalt tatsächlich als Kleid, Hülle, damit man den Offenbarer tasten und sehen kann (vgl. Irenaeus, Adv. Haer. I, 9, 3: ein corpus visibile und palpabile, ed. W. W. HARVEY, Cambridge 1857, I, 82 und 85).

[41] In Anklang an Ap xxi 3? Er ward Fleisch: das verb ⲉⲓⲣⲉ hat zweierlei Bedeutung: machen und werden. Interessant ist zu bemerken, dass Al Ghazâlî in einer polemischen Schrift die Übersetzung "ward Fleisch" (Lat.: factum est) kritisiert, weil das Koptische "Er machte Fleisch und nicht er ward Fleisch hat" (R. CHIDIAC, *Al Ghazâlî-Refutation Excellente de la Divinité de Jésus Christ d'après les évangiles*, Texte établi, traduit et commenté, Paris 1939, 51).

[42] Vgl. L. Th. LEFORT/M. WILMET, *Concordance du Nouveau Testament Sahidique*, (CSCO 124, 173, 183 und 185); Index (von R. DRAGUET) CSCO 196 (1950-1960) σκηνή Luk xvi 9, begegnet im Zitat in *Pistis Sophia* cap. 130 (TILL/SCHMIDT, *Kopt.-Gnost. Schriften*, 216); ebenfalls im Zitat bei Clemens Alexandrinus, *Quis dives* ... 31/32.

[43] Vgl. W. E. CRUM, *Coptic Dictionary*, Oxford 1939, 66ᵃ, 580 und 656. Zu beachten ist, dass das Sahidische in 2 Petr i 14 σκήνωμα mit ⲥⲱⲙⲁ wiedergibt! Bekanntlich wird die sahidische Übersetzung Anfang des ersten Jahrhunderts fertig gewesen sein. Die Nag Hammadi Codices werden jetzt wohl uni sono Mitte bzw. nach Mitte des vierten Jahrhunderts datiert; der koptische Dialekt der Codices ist meistens das

σκηνόω begegnet fünfmal im griechischen N.T. In Ap. xii 12; xiii 6 und xxi 3; Joh. i 14 werden im Sahidischen Formen des Verbums ΟΥⲰϨ, wohnen (*bleibendes, beständiges wohnen*) verwendet, mit Ausnahme von Ap. vii 15, wo das … σκηνώσει ἐπ᾽αὐτούς, folgendermassen übersetzt wird: ϥⲚⲀⲢ̄ ϨⲀⲒⲂⲈⲤ ⲈⲢⲞⲞⲨ : Er wird sie überschatten (Boh. hat ⲈϥⲈⲈⲢϬ ΗⲒⲂⲒ ⲈⲬⲰⲞⲨ, wodurch das ἐπ᾽αὐτούς wörtlich wiedergegeben wird). Das Kompositum κατασκηνόω (Mt. xiii 32; Mc iv 32; Luk xiii 19 und Apg ii 26 im griechischen N.T.) wird im Sahidischen ebenfalls mit dem Verb ΟΥⲰϨ übersetzt, vgl. MICHAELIS hinsichtlich dieses Kompositums: "…das Kompos. κατασκηνόω soviel häufiger als das Simplex…, (weil) …κατα- hierbei den Gedanken des längeren Verweilens noch hat unterstreichen sollen".[44] Wenn man versucht — unbeschadet einer mehr sachgemässeren Untersuchung — eine Folgerung zu ziehen, so drängt sich m.E. die Sicht auf, dass ⲤⲔΗⲚΗ tatsächlich ein im Koptischen eingebürgertes Lehnwort war; des weiteren, dass der Aspekt des Beständigen in den koptischen Äquivalenten des Substantivs "Zelt" und des Verbs "wohnen" deutlich hervortritt und schliesslich, dass auch an obigem Material illustriert werden könnte, dass ebenfalls die koptische Übertragung an einigen Stellen (siehe oben bei Joh. i 14 (sah); 2Cor v 1.4; Apg vii 46 und 2Petr i 13 weiter Hebr. xi 9 und zumal Ap vii 15) ein "buntes Kolorit" aufzeigt![45]

Zelt, Wohnen und Gewand

PT 47:14-15 im Kontext des Gnostizismus

I. Zu ⲤⲔΗⲚΗ

Dass im gnostischen Denken, Welt und Körper des Menschen als "Wohnung" bezeichnet werden, wie auch des näheren nuanziert, wird wohl keinen wundernehmen.

Ist doch das gnostische Denken als ein "Raumdenken" zu charakterisieren. Man hat schon öfters versucht, "dem Kern" des Phänomens des Gnostizismus und der Gnosis überhaupt näher zu kommen mittels Aufzeigen von Grundzügen.[46] Wie dem auch sei, Hans JONAS hat m.E. das gnostische Raum-Erlebnis in seiner Eigenart als Grundphänomen des gnostischen Denkens und Selbstverständnisses über-

---

Sahidische mit (sub)achmimischem Eigenart. Noch sei bemerkt, dass auch die etwas spätere bohairische Übersetzung des NT wie die sahidische an allen 20 Stellen (einschliesslich also Hebr. xi 9) σκηνή hat, *nur* das ⲤⲔΗⲚΗ geschrieben wird ⲤⲔⲨⲚΗ, siehe A. BÖHLIG, *Die griechischen Lehnwörter im sah. und boh. Neuen Testament*, München ²1958, 102. Weiter hat sie 2Kor v 1.4; Apg. vii 46; 2Petr. i 13 ünd 14: ⲘⲀ Ⲛ̄ϢⲰⲠⲈ. Bemerkenswert ist es, dass sie jedoch in Ap. xii 12; xiii 6; xxi 3 wie Joh. i 14 das Verb ϢⲰⲠⲈ- statt ΟΥⲰϨ hat.

[44] *ThWNT* VII (*s.v.* κατασκηνόω), 390 oben.

[45] H. J. VOGELS, *Handbuch der Textkritik des Neuen Testaments*, Bonn ²1955, S. 77. Allem Anschein nach sind die genannten bemerkenswerten Übertragungen nicht auf diesbezügliche besondere griechische Vorlagen zurückzuführen.

[46] So die "Gnosis/Gnostizismus-Definition" der Tagung in Messina (siehe *Le Origini*, XXIX-XXXII).

haupt, ganz treffend skizziert: "die Beängstigung durch das Riesen-
hafte, Unabsehbare des Welt-Raumes" einerseits; "die Welt, bei aller
erschreckenden Grösse, ein geschlossenes *Gehäuse* (von mir, H. unterstrichen) eigener Gesetzlichkeit — 'haec cellula creatoris' (Marcion)"
andererseits.[47] Demgemäss ist die Vorstellung bez. Himmel und Welt
massiv räumlich (Abstieg und Aufstieg)!

In all diesem war das Raum-Erlebnis der Antike und der Gnosis
wesentlich gegensätzlich.[48] Mit COLPE möchte ich die Kategorie der
"Behausung" als sachgemäss aufführen, weil sie dem gnostischen
Anliegen und dem Wortlaut der gnostischen Dokumente gerecht
wird.[49] Nun ist auch das selige Verweilen im Lichte, in der Lichtwohnung, ein Wohnen; kann doch die Menge der Erlösten als "Haus"
bezeichnet werden.[50] Wir werden es so gleich in der PT sehen.
Im Gegensatz zur Lichtwohnung jedoch wird das (zeitweilige) Dasein
in der materiellen Welt als ein Wohnen in einer niederen, engen,
finsteren, hinfälligen Wohnung qualifiziert. Das Wohnen wird also
sehr deutlich typisiert. Die Welt als Gefängnis (tatsächlich aufs engste
umzirkt!) fanden wir im AJ Codex II, 31:4-5. Aber auch "das
zeitweilige und Durchgangshafte des weltlichen Aufenthaltes"[51] wird
durch die Qualifizierung der Welt als "Herberge" bekanntlich mar-
kiert.[52] Schliesslich sei betont, dass, was im Grossen von der Welt gilt,

---

[47] JONAS, *Gnosis* I, 100-101.

[48] JONAS, 163 Anm. 1. Vgl. für das "Raum-Denken" L. SCHOTTROFF, *Animae naturaliter salvandae*, in: *Christentum und Gnosis* (Herausg. W. ELTESTER), Berlin 1969, 71: "Erlösung ist als Ortsveränderung vorgestellt...". Weiter noch: SCHOTTROFF, *Der Glaubende*, 95; MUSSNER bei: J. P. MIRANDA, *Der Vater, der Mich gesandt hat...* Bern/Frankfurt 1972, 56, Anm. 2, und J. BLANK, *Krisis. Untersuchungen zur joh. Christologie und Eschatologie*, Freiburg iBr., 1964, 192, wo auch nach JONAS, *o.c.*, 100ff. verwiesen wird.

[49] C. COLPE, *Die Religionsgeschichtliche Schule.* Darstellung und Kritik ihres Bildes vom gnostischen Erlösermythus, Göttingen 1961, 187-188 COLPE weist beim Terminus "Behausung" hin auf Michel in *ThWNT* V s.v. ὄικος: 125, wo in Anm. 15 nun wieder nach JONAS *o.c.*, 101 verwiesen wird!

[50] Siehe im folgenden die Stellen in der PT. Für die Wohnung des Demiurgen vgl. SAGNARD, *o.c.*, 518. Zum ganzen: Michel, *a.c.*, 125; E. H. PAGELS, *The Johannine Gospel in gnostic Exegesis...* Nashville/New York 1973, 70.

[51] JONAS, *o.c.*, 101.

[52] JONAS, *o.c.*, 101-102 und 912; Sagnard, *o.c.*, 183-184 und 235, Anm. 6. Zum Bild der Lichtwohnung, vgl. man Ph. VIELHAUER, *Oikodome. Das Bild vom Bau in der christlichen Literatur vom N.T. bis Clemens Alexandrinus*, Karlsruhe 1940, 36-37 (unter Verweis auf JONAS, *o.c.*, 100ff.!); 40-41 und 52. Zum methodischen Problem (Jonas' phänomenologischer Ausgangspunkt und Benützung seiner Arbeit durch die neutestamentliche Wissenschaft) siehe COLPE, *o.c.*, 57ff. Zu VIELHAUERS Oikodomestudie, vgl. ebenda 60!

im Kleinen ebensehr vom Körper gilt: die Symbole alternieren oft miteinander.[53]

Wenden wir uns nunmehr den Wohnungs-Stellen in der PT zu.

37:20-22: "Und die Stimme, die entstand aus meinem Gedanken, der drei *Bleibestätten* (ⲘⲞⲚⲎ) bildet, hat (als) eine Stimme einen Logos in sich". Der Gedanke, die Protennoia also, "est la Monade, la Maison unique, dans laquelle il y a trois demeures".[54] Die drei Aufenthaltsräume sind Vater, Mutter und Sohn, bzw. Gedanke, Stimme und Wort, und bilden zusammen die drei Manifestationen der Protennoia: Dreiheit in der *Einheit* jedoch!

40:21: (über jene) "im *Hause* (Ⲏⲓ̈) des Lichtes".

41:32: "*Mein Haus*" (Ⲏⲓ̈) nämlich der Protennoia für die Ihrigen.

43:13-14: "Und die Lose der Heimarmene und die, die die *Wohnungen* (ⲞⲓⲔⲞⲤ) durchmessen, gerieten in Erschütterung" (nämlich durch den von der Protennoia bewirkten Donner). Es handelt sich hier um die kosmischen Mächte, die durch Protennoias Stimme in Unruhe geraten. Die Wohnung als elende Begrenztheit! Vgl. auch AJ 72:3-11.[55]

43:22: "Und unser ganzes *Haus* (Ⲏⲉⲓ) wurde bewegt". Das Haus, der Raum der beunruhigten Archonten und Mächte.

44:26: "Dieser, durch den das unwissende Chaos uns (zur) *Wohnung* (ⲘⲀ ⲚϬⲞⲈⲓⲗⲈ)[56] wurde". Klage der Archonten und Anklage: selbst Ihr Haupt, der Archigenetor, verstand die Stimme und ihr Woher nicht!

45:35: lakunöse Stelle. Jedoch ist es begründet zu lesen: "...*ihre Woh*(*nung*) (ⲘⲀ Ⲛ[ϣⲱ]ⲡⲈ)". Wohl das Lichthaus der zur Ptotennoia Gehörigen".

46:28-31: "(Ich, der Logos bin) das Auge der drei *Bleibestätten* (ⲘⲞⲚⲎ), während (eine) Stimme aus einem Gedanke entstanden ist. Und ein Wort aus der Stimme". Das Auge ist der dritte Aspekt der Einen Protennoia, die Monade. Er heisst der Sohn, das Wort oder der Sohn des Menschen. Er ging aus dem Lichte (dem Vater, der Protennoia)[57] hervor und bringt Ihm Ehre (vgl. 38:5-6 und 25).

---

[53] JONAS, *o.c.*, 102 Anm. 1.

[54] Y. JANSSENS, *a.c.*, 396. Dass μονή deutlich den Charakter des Bleibenden hat, wird von HAUCK in *ThWNT* s.v. μονή (IV, 584) deutlich expliziert!

[55] Vgl. Y. JANSSENS, *a.c.*, 406/407 und eadem in *Muséon* 84 (1971), 427.

[56] Auch ϬⲞⲈⲓⲗⲈ bedeutet "wohnen" und deswegen ⲘⲀ ⲚϬⲞⲈⲓⲗⲈ, Wohnort. Die beiden Wörter sind synonym, obwohl man sagen könnte, dass ⲞⲨⲰⲜ mehr die Nuance der κατοικία trägt, während ϬⲞⲈⲓⲗⲈ mehr die der παροικία.

[57] Man beachte wie es im Gnostizismus als ein ihm eigentümliches hermeneutisches Prinzip möglich ist, eine Hypostase immer weiter zu reduplizieren. Vom 'Sohn' gilt

Man beachte: der Demiurg ist blind,[58] der Logos sieht nicht nur "den Vater", sondern ist zumal dessen Auge![59] In der Sophia Jesu Christi, wird der Sohn, der Mensch, auch: "Adam, das Auge des Lichtes" genannt.[60]

50:12-14: "Und ich (nämlich die Protennoia, H.) stellte ihn (nämlich Jesus 50:10, H.) hin in die *Wohnungen* (ⲙⲁ ⲛ̄ϣⲱⲡⲉ) seines Vaters. Und nicht erkannten mich, die da wachen über ihre *Wohnungen* (ⲙⲁ ⲛ̄ϣⲱⲡⲉ)". Vgl. für letzteres oben 43:14. Jesus aber erreicht das Lichthaus, welchem er ja doch gehört ... sei es denn, dass die Protennoia gemeint ist!

Der Deutlichkeit wegen, haben wir oben bei wichtigen Stellen den ganzen Kontext wiedergegeben. Ebenso erscheint es mir wünschenswert, unten in den Anmerkungen aus anderen Traktaten solche Stellen aufzuführen, die sich m.E. als Sachparallelen erweisen, hellt doch der diesbezügliche Sachkomplex (Wohnung, wohnen, Gewand) im ganzen Gnostizismus auf.[61]

---

was vom "Vater" gilt, sie sind letzten Endes beide ein und derselbe. In der "Heils-geschichte" des Gnostizismus musste und konnte — mittels des christlichen Kon-zeptes des "Menschensohnes"? So Colpe — der Prozess oder aber der *Re-zess*(!) zur Erlösung der Gnostiker doch "personhafte" Umrisse erhalten. Vgl. C. COLPE, New Testament and Gnostic Christology, in: *Religions in Antiquity. Essays in memory of E. R. GOODENOUGH* (ed. J. NEUSNER), Leiden 1968, 240-241. Auch in *Die Religions-geschichtliche Schule*, 107: "die (den Grundgehalt) symbolisierenden, hypostatisch verselbständigten Begriffe wechseln bis zur Verwirrung".

[58] Der Name des Demiurgen "Samaël" z.B. meint der "Blinde Gott". Vgl. JONAS, *o.c.*, 384-385 Anm. 2. Zum dort genannten "Hypostase der Archonten" vgl. jetzt auch R. A. BULLARD, *The Hypostasis of the Archons*, Berlin 1970, 52-53 und ebenso bez. "Samaël" A. BÖHLIG / P. LABIB, *Die Koptisch-Gnostische Schrift ohne Titel aus Codex II von Nag Hammadi*, Berlin 1962, 49.

[59] Vgl. auch MICHAELIS (s.v. ὀφθαλμός), *ThWNT* V, 376: "die Redeweise, die Augen statt der sehenden Person zu nennen".

[60] Vgl. Y. JANSSENS, *a.c.*, 397. "Die Sophia Jesu Christi" (in: W. C. TILL, *Die Gnostischen Schriften des koptischen Papyrus Berolinensis* (oben Anm. 23)), 100:14 und 108:10-11.

[61] Interessante Stellen sind: *Unbekanntes altgnostisches Werk* (ed. SCHMIDT/TILL, *o.c.*, 335): (Der Monogenes) 'ist das Haus des Vaters und das Kleid des Sohnes'. Vgl. Y. JANSSENS, *a.c.*, 347-348. Sehe auch in den Nag Hammadi Texten:
CODEX I (Jung): *Epistula Jacobi Apocrypha* 13:3-6: "Ich manifestiere mich Ihnen, ein *Haus* (ⲏⲉⲓ̈) bauend, das für euch sehr nützlich ist, (weil) ihr unter ihm Schutz (ⲅ̅ⲁⲉⲓⲃⲉⲥ) findet". Die himmlische Wohnung durch Jesus gebaut für die seine. (ed. M. MALININE u.A., Zürich/Stuttgart 1968). Siehe für den Charakter der Schrift, S. XXIX/XXX und J. ZANDEE, Gnostische trekken in een apocryphe brief van Johannes, *NThT* 17 (1962/3), 401-422. Zu 9:2-8 siehe unten bei "Wohnen". *Evangelium Veritatis* 25:21-25: "Es ziemt uns also vor allem dafür Sorge zu tragen, dass das *Haus* (ⲏⲉⲓ) heilig sein wird und stille für die Einheit" Der Leib als Haus oder Herberge,

Zusammenfassend wäre zu bemerken, dass es wohl nicht zufällig ist, dass MONH nur in Bezug auf die Räume der "dreifaltig Eine" Protennoia angewendet wird. So wird doch betont, dass — wie auch immer im Kosmos sich manifestierend — die Protennoia ihre *Bleibe-*stätte bei sich selbst im Licht hat und behält! Die anderen Wörter alternieren miteinander.

Dass nun in 47:15 nicht eines dieser koptischen Wörter für "Wohnung" benützt wird, sondern das griechische Lehnwort CKHNH hat m.E. sehr bestimmte Gründe. Siehe unten.

II. *Zu Wohnen*

Dass das Verb OYWϨ, wohnen, in unserem Traktat begegnen würde, ist bestreitbar auf Grund der sehr slechten Erhaltung von p. 42:31-34, so dass — wenn überhaupt das erhaltene ЄϤOYHϨ N̄[, nicht zu ЄϤOYHϨ N̄CA (folgen) zu ergänzen sei und deswegen nicht "während er wohnt" bedeuten würde — es hinsichtlich des unsicheren Kontextes nicht möglich ist, diesem Wohnen einen guten Sinn abzu-

---

vgl. SAGNARD, *o.c.*, 184. Zum Begriff "Haus" in den genannten Schriften vgl. *Epistula Jacobi* (Edition, 69/70) und *Evangelium Veritatis* (Supplementum, 13).

CODEX V: *Die Apokalypse des Adam* 77:9-12: "Und kommen wird die Herrlichkeit und sein in heiligen *Häusern* (HЄI), die sie sich erwählt hat". Es handelt sich hier um das "Täuschungsmotiv": der Phoster kommt zum dritten Mal zur Erlösung. Haus ist hier "Gestalt" nahezu Gewand, vgl. dazu Jonas, *o.c.*, 102 und A. BÖHLIG/P. LABIB, *Koptisch-Gnostische Apokalypsen aus Codex V von Nag Hammadi*, Halle/Wittenberg 1963, 90.

CODEX VI: *"Die ursrpüngliche Lehre"* 27:25-27: "Unsere Seele ist krank, weil sie in einem *Armutshaus* (HЄI M̄MNTϨHKЄ) ist..." M. KRAUSE/P. LABIB, *Gnostische und hermetische Schriften aus Codex II und Codex VI*, Glückstadt 1971. Vgl. noch K. M. FISCHER in *Gnosis und NT* (sehe Anm. 8), 257.

CODEX VII: *"Der Zweite Logos des Grossen Seth"* *50:10-12:* "Sie jubelten, nämlich das ganze *Haus* (HÏ) des Vaters der Wahrheit". Hinsichtlich des Entschlusses des Erlösers, dass er zur Rettung absteigen wird. Vgl. 59:19 "...unserem *Hause*" (HЄI), *51:5-7:* Die Sophia bereitet Orte für den Sohn des Lichtes in Zusammenarbeit mit: "den Elementen..., die unten sind zum Bau der *leiblichen Häuser* (HЄI N̄CWMA-TIKON)". Vom Erlöser: 51:20-23: "Ich suchte ein *leibliches Haus* (HЄI NCWMA-TIKON). Ich warf den hinaus, der vorher in ihm war". Dieser war: 51:34-52:1: "ein weltlicher Mensch". Austreibung der von den Archonten geschaffenen Seele, damit "Christus" dort einkehren kann! Wir begegnen in diesem so merkenswerten Traktat ("ein Kompendium... wichtiger gnostischer Gedanken" — Berl. Arbeitskreis bei der Übersetzung in *ThLZ* 100 (1975), 97) einem ausgesprochenen Doketismus! Siehe S. 55 und 56 (Täuschungsmotiv; das Verlachen in der Höhe, wenn ein anderer gekreuzigt wird usw). Eidtion von M. KRAUSE in *Christentum am Roten Meer* (herausg. von F. ALTHEIM und R. STIEHL) Bd II, Berlin 1973, 106-151.

[62] Der Berliner Arbeitskreis las ЄϤOYHϨ NCA(= folgt), Y. JANSSENS ЄϤOYHϨ "habitant" (*a.c.*, 374-375). Die vom Berliner Arbeitskreis vorausgesetzte Fassung des koptischen Textes hat jedoch bessere Gründe. Ihm standen übrigens mehr Materialien

gewinnen.[62] Es plädiert m.E. sehr vieles für die vom Berliner Arbeitskreis befürwortete Lesung des Textes eingedenk der Sachparallele im
Tractatus Tripartitus (Codex I) p. 73:30-36![63]

Es ist bemerkenswert, dass das Vérb "*Wohnen*" in der PT sonst
nicht begegnet. *Merkwürding jedenfalls, dass es an der von uns untersuchten Stelle 47:14-15 nicht begegnet!* Es ist dies ja doch der *Angelpunkt*
der von uns im Hinblick auf Joh. i 14 angeregten Frage. Um so
merkwürdiger, weil der Gedanke des bleibenden Verweilens im 'Wohnen' enthalten, wohl im, der PT so verwandten, AJ in Anbetracht
Joh. i 18 auf bedeutende Weise begegnet!

Und zwar *AJ 26:13*, im Kontext 11-14: "Denn von uns erkannte
keiner, wie es sich mit dem Unermesslichen verhält, ausser *der in
Ihm gewohnt hat* (ⲡⲉⲛⲧⲁϥⲟⲩⲱϩ ⲛ̄ϩⲏⲧϥ̄). Er ist es, der uns das
gesagt hat". Die Parallelstellen haben: "... ausser der, der in Ihm
gewohnt hat (Text schlecht erhalten)...". (Codex *III, 7:1ff.*, von Till
in seiner Ausgabe schon erwähnt[64]) "... ausser dem, der in Ihm
gewohnt hat ..." (Codex *II, 4:17*, wo übrigens der Text ⲟⲩⲱⲛϩ ⲉⲃⲟⲗ
(offenbart) hat, siehe jedoch Apparat z.St.) und "...ausser der, der in
Ihm *gewohnt hat ...*" (Text wiederum schlecht erhalten, Codex *IV,
8:19*).[65] In der längeren Version (Cod. II und IV) folgt augen-
blicklich: "— das ist der Vater — denn dieser ist es der es uns
gesagt hat". Sonst lesen alle drei das Verb ⲟⲩⲱϩ, II, 4:17 mitgezählt.
Nun ist in diesen Aussagen der Anklang an Joh. 1:18 besonders
auffällig.[66]

Zumal da das "εἰς τὸν κόλπον" des griechischen Textes, in den
koptischen Übersetzungen getreu wiedergegeben (sa: ϩⲛ ⲕⲟⲩⲛϥ,
bo: ϧⲉⲛ ⲕⲉⲛϥ̄), zu: "*in Ihm gewohnt hat*" modifiziert worden ist.[67]

---

zur Verfügung (vgl. *a.c.*, 734 Anm. 6). Der an dieser Stelle vorausgesetzte Text wird
ibid., 746, Anm. 17, wiedergegeben. Ich möchte dem Kreis hier beistimmen, nicht
zuletzt durch die oben von mir angeführte Sachparallele.

[63] R. KASSER u.a., *Tractatus Tripartitus*, pars I De Supernis (*Codex Jung* fol. xxviʳ-
fol. liiᵛ) Bern 1973.

[64] TILL, *Die Gnostischen Schriften*, z.St. Für die Numerierung des Codex III als I
(nach DORESSE) vgl. die Tabelle bei David M. SCHOLER, *Nag Hammadi-Bibliography*
1948-1969, Leiden 1971, 111f.

[65] M. KRAUSE/P. LABIB, *Die drei Versionen des Apokryphon des Johannes im koptischen Museum zu Alt-Kairo*, Wiesbaden 1962, 57, 119 und 206.

[66] Siehe: Y. JANSSENS, *Muséon* 83 (1970), 165 und 84 (1971), 53: "Bref, ce verset
de *Ioh.* nous paraît un peu comme une toile de fond de notre Apocryphon — au moins
dans ses éléments chrétiens". In: W. FOERSTER, u.a., *Die Gnosis* I, 144, wird in der
Übersetzung von AJ 26:14, im Text Joh. i 18 in Parenthese aufgeführt.

[67] Siehe weiter unten angesichts der Frage der Beziehung AJ/PT und Johannesevangelium.

Dies alles wird weiter profiliert, wenn wir *AJ 31:4-5* und die Parallelen
in den drei Codices mit in Anbetracht ziehen. AJ 31:4-5 liest:
"...diesen Geist, in dem er (nämlich der Erlöser, H.) *gewohnt hatte*"
(oүⲱ2 ⲛ̅[2ⲏ-), die *Parallelen jedoch* haben: "... (Geist), durch den
er *in Erscheinung* getreten war" (Cod. *III, 10:9*); "...die vollkommene Pronoia, deretwegen er sich *offenbart* hatte" (Cod. *II, 6:32*) und
"...die vollkommene Pronoia, deretwegen er sich *offenbart* hatte"
(Cod. *IV, 10:11-12*).[68] Obwohl auch hier die Diskrepanz zwischen
Cod *III* (oүⲱⲛ̅2), ebenfalls von Till im Apparat angeführt und
II/IV (ϭⲱⲗⲡ̅) — offenbaren/manifestieren und aufdecken — bemer-
jenswert ist, zumal hinsichtlich AJ 31:5, wo das "Wohnen" als
"präemanatorisch" gehandhabt bleibt, *doch* kann die folgende Schluss-
folgerung gezogen werden. Das Tiefgnostische, nämlich das uranfäng-
liche Einwohnen des Erlösers/Offenbarers (die Barbelo) im Vater,
dem Unsichtbaren Geist, wird nachdrücklich betont. Das ist die prinzipielle Grundansicht, wie mutatis mutandis vom mystischen Einwohnen
in Gott gleiches gesagt werden könnte.[69] *Wohnen im Unsichtbaren
Geist, dás ist das Wichtige, nicht das kurzfristige, wie oft auch wieder-
holte, Verweilen des Offenbarers in der finsteren, unteren Welt!* Vgl.
die ⲙⲟⲛ ⲏ in der PT 37 und 46.

Das "Wohnen" unterstreicht die Wesenhafte Identität des Unsichtbaren Geistes und der Barbelo/Ernoia, die nur kurzfristig absteigt
in die Welt was nun gerade mit: "im des Vaters Schoss" von
Joh. i 18 só nicht gemeint wird.

Dieser Gedanke des AJ ist für die richtige Interpretation der
PT 47:14,15 von grösster Bedeutung. Der Vollständigkeit halber,
müsste noch auf folgendes bez. *AJ 26:11ff.* und AJ Cod. *II, 4:17*
und *IV, 8:19* hingewiesen werden. Zum ersteren, sei erwähnt, dass
"von uns erkannte keiner ... usw" am besten als "une parenthèse,

---

[68] Es muss darauf hingewiesen werden, dass auch hier in den drei Parallelstellen,
Teile des Textes schlecht erhalten sind, vgl. KRAUSE/LABIB, *loc. cit.*

[69] Vgl. z.B. Philo, *Leg. All.* III, 46 vom "Weisen, der in der Weisheit wohnt"
(mit κατοικεῖν, hapax legomenon bei Philo!), vgl. àuch *ThWNT* V, 156 (Michel
s.v. οἶκος); BULTMANN, *o.c.*, 43 Anm. 4 bez. dieses Einwohnen, was eben nicht im
ἕν in Joh. i 14 beabsichtigt sei. Siehe auch zu Joh. i 18 (*o.c.*, 56) mit der seltsamen
Bemerkung: "...im Zuge des gnostischen Offenbarungsgedankens hier erwartet werden
könnte: dass der Sohn die εἰκών des Vaters ist". Die Aussage in AJ 26:13 "wohnen
im Unermesslichen" scheint uns angemessener. Nicht nur weil im wichtigen AJ belegt,
sondern auch weil 2ⲓⲕⲱⲛ in AJ 27:2 und 19 und Par. das *Wesen* der Ennoia/der
Barbelo, in 26:13 jedoch die Art der *Beziehung* zum Vater (wie in Joh. i 18) gekenn-
zeichnet wird.

une réflexion personnelle de l'auteur de l'Apocryphon"[70] gesehen werden könnte. Zum letzteren ist zu bemerken, dass diese Hinzufügung — "das ist der Vater ..usw" — vom Kontext her sich auf das Subjekt des "Einwohnens" beziehen möchte, was jedoch in Widerspruch stünde zum Grundgedanken: der Vater wohnt nicht im "Sohn" bevor dieser absteigt, sondern der letztere im ersteren. So kánn übrigens der koptische Text ausgelegt werden.

Schliesslich führen wir auch hier in den Anmerkungen wieder einige sachgemässe Parallelen aus anderen Traktaten auf.[71]

III. Zu ϨΒϹⲰ PT 47:17, Gewand

Wie gesagt, können in gnostischen Texten Symbole für Welt und Körper mit einander alternieren: wie die Welt eine Wohnung genannt werden kann, so z.B. auch der Körper. Die Frage, ob nun auch der menschliche Körper als Zelthaus, als Zelt, gedeutet wurde, liegt nahe. Tatsächlich kann man diese Frage bejahen, und zwar in dem Sinne, dass σκῆνος und σκήνωμα im Griechischem im übertragenen Gebrauch schon geläufige Bezeichnungen für den menschlichen Leib waren.[72] Gleiches kann im Hinblick auf gnostische Texte geltend gemacht werden.[73] Im allgemeinen jedoch trifft m.E. JONAS' folgende Fest-

---

[70] Y. JANSSENS (Muséon (1970), 165).

[71] Aus CODEX I (Jung): "Epistula Jacobi...", 9:2-8: "Denn ich bin herunter gekommen um mit euch zu wohnen (ⲟⲩⲱϨ), damit auch ihr mit mir wohnet (ⲟⲩⲱϨ), und als ich fand, dass auf euren Häusern kein Dach war, wohnte (ⲟⲩⲱϨ) ich in den Häusern, die imstande sein werden, mich bei sich aufzunehmen" Man beachte das "mit euch"! Vgl. Sah. Übersetzung Joh. i 14 oben. Im Kommentar der Ausgabe S. 61 wird auch nach Joh. i 14 verwiesen: "Cf. Jean i 14: ἐσκήνωσεν ἐν ἡμῖν". Vgl. das Janssensche "Confer" bei PT 47:14-15, siehe unten. Evangelium Veritatis, 32:33f.: "...und dass es in Euch wohnt (ⲟⲩⲱϨ), dieses Licht, das nicht aufhört".

Aus CODEX II: Das Thomasevangelium, 87:1f. (= Logion 29): "Aber ich wundere mich darüber, wie dieser grosse Reichtum wohnte (ⲟⲩⲱϨ) in dieser Armut". "Das gnostische Weihnachtsevangelium in einer Nussschale" (R. SCHIPPERS/T. BAARDA, Het Evangelie van Thomas, Kampen 1960, 91). Ausgabe: A. GUILLAUMONT, u.a., Das Thomasevangelium, Leiden 1959. Die Hypostase der Archonten 144:22f.: "Darum werden die Mächte nicht imstande sein, sich ihnen zu nahen wegen des Geistes der Wahrheit, der in ihnen wohnt (ⲟⲩⲱϨ)". Norea erhält die Versicherung, dass sie und ihre Nachkömmlinge, weil dem Licht entstammend, gegen die Mächte beschützt sind. Ausgabe: R. A. BULLARD, The Hypostasis of the Archons, Berlin 1970. BULLARD numerierte nach LABIBS Tafelband. Offizielle Numerierung würde sein: 96:22f. (Vgl. BULLARD S. 4).

[72] Vgl. MICHAELIS, ThWNT VII, 383, bez. σκῆνος (lebender oder toter Körper) und 385, bez. σκήνωμα (besonders der tote Körper); DODD, o.c., 52.

[73] Diesbezüglich ist mir ein merkwürdiges Verwaschen der termini technici aufgestossen. So meint MICHAELIS, a.c., 384 einerseits σκῆνος brauche an sich — weil geläufiger Ausdruck — noch keine Beziehung zum gnostischen Denkschema zu haben,

stellung zu: "Mehr noch ist es 'das Zelt', *vorzüglich aber 'das Gewand'* (unterstrichen von mir, H.), das den Körper als flüchtige Weltform der Seele kennzeichnet".[74] Bekanntlich begegnet der Gedanke des Leibes als Gefängnis, Grab u.ä. sehr oft[75] und ist darum noch nicht "gnostisch": man hat diesbezüglich von der "spätantiken Körperfeindlichkeit" gesprochen.[76] Es gibt hier eine Vielfältigkeit verwandter Ausdrücke. Sehr spezifisch und für die Bedeutung des Leibes als "Gewand" aufschlussreich, ist der Ausdrucke *"das Fleisch tragen"*.[77]

---

andererseits jedoch bemerkt er einige wenige Zeilen weiter: "zumal die entsprechenden gnostischen Aussagen σκηνή vor σκῆνος bevorzugen", unter Berufung auf H. WINDISCH in seinem Kommentar zum 2. Korintherbiref (zu 2. Kor. v 1ff.; kleiner Exkurs bez. des Bildes vom Zelt, in der 9ten Auflage von 1924, 384). WINDISCH jedoch handelt nur von σκῆνος und gibt gar keine gnostischen Stellen, es sei denn eine aus den Hermetica und auch dann noch immer σκῆνος! Auch die von WINDISCH genannte Stelle Sap. ix 15 hat σκῆνος. Dazu wieder MICHEL in *ThWNT* V (s.v. οἶκος), 136 Anm. 11, der übrigens WINDISCH angesichts dessen Hinweis auf Platos *Phaed* 81 C kritisiert. Er fährt fort: "Doch ist das Bild von der σκηνή (oder σκῆνος) schon vorplatonisch". Man sollte m.E. jedoch diese beide Wörter: σκηνή eigentlich — und σκῆνος übertragen verwendet, gar nicht in dieser Weise mit einander alternieren lassen! Nur wenn man σκῆνος dem Begriff "Wohnung" annähert kann man von gnostischer Anwendung reden. Auch BULTMANN, *o.c.*, 44, führt WINDISCH an. Seltsam ist auch bei Luise SCHOTTROFF, *o.c.*, 148, wo sie von "der dualistischen Terminologie (οἰκία, σκηνή)" in 2 Kor. v 1-4 redet. Dort ist eben nur σκῆνος benutzt! Sie führt in der diesbezüglichen Fussnote VIELHAUER (*Oikodome*) und BULTMANN (Exegetische Probleme) separat an, obwohl BULTMANN in seiner Fussnote nur VIELHAUER aufführt (jetz auch in *Exegetica*, herausg. E. DINKLER, Tübingen 1967, 301). ... Die Wörter σκηνή und σκῆνος werden oft in diesem Zusammenhang unterschiedslos angewendet, jedoch ohne jeglichen Grund! Vgl. übrigens ausnahmsweise Vielhauer, *o.c.*, 107.

[74] JONAS, *o.c.*, 102.

[75] Z.B.: oben bei AJ Anm. 25; *Evangelium Veritatis* 17:35. Vgl. weiter unter Vielen: JONAS, *o.c.*, 106, 259, 323 und 414; SCHWEIZER (s.v. σῶμα) *ThWNT* VII, 1086.

[76] SCHWEIZER (s.v. σάρξ) *ThWNT* VII, 151. An sich noch nicht gnostisch: Schweizer, *a.c.*, 1090. Als ein schönes Beispiel von "Körperfeindlichkeit" und zudem gnostisch anmutend, fand ich Hans CASTORPS nächtliche Meditation über den Körper in Thomas Manns, *Der Zauberberg*, 302 und 388 (Fischer T.-Bücher).

[77] So *Epistula Jacobi* 12:12-13 mit dem aufschlussreichen Kommentar S. 67, wo unter anderem auch auf AJ verwiesen wird. Da begegnet der Ausdruck ebenfalls. Die von SCHWEIZER, *a.c.*, 150 Anm. 392 noch als undeutlich gebrandmarkte Stelle AJ 65:20 ist jetzt durch die AJ Parallelen in Cod. III, II und IV klar (*Epist. Jac.*, *a.o.*; Ausgabe KRAUSE/LABIB, 96 und Apparat). Y. JANSSENS, *a.c.*, 410 führt auch das *"Unbekannte altgnostische Werk"* auf. Die Stelle lautet (Ausgabe SCHMIDT/TILL, 359): "Du bist es, der Du alle Dinge dem Menschen gegeben hast. Und er *trug* (ϥорı, vgl. unsere Stelle PT 47:16!) sie wie diese Kleider und zog sie wie diese Gewänder an und hüllte sich mit der Kreatur wie in einen Mantel ein". Gerade die AJ-Parallelen hinsichtlich der PT sind selbstverständlich wichtig. Natürlicherweise geht "Fleisch tragen" m.E. über in: "ein Gewand, ein Kleid tragen". Der Körper, das Leib als Kleid, Umhüllung. Vgl. SCHWEIZER (s.v. σῶμα) *ThWNT* VII, 1048. Zu letzterem vgl. AJ Cod. II, 31:21, wo ϭⲁⲗⲉⲥ begegnet, dass nach Crum, Coptic Dict. 809ᵇ mit "Umhüllung" (griech. στολισμός aaO) gut übersetzt wäre (zu Unrecht

Zur Sache des Leibes als "Gewand" führt VIELHAUER Stellen auf aus mandäischen, manichäischen aber auch älteren Literatur, z.B. *Thomasakten* — dem *Perlenlied* — zumal der *Epistula Apostolorum* (2. Jhdrt).[78]

Bevor wir uns auch hier nunmehr den diesbezüglichen Stellen in der PT zuwenden, sei noch im kurzen einiges im Hinblick auf die bemerkenswerte valentinianisch-gnostische Anschauung bemerkt, der Erlöser bekleide sich mit einem σαρκίον (buchstäblich: "Fleisch", ein Stück Fleisch) das nun sich ... aus *pneumatischen* Teilen zusammensetze! Der zu grundeliegende Gedanke jedoch ist, dass Christus *umhüllt* ist von den Samen oder Engeln, denen die Pneumatiker auf Erden, in der Welt korrespondieren und die beide im "Brautgemach" sich vereinigen werden, sodass gilt: "Now man has been re-united with his true Self".[79] Dieser eigenartige Gedanke enthält aber immer noch manche schwierig zu interpretieren Momente![80]

Die in Betracht kommende *Stellen in der PT* sind:

45:15-20: "Sie werden euch Throne geben, die die Throne geben; ihr werdet *Kleider* (ⲥⲧⲟⲗⲏ) empfangen von denen, die *Kleider* (ⲥⲧⲟⲗⲏ) geben. Sie werden euch taufen, die taufen. Und ihr werdet Herrlichkeit werden mit den Herrlichkeiten; diese (nämlich Herrlichkeit, H.) in

---

anders R. HAARDT, *Die Gnosis*, Salzburg 1967, S. 173 und 321 Anm. 37). Nur hätten wir dann statt bekanntes ⲃⲟⲗⲉⲥ als Neuform ⲃⲁⲗⲉⲥ. Für das An-bzw. Ablegen der Kleider (der Körper) vgl. sehr schön das *Thomasevangelium* Logion 21 und 37, vgl. ZANDEE, *a.c.*, 74 und HELDERMAN, *a.c.*, 52 und 55.

[78] VIELHAUER, *o.c.*, 38, 47, 54-55 und 181. Bez. der *Epistula Apostolorum* vgl. für die von VIELHAUER angeführten Stellen die Übersetzung in E. HENNECKE/W. SCHNEE-MELCHER, *Neutestamentliche Apokryphen* I, Tübingen ³1959, 132, 136 und 138. Bez. der *Thomasakten*, *o.c.* II, 300, 307 und 349. Wie bekannt, könnte man die Epistula "anti-gnostisch" nennen, es sei denn, dass gerade in der Sprache (wie hier im Hinblick auf "Gewand") die gnostischen Formen weiterwirkten. So findet man auch das "Täuschungsmotiv" in *Ep. Ap.* 13 (24) (HENNECKE, *o.c.*, 132) wieder. Zur "Theologie des Kleides" im Perlenlied usw.: G. QUISPEL in *Le Origini* (sehe Anm. 5), 637ff.

[79] ZANDEE, *a.c.*, 72. Vgl. auch 70f.

[80] Vgl. zum σαρκίον schon SCHWEIZER, *a.c.*, 149 und ausführlich *ThWNT* VII, 1088-1089. Schweizer hat recht, wenn er betont, dass in *Exc. Theod.* 22 die "Engel" (die "bessere" Hälfte der Pneumatiker!) eher "Stellvertreter als konsubstantial" mit den Erlösten seien (*a.c.*, 1089 Anm. 627). Jedenfalls begegnet man auch hier einer tief durchdachten Lehre der Erlösung (vgl. dazu noch JONAS *o.c.*, 206 Anm. 2). Grundlegend zum ganzen Probelm A. ORBE, La Encarnación entre los Valentinianos, *Gregorianum* 53 (1972), 201-234; bes. S. 207-209 und 222f. Schliesslich SAGNARD *o.c.*, 376, 548-556 (S. 556 bez. der "difficultés et les obscurités"): wie tief durchdacht, der Gnostizismus enthält m.E. immer dunkle Züge durch die jeweilige Antwort auf die Frage des "unde malum". Für das Pleroma als "Kleid des Sohnes", vgl. "Unbekanntes altgnostisches Werk" cap. I (SCHMIDT/TILL *o.c.*, 335).

welcher ihr zu Anfang wart! Gewand, hier στολη[81], gehört zu den Heilsinsignia, wie sie auch erwähnt werden bei der Wiederherstellung der Ordnung innerhalb des Pleromas: *38:19-22*, wo Barbelo/der vollkommener Sohn den Äonen den ihnen gebührenden Ruhm gibt: "Er gab ihnen die Herrlichkeit und er gab ihnen die Throne. Er stand in der Herrlichkeit, wodurch er sich verherrlichte. Sie priesen den vollkommenen Sohn". Vgl. 38:4, wo ebenfalls die Protennoia/ Vater "im eigenem Licht stand". Die Verherrlichung gilt an unserer Stelle also den Pneumatikern, die zum Heil erweckt wurden und auf die Stimme hörten. Siehe weiter unten, auch in anderen Traktaten. In der PT wird das dem Demiurg gestattete Heil (in der μεσότης) übergangen (anders als z.B. in valentinianischem Schrifttum.[82]

47:16/17: "Und ich trug ihre *Kleidung* (ϩⲃⲥⲱ)[83] eines jeden". Galt das unmittelbar vorangehende "Und ich manifestierte mich in *der Gestalt ihres Aussehens* (ⲡⲉⲓⲛⲉ ⲛ̄ⲧⲟⲩϩⲓⲕⲱⲛ)", der menschlichen Gestalt, dem Körper überhaupt — ⲉⲓⲛⲉ, die Ähnlichkeit (ὁμοίωμα) vgl. 49:14 bez. der Ähnlichkeit der Mächte — die Frage ist akut, was denn hier mit dem Gewand eines jeden gemeint sei. Y. Janssens z.St. ist folgender Meinung: "ce 'vêtement' pourrait désigner le corps, mais comme celui-ci a déjà été désigné par 'l'image', il faut sans doute prendre le 'vêtement' au sens strict".[84] Ich teile ihre Meinung nicht. Und zwar aus folgenden Überlegungen. Wie oben gesagt, darf man die drei Teile der PT nicht só trennen, dass man die beliebte Form der Vorwegnahme, des Präludieren aus dem Auge verlieren sollte. Schon in 36:13ff. wird auf die "Brüder" (47:23); die "Teile" (40:13; 41:21); die "Glieder" (49:19) zumal "den Samen" (36:16 und 50:16) gezielt. Sie sind vor dem dritten Kommen der Protennoia in die Welt selbstverständlich schon da als die "Brüder" usw, der Protennoia. Obwohl es — könnte man sagen — eine gewisse Periodisierung der gnostischen "Heilsgeschichte" gibt, das dreimalige Kommen, wovon das letzte den gnostischen Kairos bedeutet (das Kommen

---

[81] Siehe zu στολή WILCKENS (s.v.) *ThWNT* VII, 688 (zumal Material mit Bezug auf die Mysterienkulte). Auch ORBE, *a.c.*, 222. Das Wort besagt den besonderen Charakter der Kleidung, anders als ἱμάτιον.

[82] Vgl. u. das von Y. JANSSENS, *a.c.*, 345-348 gebotene. SAGNARD, *o.c.*, 193, 195.

[83] Etymologisch nicht mit ϩⲁⲓⲃⲉⲥ verwandt.

[84] Y. JANSSENS, *a.c.*, 409. Übrigens wäre mir nicht deutlich, was Gewand im eigentlichen Sinne hier besagen könnte. Das ⲟⲩⲟⲛ ⲛⲓⲙ (Jedermann) verbietet schon eine solche banale Auslegung.

des Logos) vgl. die Futura in 42:19)[85] — dòch ist *das entscheidende Thema, der rote Faden in der PT, das Wirken der Protennoia in den ihrigen.* So 36:13ff.: "Ich bin der Ruf, rufend in einem jeden, so dass sie (mich) erkennen durch sie (= die Gnosis 36:10), weil ein Same in ih(nen) ist" (so mit dem Berl. Arb. kreis).

Diese Pneumatiker also "haben kein Ende" (36:19 und 42:12) und ihnen gilt auch das in 42:15ff. gesagte: "Ich (die Protennoia, H.) bin es, die den Klang des Rufes ertönen lässt in den Ohren derer, die mich erkannt haben". Als besondere Gabe der Protennoia wurde auch den Ewigen Heiligen Geist über sie ausgegossen (45:29-30). Es gibt ein *äusserliches* Wirken des Offenbarers (die Stimme in ihren Ohren, der Logos) *und ein innerliches.*[86]

---

[85] Vgl. diesbezüglich M. L. PEEL, Gnostic Eschatology and the New Testament in *Essays on the Coptic Gnostic Library*, Leiden 1970, 141-165.

[86] Dieses innerliche Wirken im Gnostiker wird in den Texten sachgemäss erhellt durch die Bezeichnung des menschlichen Körpers als σκεῦος, Gefäss. Hierbei ist zu beachten, dass σκεῦος in diesem Zusammenhang nicht die pejorative Konnotiz des Leibes als Gefängnis der Seele in sich zu tragen braucht, ist doch die Frage, wie bzw. von wém das Gefäss "gefüllt" wird ...! Im Spätjudentum wird der Mensch gelegentlich dargestellt wie ein Hohlgefäss, das eben Gott oder Teufel beherbergen kann (vgl. MAURER (s.v. σκεῦος), ThWNT VII, 361, mit Hinweis u.a., auf *Test. Naphthali 8, 6*), wobei noch zu bemerken wäre, dass im profangriechischen, vorneutestamentlicher Zeit σκεῦος nicht für den Leib als Gefäss der Seele verwendet wird (MAURER, *a.c.*, 359). In gnostischen Texten jedenfalls ist öfters vom Leibe als Gefäss die Rede, entweder im positiven oder negativen Sinne, je nachdem die Wesensart des "Inhabers". Wenn der Offenbarer "Inhaber" ist bzw. "das Gefäss" füllt, so tritt m.E. durch die Anwendung des Wortes σκεῦος auch die Heilsnotwendigkeit (siehe unten S. 206) hervor: muss Er doch sich sammeln mittels Füllens der "Gefässe" in jeglicher Menschengeneration. Vgl. im Simon Magus-Schrifttum bez. der Ennoia, wie sie "durch Jahrhunderte wie von Gefäss zu Gefäss in immer andere weibliche Körper wanderte" (JONAS, *o.c.*, I, 355). Folgende Beispiele seien herbeigeführt. Aus CODEX I: *Evangelium Veritatis, 25:33-35*: "...anstatt der schlechten *Gefässe* (ⲤⲔⲈⲨⲞⲤ) kommen volle, welche vollkommen werden". Dann *26:8-11*: "...entstand eine grosse Verwirrung unter den *Gefässen* (ⲤⲔⲈⲨⲞⲤ), denn einige waren geleert, andere waren gefüllt". Bez. der "Verwirrung" (auch 26:15f.) oben S. 193 und zumal in unserer *PT 43:14-20*: gleicher Gedanke der Erschütterung! Schliesslich *36:20-25*: (bez. der Vollendeten) "Denn die vollen *Gefässe* (σκεῦος) sind es, die man zu salben pflegt. Wenn sich aber die Salbe eines ablöst, fliesst es aus. Und die Ursache, dass es mangelhaft wird ...". An allen genannten Stellen begegnet der Gedanke der Vollheit (die Pneumatiker) und des Mangels (wie die gefallene Sophia) vgl. ZANDEE, *a.c.*, 37 und 61 (das τελεῖν und ὑστέρημα zur oben genannten Stelle *Ev. Ver.* 36). Aus CODEX II: "*Das Philipposevangelium*", *111:5-9* (log. 51): "Die Glass*gefässe* (ⲤⲔⲈⲨⲞⲤ ⲚⲀⲂⲀⳠⲎⲈⲒⲚ) und die Ton*gefässe* (ⲤⲔⲈⲨⲞⲤ ⲂⲂⲀⳢⲈ) entstehen durch das Feuer. Aber die Glass*gefässe* (ⲤⲔⲈⲨⲞⲤ-), wenn sie zerbrechen, werden wieder hergestellt. Denn sie sind aus einem Hauch (ⲠⲚⲈⲨⲘⲀ) entstanden". Die berufene Pneumatiker, die Glassgefässe, sind der Erlösung sicher! (ed. W. C. TILL, *Das Evangelium nach Philippos*, Berlin 1963). "*Schrift ohne Titel*" (Ursprung der Welt): *163:3-4*: "Als sie (die Ar-

Das letztere wird in der PT pointiert ausgedrückt durch "verborgen
in ihnen" nämlich den Pneumatikern. Es ist das also im positiven
Sinne gebraucht, ganz entgegengesetzt zum Verborgen-Sein der Protennoia für die getäuschten(!) Mächte (so 47:22/23; 49:18-20). Wie
die Seele im Körper verborgen ist,[87] so wirkt 'die Protennoia auf
verborgene Weise ,in ihrem Samen. Sie ruft *in einem jeden* (36:15)
und manifestiert sich *in* allen denjenigen, die sie erkannt haben
(36:22-23); so auch 47:18: "ich verbarg mich selbst *in ihnen*":
Y. Janssens nennt das mit Recht *innewohnendes Wirken*: "action
intérieure" und "présence mysterieuse du divin *en eux*".[89] Sehr viel-
sagend ist 45:21-22: "Und ich verbarg mich *in einem jeden*, ich
manifestierte mich *in ihnen*" (vgl. unsere Stelle 47:18) als entscheidend
47:22/23 entgegengesetzt: "Und ich verbarg mich in ihnen, *bis* ich
mich meinen Brüdern manifestiere": hier sind natürlich die Mächte,
die ewig Getäuschten, gemeint! Man beachte den fast gleichen
Wortlaut![90] Ich fasse zusammen: die Protennoia sammelt durch ihre
innerliche und äusserliche Offenbarungsarbeit ihre Teile, ihre Spermata
wieder ein.[91] *Dazu ist sie in der fleischlichen Umhüllung*[92] *eines jeden*

---

chonten. H.) aber Adam vollendet hatten, legte er ihn in ein *Gefäss* (ⲤⲔⲈⲨⲞⲤ)...
"und *163:33-36*: die von Sophia-Zoè gesandte Eva kommt "um Adam, in dem keine
Seele war, zu erwecken, damit die, welche er erzeugen würde, *Gefässe* (ⲤⲔⲈⲨⲞⲤ)
des Lich(tes) würden". Der *Golem* wird homo salvandus! Vgl. auch Adam als erster
der "Kette des Heils". Zu beachten, dass die Heilsgefässe ἀγγεῖον genannt werden
(so auch Philo, *Quod. det.* 170 und *Migr* 193 bei Maurer Th*WNT* aO S. 361). Zur
Stelle JONAS, *o.c.*, 403. Ausgabe: A. BÖHLIG/P. LABIB, *Die kopt.-gnost. Schriften* z.St.
"*Das Buch des Thomas*": *141:6-7*: "Denn das *Gefäss* (ⲤⲔⲈⲨⲞⲤ) ihres Fleisches
(ⲤⲀⲢⳌ) wird vergehen". Das äusserliche des Menschen soll und wird vergehen.
(Ed: KRAUSE/LABIB *loc. cit.*).

[87] Vgl. u. A. SCHWEIZER, *a.c.*, 150 Zeile 10ff.

[88] Vgl. bez. des gnostizistischen Einwohnens z.B. *Acta Thomae* 88, 148 und 156
(in HENNECKE/SCHNEEMELCHER, *o.c.*, II, resp. 343, 366 und 368).

[89] Y. JANSSENS, *a.c.* resp., 394 und 409.

[90] Der Berliner Arbeitskreis übersetzt die ganze Passage dem Sinne des koptischen
Wortlauts zuwider (ⲯⲀⲚⲦⲞⲨⲞⲚⳌⲦ' = *bis* ich, nicht: *um* mich usw, Sp. 743).
Siehe schon oben S. 185 Zumal gleicher Wortlaut 49:19 verbietet das grammatisch an sich
mögliche "um ... damit ...", das übrigens seltener ist. Vgl. W. C. TILL, *Koptische
Grammatik*, Leipzig ²1961, 158/159. Gerade das "bis" trifft hier zu: wenn alle Pneu-
mateile eingesammelt sind, ist das Treiben der Mächte doch ganz uninteressant! Spielt
beim Abstieg das Täuschungsmanöver eine wesentliche Rolle: "Anders verfährt er bei
seinem Aufstieg, da er die Mächte beim Abstieg ja schon faktisch überwunden hat.
Er führt sie nun im Triumph gefangen" — Karl Martin FISCHER, *a.c.*, 259. In der PT
wird die Protennoia sogar beim letzten Aufstieg noch nicht erkannt, worauf jedoch
gleich folgt: "Denn ich bin *ungreifbar* samt meinem Samen" (50:15).

[91] Vgl. JONAS, *o.c.*, 140 und HENNECKE/SCHNEEMELCHER, *o.c.*, I, 195 bez. des
Zitates aus einem Philippusevangelium bei Epiphanius (*Panarion* 26, 13).

[92] Auch diesbezüglich sind SAGNARDs Bemerkungen über die "Enveloppements"
(*o.c.*, 242-243) aufschlussreich.

Pneumatikers da. Dabei wird gar nicht auf die "Individualität"[93] eines Geisttragenden geachtet, sondern nur auf ihn als die *jeweilige Umhüllung eines jeweiligen Samens.* Deswegen verstehe ich die Kleidung, das *Gewand in 47:17* als ·Bezeichnung des *Körpers eines jeden* (Pneumatikers), wie die Protennoia in einem jeden (45:21) verborgen war. Das ϕOPI in 47:17 erinnert ohnehin an das "Fleisch tragen", siehe oben.

48:8f.; 48:15; 49:10f.; 49:29/30: Wir fassen das auf diesen Seiten Gesagte folgendermassen zusammen. Die Stelle 48:1-10 ist schlecht erhalten "Dies alles legte ich an, ihm jedoch zog ich es aus (Verb ⲔⲰⲔ ⲀϨⲎⲨ);[94] ich bekleidete ihn mit strahlendem *Licht*; das ist das der *Erkenntnis* des Gedankens der Vaterschaft". 48:15: "Und ich übergab ihn denen, die *Gewänder* (ⲤⲦⲞⲖⲎ) geben 48:16: Jammon, Elasso, Amēnai. Und sie zogen ihm an ein *Gewand* (ⲤⲦⲞⲖⲎ) (von) den *Gewändern* (ⲤⲦⲞⲖⲎ) des Lichts".[95]

Es handelt sich hier um den Menschen, der von jeglicher Finsternis entkleidet wird, welche dann die Protennoia "auf sichselbst legt(!)".[96] Weiterhin wird von "Täufern" (48:18-21) gesprochen; von "denen, die *Throne* geben (vgl. oben 45:15ff)"; von "denen, die Herrlichkeit geben (48:24f)" usw.

In *49:10ff* wird das dreimalige Kommen der Protennoia wie bekannt (oben S. 185) nochmals — auf eine sehr kurze, pointierte Formel gebracht—erwähnt: "... manifestierte ich mich. Und unter den Kräften, als ob (ϨⲰⲤ) ich einer von ihnen wäre; unter den Söhnen des Menschen aber, als ob (ϨⲰⲤ) ich ein Sohn des Menschen wäre". In 49:28-30 folgt die beziehungsvolle Aussage: "Er entkleidete sich vom *Gewand* (ⲤⲦⲞⲖⲎ) der Unwissenheit und bekleidete sich mit strahlendem Licht". Man beachte die Betonung der Aktivität des Pneumatikers, in welchem doch die Protennoia selbe wirkt! Zum Schluss teilt in 50:10f die Protennoia mit, dass sie sich "mit Jesus bekleidet hat" vgl. schon 49:10f: "Ich bekleidete mich (wie) der Sohn des Archigenetor". Wie in 47:17 benützt die Protennoia also den menschlichen Körper als Gewand, wobei der Jesus-Name wie

---

[93] Vgl. COLPE, *New Testament and gnostic christology*, 237 im Hinblick auf den Himmelmenschen, der ... "encompasses the entire world with his corporeal counter-images, that is, earthly men". Auch SAGNARD, *o.c.*, 243: Le "Spirituel" ... au Plérôme en tant que pur "pneuma".

[94] Hier begegnet wieder der Gedanke der "guten Nacktheit", die γύμνωσις vgl. HELDERMAN, *a.c.*, 53-55, SCHOTTROFF, *o.c.*, 140-154.

[95] Vgl. für die hier begegnenden Namen der behütenden Helfer: Y. JANSSENS *a.c.*, 410.

im AJ das Ganze "christlich frisiert". Jedoch ist völlig klar: "Le docétisme de l'auteur nous paraît évident".[97]

Abschliessend führen wir noch sachgemässe Parallel-Stellen aus anderen Traktaten unten auf.[98]

---

[96] Das Koptische [ⲁⲉ]ⲓⲧⲁⲁⲩ ϩⲓⲱⲱⲧ (vgl. CRUM, *o.c.*, 394) unterstreicht, dass die Protennoia alle diese Sachen der finsteren Welt mühelos "auf sichselbst legt" so den einzelnen Pneumatiker, den Samenteil befreiend. Das ist keine "Stellvertretung" sondern dem Unüberwindlichen Licht eben gebührend!

[97] Y. JANSSENS, *o.c.*, 411. Siehe zu PT 48 und 49 daselbst, *a.c.*, 409ff.

[98] Aus CODEX I (Jung): *Evangelium Veritatis* 20:28-32: "Bis zum Tode erniedrigt er sich, während das ewige Leben ihn bekleidet (Verb ϯ ϩⲓ-) Nachdem er ausgezogen hat die vergänglichen *Fetzen* (ⲡⲗϭⲉ), hat er die Unvergänglichkeit angezogen (ϯ ϩⲓ-)". So wird Jesu Kreuzestod gedeutet. Vgl. jetzt auch: Elaine H. PAGELS, *The Gnostic Paul, Gnostic Exegesis of the Pauline letters*, Philadelphia (USA) 1975, 98; SCHWEIZER, *a.c.*, 1083 diesbezüglich.

Aus CODEX II: *Das Evangelium nach Philippos* 105:19-22 (Log. 24): "Auf dieser Welt sind die, die die *Gewänder* (ϩⲃⲥⲱ) anziehen, wertvoller als die *Gewänder* (ϩⲃⲥⲱ). Im Reiche der Himmel sind die *Gewänder* (ϩⲃⲥⲱ) wertvoller als die, die sie angezogen haben...". Das Himmelgewand, siehe oben zu Lichtwohnung; VIELHAUER, *o.c.*, 109 über das Lichtgewand, das im Jenseits existiert. *Ev. Philip.* 104 und 105 bez. der Auferstehung: A. H. C. VAN EIJK, The Gospel of Philip and Clement of Alexandria, *VigChr* 25 (1971), 94-120.

Aus CODEX VI: *Die Taten des Petrus und der zwölf Apostel* 9:15-19: "Er löste das *Gewand*, (ϩⲃⲥⲱ), das er anhatte, in dem er sich für uns geändert (verkleidet H.) hatte, indem er uns wahrhaftig offenbarte, dass er es war!" Eine sehr interessante Stelle! Hier spricht der Offenbarer Lithargoël/Jesus auf Petrus' Frage woher er ihn (Petrus) kenne. Die Apostel werfen sich nach obiger Antwort und Manifestation(!) demütig zu Boden. Hier ist "Gewand" doch wohl eigentlich gemeint, obwohl m.E. die symbolische Bedeutung (Gewand ist Körper) mitklingen dürfte. Über den Charakter dieses Traktates: M. KRAUSE, Die Petrusakten in Codex VI von Nag Hammadi, in: *Essays on the Nag Hammadi Texts in honour of Alex. Böhlig* (NHS III), Leiden 1972, 36ff. 47 und 54-56.

Aus CODEX VII: "*Die Paraphrase des Sêem*". Gewand, Feuergewand des Erlösers begegnet hier sehr oft. So z.B.: *18:1-5.12-14*: "Dann legte ich nach dem Willen der Grösse, mein *Lichtgewand* (ϩⲃⲥⲱ ⲛⲟⲩⲟⲉⲓⲛ) ab. Ich zog ein anderes *Feuergewand* (ϩⲃⲥⲱ ⲛⲕⲱϩⲧ) an, das keine Form hat..." (12-14:) "Ich ging hinab in das Chaos, damit ich das ganze Licht von ihm befreie". Und *38:29-39:10*: "Wenn ich nämlich die Zeiten vollende, die mir auf der Erde bestimmt sind, dann werde ich von mir werfen mein (Finsternis-Gewand) und auf mich scheinen wird mein *Gewand* (ϩⲃⲥⲱ), das keinen Zwilling hat (= einmaliges H.). Und alle meine andere *Gewänder* (ϩⲃⲥⲱ), die ich in allen Wolken angelegt habe, stammten vom Staunen des Geistes. Die Luft nämlich wird an mein *Gewand* (ϩⲃⲥⲱ) gelangen. Es (= mein Gewand H.) wird nämlich leuchten und alle Wolken erreichen bis hinauf zur Wurzel des Lichtes". Wir begegnen sowohl dem Täuschungsmotiv wie auch dem himmlischen Lichtgewand (siehe oben beim Evangelium nach Philippos!), das hier jedoch "soteriologische" Bedeutung hat ("saving function" — F. WISSE in seinem Aufsatz "The Redeemer Figure in the Paraphrase of Shem" in *Essays on the Coptic Gnostic Library*, 134). Der Offenbarer ist Derdekas, der Empfänger der Offenbarung Shem und die seinige. Textausgabe in: *Christentum am Roten Meer*, 1-105. Auch im "*Unbe-*

Zusammenfassung

Wir möchten nunmehr das oben genannte einschlägige Material geltend machen und daraus einige Folgerungen ziehen, so dass *das Janssenssche "confer"* — ein Vergleich, der an sich allen Deutungen Raum lässt — die notwendigen Konturen erhält. Oben (S. 197) wurde schon darauf hingewiesen, dass — wenn in gnostischem Schrifttum von *"Wohnen"* die Rede ist — sich dieses Wort und der ihm inhärente Gedanke des *bleibenden* Anwesend-Sein, ausdrücklich auf den Unsichtbaren Geist, die Lichtwelt schlechthin bezieht.[99] In ihm nur wohnt der Offenbarer, wohnen im eigentlichen Sinne letzten Endes die Pneumatiker, die Erlösten. Dieses Anliegen nun wird in *PT 47:14.15 auf originelle Weise* unterstrichen!

Der Logos manifestiert/offenbart sich den Seinigen in menschlicher Gestalt, ja erträgt aus Heilsnotwendigkeit den menschlichen Körper eines jeden Pneumatikers und wirkt, wie vorher, auch auf verborgene Weise in ihnen. Die Manifestation findet in der Welt der berufenen Menschen statt: in ihrer Umwelt. *"In ihren Zelten…" deutet also m.E. die menschliche Wohnwelt an, die als Schauplatz für diese Manifestation dienen muss: kurz: die notwendige Szenerie (abgeleitet von* σκηνή *in der Bedeutung Bühne!), in der der Weckruf erklingt!*

Hierbei ist in *PT 47:14.15 die Pointe von Joh. i 14 absichtlich*

---

kannten altgnostischen Werk" begegnet öfters das Lichtgewand (z.B. 250 in der SCHMIDT-TILLSchen Ausgabe, 352).

Aus CODEX VII: *"Die Lehren des Silvanus"*. Diese Schrift ist recht merkenswert! Obwohl nicht gnostisch im eigentlichen Sinne — der höchste Gott z.B. wird identifiziert mit dem Demiurgen; die Christologie ist nicht doketisch — *doch* enthält sie gnostische und gnostizierende Züge, atmet eine tiefpessimistische Sphäre, warnt vor einem tierischen Leben und kennt immerhin auch das Täuschungsmotiv. Siehe die Untersuchungen von Malcolm L. PEEL/Jan ZANDEE, The teachings of Silvanus, *NT* 14 (1972), 294ff.; diesbezüglich 307/308 und von Jan ZANDEE, Die Lehren des Silvanus in: *Essays … in honour of Alex. Böhlig*, 144ff.; diesbezüglich 147 und 152. Weiter: Berliner Arbeitskreis, *Die Bedeutung der Texte…*, 63. *103:32-104:1:* "*Wie viele Gestalten* (ⲈⲒⲚⲈ) *hat Christus um deinetwillen angenommen! Obwohl er Gott war, wurde er unter den Menschen als Mensch* (ⲆⲰⲤ) *er(fun)den!*". Die "trotzige" Menschenseele wird hier angeredet. Und weiter heisst es von Christus: *111:4-6:* "der den Menschen *anzog* (ⲞⲨⲖⲈ) und Gott ist, der göttliche Logos". Siehe die "Facsimile Edition" z.St. Auch von diesem Text lieferte der Berliner Arbeitskreis eine Übersetzung in *ThLZ* 100 (1975), 7-23.

[99] Man könnte diesbezüglich die oben genannten Stellen, *Thomasevangelium* Log. 29 und *Epistula Jacobi* 9:2ff., zu den Ausnahmen rechnen. Das Wohnen begegnet hier im eigentlichen Sinne, sei es nur, dass auch hier der gnostische Offenbarer spricht. Jedoch sollte man im Auge behalten, dass das Thómasevangelium seine Eigenart in seinen Beziehungen zu den Evangelien findet und die Epístula in ihrem Hintergrund des frühchristlich-gnostisch/gnostizierenden Ägypten! (vgl. S. 198).

umgedeutet. In diesem Text wird ein reelles Wohnen der Person Jesu als langfristiges Bleiben unter/mit den Menschen[100] angegeben, in jenem wird angedeutet, dass der Offenbarer (Barbelo/Protennoia) eben *nicht* selber unter/mit den Menschen arteigen wóhnt, sondern nur ihre Umwelt als Szenerie und ihre Körper als Umhüllung braucht um nach Art einer Person[101] sein Wort hören zu lassen, wenn auch in einer kurzfristigen Manifestation. Wir begegnen hier einem reinen Doketismus.[102] Das Lehnwort ᴄᴋʜɴʜ (Zelt, nicht Leib), das sich — so weit ich jedenfalls sehen kann — in den Nag Hammadi-Schriften nur hier[103] findet, wurde als geläufiges Lehnwort nunmehr im Hinblick auf Joh. i 14 gewählt, jedoch nicht in der dortigen Verbalform, sondern als Substantiv, so dass dieses Wort nun stricto sensu betonen konnte, dass die Szenerie der Menschenwelt nur kurz da sei, ja dass sie bald abgebaut sein würde, wie das mit Theatergerät üblich ist. Die Umdeutung von Joh. i 14 scheint uns klar: "Wohnen" ist nur der Lichtwelt, dem Sein im Unsichtbaren Geist vorbehalten (PT 37:21; 46:29r.; AJ 26:13).

Die "Inkarnation" ist nur Manifestation in der Umwelt der Auserwählten. Wie im AJ: 26 (und Par.) Joh. i 18 umgedeutet wurde und im — dem AJ verwandten — valentinianischen Schrifttum (Ptolemaeus!) auch Joh. i 14 umgedeutet bzw. hineininterpretiert wurde,[104]

---

[100] Vgl. mit Recht Michaelis in *ThWNT* (s.v.) VII, 388. Anders: S. van Tilborg, "Neerdaling" en incarnatie: de christologie van Johannes, *TTh* 13 (1973), 20ff.: "De vleeswording van het woord was als het verblijf in een tent zo korststondig en voorlopig" (32). Angesichts der johanneïschen Christologie sehr zutreffend: C. Colpe "For every earthly man, he (nämlich der Logos) becomes one of their own kind and shares their sin and their death. This is more than and different from the mere temporalization and historization of a mythological happening. It is, first and foremost, something substantially and phenomenologically new...", *N.T. and gnostic Christology*, 237; im gleichen Sinne bez. der Person Jesu, C. H. Dodd, *o.c.*, 249 ("a real person"). Siehe weiter oben S. 190, Anm. 40.

[101] Vgl. Karl Martin Fischer, *a.c.*, 262: "Die Verschwommenheit der vorchristlichen gnostischen Erlöser ist systembedingt". Keiner von ihnen ist eine konkrete Gestalt sondern hat einen Scheinleib (*ebda*).

[102] Vgl. Y. Janssens, *a.c.*, 411; Colpe in *RGG*[3] II, 1652.

[103] Ich möchte nur noch hinweisen auf das Lehnwort ᴨⲩⳖʜ in "Zweiter Logos des grossen Seth" in *Codex VII* p. 56:26: "...als ich in ihren *Toren* (ᴨⲩⳖʜ) war, nahm ich ihr Aussehen an...", *Christentum am Roten Meer*, 121. In anderem ("negativem") Sinne ᴨⲩⳖʜ in PT 41:9.

[104] Zu bedenken, dass der Valentinianer Herakleon den ersten erhaltenen Johannes-Kommentar schrieb! Bez. Ptolemaeus' Interpretation von Joh. i 14, siehe Irenaeus, *Adv. Haereses* I, 8, 5 (auch I, 9, 3; dazu Pagels, *Joh. Exeg.*, 42/3. Harvey, *oc.* I, 74-85; vgl. weiter Foerster u.A., *Die Gnosis* I, 191-193; Sagnard, *o.c.*, 307-311). Zum gnostischen Gebrauch des NT, vgl. Y. Janssens, *Muséon* 84 (1971), 53, Sagnard, *o.c.*, 311.

so möchten wir glauben, dass wir unsere These, dies sei auch in der
— dem AJ und dem valentinianischer Denken nahen — PT 47:14.15
der Fall, genugsam unterbaut haben. Das Janssenssche "Confer"
wäre in diesem Sinne zu verstehen. Die PT hat m.E. denn auch
nicht eine 'hauchdünne christliche Firnis":[105] dafür ist die Umdeutung
zu bewusst *polemisch* im Hinblick auf Joh. i 14!

Wir möchten daher auch die eingangs zitierte Aussage des Berliner
Arbeitskreises über die PT (zumal den 3. Teil) als Sachparallele zum
Prolog des vierten Evangeliums[106] in dem Sinne, dass "das Licht mehr
von der Protennoia auf den Johannes-Prolog fällt" mit Y. JANSSENS
— siehe oben — umkehren: das Licht falle mehr vom Johannes-
Prolog auf die PT. Um diese Meinung zu begründen und deren
Trageweite im grösseren Rahmen übersehen zu können, wollen wir
zur "religionsgeschichtlichen Szenerie" der PT 47:14.15 folgendes
bemerken.

Oben (S. 184) wurde die Bemerkung des Berliner Arbeitskreises, dass
"unser Text eine glänzende Bestätigung der längst vorhandenen
Hypothese" sein könnte — im Hinblick auf den Johannes-Prolog,
schon erwähnt. Jetzt möchten wir die Frage aufwerfen, ob es nicht
angemessener sei, erst die Einwände, welche gegen diese Hypothese
als solche, gerade aus religionsgeschichtlicher Sicht erhoben werden
können, zu erwägen, bevor man über eine "glänzende Bestätigung"
reden sollte. Die betreffende Hypothese "im Wirkungsfeld der Johannes-Interpretation R. BULTMANNS", basiert wie bekannt auf dem
"Mythus vom Erlösten Erlöser".[107] Obwohl aus guten Gründen schon
den Ausdruck Salvator Salv*andus* anstatt Salv*atus* zu bevorzugen
ist,[108] sind noch folgende Fragen von grundlegender Bedeutung.
Zunächst einmal, ob es methodisch zu empfehlen ist, aus bestimmten
Texten einen gnostischen "Grundmythus" wie vom "Erlösten Erlöser"
zu erschliessen und diesen dann gerade mit Rücksicht auf die Interpretation des Johannesevangeliums anzuwenden. Ich glaube mann
sollte diesbezüglich ernsthafte Bedenken hegen.[109] Weit wichtiger

---

[105] So der Berliner Arbeitskreis, in: TRÖGER, *Gnosis und N.T.*, 75.

[106] *A.c.*, 733; dasselbe in TRÖGER, *Gnosis und N.T.*, 76.

[107] Vgl. unter anderem H. M. SCHENKE, Die neutestamentliche Christologie und der
gnostische Erlöser, in *Gnosis und N.T.*, 205ff. Diesbezüglich 210.

[108] COLPE, *Religionsgeschichtliche Schule* 174 und 187-190.

[109] BULTMANNS "Grundmythus" im Aufsatz in der *ZNW* (1925), 104 (jetzt auch
in Exegetica, 59); bei COLPE, *o.c.*, 172. Zu den beiden Säulen unter Bultmanns
Grundmythus, SCHENKE, *o.c.*, 210. COLPES Bevorzugung anderer Kriterien: ebenda
187-188, 'So kam es zu dem in den Geisteswissenschaften nicht allzu häufigen Sachverhalt, dass ein Teil der Forscher immer mutiger zur immer vollkommeneren Dar-

noch ist die Frage, welche der beiden folgenden Formeln angesichts des Angelpunktes der gnostischen Soteriologie als die angebrachtere vorzuziehen wäre: warum und wie *der Erlöser Mensch* wurde, oder: warum und wie der *Mensch* (der Gott "Mensch")[110] *Erlöser* wurde. Es ist COLPES unschätzbares Verdienst, die Differenzierung mittels dieser beiden Formeln als berechtigt im Hinblick auf die Quellen, wie als notwendig der Deutlichkeit wegen, ans Licht gebracht zu haben.[111]

Die Bedeutung dieser Differenzierung ist für die weitere Erforschung von Gnostizismus und Neuem Testament folgenschwer. Es mutet einem die Beziehung seltsam an, wenn man z.B. einerseits erfährt, dass "die betreffende Rahmen-Konzeption der Gnosis (nämlich bez. der Auffasung BULTMANNS-H.) längst nicht mehr vertretbar" sei, andererseits: "was nun das vierte Evangelium anbelangt ... so ist es als Ganzes von der gnostischen Erlöser-Vorstellung bestimmt. Der allgemeine Nachweis dafür ist auf breiter Basis längst erbracht, besonders von R. Bultmann ... die neuen Quellen lassen das bereits Erkannte noch deutlicher werden.[112] Oder: "Das Gnosisbild, das Bultmann in seinem Kommentar voraussezt, ist durch die Textfunde von Nag Hammadi überholt. Endgültig überholt sind nun aber auch alle Thesen, die die Gnosis für nachchristlich oder zumindest ihre Erlöseranschauung als christliche Beeinflussung erklären.[113] Und als

---

stellung eines schliesslich "gnostischer Erlöser mythus" genannten Objektes fortschritt, während sich ein anderer Teil immer skeptischer dagegen sträubte" (COLPE, *o.c.*, 10, 65-66). Wichtig sind SCHENKES Bemerkungen zum Ursprung, Wesen und Entstehungsort der Gnosis in seinem Beitrag "Hauptprobleme der Gnosis" *Kairos* 7 (1965), 114ff.; zumal 118/119. Auch in *Gnosis und N.T.*, 210-211.

[110] Zum Gott 'Mensch' Jonas, *o.c.* I, 303 und 348; H.-M. SCHENKE, *Der Gott "Mensch" in der Gnosis*, Göttingen 1962.

[111] "... it follows that one may no longer ask where and how the Redeemer became man. Instead, one must ask where and how *man became Redeemer*. Here I would like to assume that this *structural change* took place in a Gnosis which absorbed and assimilated the Christian Son of Man into its speculations over the heavenly man which was already known to Gnosis" in "N.T. and gnostic christology", 237. Gleiches in *Religionsgeschichtliche Schule*, 206 und in *ThWNT* (s.v. ὁ υἱὸς τοῦ ἀνθρώπου) VIII, 415-416 und 479-480. Man vergleiche aber schon FOERSTER in *ThWNT* (s.v. σωτήρ) VII, 1019-1020!

[112] SCHENKE in *Gnosis und N.T.*, bzw. 210 und 225.

[113] FISCHER in *Gnosis und N.T.*, 249. Es ist sonderbar, dass L. SCHOTTROFF, die sie sich deutlich bekennt zur "Bultmannschen" Formel "Der Erlöser wurde Mensch" (*o.c.* 99 und 113), COLPES Ausführungen in *ThWNT* VIII 415ff und 478ff. mit Zustimmung zitiert auf Seite 103 Anm. 4, *ohne* jedoch zu erwähnen, dass COLPE a.a.O. gerade áuch die Formel von der Menswerdung des Erlösers bestreitet (*o.c.* 480 vgl. auch *Rel. Schule*, 206).

letztes Beispiel: "Die Menschwerdung des Erlösers, wie sie Joh. bietet, ist (entgegen Bultmann) nicht in der Gnosis belegt ... Gerade der Doketismus ist ein Beweis dafür, dass die Gnosis die Menschwerdung des Erlösers nicht kannte.[114] Es fällt auf, dass man hier, trotz aller unerlässlichen Änderungen durch die "neuen Funde", an dem Gedanken, die gnostische Erlösergestalt sei das arteigene Primäre (und darum: die Menschwerdung *des Erlösers*!), als einem unerschütterlichen, ein für allemal festgestellten Axiom festhält. Bultmanns Festellung: "Indessen ist der Gedanke der Menschwerdung des Erlösers nicht etwa aus dem Christentum in die Gnosis gedrungen, sondern ist ursprünglich gnostisch; er ist vielmehr schon sehr früh vom Christentum übernommen und für die Christologie fruchtbar gemacht worden,[115] ist trotz aller Nuancen in seinem "Wirkungsfeld" die Konstante geblieben, wie wir eben sahen. Hier bildet COLPES Anmerkung: "Diese Frage nach der Erlöserwerdung des "Menschen" in der Gnosis dürfte dem wirklichen Sachverhalt gerechter werden als die umgekehrte nach der "Menschwerdung des Erlösers"! Die Hinweise, die BULTMANN (*o.c.*, 10) zu diesem vermeintlich gnostischen Topos gibt, treffen am Kern der Sache völlig vorbei", einen starken Gegensatz.[116] Man sollte es nun aber nicht bei diesem Gegensatz lassen, zumal angesichts des neuen Fundes. Eine neue Diskussion ist erforderlich.

Dies um so mehr, weil auch die *Weisheitsgestalt* — so äusserst wichtig bei der Exegese von Joh. i 14[117] — manchmal und namentlich im "Wirkungsfeld BULTMANNS" als zum "Erlösermythus" gehörig, betrachtet wird.[118] Und man muss fragen, ob das berechtigt ist. Die geäusserten Bedenken sind nämlich aller Aufmerksamkeit wert![119]

---

[114] Kurt RUDOLPH, *o.c.*, 306.

[115] BULTMANN, *o.c.*, 10/11 (vgl. 38 und 39).

[116] COLPE, *o.c.*, 206 Anm. 2. So auch VAN UNNIK unter Hinweis auf COLPE (W. C. VAN UNNIK, Balans: 20 jaar na een keerpunt in het onderzoek van de Gnostiek, *NedThT* 23 (1969), 189-203. Diesbezüglich 201: "Het grondige boek van Colpe, "Die religionsgeschichtliche Schule", heeft de wortels doorgezaagd, waarop Bultmanns reconstructie berustte". Vgl. auch Seite 193!.

[117] Vgl. BULTMANN, *o.c.*, 44; in *Exegetica* 13-14 und 98; W. A. MEEKS, The Man from Heaven,*JBL* 91 (1972), 46; SCHOTTROFF, *o.c.*, 108; MICHEL (s.v. οἶκος) *ThWNT* V, 156; MICHAELIS (s.v. σκηνή) *ThWNT* VII, 373 und 390 und R. SCHNACKENBURG, *Das Johannesevangelium*, Freiburg ³1972 I, 244. Die Konstante in allen Erörterungen ist immer Sirach xxiv 8.

[118] SCHENKE, *a.c.*, 206 und 209.

[119] COLPE, *o.c.*, 193: derselbe in *ThWNT* VIII, 414 und 415; H. HEGERMANN, *Die Vorstellung vom Schöpfungsmit er im hellenistischen Judentum und Urchristentum*,

Überlegungen methodischer Art hinsichtlich des jeweils herangezogenen oder nicht herangezogenen religionsgeschichtlichen Vergleichsmaterials wie auch die Rückdatierung z.B. gnostischer Vorstellungen aus späterer Zeit,[120] führen m.E. dazu, die oben angeführte Aussage des Berliner Arbeitskreises, die PT sei "eine glänzende Bestätigung der längst vorhandenen Hypothese", als verfrüht betrachten zu müssen. Wir hoffen mit unserer Untersuchung der PT 47:14-18 ein wenig dazu beigetragen zu haben, dass man sich von den in der PT enthaltenen Gedanken ein genaueres Bild wird machen können, nachdem Y. JANSSENS die Tür zu diesem Arbeitsweg geöffnet hat.[121]

(abgeschlossen 1. März 1976).

Berlin 1961, 70 und 83; B. L. MACK, *Logos und Sophia. Untersuchungen zur Weisheits-theologie im hellenistischen Judentum*, Göttingen 1973, 18.

[120] Zum ersteren vgl. BLANK, *o.c.*, 19 und 79; zum letzteren COLPE, *o.c.*, 65; R. McL. WILSON, "Gnosis, Gnosticism and the N.T." in: *Le Origini* (sehe Anm. 5), 516; E. FASCHER, *Die Korintherbriefe und die Gnosis, in: Gnosis und N.T.*, 289 und H.-Fr. WEISS, Paulus und die Häretiker, in: *Christentum und Gnosis*, 125.

[121] Y. JANSSENS, *a.c.*, 413.

INDEX OF AUTHORS

INDEX OF SUBJECTS

INDEX OF REFERENCES

A. OLD TESTAMENT

B. APOCRYPHA, PSEUDEPIGRAPHA, AND OTHER EARLY JEWISH LITERATURE

C. NEW TESTAMENT

D. ANCIENT CHRISTIAN LITERATURE

E. THE NAG HAMMADI LIBRARY

F. CLASSICAL LITERATURE